From Shakespeare to Existentialism

FROM SHAKESPEARE
TO EXISTENTIALISM:
AN ORIGINAL STUDY

*Essays on Shakespeare and Goethe; Hegel
and Kierkegaard; Nietzsche, Rilke, and
Freud; Jaspers, Heidegger, and Toynbee*

BY WALTER KAUFMANN

Princeton University Press
Princeton, New Jersey

TYPOGRAPHY BY SUSAN SIEN

Published by Princeton University Press, Princeton, New Jersey
In the United Kingdom: Princeton University Press, Chichester, West Sussex

AUTHOR'S NOTE

*All translations from the German, poetry as well as prose, are
mine. Much of this material has never before been offered in
English.*

Princeton University Press books are printed on acid-free paper, and meet
the guidelines for permanence and durability of the Committee on Production Guidelines for Book Longevity of the Council on Library Resources

From Shakespeare to Existentialism was originally published by the Beacon Press in 1959. The Anchor Books edition was published in 1960.

First Princeton Paperback printing, 1980

9   8   7   6

TO THE MILLIONS MURDERED
IN THE NAME OF FALSE BELIEFS
BY MEN WHO PROSCRIBED CRITICAL REASON
THIS BOOK IS DEDICATED

Contents

Preface (1979)

In the summer of 1979 I traveled around the world for the fourth time, visiting half a dozen countries to which I had been before. Upon arriving at San Francisco from Tokyo, I drove to the Monterey Peninsula and Big Sur. There I explored some of the same sights more than once, although I had been there several times before. Suddenly it struck me that it was odd that instead of seeking out new places I keep returning to so many that keep fascinating me. Yet some people invest in a summer house and go back there year after year. At least my repertory is larger than that. Then it occurred to me, as the sea showered the rocks with veils of lace, that it is no different in the realms of scholarship. We are, most of us, of one piece.

I keep going back to the same men, deepening my understanding of them. Yet even as my most recent photographs of India and Bali do not supersede those taken some years ago, the essays in this volume are not, I think, dated.

Of course, this is an unusually personal approach to scholarship. But even in 1949, when my first two articles on Goethe appeared on the occasion of the poet's two hundredth birthday, I stressed the intimate connection between character and work as well as the philosophical dimension of much of the greatest poetry. These themes recur in many of the other essays in this volume, and they have remained characteristic of my work ever since.

Some philosophers are interested primarily in words, in systematically misleading expressions, or in odd propositions that they find in the writings of their predecessors. Many more con-

cern themselves primarily with arguments. All these approaches
are legitimate if not particularly humanistic. It is no less legitimate, though certainly less fashionable, to view the writings of
philosophers and poets as expressions of human beings and to
inquire about their central concerns and their experience of life.

In any case, even a stringent academic taste permits some references to the author in a preface, and when a collection of essays that has been in print continuously for twenty years is reprinted again in the twenty-first by a different publisher, he is
expected to explain its relation to his more recent work.

To two of the ten men to whom these twenty essays are devoted I have not returned: Jaspers and Toynbee. There was no
need to return to Toynbee. I aimed to show in the last chapters
of this book that he was vastly overrated, and this view, originally shared by only a few others, has won the day. Nor do I
seem to stand alone in finding little nourishment in Jaspers.

Most of the essays in this book were inspired by great admiration. That is true not only of Shakespeare and Goethe, Hegel
and Nietzsche, Rilke and Freud, but also of Kierkegaard. But
admiration, of course, does not entail agreement.

To Shakespeare I returned in *Tragedy and Philosophy* (1968,
Princeton University Press 1979) and in the last part of *Man's
Lot* (1978), which was also issued separately under the title *What
is Man?* To Rilke, in the first part of the same trilogy, which was
also issued separately as *Life at the Limits*. To Hegel I devoted a
whole book (1965), and to Kierkegaard another essay (1962),
which is included in my *Existentialism, Religion, and Death*
(1976). Freud is the subject of a chapter in *The Faith of a Heretic*
(1961). And now I am publishing another trilogy, *Discovering
the Mind*, which consists of three volumes: *Goethe, Kant, and
Hegel* (1980), *Nietzsche, Heidegger, and Buber* (1980), and
Freud versus Adler and Jung (1981).

These books build on some of the essays collected in the present volume and sometimes refer to them. Some of the essays
brought together here have also been reprinted in anthologies,
but naturally not all have had an equal impact. Referring specifically to the first two Hegel essays as well as to my *Hegel*, An-
thony Quinton said in *The New York Review of Books* in 1975:
"In the United States the revival of interest in Hegel was initially
the work of Walter Kaufmann." But my essay on Heidegger's

later thought has not been so fortunate. His star is still in the ascendance, especially in the United States, and it is for that reason that I have returned to him in the second volume of *Discovering the Mind* to finish the job, if possible. But this critical animus is reserved largely for Heidegger and Toynbee. Most of the chapters are inspired by enthusiasm, if not love.

The essays closest to my own heart have not had the greatest impact. Chapters 12 through 14 deal with matters of which relatively few scholars seem to have had much experience. Yet most scholars seem to assume implicitly that the men about whose works they write were on the whole not very different from themselves. Often this does not seem to be the case. Again we face the question of the man behind the work, or rather *in* the work. I feel that those three chapters may still contribute something to the understanding of Nietzsche and Rilke, poetry and art.

These essays first appeared in book form in 1959, and some additions were incorporated in the first paperback edition a year later. It would not make sense to revise them now, or to update the Bibliography significantly. But I have made a few small changes in the Bibliography, beginning on page 430.

I am grateful to the Princeton University Press for bringing together under its imprint four of my books. The relationship of this one to the other three is so close that it does not need laboring.

Preface (1960)

The history of a book may constitute a large part of the author's life—and therefore concern him alone. Yet false assumptions about the genesis of a work may abet serious misconceptions of the writer's valuations.

Many a chapter in this book was rewritten again and again, some passages easily twenty times, before a preliminary version appeared in some book or journal—a piece of a work in progress. Eventually the time came to worry and work over these chapters, along with others not yet published and still others yet to be written—a time of rewriting and polishing and rewriting again until the book was ready to be offered to a publisher. Accepted and threatened with the relative permanence of print, a manuscript cries out for final scrutiny and hundreds of last-minute changes: here the prose could be tightened, there a phrase might be brought a little closer to perfection. Some writers gladly leave such tasks for editors; I should as soon request another man to see or suffer, live or love for me. For writing is a form of seeing and of suffering, of life and love.

After that, what reaction would be most amusing: to have the book read as an explication of the first two chapters, which in fact were written last? or to find the whole considered as a casual collection of a score of miscellaneous essays? or to be congratulated on publishing a book a year? My *Critique of Religion and Philosophy* had appeared only a year earlier, in 1958. But a book a year? Rather, two books in nine years; or, counting my *Nietzsche,* originally issued in 1950, three books in thirty-eight years. The volumes which I translated and edited were by-products.

My books are not noncommittal. They praise what is rarely praised. But today "commitment" is associated with the refusal to stand alone, and "nobility" is not in favor. In this book "nobility" means being hard with oneself, making demands on oneself, devotion.

People use moral terms without thinking about them. They confound devotion with devoutness, and humility with meekness. Yet nothing makes one more conscious of one's limitations than bold aspirations, which are not self-effacing. People decry ambition, but ambition teaches humility. One need not be a Freudian to see that, but it helps to know Freud, the undevout, devoted man in whom humility and pride were fused.

Love, unlike nobility, is popular and frequently commended as if, even when the word is not used as a euphemism, it were most enjoyable. But what do those know of love who do not know that it is a cross? Surely, the Buddha was right that love is the fountainhead of hurt and misery, suffering and despair. He also taught that life and love were not worth while. But to take this cross upon oneself with open eyes, that is nobility, that is devotion, that makes life worth while.

In the first chapter, partly in an effort to provoke, nobility, even when not fused with love, is considered with a great deal of respect. We are used to distortions of the history of ethics and aesthetics, and it is worth pointing out that Aristotle and such celebrated tragedies as *Oedipus Rex* and *Hamlet*, *Coriolanus* and *Julius Caesar* confront us with a great tradition in which nobility is not associated with love. Here is dedication, courage, and severity against oneself, but no love. This is not the acme of humanity but an interesting contrast to that modern cult of sentiment which does not issue from tremendous depths of feeling but, quite to the contrary, from lack of depth and feeling. People enjoy feelings which are not intense enough to torment them, and think it would be nice to feel what they do not quite feel. If the treatment of this problem in the first chapter should be provocative to the point of misleading the reader about my own valuations—which matter far less than the attempt to make the reader reconsider *his*—the

Rilke poem and the comments on it early in the thirteenth
chapter may take care of that.

Perhaps one has to know what it means to be burnt alive
to understand Shakespeare's thought, or outcry, that being "as
stone" may be a mark of superiority. Michelangelo did. When
Giovanni Strozzi composed a stanza on Michelangelo's statue
of Night, saying she was so alive that if you spoke to her she
might awaken and reply, the sculptor responded:

> *Sweet is my sleep, but more to be mere stone,*
> *So long as ruin and dishonor reign;*
> *To hear nought, to feel nought, is my great gain:*
> *Then wake me not, speak in an under-tone.*

This is John Addington Symond's translation.[1] Rilke rendered
the same lines into beautiful German verse.

Those who know the longing to be marble because they
know the pain of passion, and still would not surrender what
torments them, may attempt to pour their most intense emotion into sculptured stone, or tone, or prose, to create something that, moving others, is itself as stone. Such ambition can
become another passion, another devotion, another source of
suffering. It can also give one's life some meaning. And one
of its bounties is that it protects against the laughable conceit that one has been successful.

To mold the language to reflect experience, to disturb assurance and dislodge presumptions, and to inform to stimu-
late, not end, inquiry—such goals preclude more than partial
success. This book is a fragmentary account of a voyage of
discovery and an invitation to set sail. This new edition is un-
cut. Some small changes have been made, including several
additions, in Chapters 1, 2, 3, 10, 14, 16, and 18.

Let us return once more to Michelangelo who, like few, if
any, artists confronts us with definitive alternatives. As one
sometimes compares people to animals, plants, materials, and
drinks, one may perhaps compare a book to some of Michel-

[1] *Renaissance in Italy*, vol. I, p. 767, in the Modern Library
edition.

angelo's masterpieces, merely to indicate ideal types, completely disregarding levels of achievement. Surely my books are more like the master's Slaves, struggling out of the stone, unfinished, than like his Pieta in St. Peter's. Some readers, alas, will feel reminded more of his Last Judgment. But I should rather like to think of these books as torsos—a beginning rather than a final statement, groping rather than definitive, not sicklied over by the deadly cast of scholarship but a challenge.

W. K.

February 1960

Preface (1959)

This book is the fruit, albeit not the only one, of almost ten years' work. Drafts for various chapters have appeared here and there, but all of them have been revised, for the most part very extensively. One can—and unfortunately almost every reader will—begin with any chapter that may strike his fancy. Read straight through, however, the book traces a historical development—and gradually various themes are developed. Even those who read only the first four chapters before they begin to skip will find more in the later chapters than readers who approach nonfiction as a kind of smorgasbord.

The outlook toward which this book points is developed more fully in my *Critique of Religion and Philosophy*. Here are some of the historical studies out of which my *Critique* has grown; there are some of my own conclusions. Alas, it works the other way around, too, and a few contentions in the present volume had to be backed up by references to my *Critique*.

This is certainly not positivistic historiography but writing that comes perilously close to existentialism, although Heidegger and Jaspers are sharply criticized in both books, and Toynbee is accused, among other things, of being an existentialist historian. But we need not choose between positivism and existentialism of that sort any more than between Christianity and materialism. One can write with—and can remember that the men one writes about had—"dimensions, senses, affections, passions," without embracing the profoundly unsound methods and the dangerous contempt for reason that have been so prominent in existentialism.

While this book has considerable continuity, it is certainly not Procrustean, and the ten subjects of this study are not reduced to grist for the author's mill. The approach varies in almost every chapter, and a juxtaposition of "Nietzsche and Rilke" leads to a more systematic discussion of "Art, Tradition, and Truth," and hence to an essay on "Philosophy Versus Poetry." Throughout, the interrelations of poetry, religion, and philosophy are emphasized; and so are a few remarkable falsifications of history. One conclusion may be anticipated. The book denies that "Beauty is truth, truth beauty"; but it finds both in Shakespeare and neither in Toynbee.

Shakespeare is seen in an unconventional perspective, and so are the other nine men studied in this volume: Goethe, Hegel, and Kierkegaard; Nietzsche, Rilke, and Freud; Jaspers, Heidegger, and Toynbee. It is part of the purpose of this book to view them all in a new light—not only singly but also as figures in a story that begins and ends in England but unfolds for the most part in Germany. No attempt is made to be "complete" by padding this revaluation either with obeisances to Schiller, Schelling, and Schopenhauer—who are merely noticed occasionally, from a distance—or with capsule outlines of the views of those considered. This book deals intensively with a few men and is more concerned with issues and interpretations than with the recital of facts and events which may be found in good encyclopedias. Every chapter tries to make a few points, and not one tries to repeat what can be readily found elsewhere.

Whatever else might be said in this Preface is said in the first two chapters. My own view of life is made plain in Chapters 1 and 2, and 12 through 14, though not only there. I agree with Paul that love is more important than faith and hope; but so are honesty, integrity, and moral courage. The world needs less faith and more love and nobility.

W. K.

From Shakespeare to Existentialism

I

SHAKESPEARE: BETWEEN SOCRATES AND EXISTENTIALISM

That history is at least often written from a point of view —and that the Nazis and the Communists developed different accounts, not only of the recent past, but of the whole development from ancient Greece to modern times—is now a commonplace. But that a warped and tendentious view of the present age and its relation to the past is current in our midst and more indebted to Christianity than to any political ideology requires showing.

It would be tedious to present a catalogue of noteworthy offenders and to argue, one by one, with each. And it would be silly to suppose that they conspired with each other. What the guilty writers share is not a platform or a set of dogmas but a deep dissatisfaction with the time in which it is their lot to live.

This widespread feeling, like many another, was formulated definitively by T. S. Eliot. He persuaded millions that the modern world is a waste land, and he proclaimed (in *After Strange Gods*) that "the damage of a lifetime, and of having been born in an unsettled society, cannot be repaired at the moment of composition." Thousands of writers feel sorry for themselves, and some who do not greatly admire Eliot believed Gertrude Stein when she blamed society for her inability to write better and when she told them that they were a lost generation.

This self-pity and self-deception involve, among other things, a comprehensive distortion of history. It is not uncommon for modern writers to talk themselves and others into the fancy that our generation is unique in having lost the motherly

protection of a firm religious faith, as if Socrates and Shakespeare had been reared with blinders and as if the Renaissance,
the Enlightenment, and the nineteenth century were all contemporary inventions. Some turn such men as Socrates and
Shakespeare into honorary Christians; others sob wistfully
about Dante and Aquinas.

Godless existentialism is pictured as the philosophy of our
age: the modern poet is not offered the fine edifice of Thomism, as Dante was; he is confronted, we are told, by a bleak
doctrine that proclaims that man is not at home in the world
but thrown into it, that he has no divine father and is abandoned to a life of care, anxiety, and failure that will end in
death, with nothing after that. Poor modern man!

In fact, a disillusionment that used to be the prerogative of
the few has become common property; and what exhilarated
Socrates and Shakespeare, who were in a sense sufficient to
themselves, is found depressing by men who lack the power
to find meaning in themselves. It has almost become a commonplace that the modern artist has lost contact with his audience and that the public no longer supports him as in previous
ages. In this connection one simply ignores Rembrandt and
Mozart, Villon and Hölderlin, Cézanne and Van Gogh. Hundreds of works by modern artists hang in museums largely
because the public is so eager to treat unconventional artists
better than former ages did. But Rembrandt did not need a
public: he had his work and himself. Many moderns are not
satisfied with themselves and their work and blame their failures on the absence of a cultured audience.

There have never been so many writers, artists, and philosophers. Any past age that could boast of more than one outstanding sculptor or philosopher the whole world over and of
more than three good writers and painters wins our admiration as unusually productive; and many an age had none of
great distinction. It is not the public that is at fault today but
the excess of pretenders. But instead of recognizing their own
lack of excellence, many resort to styles that will allow them
to charge their lack of success to the obtuseness of the public.

Rembrandt had the ability to maintain a great reputation
but preferred to paint in his own way, saying in effect, as

Shakespeare's Coriolanus says when he is exiled: "I banish you. . . . There is a world elsewhere."

Shakespeare came to terms with the obtuseness of his public: he gave his pearls a slight odor of the sty before he cast them. Far from cheapening his art, he turned the challenge of a boorish, lecherous, and vulgar audience to advantage and increased the richness and the subtlety of tragedy so vastly that age cannot wither it, nor custom stale its infinite variety.

A stupid public need not always be a curse. It can be a challenge that turns the creator to search within or that leads him to amuse himself by treating his contemporaries to jokes at which they laugh without understanding more than is needed to keep them entertained. Few genuine artists care to be fully understood or esteem those who are profuse in their appreciations. Praise is wanted mainly as a consolation for one's failures.

Some modern writers with intellectual pretensions deal with sex and use four-letter words to register a protest and to get their books denounced, either to insure their success or to excuse their failure. Their preoccupations are with success or failure and with sex as a means to one or the other.

Shakespeare dealt with sex and used four-letter words as a concession to his audience and for humor's sake, not to antagonize and not from boldness and least of all because he had nothing else to offer, but incidentally as one more element in the complexity of his creations. Shakespeare's poetry is the poetry of abundance. There is laughter in it and despair but no resentment or self-pity. He was not even intent on fame and did not see to it that his works were painstakingly committed to print. He knew the view that man is thrown into the world, abandoned to a life that ends in death, with nothing after that; but he also knew self-sufficiency. He had the strength to face reality without excuses and illusions and did not even seek comfort in the faith in immortality. In his last play, *The Tempest*, which is so fanciful on the face of it, this complete freedom from fancy gains consummate expression:

> *. . . like the baseless fabric of this vision,*
> *The cloud-capp'd towers, the gorgeous palaces,*

The solemn temples, the great globe itself,
Yea, all which it inherit, shall dissolve;
And, like this insubstantial pageant faded,
Leave not a rack behind. We are such stuff
As dreams are made on, and our little life
Is rounded with a sleep.

We have been told that Shakespeare was a Christian. Some say he was a Protestant; others, he was a Catholic. Some say that he extolled the Christian virtues. Faith? Hardly. Hope? Certainly not. But love, of course. In the end, the whole suggestion is reducible to the absurd assumption that a man who celebrates love must have been a Christian. Goethe's *Iphigenie*, Sophocles' *Antigone*, Hosea, and the Song of Songs remind us of the baselessness of this Christian imperialism that would like to monopolize love.

Shakespeare is closer to Goethe than he is to Luther, Aquinas, or the Gospels—and still closer to Sophocles. Cordelia and Desdemona are feebler sisters of Antigone, and Shakespeare shares the Greek tragedian's tragic world view: even without moral transgressions human beings sometimes find themselves in situations in which guilt is unavoidable, and what is wanted at that point is neither faith nor hope but courage. As Shaw says in *Heartbreak House*: "Courage will not save you. But it will show that your souls are still alive." There is no hope and no redemption after death. Life is its own reward; and if death should be the wages of sin, it still need not be ignominious. Courage will not save you, but there is a difference between death and death.

The word "Christian" has so many meanings that the absence of faith and hope from Shakespeare's world view may not make him un-Christian in the eyes of those who cannot conceive of any excellence that is not Christian. Nor is there any point in claiming that Shakespeare, or anybody else, was "un-Christian" in *all* senses of that word. But he celebrated *this* world in a most un-Christian manner: its beauties and its grossness; love between the sexes, even in its not particularly subtle forms; and the glory of all that is transitory, including intense emotion. Suffering and despair were to his mind not revelations of the worthlessness of *this* world but experiences that, if intense enough, were preferable to a more mediocre state. "*Ripeness* is all," not faith, hope, even charity, but that maturity of which love, disillusionment, and knowledge born of suffering are a few important facets.

2

They that have power to hurt and will do none,
That do not do the thing they most do show,
Who, moving others, are themselves as stone,
Unmoved, cold, and to temptation slow:
They rightly do inherit heaven's graces
And husband nature's riches from expense,
They are the lords and owners of their faces,
Others, but stewards of their excellence.
The summer's flower is to the summer sweet,
Though to itself it only live and die,
But if that flower with base infection meet,
The basest weed outbraves his dignity:
For sweetest things turn sourest by their deeds;
Lilies that fester smell far worse than weeds.

This sonnet, XCIV, celebrates Shakespeare's un-Christian ideal, which was also the ideal of Nietzsche, who expressed it, not quite three centuries later, in the chapter "On Those Who Are Sublime" in *Zarathustra*. Those who find Shakespeare's first two lines puzzling will find an excellent commentary in Nietzsche:

One who was sublime I saw today, one who was solemn, an ascetic of the spirit; oh, how my soul laughed at his ugliness! . . . As yet he has not overcome his deed. . . . As yet his torrential passion has not become still in beauty. Verily, it is not in satiety that his desire shall grow silent and be submerged, but in beauty. Gracefulness is part of the graciousness of the great-souled. . . . There is nobody from whom I want beauty as much as from you who are powerful: let your kindness be your final self-conquest. Of all evil I deem you capable: therefore I want the good from you.

Verily, I have often laughed at the weaklings who thought
themselves good because they had no claws.

In a note published posthumously in *The Will to Power*
(§983), Nietzsche compressed this vision into half a dozen
words: "the Roman Caesar with Christ's soul." Shakespeare,
too, celebrates the man who has claws but does not use them.
Or, as he put it in *Measure for Measure* (II, ii):

> *O, it is excellent*
> *To have a giant's strength; but it is tyrannous*
> *To use it like a giant.*

In a good book on *The Sense of Shakespeare's Sonnets*, Edward Hubler tells us that "On first reading the [ninety-fourth]
sonnet, we shall, of course, notice the irony of the first eight
lines. . . . It is preposterous on the face of things to proclaim
as the inheritors of heaven's graces those who are 'as stone.'
It can be other than ironical only to the cynic. . . ."

What seems "preposterous" to a Christian reader need not
have struck a Roman or a Spartan as unseemly. We need only
to recall some of the heroes of republican Rome—the first Brutus or Scaevola. Caesar, too, was one of those "who, moving
others, are themselves as stone." Notice the difference between
his affair with Cleopatra and poor Antony's. Shaw underlined
this point: his Caesar knows he has forgotten something as he
is about to leave Egypt, but cannot remember what it is. And
then he realizes that he almost left without saying goodbye
to Cleopatra. The historical Caesar literally moved Cleopatra
to Rome, without letting her interfere with his work.

Caesar, to cite Nietzsche's great tribute to Goethe from his
Twilight of the Idols, "might dare to afford the whole range
and wealth of being natural, being strong enough for such
freedom." And not only Caesar and Goethe but Shakespeare
himself might well be characterized in Nietzsche's words as
"the man of tolerance, not from weakness but from strength,
because he knows how to use to his advantage even that of
which the average nature would perish."

Poetic liberties that would have ruined a lesser poet are
used to advantage by Shakespeare, whose moral tolerance does

more to educate the heart than a whole library of sermons. And Shakespeare, no less than Caesar, was one of those "that have power to hurt and will do none" and "who, moving others, are themselves as stone." Cassius was irritated by Caesar's excessive power to hurt without appreciating that Caesar had no mind to use his power like a giant. And how much hurt could Shakespeare have inflicted with his rarely equalled power to express himself! Those romantic souls who would rather not believe that Shakespeare, the poet, moving others, was himself as stone, might well recall that Shakespeare was an actor, too.

The interpretation that insists that the first eight lines must be ironical depends on the strange assertion that "The first line is tauntingly obscure, and an understanding of the poem cannot proceed without an interpretation of it." The second half of that sentence is true enough, but the first line is not at all obscure. As Edward Dowden understands it rightly in his standard edition of the sonnets, it refers to those "who can hold their passions in check, who can refuse to wrath its outbreak" or, to approximate the wording of the line, to those who have power to hurt but refrain from using it to hurt. There is no irony at all in praising men like that. As Dowden says: "True, these self-contained persons may seem to lack generosity; but then, without making voluntary gifts, they give inevitably, even as the summer's flower is sweet to the summer, though it live and die only to itself."

Such self-sufficiency is not a part of popular morality. "Physician, help yourself: thus you help your patient, too. Let this be his best help that he may behold with his eyes the man who heals himself," says Nietzsche's Zarathustra in his discourse "On The Gift-giving Virtue"; and the chapter "On The Friend" is a fine commentary on Shakespeare's sonnets, too.

It is only in a world view that does not seek a meaning for this life and this world beyond, after death, that experience becomes an end in itself, especially the experience of those who embody mature perfection, "though to itself it only live and die."

The apprehension may remain that such perfection and such power are profoundly dangerous. Cassius considered

Caesar dangerous, and Coriolanus, Macbeth, and Othello met
"with base infection." But that is part of the point of this sonnet and of Shakespeare's tragic view: "Lilies that fester smell
far worse than weeds."

Those who reconsider Hamlet's character in the light of this
sonnet may gain a deeper understanding of him. Although he
is hardly the man whom the sonnet celebrates, he is surely
one of those "that have power to hurt and will do none, that
do not do the thing they most do show"; and his relation to
Ophelia, for example, is well described by these lines:

> Who, moving others, are themselves as stone,
> Unmoved, cold, and to temptation slow.

3

The idea of one who, moving others, is himself unmoved
comes from Aristotle, who thus pictured God. It is also to Aristotle that Nietzsche's word "great-souled" refers; and to the
reference in the chapter "On Those Who Are Sublime" one
may add an underscored remark in Nietzsche's notes, published posthumously in The Will to Power (§981): "there is
nothing romantic about greatness of soul."

In their rebellion against romanticism, modern critics, culminating in T. S. Eliot, have gone back to Christianity and
have glorified the Middle Ages without realizing that this was
the very course that the early romantics took, too—Novalis, for
example, and Friedrich Schlegel, who became a Catholic. The
modern opponents of romanticism have tried to go back to
Dante and Aquinas, not to Aristotle, Socrates, and Sophocles,
and, moreover, to a very partial, rather romantic, conception
of Dante and Aquinas.

This kind of literary criticism was bound to compromise itself when it tried to deal with Shakespeare, who is an embodied refutation of its quaint norms and its weird dichotomy
of Christian and romantic. Eliot's confident assertions that
Hamlet "is most certainly an artistic failure" and that Shakespeare had "an inferior philosophy" sum up the matter. Certainly, those who champion Aquinas and condemn the Refor-

mation, the Renaissance, and Shakespeare, while ignoring
Aristotle, Socrates, and Sophocles, should not be considered
guardians of "tradition."

Once the Greeks have been read out of history, with no
place left for Shakespeare either, recent history is bound to
be falsified no less. Goethe must go, too, together with his
models. Certainly, there is no room now for *his* opposition to
romanticism which, if once admitted, would explode the false
dichotomy of either nineteenth-century romanticism or Christianity. Indeed, Goethe is not read but simply classified—as a
romantic! And Hegel's critique of romanticism is ignored, too.

Kierkegaard enjoys a certain vogue, but there is no room for
the things that mattered most to him. His opposition to apologetics and his central claim of the absurdity of Christian faith
are disregarded together with his vehement *Attack on Christendom*, and he is turned into an apologist. This looks dishonest, but the way in which history has been rewritten does
not make it possible for our critics to discern how anyone
could consider Christianity absurd. If they had read Aristotle
rather than Aquinas they might understand.

Nietzsche, the first great philosopher to celebrate the tragic
outlook that pervades the work of Shakespeare and the first in
modern times to celebrate the great-souled man of Aristotle's
Ethics, is now viewed as a half-mad, eccentric critic of "tradition" who attempted, single-handed, to turn all things upside
down.

Rilke, the greatest pagan religious poet since Hölderlin, is
posthumously christened; Kafka is turned into a misty mystic,
and then Heidegger confronts us all at once with an allegedly
distinctly modern philosophy of alienation. The critics who
have given us this picture are themselves alienated from a
magnificent tradition that culminates in Heidegger—"not with
a bang but a whimper."

To redress this falsification of history one must go back to
classical Greece—not to the pre-Socratics to whom Heidegger
wants to return. A simple reading of a couple of pages from
Aristotle's *Nicomachean Ethics* is sufficient to give anyone a
new perspective on Shakespeare's ninety-fourth sonnet, his

Coriolanus, and his other tragedies, and on Goethe and Nietzsche, too.

The good man ought to be a lover of self, since he will then act nobly, and so benefit himself and aid his fellows; but the bad man ought not to be a lover of self, since he will follow his base passions, and so injure both himself and his neighbors. (IX, 8)

A person is thought to be great-souled if he claims much and deserves much. . . . He that claims less than he deserves is small-souled. . . . Greatness of soul seems . . . a crowning ornament of all the virtues. . . . Great honours accorded by persons of worth will afford [the great-souled man] pleasure in a moderate degree: he will feel he is receiving only what belongs to him, or even less, for no honour can be adequate to the merits of perfect virtue, yet all the same he will deign to accept their honours, because they have no greater tribute to offer him. Honour rendered by common people and on trivial grounds he will utterly despise. . . . He . . . will be indifferent to other things as well. Hence great-souled men are thought to be haughty. . . . The great-souled man is justified in despising other people—his estimates are correct; but most proud men have no good ground for their pride. . . . He is fond of conferring benefits, but ashamed to receive them. . . . He returns a service done to him with interest, since this will put the original benefactor into his debt in turn. . . . The great-souled are said to have a good memory for any benefit they have conferred, but a bad memory for those which they have received. . . . It is also characteristic of the great-souled men never to ask help from others, or only with reluctance, but to render aid willingly; and to be haughty towards men of position and fortune, but courteous towards those of moderate station . . . and to adopt a high manner with the former is not ill-bred, but it is vulgar to lord it over humble people. . . . He must . . . care more for the truth than for what people will think; . . . he is outspoken and frank, except when speaking with ironical self-deprecation, as he does to common people. . . . He does not bear a grudge. . . . He is . . . not given to speaking evil himself, even of his enemies, except when he deliberately intends to give offence. (IV, 3)

Most modern admirers of Aristotle pass over such passages in embarrassment though they offer nothing less than Aristotle's notion of ideal manhood—and then Shakespeare's ninety-fourth sonnet seems "preposterous" to them. For it does not celebrate the Christian saint but Aristotle's great-souled man.

In Shakespeare's tragedies, Coriolanus is the outstanding example of a great-souled man. But he is not the only one. Take Othello's last speech: "I have done the state some service, and they know't. . . ." T. S. Eliot does not like Othello's attitude: "What Othello seems to me to be doing in making this speech is *cheering himself up*. He is endeavoring to escape reality, he has ceased to think about Desdemona, and is thinking about himself. Humility is the most difficult of all virtues to achieve. . . ." Indeed, Othello is not humble nor a Christian; he is a great-souled man. Nor did Shakespeare write his tragedies about saints. Does that make them artistic failures in comparison with modern plays about saints? Eliot's remarks on Othello occur in his *Shakespeare and the Stoicism of Seneca,* where Shakespeare is contrasted with Dante by way of showing that the philosophy behind Shakespeare's works was "inferior." But Eliot makes it rather easy for himself when he contrasts Aquinas with Seneca, not with Aristotle. To be sure, Shakespeare was no Aristotelian, and in many ways he was not "classical." In some ways his style was even anticlassical. He did not conform to Aristotle's aesthetic canon, as we have it in the *Poetics;* nor was Nietzsche an Aristotelian. But their un-Christian ethics do invite comparison with Aristotle, if only to correct the warped perspective that has become the norm.

Nor should we overlook Aristotle's comment, in the portrait cited: "The great-souled man is justified in despising other people—his estimates are correct." Surely, Shakespeare's acid contempt for men and women is one of the central motifs of his tragedies. It is part of the point of that famous scene in *Julius Caesar* in which Antony sways the populace with his celebrated speech, "I come to bury Caesar, not to praise him."

It is marked throughout *Coriolanus*. It is the background of Hamlet's melancholy. To be sure, we cannot simply ascribe to the poet Coriolanus' attitude, but it is surely extraordinary that Shakespeare should have chosen such a theme and then done his successful best to make us sympathize with such a hero whom, but for the poet's art, we should most likely loathe. We cannot identify Shakespeare with Hamlet, but what, if not his own experience, could have moved the poet to endow his prince with such persuasive disillusionment about mankind? Was this extreme of bitterness required by the plot or for purely aesthetic reasons? And in the case of *Caesar* it is clearly not Marc Antony who tells us that the people's voice is not the voice of God, but rather the dramatist who leads us to share a profound contempt for the mass of men.

One play alone might not warrant an inference about the poet's views, even as one of Faulkner's novels by itself might be considered insufficient to back up the claim that he is not an optimist and by no means persuaded that the introduction of machines will solve most human problems. But the body of a writer's major works may make conclusions of this sort quite reasonable, and the tragedies of Shakespeare reveal something of a pattern.

The drama in which Shakespeare's tragic period culminated, *Timon of Athens*, is single-mindedly devoted to the theme that almost all men are despicable, but it is rarely discussed. Yet *Timon* is instructive, not only because it shows how deeply disillusioned Shakespeare was, but also because in the first part of the play we see a classical, non-Christian love in action.

In the early scenes, Timon loves wealth and luxury and sensuous pleasures, without in the least approximating either the portrait of the rich man that we find in the New Testament or the kind of sensuousness that we associate, for example, with the young Augustine. Timon loves his bounty because he can use it to purchase delights for others as well as himself: he loves wealth and pleasures because he can share them. He reminds us of the celebrated Aristotelian dictum that property should be private, but the use of it common. To be sure, the pleasures of this world are transitory, even the pleasure of giving, which Timon had prized above all others. But what galls Timon is not the loss of his wealth and sensuous delights: only man's ingratitude, man's meanness, man's lack of nobility elicits those resounding curses that fill all his later speeches, of which there are many. Even then the poet lavishes nobility on Timon to induce the audience and the reader to sympathize with him and to share his loathing for most men. Nor does Timon's disillusionment lead him beyond this world: he only wants to

> *Lie where the light foam of the sea may beat*
> *Thy grave-stone daily.* (IV, iii)

With *Timon of Athens* Shakespeare spent that fury of which his great tragedies from *Caesar* and *Hamlet* to *Lear* and *Coriolanus* are enduring monuments. He purged his soul, not by austerities or penances, but by giving free vent to his feelings.

It will never do to ignore *Timon*, even though some of the less important scenes were probably not written by Shakespeare. If we went to the absurd extreme of conservative caution and supposed that only Timon's major speeches were by Shakespeare, we could not escape the question: How full must the poet's heart have been if he took up a theme like that to write such hymns of generosity and, then, disdain?

Having poured out his fury, he did not become converted, nor did he renounce this world. He achieved a poetry of disillusionment without resentment. He did not renounce Macbeth's great insight that

> *Life's but a walking shadow, a poor player*
> *That struts and frets his hour upon the stage*
> *And then is heard no more: it is a tale*
> *Told by an idiot, full of sound and fury,*
> *Signifying nothing.* (V, v)

Shakespeare found some beauty, though no cosmic purpose, in this tale. And this fairy-tale charm and the gentle humor of absurdity became dominant in his last plays. Courage loses all shrillness; disillusionment, all bitterness. And when he writes in *The Tempest* that the great globe itself shall dissolve

And, like this insubstantial pageant faded,
Leave not a rack behind

and that "our little life is rounded with a sleep," most readers
are aware of little but the poetry and hence are ready to believe those critics who maintain that Shakespeare had no world
view—or even that he was a Christian.

4

Shakespeare's tragic world view is ignored not only by those
critics who are much too democratic to allow for the bare possibility that our greatest poet might have felt such a profound
contempt for most men. Antiliberal critics also manage to present us with dichotomies in which the tragic view is simply
overlooked. Take T. E. Hulme's pioneering essay on "Romanticism and Classicism," which exerted a profound influence
and is therefore reprinted as the first selection in Stallman's
anthology of *Critiques and Essays in Criticism.* Romanticism,
says Hulme, views man as "an infinite reservoir of possibilities"
and pins its faith on progress. The classical view is "the exact
opposite" and holds that man is a "limited animal whose nature is absolutely constant. It is only by tradition and organisa-
tion that anything decent can be got out of him." And Hulme
adds that "the Church has always taken the classical view
since the defeat of the Pelagian heresy and the adoption of
the sane classical dogma of original sin."

It takes a systematic abuse of terms to find the dogma of
original sin "classical." Only ignorance of classical Greece can
keep us from understanding Kierkegaard's insistence that the
dogma is absurd, or Paul's illuminating remark that his preaching seemed "unto the Greeks foolishness."

Shakespeare, like the Greeks before him and Nietzsche after
him, believed neither in progress nor in original sin; he believed that most men merited contempt and that a very few
were head and shoulders above the rest of mankind and that
these few, more often than not, meet "with base infection"
and do not herald progress. The prerogative of the few is
tragedy.

The tragic world view involves an ethic of character, not, like the Gospels, an ethic of otherworldly prudence. In the Sermon on the Mount alone, the word "reward" recurs nine times, the idea of reward at least another nineteen times, and the threat of dire punishments at least a dozen times, before the Sermon is concluded with the express assertion that those who do as they are bidden are "wise" while those who do not are "foolish." As Guenther Bornkamm, a German Protestant theologian who dislikes the idea of prudence, is forced to admit in his learned monograph on *Der Lohngedanke im Neuen Testament,* "the New Testament does not know the idea of the good deed that has its value in itself."

The tragic hero has no reward. The tragic view knows, as Christianity does not, genuine self-sacrifice. To readers accustomed to the modern falsification of history, this sounds paradoxical. In his chapter on "The Ethic of Jesus" in *An Interpretation of Christian Ethics,* Reinhold Niebuhr, another champion of original sin, argues in effect that the absence of the idea of genuine self-sacrifice from the Christian ethic "merely proves" that *no* ethic can maintain such an ideal. One does not have to cite Mahayana Buddhism, the life of Moses, and the teachings of some of the Hebrew prophets to refute this claim: the great tragedians will do.

Sophocles' Antigone goes to her death without the least hope of reward. It is her duty and not the fulfillment of her hopes that demands self-sacrifice. The tragic hero accepts as his own a guilt that is at the very least not only his own and sacrifices himself, like Oedipus and Hamlet, to lift a curse from his society and to transcend futile mediocrity in the sheer glory of self-immolation.[1]

In Shakespeare's works, this point is perhaps most emphatically made in *Troilus and Cressida,* one of the two great comedies of Shakespeare's tragic period, written shortly after *Hamlet.* Here the same loathing for most men that finds expression in the tragedies is given a comic twist. The victorious Greeks are pictured as despicable men—none more so than their great-

[1] Bornkamm, Niebuhr, the New Testament, and *Antigone* are discussed more fully in my *Critique of Religion and Philosophy,* §§58, 68, and 77.

est heroes: Ajax, Diomedes, and Achilles. Menelaus is dismissed as a cuckold, and the celebrated Helen, as a whore.
When Paris asks Diomedes,

> *Who, in your thoughts, merits fair Helen best,*
> *Myself or Menelaus?*

Diomedes answers him:

> *Both alike:*
> *He merits well to have her, that doth seek her,*
> *Not making any scruple of her soilure,*
> *With such a hell of pain and world of charge,*
> *And you as well to keep her, that defend her,*
> *Not palating the taste of her dishonour,*
> *With such a costly loss of wealth and friends:*
> *He, like a puling cuckold, would drink up*
> *The lees and dregs of a flat tamed piece;*
> *You, like a lecher, out of whorish loins*
> *Are pleased to breed out your inheritors:*
> *Both merits poised, each weighs nor less nor more;*
> *But he as he, the heavier for a whore.* (IV, i)

It is widely believed that the ironical attitude toward classical antiquity that finds such hyperbolic expression in these lines is something novel in the twentieth century. Clearly, it is not. Nor is this debunking attitude confined to the scurrilous and scurvy Thersites and to Diomedes, quoted here; the play is based on the assumption that Diomedes is right. And Hector, the one truly magnanimous hero in this play, accepts this view.

He proposes to "let Helen go." He has no wish "to guard a thing not ours nor worth to us." When his brothers protest, he replies: "She is not worth what she doth cost the holding." Then Cassandra prophesies the failure of their efforts and concludes: "Troy burns, or else let Helen go." It is without faith in his cause and without hope that Hector nevertheless decides to fight. His last long speech in this scene (II, ii) leaves no doubt about that. There is no inkling of faith, hope, or prudence in his virtue.

Hector's adoption of a cause that he himself considers

clearly contrary to the laws of morality lacks that poetry of statement that transfigures Macbeth, and Hector barely falls short of being a tragic hero. Although Shakespeare's conception of his death breathes a bitterness exceeding the account of Homer, it lacks tragic grandeur.

> HECTOR: *I am unarm'd; forego this vantage, Greek.*
> ACHILLES: *Strike, fellows, strike, this is the man I seek.*

Hector falls, and Achilles commands his Myrmidons:

> *Come, tie his body to my horse's tail;*
> *Along the field I will the Trojan trail.*

A page later, the play concludes with a humorous epilogue by Pandarus.

The difference between comedy and tragedy—as is more evident here than almost anywhere else—lies in the point of view. In essentials, *Troilus and Cressida* agrees with *Hamlet;* if anything, the poet's disillusionment has become still deeper in the comedy: he no longer expects anything of men and has ceased to be disappointed by their meanness and stupidity, their lechery and their disloyalty. He almost seems more concerned to show that those who dwell on these faults are in danger of becoming doubly mean by their resentment, like Thersites. The noble man, like Hector, wastes few words upon the wretchedness of mankind and lives and dies nobly.

In *The Birth of Tragedy,* Nietzsche pictured Socrates as the man whose rationalism brought an end to the tragic era and, with real reverence, blamed him for the demise of tragedy. There is some truth in this view; yet Socrates may also be viewed as a tragic hero. Socrates' *Apology,* as Plato has recorded it, shows him going to his death without as much as thinking of the possibility of a reward after death. Like Antigone, he will not compromise his duty, as he sees it, to avert self-sacrifice. Rather than live on in enforced mediocrity, he attains his greatest height in facing death with open eyes. He even anticipates Shakespeare, and differs from Sophocles, in finding the occasion not unfit for humor, biting irony, and mocking laughter. That he was deliberate in fusing the sublime and the ridiculous, Plato assures us at the end of his

Symposium, where Socrates compelled Aristophanes, the comic poet, and Agathon, the tragic poet, "to admit that the genius of comedy was the same with that of tragedy, and that the true artist in tragedy was an artist in comedy also." Shakespeare's sonnets are full of echoes of this dialogue.

Nietzsche coupled his highest tributes to Socrates' *Apology* with the express assertion that it was from this great speech that "*Plato* seems to have received the decisive thought as to how a philosopher ought to behave toward men." He failed to notice, like everyone else, that at least some features of Aristotle's conception of the great-souled man were also influenced by Socrates' *Apology.*

Here is the man who "claims much and deserves much"; who is "justified in despising other people"; who "is fond of conferring benefits but ashamed to receive them"; who remembers well the benefits he has conferred; who refuses to ask for consideration and is "haughty towards men of position and fortune"; who cares "more for the truth than for what people will think"; who "is outspoken and frank, except when speaking with ironical self-depreciation"; and who speaks evil of his enemies only "when he deliberately intends to give offence."

Those who have come to see all things in the perspective of Christian norms that have been made comfortably bourgeois admire Aristotle from a distance but profess to be embarrassed when confronted with his own ideal. They praise Socrates after christening him, preferably as an Anglican. They acknowledge Shakespeare's greatness but find his ninety-fourth sonnet "preposterous" or tell us that, of course, he did not mean it, and they force some kind of Christian reading on his tragedies unless they dismiss them as mere poetry.

They do not realize that possibly the noblest world view of them all has here found perfect form—without the swaggering terminology and the strutting obscurantism with which some of the same ideas are associated in modern philosophic prose. Even with the word "nothing" Shakespeare had his sport; the confrontation with death is there no less than resolution, man's abandoned state, and above all the sheer absurdity of life. And what remains to man? The liberating feeling of pervasive disillusionment; the joy of honesty, integrity, and courage; and the grace of humor, love, and comprehensive tolerance: in one word, nobility.

5

On one important point, Shakespeare seems to be closer to the Christian view than to that of some existentialists. He appears to believe in absolute moral laws. When Hector, in *Troilus and Cressida,* expresses his lack of faith in the Trojan cause, he says:

> *If Helen then be wife to Sparta's king,*
> *As it is known she is, these moral laws*
> *Of nature and of nations speak aloud*
> *To have her back return'd: thus to persist*
> *In doing wrong extenuates not wrong,*
> *But makes it much more heavy.*

In the immediately following lines, he nevertheless accepts his brothers'

> *resolution to keep Helen still,*
> *For 'tis a cause that has no mean dependence*
> *Upon our joint and several dignities.*

He puts his own resolve and dignity above "the moral laws of nature and of nations."

The rest of the play makes it possible that Hector's speech with its unexpected conclusion is meant to be funny. Moreover, Troilus has argued in the very same scene: "What is aught, but as 'tis valued?" Hector might speak for himself alone, not for the poet, when he replies: "But value dwells not in particular will."

The conception of absolute moral laws, however, is encountered in some of the other plays, too. In *Othello* and *Macbeth,* in *Lear* and in *The Tempest,* there is little or no question about what is good and what is evil. Some of Shakespeare's characters have some claim on our sympathy or even our admiration in spite of the evil they do, but there is no doubt that it is evil. Again and again it is assumed, and we are led to feel, that not only the moral laws of nations have been outraged but the moral laws of nature, too. Is Shakespeare a Christian after all? It may be more to the point that he agrees with Sophocles and the Greeks.

At least one play, however, has an emphatically un-Greek conclusion. That is the other great comedy of the tragic period, *Measure for Measure*, in which everybody is forgiven in the end. According to a current usage that is conditioned by liberal Protestantism, which in turn has been influenced by post-Christian poets like Shakespeare and Goethe among others, this conclusion is clearly "Christian." But it is sharply at variance with the teachings not only of the Catholic Church and the Reformers but of the Gospels, too. The ideal of universal forgiveness has always been condemned as a heresy.

In *Measure for Measure*, moreover, Isabella's Christian virtue comes very close to being ridiculed; for example, when she says:

> Then, Isabel, live chaste and, brother, die.
> More than our brother is our chastity. (II, iv)

Or when she replies to a man who suggests that after all she might consider sacrificing her chastity—not to him—to save her brother:

> Die, perish! Might but my bending down
> Reprieve thee from thy fate, it should proceed:
> I'll pray a thousand prayers for thy death,
> No word to save thee. (III, i)

We need not concentrate on single speeches. The play begins with the merciful Duke's attempt to remedy the license that has developed in the wake of his own loving tolerance. He delegates his authority to one who is less forgiving and quite willing to enforce justice. But the man intent on judging others quickly succumbs to temptation, and in the end we are returned to the rule of mercy, with forgiveness for all. The play invites comparison with Tolstoy's heretical conception of the Gospel as a plea for anarchy, but if Shakespeare ridicules the pretensions of churches, whether Catholic or Calvinist, he is no less remote from Tolstoy's fanatic moralism and rabid denunciations of sex and sensuality.[2]

What we find in Shakespeare is a world-embracing tolerance that would punish no man, for the poet is above resentment. But this tolerance is coupled with a vast contempt for most men. What the poet admires is nobility, and the noble man despises without the least wish to inflict hurt. He exercises charity—an *agape*, to use the Greek word, that comes from a height and is distinct from his *eros*, his aspiration for perfection. If this aspiration meets with base infection, it may devour charity, as it does in Macbeth. One need not be a Christian or a believer in natural law to feel, as Shakespeare does, that Macbeth *has* met with base infection and that his deeds are evil; or to see Lear's folly and Goneril's wickedness; or to condemn the actions that the poet ascribes to Richard III.

The noble man who is corrupted and festers violates the laws of nature in the same sense as other disturbances of the natural order, enumerated, for example, in *Lear*. You may say, and many of us should prefer to say, that diseases and corruption are perfectly natural and part of the way of the world. That does not annihilate the difference between health and sickness. Shakespeare assumes that the corruption of a noble nature and its degradation to the level where it becomes involved in base deeds is comparable to an infection. This parallel does not extend to every transgression of the moral laws of nations: one can transgress man-made laws and remain healthy. But Shakespeare's great evildoers do not merely flout convention; they become ignoble and base.

Shakespeare's non-Christian outlook is particularly clear in the two tragedies in which we encounter a profound moral perplexity: *Caesar* and *Hamlet*. In the end, it seems relatively unimportant whether Brutus and Hamlet made the right decisions. Faith, hope, and charity are out of the picture no less than conventional right and wrong. Yet a standard remains:

[2] An interesting summary of "Tolstoy's Attack on Shakespeare" may be found in *The Wheel of Fire: Interpretations of Shakespearean Tragedy* by G. Wilson Knight, one of the best and most philosophical of Shakespeare scholars.

nobility. When Hamlet dies, Horatio says: "Now cracks a
noble heart." Antony's tribute to Brutus is, if possible, still
more famous: "This was the noblest Roman of them all." Unlike the others who did what he did, too, Brutus was free of
envy, honest and gentle,

> *and the elements*
> *So mix'd in him that Nature might stand up*
> *And say to all the world "This was a man!"*

His un-Christian suicide does not diminish his integrity. And
in a later Roman play, Cleopatra actually achieves greater nobility than she ever had in life when she dies of her own hand,
or rather of the bite of the serpent, the Christian symbol of
evil.

Shakespeare is—at this point, too—far closer to Socrates and
Nietzsche, to Aristotle and Goethe than he is to the evangelists
or St. Augustine, to Aquinas, Calvin, Kierkegaard, or T. S. Eliot. His work stands as a monument of a tradition that is frequently forgotten today, and it celebrates the riches of a world
without God.

6

"Having been born in an unsettled society"—to use Eliot's
fine phrase once more—need not entail any fatal "damage,"
though the fairy tale of a distant "golden" past is old indeed.
Today many intellectuals believe it and endow some past age
—usually the Middle Ages—or even all ages save our own, with
a halo. The witness against such myths—not only by historians
—is impressive. Robert Bridges wrote one of his finest poems on
the "Nightingales" to insist that their home is not "beautiful"
but "barren." Hermann Hesse, in a poem entitled "After reading in the *Summa Contra Gentiles*," suggests that serenity may
be an optical illusion due to distance and that some tormented
soul of our time may yet become a paradigm of tranquillity
to future ages. Nietzsche concluded *The Birth of Tragedy*, saying of the Greeks: "How much did this people have to suffer
to become so beautiful!"

There is no need to pit authority against authority. "Having been born in an unsettled society" is the condition that Elijah and Jeremiah, Plato and Aristotle, Paul and the Buddha, Leonardo and Michelangelo, Shakespeare and Spinoza have in common. Perhaps Dante, who lived in exile, and Aquinas, who saw his religion menaced by the discovery of Aristotle's pagan world view, should be added to this list.

It may seem fitting that pumpkins should grow on huge trees, and acorns on the ground, but that is not the way the world is. Wheat grows where the ground has been torn open and plowed; edelweiss, in the cracks of Alpine rocks, over the precipice; and great prophets and philosophers, poets and artists generally grow in unsettled societies, on the brink of some abyss.

The modern world *is* a waste land, but the world never has been—and surely never will be—a flower garden. What we make of that is largely up to us. Eliot's sterile waste land is the setting for Hemingway's fishing trips and bull fights in *The Sun Also Rises;* and Hermann Hesse, in *Der Steppenwolf,* shows us a sensibility that embraces Eliot's experience as well as Hemingway's—and Mozart's, too. The fragmentation and ugliness of the modern world are undeniable. What needs to be denied is that the world of Dante and Aquinas was less ugly, crude, and cruel. Greatness is possible, but exceptional, at all times.

Blaming one's failings on the *Zeitgeist* involves self-deception. Our age may well have more than its share of great writers. That is no consolation for those highly sensitive and often lovable souls whom a modern poet has caricatured with definitive malice. Edwin Arlington Robinson may not have been a great poet, but he did not blame his time for that, and in his best-known poem he ridiculed those whom self-pity leads to distort history:

> *Miniver cursed the commonplace*
> *And eyed a khaki suit with loathing;*
> *He missed the medieval grace*
> *of iron clothing.*

> *Miniver Cheevy, child of scorn,*
> *Grew lean while he assailed the seasons;*
> *He wept that he was ever born,*
> *And he had reasons.*[3]

[3] Stanzas 6 and 1 of "Miniver Cheevy," originally published in *Scribner's Magazine* in March 1907, reprinted in *The Town Down the River*, Charles Scribner's Sons, New York 1910, and quoted here with the publisher's permission.

2

DIALOGUE WITH A CRITIC

CRITIC: Your tone is peremptory, and your thesis almost ridiculous. The modern situation *is* unprecedented; and the lot of the sensitive, deeply depressing.

AUTHOR: Being more sensitive than others means suffering more. That has nothing to do with modernity. Or do you think you suffer more than Michelangelo, Shakespeare, or Goethe?

CRITIC: "When man becomes mute in his agony," said Goethe, "a god gave me to say what I suffer." That gift makes up for a great deal.

AUTHOR: Then you admit that what so many modern artists, intellectuals, and writers really resent is not the age in which they live but their own lack of genius.

CRITIC: The age is responsible for the impossibility of any real genius in the arts today. We lack the hard core of a recognizable public that we might address. The elite is gone. The common background of knowledge, tastes, and manners has disintegrated. One lives in a vacuum.

AUTHOR: The conclusion you try to prove is false. There is no lack of real genius.

CRITIC: Do we have a Shakespeare or a Michelangelo?

AUTHOR: Only one age had a Shakespeare; only one a Michelangelo. In Elizabethan England poetry flourished, but sculpture, painting, and philosophy did not.

CRITIC: We have no artists of the first rank in any field.

AUTHOR: We have no dramatist like Shakespeare; but what age besides his own did? Epstein is no Michelangelo but compares favorably with the best sculptors of many other centuries. Rilke may well have been one of the greatest poets of all time, and the twentieth century has had more than its share of other good poets. Few novelists and architects have excelled our best ones. Russell, Whitehead, Wittgenstein, and Santayana do not equal Plato, but few generations have done better.

CRITIC: I don't want to find fault with all the men you mention, one by one. I'll even concede that most of them have met with more acclaim than many of the great men of the past had in their own day. But for every name you mention there are thousands who are wretched. Was that always the price for every genius?

AUTHOR: Wretchedness used to take different forms, and in many countries, especially in Asia and Africa, it still does. Today some of those who in other ages would have lived in squalor get an education and achieve unprecedented comfort. Still they lack the talent to turn self-awareness into a creative asset. But few remain wretched for long: the vast majority return to comfortable blindness before they are thirty. They still read, but mainly magazines; and they are reasonably happy.

CRITIC: But there is a large class of unhappy people who are only too aware of their position in the world. They worry about its meaning and feel alienated, frustrated, and futile.

AUTHOR: That is the price you have to pay for compulsory education. If you find it too heavy, there are two alternatives. Either you make education a rare privilege and keep the masses illiterate; or you substitute indoctrination for education. In the latter case, you have to supplement your system with censorship and inquisition, secret police and concentration camps. That is an entirely workable remedy for the ills of which you have complained, but perhaps you will agree that these alternatives are worse than our present system, which engenders the desire to be a great writer or artist in hundreds, who, sooner or later, are bound to feel frustrated when they discover that they lack the talent.

CRITIC: Why not have indoctrination without censorship and concentration camps?

AUTHOR: The confused, half-hearted Platonism that is championed, for example, by T. S. Eliot in his *Idea of a Chris-*

tian Society is unworkable. Without the unsentimental methods of Plato and Aquinas you cannot achieve that uniformity of outlook, that authority of dogma, that agreement in belief and values that Eliot demands to cure the failings of the democratic system. In our present syncretistic age with its unprecedented possibilities of travel and communication, we should have to go beyond Plato's Nocturnal Council and Aquinas' Inquisition and approximate the nightmare of George Orwell's *Nineteen Eighty-Four*.

CRITIC: I am not trying to defend Eliot's book. His arguments are simple-minded: "If you will not have God (and He is a jealous God) you should pay your respects to Hitler or Stalin" (p. 64). Why? He confronts us with alternatives that leave out of account a large body of thought. And, though as a poet he is famous for his irony, and though he surely is not ignorant of Dostoevsky's Grand Inquisitor, he never seems to notice how ironical his blithe equation of Christianity with blind conformity must seem to anyone who has not quite forgotten Jesus' gospel. Eliot's book scarcely merits detailed criticism: even his admirers are embarrassed by it. But some of the ills that bother him are real enough. The tightly knit elite, composed of men who knew each other, is a matter of the past: the serious writer and artist have lost their audience.

AUTHOR: Their audience is larger than ever before. We not only have the printing press but art books, reproductions, radio, and records. The small elites of former ages have been replaced by a huge, but widely scattered, class of people who are much less homogeneous but no less appreciative and even hungry.

CRITIC: They are far away. Writers and artists do not belong. They have lost the respect of the less educated and less sensitive majority. They are exiles.

AUTHOR: Instead of either being oppressed by the nobility or themselves thriving on the sweat of their inferiors, they live on the margins of society. Many are lonely. That sounds sad. If you said that they are left alone, it would sound more cheerful. Moreover, those whose excellence prevails have more prestige than any of their predecessors had in their day.

CRITIC: Not as much as movie stars or athletes.

AUTHOR: More than Rembrandt, Dante, Plato, or Spinoza enjoyed in their day. You must not compare the prestige of the living with that of the dead. It takes time to survive ephemeral reputations. A celebrated saying in the Gospels would be truer if it were revised to read: A prophet is not without honor, save in his own time.

CRITIC: Surely, things are worse today than ever.

AUTHOR: Socrates was put to death; Aristotle fled lest the Athenians should sin twice against philosophy; Dante, like Anaxagoras, was exiled. Rembrandt all but starved to death. Mozart had a pauper's funeral. How would you gauge Plato's sense of alienation or Spinoza's? Was the author of *Hamlet* and *Timon* less lonely than the writers of today? Did he have an audience that responded to the infinite complexities of his creations? Was he appreciated like Thomas Mann or T. S. Eliot who, in middle age, could read whole libraries of adulating "criticism" of their works? Was there any seal of international approval that one might compare with the Nobel Prize?

CRITIC: You have a flair for inconvenient facts. But there are unprecedented factors. We have weapons of destruction that threaten to wipe out mankind. That creates a sense of futility.

AUTHOR: The prime source of any feeling of futility, frustration, and anxiety lies in the self. Shakespeare could face the thought that the great globe itself would "leave not a rack behind" and that life is "a tale told by an idiot" without being overwhelmed by self-pity.

CRITIC: Naturally, if all men were Shakespeares we should not have the problems that we do have. That is a truism, but hardly helpful or illuminating.

AUTHOR: It might help a little, though hardly much. Some people who now blame their time for many of their shortcomings might recognize their self-deception. A few might even acquire a greater sense of dignity, responsibility, and purpose when they realize to what extent the source of their complaints lies in themselves. In any case, self-knowledge is better than resentment. The truth of a diagnosis does not depend on therapeutic success. If a man persuades himself and others that he is possessed by demons or tortured by spirits, it is not terribly helpful if we tell him that he has a cancer that is probably incurable. But it is honest, and it keeps people from looking in the wrong direction, wasting time and energy on futile plans. Above all, it is illuminating to see what ills are connected with what gains; to know the price one has to pay for widely hailed advances; and to have a clear conception of the possible alternatives.

CRITIC: What is new is that our values are hollow. A play like *Death of a Salesman* shows what is wrong. It is a *modern* tragedy, and what is tragic today is not what was tragic in former times.

AUTHOR: It is hardly a tragedy. Classical tragedy deals with the uncommon individual whom we look up to in the beginning and who is somehow superior even in his destruction. *Death of a Salesman* is meant to be about a common case, and the hero is pathetic.

CRITIC: Let us not quibble about words.

AUTHOR: Equally pathetic individuals must have abounded in all ages, and the majority of mankind has been, and still is, far worse off; but the poets of former ages did not write about such men—at least not tragedies.

CRITIC: Are you finding fault with Arthur Miller?

AUTHOR: Not at all. The fact that playwrights in the past did not indict the hollow values of their day—if it is a fact—does not in any way prove that the modern age must be inferior. More power to the men who criticize the hollow values of their time! But consider Miller's play, *The Crucible*, or Ibsen's *An Enemy of the People:* those, too, are indictments of the age. Still, they have heroes. "The enemy of the people" is an uncommon individual who is not pathetic, a man who echoes Kierkegaard's dictum that "wherever there is a crowd there is untruth." Arthur Miller's splendid adaptation of that play became a great success—in a tiny theater in Greenwich Village. It never met with the wide acclaim accorded *Death of a Salesman*, because most people would rather look down on Willie Loman than look up to Dr. Stockmann. Indeed, I am not finding fault with Arthur Miller: it is not *his* fault that the public does not enjoy his criticisms unless they are palliated by a protagonist whom one can pity. It is not *his* fault that the only victim of Hitler who has caught the imagination of the mass is not one of the many who defied him but a little girl, Anne Frank.

CRITIC: At least you admit that our values have become hollow.

AUTHOR: You judge Elijah's age by him; Socrates' time by him; Shakespeare's by him; but ours by the values of the mass. And then you think that you have proved that today is the low point of history. The values of the mass are always hollow. But critics often talk as if things had been better in the past. For some of the Hebrew prophets, the years in the wilderness became a golden age; for Moses, they were hardly that: how could he forget the golden calf! We think of the age of the great prophets as a kind of golden age, struck by the succession of the titans from Elijah and Amos to Jeremiah and the Second Isaiah; but to them their own age could scarcely have been worse.

CRITIC: I had begun to think that you considered our time the golden age.

AUTHOR: Those who see it that way and gloat over progress seem as strange to me as those who would like to go back to the womb of the Middle Ages. Of course, we have made progress in a great many ways; nor did the Middle Ages lack attractive features. But as far as man's condition is concerned I agree more with Ecclesiastes and the great tragedians. The forms of self-deception change a little, but the tragedy of Oedipus is timeless. So is Antigone's. So is Job's.

CRITIC: Are you then opposed to all attempts to criticize present conditions and to correct injustices?

AUTHOR: Not in the least. Criticism and the fight against injustice are ingredients of the best life one can live. But I am less optimistic about the results than you are. Failure is no argument against nobility.

CRITIC: Do you consider all ages equally bad?

AUTHOR: Whether a man would as soon live today or not depends on whether he would as soon be himself or not. The primary yes is self-affirmation; the primary no, resentment of oneself.

CRITIC: I understand you better now, but two things bother me as much as ever. The first is that your approach involves you constantly in slurs upon the character of those with whom you disagree. "Resentment of oneself." There is something nasty about your criticism. Most men *are* revolting; but when you write about them you might show some sympathy. It would make your criticism more effective.

AUTHOR: I don't find people disgusting. What I oppose is the book, the write-up, the public personality, its influence and what it stands for—but when I meet the man I like him. I admire his virtues, am saddened by his weaknesses, am sorry if he drinks too much, but like him for all that. How I feel about him personally is nobody's business—not even *his*. As Goethe once said: "If I love you, what concern is that of yours?" But the books that the man himself saw fit to publish and his impact don't enjoy the same immunity. I can like and even admire men with whom I differ, and still represent the type by quoting E. A. Robinson:

> *Miniver coughed, and called it fate,*
> *And kept on drinking.*

CRITIC: Are you insinuating that all the writers who disagree with you are alcoholics?

AUTHOR: Of course not. But these lines are appropriate because they make us feel that a man's drinking cannot be blamed solely on the paltry times in which he lives. Still, men's faults differ. Sympathy is individual and refuses to see a man's problems and failings merely from the outside as typical. But when you write, sympathy prevents you from publicizing what is personal.

CRITIC: But *you* do not deal with the books only. You try to deal with the human reality behind the book.

AUTHOR: Insofar as it is typical, making allowance for scores of variations, which, probed individually, elicit sympathy. But if, in decency, we stop short of the personal, what we see is often comical. It is more discreet to laugh than to expose what merits tears.

CRITIC: The love and sympathy you claim to feel are nowhere evident. Your criticism would be more persuasive if you would express them here and there.

AUTHOR: Let politicians make a show of sympathy to help their cause.

CRITIC: It is perverse to conceal your sympathy and to appear to loathe men whom in fact you like.

AUTHOR: I criticize T. S. Eliot, for example, but am certainly not blind to his virtues. That he has always had the courage of his convictions is one of the least of these. His collection of some of his later essays, *On Poetry and Poets* (1957), shows that he also possesses the courage for an attack on his convictions. This is especially plain in his pieces on Milton, on Goethe, and on "The Frontiers of Criticism." Of one of his earlier remarks on Goethe, for instance, he now says that it is "interesting because it enunciates so many errors in so few words" (p. 256). His third excellence is still more uncommon: he only writes when he has something to say. To be sure, occasionally he still presents his idiosyncrasies as solemn dogmas, but the predominant note in his later essays is one of humility, humanity, and honesty. His vast reputation has not hardened him; he has continued to grow.

CRITIC: If you feel that way about him, why do you single him out for attacks?

AUTHOR: A writer can do worse than to criticize primarily men he respects. But he becomes a bore if he introduces every stricture with three bows. If you try to swim against the stream, you will never get anywhere if you feel obliged to atone for every yard you gain. If I ever succeeded in reversing the current and found that nobody saw any good at all in the men whom I had fought, there would be time enough then to feel thoroughly embarrassed. To forestall that, I try to buck currents that seem far too strong to make that likely. And that is another reason for picking strong opponents.

CRITIC: They may be strong; but surely you do not really like them. After all, you charge some of them with self-deception and dishonesty.

AUTHOR: I certainly do not admire all of them, but I can still feel that they are troubled human beings. Yet it would be insufferable to write about them in that vein.

CRITIC: Then correct their errors and refrain from casting aspersions on the men behind the books.

AUTHOR: If a writer and his followers want to eat their cake and have it, too, that deserves exposure. But why each of them is unable to resist this urge is a private matter. If an outlook involves self-deception or if the most popular historian of the age lacks the historian's conscience, that merits public attention. But it would be impertinent to publicize, or to speculate in print about, the personal weaknesses behind these failings, though they might elicit our sympathy. Must I either condone falsehood and irresponsibility or forget that the other fellow is a human being like myself? We should speak out boldly but should retain enough humanity to realize that the men we criticize may well be loyal friends and loving fathers and foes of injustice who in many ways are much more admirable than a lot of men with whom we happen to agree, not to speak of ourselves.

CRITIC: But self-deception and dishonesty are such terrible charges that you cannot gloss them over with such compliments.

AUTHOR: Hamlet deceives himself. He is dishonest. Does that in itself establish that he is in no way admirable? What of Lear? Of Jacob in the Book of Genesis? Of Faust? Of Raskolnikov? Your moralism is subliterate.

CRITIC: But you are dealing with real people and not with characters in works of fiction.

AUTHOR: Great literature is no mere make-believe. What I learn from it carries over into real life.

CRITIC: But the great poets show us both sides and go out of their way to enlist sympathy for men whom otherwise we might despise. You, on the contrary, concentrate precisely on the failings of men whom we might admire, and then you protest your sympathy.

AUTHOR: I don't protest my sympathy. It does not enter into the picture. It is a private matter. I feel no resentment, and that is my good fortune: it concerns me and not the men I criticize. If a man distorts history or indulges in fallacies, and his account is widely accepted, it is worth-while to show how wrong he is. There is no point in adding a chapter about his

being a fine fellow for all that. And it would be downright
wrong to refrain from speaking up because I like him. The
truth, as Aristotle said, is a greater friend.

CRITIC: Still, you might at least develop your opponent's
view from the inside, as if it were your own, before you criticize it.

AUTHOR: That might well be more effective, but it is too
histrionic for my taste. That approach is sound when you concern yourself with views that have few champions and seem
alien to your audience: writing about the religions of India,
for a Western audience, you can do no less. But when you
deal with the idols of the day, writing for people who are in
the habit of admiring what you criticize, that would be a
waste of time and space, a comic detour. I have little hope
that this convinces you; but you said a while ago that two
things bothered you. What was the other one?

CRITIC: One reason why you have failed to convince me
on so many points is that you touch so blithely and so briefly
on so many matters. You mention names, venture suggestions,
make allusions and then do not follow them up. You might
deal with one man at a time, or at most with two.

AUTHOR: I have tried to make out a prima facie case, showing that a view that at first glance must seem strange to many
people has in fact some plausibility. The rest of the book develops most of my suggestions rather in the manner you propose. And I'll make one other concession to you: I shall on
the whole speak well of the dead and ill of the living. Instead
of congratulating our time, I shall try to criticize some of its
idols. Many of my specific claims are surely irrefutable, but
my over-all views cannot be demonstrated beyond the shadow
of a doubt. As they are gradually developed, however, they
should at least make sense. And even if you still can't accept
them without reservations, you may find your understanding
of many men and issues deepened. Some things that now seem
doubtful to you may well become certain in due course, while
many more that had seemed certain should become problematic. Being right matters less than making people think for
themselves. And there is no better way of doing that than being provocative.

3

SHAKESPEARE VERSUS GOETHE

In a conversation with Eckermann (March 30, 1824), Goethe, at the height of his fame, rejected the notion that Tieck, a German romantic, might be his equal and added: "It is just as if I were to compare myself to Shakespeare who also did not make himself and who is nevertheless a being of a higher order to whom I look up."

The most enthusiastic admiration is also evident in Goethe's autobiography and in his essay "Shakespeare without End" and above all in *Wilhelm Meisters Lehrjahre*. The account of Wilhelm's first acquaintance with Shakespeare, in Book III, becomes a veritable paean before giving way to the author's long reflections on *Hamlet;* and in the second chapter of Book IV it is intimated that Goethe named his hero, who was to occupy him for fifty years, after Shakespeare.

As Goethe was well aware, his reverence for the English poet did not preclude some profound differences between his hero and himself. An analysis of some of these differences throws light on Goethe's modernity and relative proximity to us and may help those who are more intimate with Shakespeare to gain an approach to Goethe. But there is no need for any piecemeal juxtaposition. We can first sketch a picture of Shakespeare, unorthodox in some respects, and then concentrate on Goethe.

Discussion of a very few of Shakespeare's dramas will suffice to suggest two major points that are interrelated: these plays are not primarily psychological, notwithstanding the poet's psychological penetration; and the crux of these plays is that

the hero belongs to, and lives in, a world of which the other
characters have no inkling.

2

The insistence on fully explaining all behavior psychologically is a relatively recent development; and applied to some
of the most remarkable works of literature, it falls flat. Take
Judas' betrayal of Jesus. Scripture offers no psychological explanation but intimates the inevitability of predestination; and
any effort to explain this act in terms of a single motive—
whether jealousy, disappointment, or politics—trivializes it.

It is similar with Aeschylus and Sophocles: again, the inexorable, preordained before the hero was born. It is the poet's
very point that the behavior itself is *accidental* in the sense
that it is a mere means to a predetermined conclusion that
would have been inescapable, no matter what the hero might
have done; and the hero's behavior is *necessary* only insofar
as it leads to his undoing. Hence, that suspense on which
modern writers rely to such a great extent is lacking. The
Greek dramatist chose themes that ensured that his audience
would know the outcome in advance—the conclusion was predetermined in this sense, too—but it did not occur either to the
poet or to his public that this might in any way detract from
the power of his work. Just this was found in the unfolding
of what *had* to come to pass. Nor does our knowledge of the
outcome of a drama, or of the Bible stories, lessen our sense of
Jacob's or of David's anguish, of Jeremiah's agony or Ajax'
madness. The majesty of passion here portrayed is scarcely
touched by most psychological analyses, the relevance of
which almost invites comparison with chemical analyses of
paintings: they reveal something about the artist's medium,
not his meaning.[1]

[1] Here, too, Freud is far profounder than many of his followers.
In his *Traumdeutung* (1900), he concluded the famous footnote in
which he offered his psychoanalytic interpretation of *Hamlet* by saying expressly: "Just as, incidentally, all neurotic symptoms—just as
even dreams are capable of overinterpretation, and indeed demand
nothing less than this before they can be fully understood, thus ev-

This parallel between Greek tragedy and Scripture is not of the surface: Aeschylus and Sophocles have what one might call a religious dimension. They transcend the social sphere and represent something of cosmic significance, beginning perhaps with divine oracles and ending in death or madness, as if some vastness from beyond rushed in, or welled up, to crack man's pretentious brain. There is the chorus to remind us constantly of the ritual origin of the drama and of its function in religious festivals. The dramas became entertainment without ceasing to be revelations. And only in Euripides, where the attempt to psychologize the characters has taken definite form, the gods appear *ex machina,* unmotivated and not quite appropriately. For the attempt to motivate the action psychologically leads us to expect that there will be no supernatural intervention.

In Shakespeare there are no deities, and the dramas are so excellent as entertainment—and we are sometimes told that he wrote only to entertain—that we are easily led to assume that no ritual or religious elements remain. His outstanding interest in human motivation, moreover, suggests that all the action in his tragedies is meant to be explainable in terms of some prominent motive. And yet this exoteric view does not account for those levels of meaning that raise Shakespeare's plays above mere entertainment and invite comparison with Aeschylus, Sophocles, and the Bible. For his greatness is certainly not solely a function of his use of language.

There is, of course, one level of meaning on which *Othello,* for example, is the tragedy of jealousy, and the play does not lack consistency on this psychological plane. Iago is deeply wounded, having been passed by when Othello made Cassio his lieutenant, though he had less seniority and combat experience. Nor is Iago jealous of Cassio alone; he also hates Othello because he suspects that the Moor has seduced his

---

ery genuine poetic creation, too, has presumably issued from more than one motive and more than one stimulus in the poet's soul and permits more than one interpretation." But it is only the simplicity of a single explanation that appears to remove all mystery. (Cf. section 77 of my *Critique* for a contrast of Freud and Fromm along these lines.) Overinterpretation restores the sense of mystery.

wife, Emilia, and he envies Othello his beautiful Desdemona.
If one analyzes the drama psychologically, it is surely Iago that
has an inferiority complex—not, as Margaret Webster has suggested, Othello.

Iago is consumed by *ressentiment* against Othello, Desdemona, and Cassio—*ressentiment* in precisely the sense in
which Nietzsche introduced the term into psychology. Nor
does this interpretation conflict with A. C. Bradley's when he
claims in effect that Iago is motivated by what Nietzsche
called "the will to power." Undoubtedly, he does enjoy a sense
of power in manipulating others, in creating situations, and in
sending those who hurt him to their doom. But that his will to
power manifests itself so vengefully is surely due to his
ressentiment—especially against the Moor. He cannot forgive
Othello his "constant, loving, noble nature," which is a living
reproach to him; nor can he forgive him that, in spite of his
black skin, Desdemona prefers him. And the thought that perhaps his own wife does, too,

> *Doth like a poisonous mineral gnaw my inwards;*
> *And nothing can, or shall, content my soul,*
> *Till I am even'd with him, wife for wife;*
> *Or, failing so, yet that I put the Moor*
> *At least into a jealousy so strong*
> *That judgment cannot cure.* (II, i)

He wants to be equal because he cannot endure Othello's superiority; and, if it cannot be accomplished "wife for wife,"
Othello must be pulled down to Iago's own miserable level,
"into a jealousy so strong that judgment cannot cure." He must
cease to be Othello, the "most dear husband" of Desdemona.
He must be destroyed—preferably in a manner entailing her
destruction and Cassio's as well. It is Iago rather than Othello
who is pictured with the most uncanny psychological penetration, for the Moor's conduct hardly requires any similar
analysis.

> *The Moor is of a free and open nature,*
> *That thinks men honest, that but seem to be so,*
> *And will as tenderly be led by the nose,*
> *As asses are—*

thus Iago describes him at the end of the first act; and seeing
that Othello assumes Iago's honesty without the slightest
doubt, he cannot fail to be persuaded by the overwhelming
evidence of Desdemona's illicit relation with Cassio with which
Iago confronts him. He then consents to Cassio's death and
himself smothers Desdemona.

If this were all there is to the drama, it would be superb
theater, distinguished by the incredibly keen characterization
of Iago and the magnificent poetry of some of the speeches.
This would be sufficient to ensure the play a high rank, but it
has yet another dimension.

To begin with Iago, his scheme is motivated, but the full
magnitude of his wickedness is unaccounted for. Since he is
so villainous, the motives outlined here make his behavior
plausible; but no attempt is made to explain his initially evil
nature, without which all these provocations could not have
occasioned such diabolical actions. Perhaps this is even underscored in the last scene:

> *I look down towards his feet;—but that's a fable:*
> *If that thou be'st a devil, I cannot kill thee.*

And in the last lines of the play he is again referred to as a
"hellish villain."

A modern writer might well have been tempted to carry the
psychological motivation beyond the point where Shakespeare
stopped. Yet this is not a fault of Shakespeare's art but an important clue to his conception of the drama. Any further explanation would have threatened to trivialize Iago's wickedness, to explain it away and to reduce his terrifying stature.
As he stands, Iago invites comparison with Judas or the serpent
in Eden. What he does is enigmatic and inevitable; and to ask
why he is evil or why Othello is deceived by him is almost
like asking why the end is tragic. Why did Prometheus steal
fire from heaven? Such questions miss the point, and Shakespeare's tragedies retain something of the sacramental quality
of the Greek drama and the Bible.

Iago is no exception: in *Hamlet* the action is propelled by a
ghost; in *Macbeth*, by witches. Nor are these spirits *dei ex
machina*, extraneous to the action, interfering in it inappropri-

ately, and hence more or less objectionable. They bring about an action that would lose its essential character without them, and they point to a suprapsychological significance that raises the drama beyond mere accident. They create that "numinous" atmosphere—to use Rudolf Otto's apt word for what is simultaneously majestic, awe-inspiring, overpowering, and fascinating—that is of the essence of Shakespeare's great tragedies and gives them the depth and intensity of the religious experiences that Otto describes.

This numinous quality that becomes incarnate in ghosts and witches is by no means confined to spirits but is found in those tragedies, too, in which no supernatural beings make their appearance. Lear has something of this: his conduct in the first scene suggests less—as Goethe characteristically supposed—insufficient motivation than the inevitability of an ancient myth. His titanism is inseparable from this. And in *Macbeth*, too, the witches' numinous quality is reflected by the hero whom they choose as the vehicle of destiny. Nor does Othello lack this dimension, nor Caesar and Coriolanus, nor even such gentler souls as Richard II and Hamlet. Some details of their characters are drawn with the most admirable psychological skill, but in each case the hero is raised to the unquestionable majesty of myth.

3

To achieve this effect, Shakespeare relies not only on occasional contacts with ghosts or witches but above all on a radical distinction between the hero and the other figures in the play. Like Saul, the hero is "higher than any of the people from his shoulders and upward"—a man marked and set apart, one with a destiny, a tragic figure. It is one of the most crucial features of these tragedies that the hero is never understood by any other character in the play. The fact that Shakespeare's heroes generally do not soliloquize about the failure of other men to understand them does not prove that they are understood but only that Shakespeare does not romanticize his heroes; and, again, this is not a failure of his art but an essential feature of his greatness. Instead of becoming pathetic, his heroes retain the stature of majesty; instead of being mere projections of author, reader, or audience, they _are_ what others think or dream they are, and they retain the full impact of myth.

Instead of having Othello tell us that his stature precludes his being understood by any of the others in the play, Shakespeare composed a murder scene in which Othello acts and speaks in a manner that convinces us that he lives in a world in which none of the others could participate. Iago has succeeded in his scheme insofar as the Moor kills his wife, but he has patently not succeeded in reducing Othello to his own level. The scene is the most numinous in the whole drama, awe-inspiring rather than fearful, and Othello, instead of frothing at the mouth with jealousy, acts with a solemn majesty that suggests the hierophant. Desdemona, Iago, and the others in the play, as well as most readers and listeners, to be sure, take that for "a murder, which I thought a sacrifice."

Othello's lines in this scene underscore the inadequacy of the purely exoteric interpretation of the action and suggest another level of meaning—even as Shylock's famous speeches, "Signior Antonio, many a time and oft . . ." and "Hath not a Jew eyes? . . . ," underline the insufficiency of any reading that sees only the comedy in _The Merchant of Venice_. There is one level on which it _is_ a comedy and on which _Othello_ is the story of Iago's villainous success. On another level of interpretation, however, Shylock is a great tragic figure; and Othello's murder, a sacrifice.

He had not thought of Desdemona as mortal; she was his very god. In that sense, there was no proportion between Othello's conception of Desdemona and the essentially inconsequential, if beautiful and faithful, object of his love. If the Moor were to understand her limitations and the sheer brevity of her existence, this would not be another insight but the catastrophic dissolution of his faith, his religion. Iago is the poet's instrument for bringing about this tragic end and does it, not by opening Othello's eyes to Desdemona's true nature —the play is not a philosophic allegory—but through a villainous deception. Nothing less would have offered a sufficient framework for the drama. In spite of these dramatic intricacies, however, what shatters Othello is essentially the realization of

Desdemona's limitations, which he immediately associates with the thought that she must die. "She must die"—that is the point of intersection of the two levels of meaning; only this spatial metaphor of intersection is inadequate insofar as it falsely suggests a complete separation of the two levels.

Macbeth presents an analogous case. The hero is ambitious but also has another dimension to which the other characters in the play are blind and which Lady Macbeth takes for mere weakness. Being extraordinarily ambitious herself, she cannot understand how he differs from her:

> *Yet do I fear thy nature:*
> *It is too full o' the milk of human kindness,*
> *To catch the nearest way. Thou wouldst be great;*
> *Art not without ambition but without*
> *The illness should attend it: what thou wouldst highly,*
> *That wouldst thou holily; wouldst not play false,*
> *And yet wouldst wrongly win. . . .*

That is how Macbeth appears to her—and to many a reader—and she rightly concludes that he would never murder Duncan unless she made him do it:

> *Hie thee hither,*
> *That I may pour my spirits in thine ear,*
> *And chastise with the valour of my tongue*
> *All that impedes thee from the golden round,*
> *Which fate and metaphysical aid doth seem*
> *To have thee crown'd withal.* (I, v)

What she fails to see is that Macbeth would be great in another way; that his desire for enhancement is different in kind from her ambition and that he is not merely more particular as regards the means; and that, once crowned, Macbeth will find that his "ambition" is unstilled, being of such a nature that no crown could satisfy it.

Indeed, Macbeth is far closer in spirit to Hamlet than to Lady Macbeth. He has a deep spirituality and an essentially lyrical soul—albeit of titanic dimensions—that finds expression in almost all of his monologues and asides. Again, there is no other character in the play who could possibly appreciate these speeches:

> Had I but died an hour before this chance,
> I had liv'd a blessed time; for from this instant,
> There's nothing serious in mortality;
> All is but toys: renown, and grace, is dead;
> The wine of life is drawn, and the mere lees
> Is left this vault to brag of. (II, iii)

> I have liv'd long enough: my way of life
> Is fall'n into the sear, the yellow leaf. (V, iii)

> Life's but a walking shadow; a poor player,
> That struts and frets his hour upon the stage,
> And then is heard no more: it is a tale
> Told by an idiot, full of sound and fury,
> Signifying nothing. (V, v)

Not a soul in the drama could respond to such melancholy any more than Rosencrantz and Guildenstern could to that of Hamlet or Bolingbroke to that of Richard II. Shakespeare's tragic heroes live in a world of their own, and this—no less than the witches and ghosts—underscores the inevitability of their disaster, which is not a matter of circumstances but destiny. Macbeth and Hamlet are doomed no less than Oedipus, called to do what they would rather not do, placed in a world that is not their own and among people who cannot understand them.

The gulf between the hero and the rest of mankind is mitigated in several tragedies by the interposition of an intermediate nobility that requires no extraordinary talent and that, in principle, need not be rare—a nobility that consists in loyalty. In *Hamlet* and *Lear* it is exemplified by Horatio and Kent; in *Timon*, by Flavius, who moves the misanthropic hero to exclaim:

> Forgive my general and exceptless rashness,
> You perpetual-sober gods! I do proclaim
> One honest man—mistake me not—but one;
> No more, I pray,—and he's a steward. (IV, iii)

We are reminded of the ninety-fourth sonnet (cited in chapter 1, section 2): men like Timon and Hamlet "are the lords and owners of their faces," while Horatio and Flavius are "but stewards of their excellence." Loyalty should be possible for all; and it is all-important in Shakespeare's godless world. It is a man-made absolute in the flood of corruption. But it is a measure of Shakespeare's disillusionment that he considered it so exceedingly rare.

When we compare Shakespeare with Aeschylus and Sophocles, the following points seem important. Shakespeare's dramas are longer and more complex, and the satyr play is absorbed by the tragedy: instead of appearing as a separate member of a series of plays, it appears within the tragedy in the form of Shakespeare's famous comic scenes. Secondly, the inevitability is rendered less obvious and tempered by a wealth of psychological detail. And, finally, the mythical stature in which most of the figures had shared in the ancient dramas is in Shakespeare restricted to the hero. These three points make Shakespeare more "modern" and mark the transition from the classical drama to the romantic. He marks the end of a world in the same sense as Michelangelo: a unified world on the verge of disintegration; the exaltation of the individual to a plane that is somehow higher than that reached by all subsequent individualism. And the poet no less than his heroes into whom he breathed his spirit may justly be called—in Goethe's previously cited words—"a being of a higher order."

4

Goethe's *Faust* has much in common with Shakespeare's dramas. The Prologue in Heaven suggests clearly that *Faust*, too, transcends the plane of psychological analysis; and there is no character in the play—except of course the Lord in the Prologue—who understands Faust. The parallel extends to another point that Francis Fergusson has stressed in relation to *Hamlet: Faust*, too, deals not only with the hero but with the society in which he lives. There is the scene "Before the City Gate" and another in "Auerbach's Keller"; and later on Gretchen's entire milieu is brought to life. If Goethe uses this social background in large part to model Faust's character that much more clearly, the same consideration applies to *Hamlet*. Moreover, where there are elements of ritual in *Hamlet* we have choruses in *Faust*, ranging from the Easter choirs to the *Dies Irae* in the Cathedral scene. Nor are ghosts lacking. Again, there is an abundance of psychological insight and much humor. Finally, Faust's character invites comparison with Hamlet's, Gretchen's with Ophelia's, and Valentine's with Laertes'.

At this point, the similarity may seem misleadingly close; and to gain a clue to the important differences, it may be well to cast a sidelong glance at Goethe's Tasso, who is in some ways even closer to Hamlet. Here, however, the differences are more obvious. While both dramas depict an individual against the background of a society, Hamlet is far lonelier than Tasso and far surpasses him in stature. In fact, we hardly exaggerate when we say: none of the other characters in the play understand Hamlet, but he does not state this expressly, while Tasso never tires of informing us that none of the others understand him, although at least half of them do. Add to this that in *Hamlet* we have a world with evil in it and with a numinous dimension, while in *Tasso* we have a world without evil and without any such dimension. In *Hamlet* we have a real society; in *Tasso*, a stylized projection of the poet's experience into an imaginary Renaissance setting. Hamlet is not pitiful and pathetic: the ghost speaks the truth and the evil situation in which he finds himself is real; while Tasso's predicament is essentially subjective, and he may to that extent be considered sick or neurotic.

These differences may help us as we return to *Faust*. For Faust, too, lacks Hamlet's stature. His practice of magic does not serve to elevate him to superhuman stature: the word *Übermensch* (superman) is actually used mockingly by the Earth Spirit, whose sight Faust cannot bear. He is as we are—merely human. The spirit with whom he *can* commune, Mephistopheles, is a devil stripped of all numinous attributes. Far from inspiring awe, he ridicules such feelings. And while he is surely one of the few truly great creations of world literature, he is a projection of human qualities—call them inhuman if you will; it is still a peculiarly human inhumanity, one that we encounter in ourselves and our fellow men. In the same vein, Faust is a projection of the poet, the reader, the audience—essentially as we are ourselves—while Hamlet is more as we think, or like to think, we are; and therefore Hamlet is more like a figure in a dream or myth.

Faust's inability to confront the Earth Spirit, his failure at the point where Hamlet and Macbeth succeed, is crucial and suggests at one blow how much more modern and how much closer to us he is. There is an implicit contrast here with more heroic times—an anticipation of Joycean irony. What is merely implicit in this abortive encounter is spun out in detail through the appearance and speeches of Mephistopheles. For Mephistopheles is an essentially modern devil. Where the nineteenth century put up with him for Faust's sake, we are much more likely to put up with Faust for Mephistopheles' sake.

Faust is not the solitary hero that we find in Hamlet: while Mephisto never quite understands him—and the Lord calls our attention to this at the very beginning—Faust never does justice to Mephisto either. In this respect one may think of Othello and Iago—a parallel strengthened by the fact that Iago-Mephisto lead Othello-Faust into responsibility for the death of Desdemona-Gretchen. But, while it is true that Iago and Othello never understand each other, Iago is evil in a sense in which Mephisto is not. We do not sympathize with Iago, and his wickedness is essentially unaccountable. Mephistopheles, on the other hand, is rather engaging, and, while his wickedness is not explicable psychologically, it is nevertheless fully accounted for, first by the Lord and then, with characteristic frankness, once more by Mephisto himself, who takes great pains to keep Faust and the audience well posted from the time of his first entrance. Decidedly, he is not mysterious but, on the contrary, an embodiment of ruthless intellectual analysis—though, fortunately for the drama, not only of that. By a stroke of genius, Goethe also associates him closely with sex and gives him the sense of humor that Faust so sorely lacks.

In sum, Faust, unlike Hamlet and Macbeth, is not a titan but as human as we are, and a would-be superman as some of us are; and Goethe goes further and creates an essentially human devil. The plot is no longer centered in a man raised above his fellows by inscrutable fate, one made to perform a hideous deed to which his own will stands in a questionable and mysterious relation (the crux of *Oedipus, Hamlet,* and *Macbeth*); instead the hero *wishes* to raise himself above other men, is eager to experience agony as well as joy, but suffers like the rest of us when confronted with grief; and, for all the ostentatious interference of spirits, his grief no less than the occasion for it is as natural as can be. And the central relation, that between Faust and Mephistopheles, is largely reducible to a formulation used by Faust in a different context: "Two souls, alas, are dwelling in my breast." Goethe found both in himself, and so do many of us.

5

Faust is etched not only against the background of his own society, which we behold in such scenes as "Before the City Gate" and "Auerbach's Keller" and in the many scenes in which Gretchen's world comes to life. There is also the Walpurgis Night and, in Part Two, the Imperial Court, civil war, a Classical Walpurgis Night, and classical antiquity as it appears in the Helena act. On the whole, it is therefore not *one* society in which Faust finds himself, as Hamlet does, or Macbeth, or Othello; rather, he transcends his own society and understands himself, and forces us to understand him, in relation to the past as well as to his own time. We must experience his society, from the small-town milieu of Gretchen to life at court, as well as classical antiquity. Faust is somehow defined through their contrast—as Joyce's Bloom, too, is to be understood fully only in contrast with the ancient Ulysses. In this respect, too, *Faust* is more modern than Shakespeare and is closer to us.

The creation of a human devil who carries humor not only into occasional comic scenes, such as Mephisto's dialogue with the student in Part One, but into almost every scene in the drama reinforces the abandonment of the framework of a single society and leads us yet further from the sacramental and

inevitable that were still characteristic of Shakespeare's tragedies. The artist becomes sovereign and subjects everything to
caustic comments: *everything* has become problematic—every
human feeling, every social institution, every received *Weltanschauung*. Faust's noble sentiments, whose often magnificent
expression delighted the nineteenth century, become foils for
Mephistopheles' sarcastic insights; in fact, this premature
brother of Nietzsche and Freud mercilessly exposed romanticism before it had yet reached its full development. The social
setting and the faith and world view that go with it are not
only used as a background for Faust's character, nor merely
questioned implicitly through the contrast with classical antiquity; they, too, become ridiculous, seen in the mirror of
Mephisto's wit.

And yet the poet is not satisfied with this by now familiar
division in the modern soul. Unable to accept his *Weltanschauung* from society, he forms his own. He employs arch-
angels, though it does not occur to him to believe in them,
ghosts, witches, wizards, various species of devils—ingeniously
invented—saints, even a *Mater Gloriosa*, but then turns around,
having finished Act V, and writes a fourth act in which the
accusations that Mephisto had raised against the Catholic
Church in Part One are substantiated before our eyes. In the
first scene of the Second Part he imitates Dante's *terza rima*
in a grandiose speech; in the last scenes he parodies Dante,
creates portable jaws of hell in contrast to Dante's awe-
inspiring portal to the *inferno*, and elevates not only Gretchen
but even Faust into his Dantesque heaven, while the Floren-
tine had sent even Francesca da Rimini to hell. Yet in the end
we get no mere collection of highly polished gems with cutting edges but a single cosmos, a world that is the poet's own
creation.

If the Helena episode should suggest to superficial readers
a wish to return to a past age or a conviction that the contemporary world lacks any such exemplary unity as could be
found in former ages, the poet's answer is clearly that, confronted with this lack of unity, he fashions a whole world out
of himself. At the moment of composition, he does repair the
damage of a lifetime. This damage, which T. S. Eliot considers

irreparable, is not so unique a feature of our age as he supposes. "Decadence," Nietzsche once wrote, "belongs to all
epochs of mankind"; and it may well be the mark of the great
poet that he goes beyond mirroring the damage and creates a
perspective in which it is transcended.

6

In an age of intolerance and terror, Goethe's singular tolerance and freedom from fear are apt to seem remote. We turn
to Dostoevsky. Not to his pamphlets, steeped in bigotry, but
to his novels in which we encounter terror in congenially
crushing proportions. We also find a world, whole and overwhelming—and new to us as if it were the poet's own creation. Yet it is not, and here may be the reason why these
novels—though plainly as great as any—seem to move *us* more
than those grown up in Dostoevsky's culture. What strikes us
as original and fresh is really reaction: flight into a past that
does not happen to be ours; acceptance of a *Weltanschauung*
that, though new to us, is long irrevocable. For us this novelist
explodes horizons and unwittingly advances tolerance—simply
by forcing us to measure our values against his. Yet in his own
context he belongs with those who despair of the damage and
of our whole modern world and try to conjure up the dead.
That he did all this with a range of human sympathies that
his worse judgment fortunately could not cure and with a passion that not only pales all other cultural necromancers but
appropriates each character in turn—that helps to make him
one of the giants of world literature.

But, if we would find passion, not less intense for being far
from terror, and scope and unity outside the pale of dogma,
not purchased for a sacrifice of vision—*one* world in which our
modern multiplicity is *formed*—then we should look to Goethe.
Here criticism, as in Mephistopheles, does not respect tradition
or propriety, and yet analysis is not unmindful of its limits,
which are recognized in humor. No occasion is left from which
irreverent reflection might be banished, not even the Prologue
in Heaven. Here we breathe our modern climate of opinion—
in which we must even ask in the end whether psychology

cannot explain the different attitudes toward majesty and mystery in Shakespeare and in Goethe.

To what extent might Shakespeare's surely troubled relation to his father—though not as difficult as Dostoevsky's—illuminate his attitudes where they are different from Goethe's? Particularly the way in which he again and again elevates one man above all others and then leads him to his doom? We cannot charge "contempt of art" and be done with such queries. But, while conceding free sway to psychology, we need not overlook the relevance of cultural developments. In his *Antichrist,* Nietzsche said, "In the son that becomes conviction which in the father still was a lie"; and a look at totalitarian countries bears him out. But we can also say, conversely: "In the son that becomes a lie which in the father still was a conviction." Whatever its psychological roots may have been, Goethe's attitude toward miracle, mystery, and authority (the trinity of Dostoevsky's Grand Inquisitor) is all that is left for us today: reflective wit, which does not halt before the numinous.

Shakespeare's less Mephistophelean attitude has not lost meaning for us; his ghosts and witches are still vivid symbols of the frontiers of the mind, and his heroes move us with the eloquence of dreams like voices from inward abysses. But symbols recognized as such evoke reflection and lose the strength to integrate a world: like Mephistopheles' minions and the legions of heaven in *Faust,* they become legitimate butts of sarcasm and themselves require integration. This, however, Goethe had the power to provide. Without the ostrich attitudes of some of the later nineteenth century, without curbing his wit, and without seeking refuge in ruins, he fashioned a whole world and repaired the damage of a lifetime. And, since the damage of his day was more like ours, he can give us what we cannot find even in Shakespeare. Surely, his age and ours is far from exemplary or exhilarating, but it is precisely this that makes Goethe himself exemplary and the experience of his personality, as reflected in his work, exhilarating.

4

GOETHE AND THE
HISTORY OF IDEAS

Students of the history of ideas are often preoccupied
exclusively with the tracing of connections between ideas. This
approach is too narrow and does not allow for the proper appreciation of some of the most influential men. A good deal of
history, and of the history of ideas, too, consists in the untiring
efforts of posterity to do justice to some *individuum ineffabile*
(to use a phrase of Goethe's). Socrates and Jesus, Napoleon
and Lincoln are cases in point. So is Goethe.

In view of his intellectual powers and interests, it is under-
standable that his ideas should have been related again and
again to what came before and after him. From the 143 volumes of his works, diaries, and letters (*Sophienausgabe*) and
the 5 volumes of his collected conversations (Biedermann's
edition) it is not hard to cull a pertinent anthology on almost
any subject. Moreover, a vast literature has grown around the
implications of his major poems, plays, and novels. In the present chapter, however, we shall concentrate on the historic impact of the poet's life and personality.

2

Goethe invites comparison with the men of the Renaissance,
Leonardo in particular, as a "universal man." As a member of
the state government in Weimar, he took his official duties
seriously and devoted a good deal of time to them; but he
took an even greater interest in the arts and in several of the
natural sciences; he made an anatomical discovery, proposed

an important botanical hypothesis, and developed an intricate
theory of colors; he directed the theater in Weimar from 1791
to 1817; and he came to be widely recognized, some thirty
or forty years before his death, as Germany's greatest poet.
That estimate still stands.

Goethe never considered himself a philosopher, but he read
some of Kant's works as they first appeared, and he personally
knew Fichte, Schelling, Hegel, and Schopenhauer. He admired
Spinoza and was also influenced by Leibniz and Shaftesbury.
At no time did he develop his outlook systematically, and in
his *Maxims and Reflections* he said: "Doing natural science,
we are pantheists; writing poetry, polytheists; and ethically,
monotheists."

The outstanding fact about Goethe is his development—not
from mediocrity to excellence but from consummation to consummation of style upon style. *Goetz* (1773) and *Werther*
(1774) represent, and were immediately acclaimed as, the
culmination of Storm and Stress. In Goethe's two great plays,
Iphigenia (1787) and *Tasso* (1790), German classicism
reached its perfection. Then, still before the end of the century, *Faust: A Fragment* and *Wilhelm Meister's Apprentice-
ship* gave a decisive impetus to romanticism, and *Meister* all
but created a new genre: the novel that relates the education
and character formation of the hero, the *Bildungsroman*. And
Dichtung und Wahrheit (3 parts 1811–14, last part 1833) is
not only a strikingly original autobiography but created a new
perspective for the study of an artist or, indeed, of man in
general: life and work must be studied together as an organic
unity and in terms of development.

The evolution of Goethe is reflected in his poetry. Perhaps
no other man has written so many so excellent poems; certainly
no one else has left a comparable record of the development
of a poetic sensibility over a period of approximately sixty
years. Anacreontic lyrics, the magnificent defiance of *Prometheus*, hymns, earthy *Roman Elegies* (1795), biting *Venetian
Epigrams* (1796), the wonderful ballads of 1798, the sonnets
of 1815, and, at seventy, the epoch-making *West-Eastern
Divan*—nothing in world literature compares with this. And in
all these periods Goethe wrote the most moving love poems,

from "Willkommen und Abschied" in his twenties to the
"Marienbader Elegie" in his seventies. These poems help to
account for the fact that Goethe's loves have been, for decades,
part of the curriculum in the German secondary schools: not
to know Friederike, Lotte, Lilli, and the rest was to be unedu-
cated.

Obviously, men so brought up would on the whole tend to
favor a self-realizationist ethic, and at least some forms of
moral intuitionism would strike them as clearly absurd. What
is good is not seen once and for all; as he develops, a man's
moral ideas change; and wisdom is attained, if ever, only in
old age. Goethe's *Maxims and Reflections* and his celebrated
Conversations with Eckermann are among the world's great
books of wisdom, but their influence does not compare with
that of Goethe's own development. It was Goethe's example
—his life and his self-understanding—rather than any explicit
teaching that led others more and more to study works of art
and points of view and human beings in terms of development.

3

The only work of Goethe's that has had an influence at all
comparable to his life is *Faust*. Partly owing to the fact that
Goethe worked on it off and on for sixty years, partly also
owing to his conception of poetry and its relation to ideas,
Faust is not only no allegory but does not embody or try to
communicate any single philosophy of life.

To be sure, *Faust* is more epigrammatic than any other great
work of literature except the Bible, and the play has enriched
the German language with more "familiar quotations" than
could be found in *Hamlet*. But for all that the drama is emphatically not didactic. Shakespeare was Goethe's model, not
Dante.

One of Goethe's *Maxims and Reflections* is as relevant as it
is concise:

It makes a great difference whether the poet seeks the particular for the universal or beholds the universal in the particular. From the first procedure originates allegory, where

the particular is considered only as an illustration, as an
example of the universal. The latter, however, is properly
the nature of poetry: it expresses something particular without thinking of the universal or pointing to it. Whoever
grasps this particular in a living way will simultaneously
receive the universal, too, without even becoming aware of
it—or realize it only later.

In one of his conversations with Eckermann (May 6, 1827)
Goethe himself applied these considerations to *Faust:*

> They come and ask me what idea I sought to embody in my
> *Faust.* As if I knew . . . that myself! . . . Indeed, that
> would have been a fine thing, had I wanted to string such a
> rich, variegated . . . life . . . upon the meagre thread of a
> single . . . idea! It was altogether not my manner as a poet
> to strive for the embodiment of something abstract. . . . I
> did not have to do anything but round out and form such
> visions and impressions artistically . . . so that others would
> receive the same impressions when hearing or reading what
> I presented.[1]

Goethe's undoctrinaire attitude is further illuminated by another remark. Only we must recall that on other occasions he
frequently referred to himself as a pagan:

> I pagan? Well, after all I let Gretchen be executed and I
> let Ottilie [in the *Elective Affinities*] starve to death. Don't
> people find that Christian enough? What do they want that
> would be more Christian?[2]

Goethe tried to picture life as he saw it and people as they
are. His primary intention was not to persuade or to instruct,
although his tolerance and freedom from resentment naturally
move us.

Goethe's attitude may remind us of the words of Spinoza,
whom Goethe so admired: "to hate no one, to despise no one,
to mock no one, to be angry with no one, and to envy no

[1] Cf. also July 5, 1827; Jan. 3, 1830; and Feb. 13, 1831.
[2] *Goethes Gespräche,* ed. Biedermann, II, 62.

one."[3] Only mockery was part of Goethe's genius—but a mockery that was free from hatred, anger, and envy. In the young Goethe it seems like the overflow of his exuberant high spirits; in the old Goethe, it seems Olympian and yet also an expression of that deep humanity that his frequent reserve concealed from casual observers.

4

While it is obvious that Goethe's heroes are not conceived as allegorical personifications, Faust has sometimes been misconstrued as an idealized self-portrait of the poet. But Goethe's male heroes are emphatically not ideals; they are partial self-projections—magnified images of qualities that, when separated from the whole personality, become failings. In Faust and Mephistopheles, in Tasso and Antonio, in Egmont and Oranien, Goethe, as it were, divides himself in half—with the result that both male leads are lesser men than the poet himself. But the creation of these splendid caricatures let him breathe more freely.

Of course, this analysis is far too neat to do full justice to the vast complexities of artistic creation, and Faust is much more than the dross of Goethe's gradual refinement. A multitude of different impressions and experiences have found their way into Faust—probably including, for example, the young Goethe's experience of Frederick the Great, whom the boy admittedly admired. The king's brilliant victories at the beginning of the Seven Years' War were wiped out by his disastrous defeat at Kunersdorf and the Russian occupation of Berlin, when Goethe was ten. But Frederick held out, shifted small forces—no large ones were left—wherever they were most needed, and never rested, though no reasonable chance of victory remained. Only the death of the Tsarina and her successor's stunning order to his troops to change sides saved the king. One is reminded of two famous lines near the end of Faust: "Who ever strives with all his power, we are allowed to save." And in his last years, when peace had come, the old

[3] *Ethics*, end of Part II.

king designed a project to drain and colonize the Oder-Bruch, which may have helped to inspire Faust's last enterprise.

It would be absurd to conclude that Faust is really a portrait of the king, who was anti-Gothic, enlightened, and immune to the charms of women. Moreover, in the text of *Faust*, the poet himself likens the Philemon and Baucis episode to the biblical tale of Naboth's vineyard; Frederick, in an exactly parallel situation, let a miller keep his mill—not as a matter of capricious grace, but in explicit recognition of the rights of man.

5

Nothing said so far gives any adequate idea of the influence of *Faust*. Goethe created a character who was accepted by his people as their ideal prototype. We shall see in the next chapter that this was by no means his intention. Nevertheless, this was the result; and it is questionable whether there is any parallel to this feat—that a great nation assigns such a role to a largely fictitious character, presented to it so late in its history.

A nation's conception of itself influences not only its attitude toward its own past but also its future behavior. Goethe's vision of Faust is therefore not only a major clue to the romantics' anthologies and historiography but also an important factor in subsequent German history. When we behold Faust sacrificing Gretchen to his own self-realization and, in Part Two, closing both eyes while Mephistopheles advances the fulfillment of his ultimate ambitions by destroying Philemon and Baucis, we may wonder if his disregard of concrete human beings and his boundless will to power over everything except himself is not part of a prophetic vision of horrors to come.

Goethe saw the dangers of a Faustian striving and attempted in a great variety of ways to dissociate himself from Faust. As will be shown in the next chapter, he came to distinguish two kinds of striving: the romantic, unconditional, and hence destructive kind Faust represents and his own classical, self-disciplined devotion to his work. These two kinds of striving correspond to, and probably helped to inspire, Hegel's contrast between the "good" and the "bad infinite." And Hegel

used his influence as a professor of philosophy in Berlin to remind his students: "Whoever wants something great, says Goethe, must be able to limit himself."[4]

Hegel's whole *Philosophy of Right* is profoundly influenced by Goethe's example—by his life rather than by any epigram. It teaches that freedom must be sought within the limitations of a responsible role in the civic life of a community and that the realm of art and philosophy does not involve a rejection of civic life but only its fulfillment. The British idealists were to teach much the same doctrine, under the dual influence of Hegel and Goethe himself.

No doubt, Goethe thought of embodying this idea in his *Faust* when he decided to let Faust end up winning land from the sea. Here was some possibility of presenting in concrete terms the limitation of a previously unconditional striving. Any number of details suggest, however, that Goethe did not go through with this notion. His whole bent was undidactic. In the end Faust still resents the here and now, is ruthless with his neighbors, and employs slave labor while he dreams of freedom in the future; and in his last scene he is not only physically blind but completely unaware of his environment and situation. Nothing whatever will come of his efforts, and, while he thinks drainage ditches are being dug, it is in fact his own grave.

6

If Hegel was profoundly influenced by Goethe himself, Schopenhauer found the quintessence of human nature—indeed, of the universe—in Faust. His metaphysical conception of the ultimate reality as relentlessly striving, blind will may be considered a cosmic projection of Faust's ceaseless aspiration.

Nietzsche, on the other hand, did not take his cue from Faust, as the popular misinterpretation of his philosophy would imply, but from the old Goethe. Departing from established estimates, he disparaged *Faust* and emphasized, like

[4] *Philosophy of Right,* addition to §13.

no major interpreter before him, the surpassing greatness of
the never popular old Goethe. Pointedly, he called the *Conversations with Eckermann* "the best German book."[5] The
greatest power was, to Nietzsche's mind, the perfect self-control and creativity of the old Goethe. One of Nietzsche's least
plausible notions, his doctrine of the eternal recurrence of the
same events at gigantic intervals, is intended partly as the most
extreme antithesis to Faust's repudiation of the present. While
Faust is willing to be damned if ever he should say to the
moment, "abide," Nietzsche says in the penultimate chapter of
Zarathustra: "If ever you wanted one thing twice, if ever you
said, '. . . Abide, moment!' then you wanted *all* back. All
anew, all eternally. . . . *For all joy wants—eternity.*" (The
contrast between Faust and Goethe will be considered more
fully in the next chapter.)

While Hegel had found in Goethe the demonstration that
the State is the proper basis and framework for the development of art and culture, Nietzsche illustrated his diametrically
opposite claim, that state and culture thrive only at each
other's expense, by also citing Goethe. Goethe had flourished
when Germany was fragmented and lacked a state, while
France was the great European power; and, after 1871, de-
feated France became a great cultural center. The Alpine re-
cluse did not take the Weimar court as seriously as the Berlin
professor had done. Nietzsche also pointed to Goethe's anti-
political opposition to the so-called Wars of Liberation against
Napoleon.

Fichte, Schelling, Schopenhauer, and Nietzsche could all
have said to Goethe what Hegel wrote to him on April 24,
1825: "When I survey the course of my spiritual development,
I see you everywhere woven into it and would like to call myself one of your sons; my inward nature has . . . set its course
by your creations as by signal fires." The full truth of this
statement, as far as Hegel is concerned, should become apparent in chapter 8. The point is not that Goethe provided convenient quotations for the philosophers. Nineteenth-century

---

[5] *Der Wanderer und sein Schatten,* §109.

German philosophy consisted to a considerable extent in a series of efforts to assimilate the phenomenon of Goethe.

The ethics of Plato and Aristotle, the Cynics and the Cyrenaics, the Stoics and the Epicureans was largely inspired by the personality, the life, and the death of Socrates. The image of the proud, ironic sage who found in wisdom and continual reflection that enduring happiness that riches cannot buy and whose character had somehow had such power that a despot, lacking self-control, seems like a slave compared with him— this wonderful embodiment of human dignity captivated all the later thinkers of antiquity, became their ethical ideal, and led to a new conception of man. Socrates' fearlessly questioning iconoclasm and his defiant decision to die rather than to cease speaking freely had an equal impact on the modern mind. His character and bearing have influenced the history of philosophy as much as any system.

Goethe is one of the few men whose personality has had a comparable influence. His character, too, became normative for others; so did some of the characters he created; and his tolerance as a man and as a poet furnishes a prime example of an ethical attitude that is above resentment.

5

GOETHE'S FAITH AND
FAUST'S REDEMPTION

Less than a year before his death, on June 1, 1831, Goethe wrote his friend Zelter, the composer, that he had practically finished *Faust:* little remained but to "wrap a few mantle folds around the finished product that it may altogether remain an evident riddle, delight men on and on, and give them something to work on."

None of the riddles in which the Second Part abounds has elicited a larger body of work than the final scene with its religious setting. For Goethe had often pictured himself as a pagan; his earlier dramas, epics, lyrics, ballads, and elegies— and the conception of Mephistopheles in *Faust* itself—did not show any great respect for Christianity; and in his Venetian Epigrams, and in many of his letters and conversations, he had frequently referred to Christian symbols with extreme contempt. There is no need for an anthology of relevant remarks or lines. Two very brief quotations from his last letters to Zelter will suffice; and it should be noted that the poet himself intended these letters for publication, as he says expressly a number of times (Oct. 31 and Nov. 23, 1831, and Jan. 3, 1832). These quotations make it clear that the end of *Faust* does not represent the renunciation of the poet's paganism or a *rapprochement* to a Catholic version of Christianity, comparable to Novalis' later poems, to the conversion of Friedrich Schlegel, or to Wagner's *Parsifal.*

Goethe calls the cross "the most disgusting thing under the sun [which] no reasonable human being should strive to exhume" (Jun. 9, 1831); and he expressly scorns Schlegel, of

whom he says that he "suffocated in the end of his rumination
of ethical and religious absurdities" and "fled into Catholicism"
(Oct. 20, 1831). Suffice it to add that Goethe had no sooner
finished Act V than he turned to Act IV, which he concluded
with a spiteful and sarcastic treatment of the church.

One can understand why some critics have wondered
whether the medieval heaven of the last scene was not meant
to be a hyperbolic blasphemy. Yet this suggestion is as wide
of the mark as the notion that it must be read as an obeisance
to traditional religion. Goethe was in earnest, but he disliked
Christianity as much as ever.

Hence, it has been argued that he bowed to Swedenborg,
from whom he certainly derived some of the mystifying symbolism of the last scene. But the more than 150 volumes of
the poet's writings, letters, and recorded conversations contain
scarcely any references to Swedenborg. A few times, Goethe
uses the image of the spirits' entering the seer (cf. *Faust*, lines
11906 ff.), and in a late "confession" he compares Swedenborg's activities to Cagliostro's "juggleries" and concludes: "a
certain superstitious belief in demonic men will never cease,
and . . . the problematically true, which we respect only in
theory, can be most comfortably coupled with lies in its execution."[1] Clearly, he did not accept Swedenborgianism. His faith
was different.

In another letter to Zelter, Goethe wrote (Aug. 4, 1803):
"One does not get to know works of nature and art when they
are finished: one must catch them in their genesis to comprehend them in some measure." A German scholar, Pniower, has
chosen these words as the motto for a book, *Goethes Faust*
(1899), in which he collected documents that illuminate its
genesis. Five years later, Gräf devoted to Goethe's own remarks about his *Faust* more than six hundred pages of the
fourth volume of his gigantic work *Goethe über seine Dichtungen*, in which he tried to assemble everything that Goethe ever
said or wrote on any of his own poetic works. The Teutonic
thoroughness of these collections makes it possible for us to
scan the vast materials in a short time—and to confine ourselves

[1] *Werke*, Ausgabe letzter Hand, XXXI, 229.

to a few important aspects of the development of Goethe's conception of *Faust*.

The fact that the poet worked on *Faust* off and on for sixty years does not prove, as is sometimes supposed, that he identified himself with the hero. Faust's redemption is not a dramatization of Goethe's confidence in his own ultimate salvation. Rather, the poet's attitude toward both the hero and the play was marked by a striking ambivalence, and in one important work after another he projected himself into radically anti-Faustian characters and lines. Wilhelm Meister, who occupied him almost as long as Faust, is the most obvious example, while Egmont, although certainly no faithful self-portrait either, is the quintessence of Goethe's anti-Faustian traits: "That I am gay and take things lightly, that is my good fortune. . . . Do I live but to think about life? Should I rather not enjoy the present moment?" And again: "If I were a somnambulist and walked on a ridgepole, would it be friendly to call me by my name to warn me, and thus to awaken and kill me? Let each man go his own way and take care of himself."

These crucial passages explain why, when Oranien wisely leaves, Egmont stays behind and falls victim to the plot Oranien had foreseen. It is noteworthy that the old Goethe, after finishing *Faust*, went back to this very scene in *Egmont* for the quotation with which he concluded his autobiography:

As if whipped by invisible spirits, the sun steeds of time run away with the light chariot of our destiny, and nothing remains to us but to hold on to the reins with calm courage, steering the wheels, now right, now left, from the stone here and the abyss there. Where it goes—who knows? One hardly remembers from where one came.

There you have the allegedly so modern, existentialist conception of *Geworfenheit*, of finding oneself thrown into the world, abandoned to one's own devices, without a benevolent father in heaven, but in Goethe it lacks both the saturnine pathos of Heidegger and the self-pity so fashionable today. To be sure, Egmont's naïve way of life and his delight in the present moment cannot be ascribed to Goethe without qualification; but he must not be credited with Faust's scorn of the

here and now. Goethe had no reason to feel suddenly, like
Faust, that he had wasted his whole life. He did not resent
himself, his lot, or man's condition.

2

Although begun earlier than *Egmont, Faust* was not finished until more than forty years later; and within limits we
can distinguish the reasons for the delay of the First and the
Second Parts. The Faust of Part One was, at first, a projection
of the poet who, as usual, let both of his male leads imperson-
ate important facets of his character. Thus Faust and Mephistopheles correspond to Tasso and Antonio. Faust represents
the young poet's profound storm and stress, while Mephistopheles reminds us continually that this style and outlook
never possessed Goethe completely. That was the conception
of the so-called *Urfaust,* before 1775—a dramatic attempt that
had no equal in German dramatic literature up to that time but
that was nevertheless held back by the poet, not to be discovered and published until 1887. Why was it withheld? Why was
only a part of it polished and published as "A Fragment" even
in 1790? And why was Part One not published until 1808,
three years after the death of Schiller, who had long insisted
that *Faust* was a masterpiece that must be completed and published?

The very excellence and power of the play seem to have
been partly responsible. Goethe's first great literary triumph—
Werther, which inspired a wave of suicides—had taught him
that great works of art are dynamite; and he prefaced later
editions: "Be a man and do not follow me." Tasso, the "intensi-
fied Werther," needed no such introduction: clearly, he was
an exaggerated projection of only part of the poet and cried
out to be united in one personality with Antonio. Faust, however, had come to life like Werther and gained an independent
existence of his own. The presence of Mephistopheles did not
suffice to establish the crucial difference between the poet and
his creature—or to counteract the intoxicating effects of Faust
on the people who were soon to hail him as the incarnation
of their national character.

Surely, the poet did not foresee the extent of Faust's influence; but the play was so personal and there was enough of himself in Faust to make him shrink from publishing the play as long as its hero, about whom he now had such mixed feelings, would be taken as an idealized self-portrait. He was not writing for effect alone but to reach clarity about himself; and he had to come to terms with Faust to come to terms with himself.

Near the turn of the century, Goethe conceived the Prologue in Heaven. Instead of raising the curtain on Faust's Gothic study, he introduced Faust indirectly through the Lord's dialogue with Mephistopheles, modeled after the prologue to the Book of Job. Mephistopheles' irreverence rules out any idea that the scene might represent a religious obeisance, but the Prologue succeeds in dissociating Goethe from Faust.

Even so, Part One was not published for another decade. This delay must be understood in terms of the poet's "classical" outlook. The author of *Tasso* and *Iphigenie* had just concluded *Wilhelm Meisters Lehrjahre* with admonitions that sound like deliberate antitheses to Faust's ambitions: "Wherever you may be . . . , work as best you can . . . and let the present be a cause of good cheer to you." And: "Man cannot be happy until his unconditional striving limits itself." And: "Whoever wants to do or enjoy all and everything in its whole humanity . . . will only spend his time with an eternally unsatisfied striving" (VII, 8 and VIII, 5, 7).

These last lines, of course, refer specifically to one of Faust's great speeches; and it should be noted that the word just rendered as "humanity" is *Menschheit*—the same word I have translated as "mankind" in Faust's speech (lines 1765 ff.).

> *Do you not hear, I have no thought of joy!*
> *The reeling whirl I seek, the most painful excess,*
> *Enamored hate and quickening distress.*
> *Cured from the craving to know all, my mind*
> *Shall not henceforth be closed to any pain,*
> *And what is portioned out to all mankind,*
> *I shall enjoy in my own heart, contain*
> *Within my spirit summit and abyss,*

Pile on my breast their agony and bliss,
Let my own self grow into theirs, unfettered,
Till as they are, at last I, too, am shattered.

Goethe must have felt how ineffective the dry antitheses of
Meister were, compared with such intoxicating lines; and by
now he was loath to be identified not only with the hero but
with the drama itself.

Christmas, 1797, he wrote in a letter (to Hirt; for the date
see Pniower §111) that he was "at the moment infinitely far
removed from such pure and noble subjects [as Laokoon], insofar as I wish to conclude my *Faust* and renounce at the
same time all nordic barbarism." And to Schiller, too, he referred to the "nordic nature" of his "barbarous production"
(Apr. 28, 1798); while in yet another letter he called it a
Hexenprodukt—a witches' brew. Finally (according to Pniower, in 1800), he took leave of *Faust* with a poem, *Abschied*
(Farewell), of which the first stanza reads:

Completed lies now my dramatic dirge
Which I concluded in the end with fright,
No longer moved by man's tumultuous urge,
No longer by the power of the night.
Who likes depicting the chaotic surge
Of feeling, when he has emerged to light?
And thus be closed, with all its sorceries,
This narrow circle of barbarities.

Instead of sending Part One to the printer, however, Goethe
now concentrated on the Helena episode of Part Two. He was
not only reluctant to split up his work and publish one half
without the other, but he was doubly averse to bring out what
he now considered the "barbarities" of Part One without balancing them immediately with a poetic reflection of his own
emergence to light and clarity.

In this he did not succeed, and eventually he consented to
the publication of Part One in 1808. But it is noteworthy that
Goethe published the Helena scenes after he had given them
their final form in 1827, while, a little later, he resisted all
suggestions that he publish the final scene of the play about

which there was no end of inquiries; and he would not even divulge the conclusion to such a trusted and respected friend as Wilhelm von Humboldt. He realized that the final scene was bound to be widely misconstrued, and he did not want to spend what little time remained to him explaining and defending it.

The outlook of the old Goethe is further clarified by the subtitle he gave to the Helena scenes when he published them —*klassisch-romantische Phantasmagorie*—and by his comments on it in a letter to Iken (Sept. 23, 1827):

The passionate discord between classicists and romanticists should finally be reconciled. That we should educate and give form to ourselves [*uns bilden*] is the most important demand; and our models would be immaterial if we did not have to fear that we might malform ourselves [*verbilden*] by the use of false models. After all, a wider and purer vision is provided by Greek and Roman literature to which we owe our liberation from monkish barbarism. . . .

It is surely odd that modern critics, who profess to be anti-romantic, although they share the romantic glorification of the Middle Ages and ignore classical antiquity, should try so often to dispose of Goethe as a German romantic poet. The labels do not ultimately matter. What is crucial is that we are not compelled to choose between nineteenth-century romanticism and twentieth-century neo-Christianity, whether it be neo-Thomism or neo-orthodoxy. We need not choose between the surging medievalism of Richard Wagner and the brittle medievalism of T. S. Eliot. "There is a world elsewhere," as Coriolanus says. Indeed, almost all of world literature lies outside this frightening alternative: not only "Greek and Roman literature," to which Goethe here refers, but also Indian literature, which was only beginning to be discovered in the West in Goethe's time; the world of the Old Testament, which, one sometimes feels, has not been discovered yet, though Michelangelo had more feeling for it than most professors of theology and Bible; Shakespeare; Goethe himself; and, more recently, Nietzsche and Rilke.

3

The sheer impossibility of equaling the beauty and the power of Part One was clearly the main reason for the long delay of the completion of Part Two. The Prologue in Heaven, which had provided a majestic opening for the drama and which was the very addition Goethe needed before he could publish Part One, required a pendant. Without that, the work must forever remain a fragment.

For a time, Goethe may have thought of evading this necessity by a bold tour de force. In 1820 (Nov. 3), he wrote to K. E. Schubarth: "Mephistopheles may win his bet only half; and when half of his guilt remains with Faust, the Old Man's right of pardon comes in immediately, for the merriest conclusion of the whole." Yet no merriment could have balanced the Prologue or provided an acceptable conclusion.

Eventually, Goethe composed what is now the last scene, emphasizing the desired symmetry by a number of parallels to the Prologue. It is as if the completion of this epilogue had broken a spell, so rapidly did Goethe then succeed in finishing the fourth act, after all the other acts had occupied him so much longer.

Goethe's reluctance to complete *Faust,* and especially the last act, must be understood in terms of two points. First, the idea of redemption by grace was almost as abhorrent to the poet as the thought of damning Faust—or anyone else—in eternity. And secondly, Goethe had come to see more and more clearly that the Faustian alternative of a radical repudiation of the present and a "bed of sloth" was utterly unsound.

4

To begin with the first point, Goethe felt that his constant activity *entitled* him to immortality: "If I work indefatigably until my end," he said to Eckermann (Feb. 4, 1829), "then nature is obligated to offer me another form of existence when the present one can no longer endure my spirit." And later in the same year (Sept. 1), he remarked, also to Eckermann:

"I do not doubt our continuance, for nature cannot get on without entelechy; but we are not all equally immortal, and in order to manifest oneself as a great entelechy in the future, one must first be one." The conversation of May 2, 1824 and the letter to Zelter of March 19, 1827 express similar ideas.

If these notions should seem murky and ill-founded, it is well to keep in mind that they come from the poet's conversations and his correspondence and are not proffered to us with the gravity of dogma. Indeed, if you catch Goethe's inflection, his stress does not fall on his dubious affirmation but on three negations. First, he rejects the Christian notion of heaven and hell. Secondly, he neither dreads death nor feels worried about his future state. And, finally, he derides the faith of those who trust that, having botched their lives, they will be compensated in another world. His attitude harks back to Socrates' confident agnosticism in Plato's *Apology:* a man should do his work with courage and intensity, serving others by making the most of his unique gifts and by encouraging others to develop theirs; and he should leave the hereafter to take care of itself.

In another conversation with Eckermann (Feb. 25, 1824), Goethe comes even closer to Socrates' sarcastic agnosticism:

Such incomprehensible things are too distant to furnish a fit subject for daily reflection and thought-destroying speculation. . . . It would be all right with me if, once this life is over, we were blessed with another; only I should like to stipulate that over there I should not meet any of the people who had believed in it here. Else my troubles would have barely begun! The pious would surround me and say: Were we not right? Did we not predict it? . . . The preoccupation with ideas about immortality is for elegant people and especially for the womenfolk who have nothing to do. An able human being, however, who wants to amount to something over here already, and who therefore has to strive, to fight, and to work daily, leaves the world to come to take care of itself and is active and useful in this one. Further, thoughts about immortality are for those who did not get the best of things over here, as far as happiness is concerned; and, I bet, if our dear Tiedge had a better lot, he would also have better thoughts.

The same attitude finds expression in Faust's retort to Mephistopheles, in the pact scene (lines 1660 ff.):

> *Of the beyond I have no thought:*
> *When you reduce this world to naught,*
> *The other one may have its turn.*
> *My joys come from this earth, and there,*
> *That sun has burnt on my despair:*
> *Once I have left those, I don't care:*
> *What happens is of no concern.*
> *I do not even wish to hear*
> *Whether beyond they hate and love*
> *And whether in that other sphere*
> *One realm's below and one above.*

In one of the last scenes of Part Two, Faust employs similarly forthright language in repulsing Care—the very specter that was to haunt the pages of Heidegger's *Sein und Zeit* exactly a hundred years later. The existentialists, too, try to exorcize Care with "resolution," but only after a dizzying display of verbal magic that might well have recalled to Goethe's mind the "monkish barbarism" he associated with the romantics and the Middle Ages. There is nothing scholastic about Faust's "resolution":

> *The earthly sphere I know sufficiently,*
> *But into the beyond we cannot see.*
> *A fool, that squints and tries to pierce those shrouds*
> *And would invent his like above the clouds!*
> *Let him survey this life, be resolute,*
> *For to the able this world is not mute.*
> *Why fly into eternities?*
> *What man perceives, that he can seize.*

Goethe felt a powerful aversion to the otherworldliness and the preoccupation with death that were so characteristic of many of the German romantics and that he considered morbid. But he did not go to the opposite extreme to accept

Prospero's imposing resignation (see chapter 1, section 3). Goethe did not believe that "the great globe itself" would "leave not a rack behind," and that "our little life is rounded with a sleep." Nor did he accept Shakespeare's tragic world view. Everywhere he experienced "how death is always swallowed by life," as he once put it in a letter to Nees von Esenbeck (Sept. 27, 1826). For this recurring death and rebirth was the heartbeat of his life.

One of Goethe's finest poems ends:

> And until you have possessed
> dying and rebirth,
> you are but a sullen guest
> on the gloomy earth.

(A translation of the whole poem is offered in section 7 of my *Critique*.) It is easier to accept this value judgment with its figurative use of the idea of death than it is to assent to Goethe's faith that death and destruction are never final. One may admire his poetic formulations of that faith, at least in the original German, and still prefer Prospero's disillusionment, coupled with Shakespeare's insistence that "The summer's flower is to the summer sweet,/Though to itself it only live and die."

In *Urworte, Orphisch*, Goethe proclaims, rather more confidently:

> No lapse of time nor any force dissolves
> A form, once coined, that through its life evolves.

And in one of his last poems, *Vermächtnis* (Legacy), which he read to Eckermann on February 12, 1829, having just completed it, he speaks in a similar vein, drawing a moral, too:

> No substance can turn into naught
> The eternal stirs in everything . . .
> The moment is eternity.

5

How is Goethe's faith reflected in Faust's redemption? In talks with Eckermann, the poet himself called attention to two lines in the last scene as a clue, especially on May 6, 1827, and on June 6, 1831. But in the first conversation, which has already been cited in part in chapter 4, section 3, Goethe added significantly that the drama contains "no idea which might be called the foundation of the whole and of every single scene." The famous lines are:

> Who ever strives with all his power,
> We are allowed to save.

That was indeed Goethe's faith; but, without qualification, these lines do not describe Goethe's ideal. What he desired and embodied was not the unconditional striving that is so characteristically Faustian and of which another typical form is encountered in *The Picture of Dorian Gray* by Oscar Wilde. The explicit repudiation of such unconditional striving in *Wilhelm Meisters Lehrjahre* has been cited above (section 2), and the sequel, *Wilhelm Meisters Wanderjahre*, was actually subtitled *Die Entsagenden*—Renunciation. Nor could Faust have written *Faust*.

Goethe's characteristic striving was not that of an undisciplined will, pushing on into infinity without hope of satisfaction like Hegel's "Bad Infinite" and Schopenhauer's "Will." Rather, Goethe was imbued with the relentless determination to educate himself and to give form to himself. Goethe's passion for classical antiquity was not a romantic flight from the present but the will to embody what he could learn from such models here and now—in his own person and his works.

If the lines, "Who ever strives with all his power,/We are allowed to save," require this qualification to characterize Goethe's striving and to do justice to his ethic, there is yet another sense in which they reflect the poet's faith without qualification: having redeemed himself, he had faith that all of the cosmos—which he pictured as a Leibnizian universe of constantly striving monads—was also redeemed. In that sense, the first of the two lines is all-inclusive, and the quotation is an expression of world-embracing tolerance.

Thus Nietzsche said of Goethe: He "created himself" as

> the man of tolerance, not from weakness but from strength, because he knows how to use to his advantage even that from which the average nature would perish. . . . Such a spirit who has *become free* stands amid the cosmos with a joyous and trusting fatalism, in the *faith* that only the particular is loathsome, and that all is redeemed and affirmed in the whole—*he does not negate any more*. Such a faith, however, is the highest of all possible faiths: I have baptized it with the name of *Dionysus*.

This "Dionysian" tolerance is beautifully illustrated by a remark Goethe made in a conversation with Falk. After expressing his disillusionment with the public, he added: "When, in the sequel of *Faust*, they come to the place where even the devil finds grace and mercy before God—that, I should think, they will not easily forgive me."

Pniower, who cites this conversation (§973) and determines that it must have taken place between 1808 and 1816, comments in part: "Goethe's utterance . . . represents either one of those mystifications which were not rare with him and with which he would permit himself a joke, now to an individual and now to the public, or a passing mood which we cannot follow up." Surely, it was a passing mood—but one that welled up from the very depths of Goethe's *Weltanschauung* and a fair sample not only of Goethe's affirmation of all being, without reservation, but also of that "divine spitefulness" without which Nietzsche, in his *Ecce Homo*, said he could "not imagine perfection."

In a similar vein, Goethe said in the same conversation:

> For thirty years almost, they have plagued themselves with the broomsticks of the Blocksberg and the monkeys' conversation in the witch's kitchen . . . , and the interpreting and allegorizing of this dramatic-humorous nonsense has never gone too well. Indeed, one should indulge in such jokes more often while one is young. . . .

That remark may well throw more light on the end of *Faust* than most contributions to the literature.

Of course, Goethe did not write a scene depicting Mephistopheles' redemption, but there was no need for that. For the Prologue (especially the Lord's last speech) and Mephistopheles' description of himself as "part of that force which would/ Do evil evermore and yet creates the good" (lines 1336 f.) leave no doubt that Mephistopheles is redeemed in the total design of the world from the very beginning.

Thus the clue to Faust's redemption should be found in Goethe's faith and not in Faust's moral merits. Faust's salvation does not prove Goethe's endorsement of his deeds, nor, as has been suggested, that Faust has in the end reached the lowest point of his career—a view that is inconsistent with his words to Care and his last speech—and is therefore in dire need of immediate supernatural intervention. Faust has not reached his nadir; neither has he perfected himself.

In the Prologue, the Lord said of Faust:

> *Though now he serves me but confusedly,*
> *I shall soon lead him out into the light.*

And in his previously cited poem "Farewell" (section 2), Goethe wrote:

> *Who likes depicting the confusing surge*
> *Of feeling, when he has emerged to light?*

Faust did not emerge into the light to attain clarity in this life, as Goethe did. The Lord—on this note the drama closes —will fulfill his promise in heaven. Thus Gretchen is told in the last scene:

> *Come, raise yourself to higher spheres.*
> *When he feels you, he follows there.*

And then the drama ends:

> *The Eternal-Womanly*
> *Attracts us higher.*

These lines, of course, were suggested to the poet by his earthly experience and bring to mind a similar passage in one

of Goethe's last great love poems, the *Marienbader Elegie*.
What Goethe lets Faust find only in heaven, he himself had
not only sought in this life, but he felt that he had found it:
redemption and fulfillment.

In his last speech, Faust says:

> *Then, to the moment I might say:*
> *Abide, you are so fair!*
> *The traces of my earthly days*
> *No aeons can impair.*

To Goethe it had been granted to say to the present moment,
not only in anticipation in the hour of death, but all his life
long, "Abide, you are so fair!" And the famous song of
Lynkeus, the Tower Warden, in the last act seems to have no
other function in that place than to remind us of this:

> *To see, I was born,*
> *To look, is my call,*
> *To the tower sworn,*
> *I delight in all.*
>
> *I glance out far*
> *And see what is near,*
> *The moon and the stars,*
> *The wood and the deer.*
>
> *In all things I see*
> *The eternally bright,*
> *And as they please me,*
> *In myself I delight.*
>
> *You blessed eyes,*
> *What you saw everywhere,*
> *It be as it may,*
> *It was, oh, so fair!*

Surely, Goethe was more like Lynkeus than he was like
Faust when, near the end, he still scorns the here and now,
exclaiming "The accursed *here!*" (line 11233). Nor was
Goethe "dissatisfied at every moment" as Faust is, even in his
dialogue with Care.

6

Faust's wager with Mephistopheles had been based on the false assumption that one could not appreciate the present without becoming a Philistine. Goethe, however, came to feel that "every moment is of infinite value" and exhorted Eckermann: "always hold fast to the present" (Nov. 3, 1823). And in his last letter to his friend Zelter, the composer, he wrote: "Fortunately, the character of your talent depends on the tone, i.e. on the moment. Since a succession of consecutive moments is, however, always a kind of eternity, it was given to you to find permanence in the transitory and thus to satisfy fully not only me but also the spirit of Hegel, insofar as I understand it."

Goethe believed and demonstrated that one can live in the present without betraying one's ceaseless striving. Faust did not learn this lesson and hence cannot find fulfillment in this life: he is in need of redemption and further instruction beyond. But in the four lines from his last speech, which we have quoted, Goethe hints at another kind of redemption. Even as Tasso and Antonio could be redeemed if only nature would "form *one* man out of the two of them" (Act 3, scene 2), Faust could find salvation by being reabsorbed into the poet's character. He would then transcend the false alternative of his repudiation of the present and the "bed of sloth"; he would be permitted to say to the moment "Abide, you are so fair!" and to share Goethe's faith—for it was no mere confidence in fame but a cosmic faith: "The traces of my earthly days/No aeons can impair."

> Zum Augenblicke dürft ich sagen:
> Verweile doch, du bist so schön!
> Es kann die Spur von meinen Erdetagen
> Nicht in Äonen untergehn.

6

GOETHE VERSUS
ROMANTICISM

In the English-speaking world, Goethe, Hegel, and Nietzsche are often classified as German romantics. In view of the ambiguity of the word "romanticism," this is hardly wrong, but it is unfortunate because it obscures the deep differences that separate these men from Novalis, Tieck, the brothers Schlegel, Schelling, Arnim, and Brentano—writers who called themselves romantics to signify their opposition to classicism. It is useful to have a common label for these rebels, and, since they themselves insisted that they were romantics, while Goethe and Nietzsche frequently made vitriolic comments on "romanticism," it seems reasonable to apply the label primarily to the men who liked it.

The early romantics—Novalis, Tieck, and the Schlegels—rebelled first of all against German classicism, as represented by Goethe and Schiller; but in the beginning they took their cue from some of Goethe's nonclassical works: *Goetz* and *Werther*, which Goethe felt he had outgrown; *Faust: A Fragment*, with which Goethe was not happy; and, above all, the first installments of his novel, *Wilhelm Meister*, which Goethe then began to punctuate in subsequent installments with antiromantic epigrams. As Goethe saw it, the romantics were opposed to all that mattered most to him; and this opposition was symbolized by the romantics' scorn of Goethe's best friend, Schiller. By the end of the century, the romantics accepted Goethe's estimate that their intentions were deeply opposed to his—and attacked him no less than Schiller.

It has often been pointed out that what Goethe and Schiller called their classicism was in fact remote from some important meanings of that word—French classicism, for example. But the primary reference of classicism is to classical antiquity, and, however far Goethe and Schiller were from that, the crucial point to note about them was their overwhelming admiration for the Greeks and Romans, especially the Greeks. It deserves emphasis, too, that the romantics did not share this admiration and began to glorify the Middle Ages.

Reaching back into the German past, Goethe had stopped with Goetz and Faust, both men of the Renaissance, and he never glorified Catholicism any more than the theology of the Reformers. Even in his storm and stress phase, Goethe had been pagan, and he never was or became anti-European. But instead of generalizing about the German romantics, we must introduce certain distinctions.

There are, first of all, the brothers Schlegel, Tieck, Novalis, and Schelling—the romantic clique. Then there is the nationalistic wave of the Wars of Liberation against Napoleon. Third, there are Hölderlin and Kleist, essentially lonely figures who were not, properly speaking, part of any movement, and to these one might add Byron outside Germany because Goethe took such an interest in him. Finally, there is romantic painting and, above all, music.

2

Goethe's attitude toward the early romantics was not entirely constant, which was due to their inconstancy more than to Goethe's. They began by paying extravagant homage to some of Goethe's works, notably *Meister*, and by opposing that hopelessly shallow version of enlightenment which was then propagated in Germany by Nicolai. Without at any time identifying himself with this movement, Goethe considered it a possibly healthy ferment. Soon, however, the romantics were dissatisfied with *Meister*, with Goethe himself—and with the present as such. That flight from the present began which is the very core of what we ought to call romanticism—something that found varied expression in a cult of the past and a yearning for the future, death-worship, and otherworldliness. To this Goethe was unalterably opposed.

Goethe thought that any such extravagant dissatisfaction with the present was generally rooted in a deep dissatisfaction with oneself—often quite justified. Novalis' otherworldliness and hymns to night and death became his forte *faute de mieux:* the sick poet was unable to enjoy this life or to prove his worth here and now. His romanticism was reducible to his sickness and his inferiority to Goethe. And the Schlegels' growing interest in Indian lore is similarly understood by Goethe as "merely a *pis aller.* They had sense enough to see that they could not do anything brilliant in the German, Latin, or Greek field." This vitriolic judgment, in a letter to Zelter (Oct. 20, 1831) recalls an earlier conversation with Boisserée (Aug. 3, 1815) in which Goethe had said of Tieck and the Schlegels: "In Spinoza we can look up what is the matter with these gentlemen: it is envy." Goethe expressed himself often in a similar vein, and some other examples may be found in my book on *Nietzsche* (chapter 12, section 6). The cult of the Middle Ages and Friedrich Schlegel's conversion to Catholicism seemed to Goethe mere forms of escape prompted by the inability to gain satisfaction with oneself—subterfuges of men who had always "wanted to represent more than nature had granted them" (to Zelter, Oct. 20, 1831).

If Goethe rather liked Schelling and felt that his views of nature were congenial to some extent, the reason was that Schelling seemed to Goethe to have corrected one of the most serious faults of romanticism: its limitless subjectivity. Schelling's essential advance over Fichte was that he proposed to view nature not as posited by the ego but as a realm with equal rights. It was this "objectivity" that Goethe liked. But, when Schelling later turned to revealed religion, Goethe had only contempt for him.

The nationalistic romanticism that came to the fore during the *Freiheitskriege* against Napoleon need not detain us because it is well known how utterly Goethe despised it; how he considered Napoleon a good European; and how consistently he urged the abandonment of any narrow nationalism and the advancement of *Weltliteratur.* There were few things he abhorred more than that fusion of nationalism and religion that later attained its apotheosis in Wagner and that Goethe denounced as "neo-German, religious-patriotic art." (The joint manifesto against *Neu-deutsche religiös-patriotische Kunst*, published by Goethe and Heinrich Meyer, is reprinted in the *Sophien-Ausgabe* of Goethe's works.)

3

Goethe's lack of sympathy for Hölderlin, who is now widely hailed as Germany's greatest lyric poet, next to Goethe, and for Kleist, who in sheer dramatic power excelled Goethe and Schiller, has often been considered proof of egotistical unkindness, sterile conservatism, and even lack of critical acumen. Goethe, of course, was a poet rather than a critic—unlike many modern writers who are primarily critics and only incidentally poets—and his chief concern was with his own creations, not with those of others. He did not deal with Hölderlin and Kleist of his own accord. He did not single them out for criticism. They approached him, and the question was whether he should go out of his way to sponsor their works or at least to encourage them and thus admit them into his own sphere. This he refused to do. Why?

Hölderlin was neither a nationalist nor a medievalist; he even excelled Goethe in his passion for the Greeks. And the work Kleist offered "on the knees of my heart" was not *Die Hermannsschlacht*—that Teutonic hymn of hatred against Napoleon—but *Penthesilea*, which dealt with a Greek theme. Nor could Goethe have known then that Hölderlin would soon become insane or that Kleist would commit suicide. There is no need to suppose that Goethe's judgment was based on any impression of their personalities, beyond what had found expression in their works. But what was expressed in these was, in both instances, that "unconditional striving" that Goethe, after his return from Italy, had condemned in the later sections of *Wilhelm Meister*.

Hölderlin's greatness as a lyric poet depends on the sovereign power with which he was able to mold language; and in this respect his verse invites comparison with the young Goethe's. But Hölderlin's poetry quite lacks that exultation in the present that inspires Goethe's hymns. What struck Goethe was that this new poetry was an incarnate repudiation of the present, a pining for the past without all possibility of fulfillment or compromise. That way lay madness.

Such considerations may well be irrelevant to any pure aesthetic judgment. But Goethe did not claim to pass such judgment. The slogan *l'art pour l'art* he would certainly have rejected no less than a utilitarian approach to art. He did not view poetry as the handmaiden of anything but—life. He wrote to save himself from suicide and madness: let Werther shoot himself and Tasso court insanity if only the poet could thereby survive and retain his sanity.

Hölderlin—comparable in this to Novalis—subordinated his life and sanity to his art: he sang himself insane even as Novalis sang himself to death. He had no will to life or sanity. Goethe was no Dr. Faustus, bartering his sanity for unheard-of artistic creativity. It was not that he had moral scruples, but his physical and mental constitution was such that poetry welled from his heart whenever suffering threatened him with death or madness; and through art he was healed—not made sicker.

Kleist's *Penthesilea* is even more insane than Hölderlin's verse, though it may well have more dramatic power than any previous German play. It is clearly the work of one who excels in tearing himself to pieces and who celebrates the very destructiveness of passion. One could call this play the antithesis of Goethe's *Iphigenie*. If all human failings are atoned by the pure humanity of Goethe's heroine, Kleist's represents these failings raised to such a pitch that Orestes, haunted by the furies of his mind, seems a paragon of sanity compared to her.

In *Penthesilea* passion has reached a depth unknown even in Shakespeare's dramas, and it is not mitigated by a balanced framework or a comprehensive vision. Kleist wallows in the beauty of Penthesilea's madness and celebrates neither triumphant life nor yet that deeper understanding that is born of suffering, but the beauty of death and insanity. To have discovered beauty where his predecessors had not found it and to have communicated it in rich and stunning language is sufficient to establish Kleist as one of the few great tragedians; it was also sufficient to earn Goethe's horror.

That this indicates some limitation on the part of Goethe,

who approximated catholicity of sympathy and understanding, is unquestionable. He was, as he himself knew, basically untragic. But he certainly did not look on himself as a universal norm or a *non plus ultra*. Rather, he considered Shakespeare "a being of a higher order to whom I look up" (cf. chapter 3, section 1). His own creativity depended on a subtle equilibrium that must be guarded against the intrusion of such meteoric forces as the geniuses of Kleist and Hölderlin. Those who accept a tragic world view may concur in Goethe's modest estimate and find Shakespeare a being of a higher order. They will yet have to concede that few men have made so much of their talents—and perhaps no other human being has written so many excellent poems.

The differences between Goethe and Shakespeare, Kleist, and Hölderlin should not distract attention from the crucial fact that all four belong to a tradition that many a modern critic has tried to read out of history, often using the device of calling the three Germans "romantics" and thus covering up the difference between them and the medievalists. But these four men furnish four examples of un-Christian poets who created works of the first rank, untutored by any creed, philosophy, or revelation, and in spite of a public that never fathomed their profundity.

4

Why was Byron not condemned by Goethe as no less romantic than the German poets whom Goethe rejected? Was not Byron's longing for Greece more like Hölderlin's than like Goethe's? Did not Byron court an early death?

As a matter of fact, Goethe's admiration for Byron was distinctly qualified. When Goethe idealized him as Euphorion in the Second Part of *Faust*, he let him disintegrate into thin air. Byron did not fulfill Goethe's hopes for the future. But Byron did not come to Goethe as a struggling young man who requested an endorsement and encouragement, like Hölderlin and Kleist. Rather, he was a poet of world-wide fame whose admiration greatly pleased Goethe at a time when his position in his own country was complicated by widespread resentment of his lack of patriotism. Byron's *Manfred* was sufficiently like *Faust,* and yet also original enough, to win Goethe's interest and respect. And Byron's love of life and the clarity of his poetic diction, no less than the apparent ease of his creation, seemed far different from the German poets—and did not foreshadow any similar developments.

5

Goethe's attitude toward romantic painting can be briefly summarized. He disliked the growing preoccupation with medieval and religious themes; and the manifesto against "neo-German, religious-patriotic art" was occasioned by a new trend in painting that was associated with men who called themselves Nazarenes. Moreover, Goethe considered much recent painting weak and sickly. His attitude toward music is far more interesting because it was in this field, not in painting, that German romanticism produced some of its finest fruits.

As a boy of fourteen, Goethe had heard the seven-year-old Mozart play the piano; and, even after Mozart's death, Goethe retained a deep affection and a loving admiration for him. Nobody's works were performed more often at the theater in Weimar during the long period when it was directed by the poet; and he wished that the composer of *Don Giovanni* might have written music for his *Faust.*

Later, Goethe developed an equal enthusiasm for Handel, and he greatly respected Bach, in whose revival Zelter, Goethe's friend, had an important share. One need only add that Goethe was sixty in 1809 and that he was primarily a "visual" person for whom the eye was man's noblest sense—Goethe's failure to welcome romantic music with enthusiasm needs no further explanation. What man of over sixty, or even seventy, whose primary concern is with literature and science, would appreciate the latest and most revolutionary developments in music, particularly in an age without radio and records?

Actually, very few of the romantic composers lived in Goethe's time or came into contact with him. Schumann and Chopin, for example, were both born in 1810, when Goethe was sixty-one. But Berlioz and Schubert sent him their music for some of his works. Berlioz' he sent to Zelter, asking for his friend's opinion, which was devastating. Schubert's annoyed him because the composer, his junior by forty-eight years, had turned the *Erlking* into a melodrama. The poet had sought to equal the simplicity of a folk song, sung by an old working woman, and considered it essential that the melody should be repeated stanza after stanza, any difference being confined to the intelligent inflection of the singer's voice. The music must be subordinated to the words. It must not use the words as an occasion for an emotional outburst.

The issue here is not reducible to the poet's vanity, as if his judgment had been warped by his resentment of Schubert's defiance of his own intentions. Goethe could not understand how anyone could possibly admire an opera while admitting that the libretto was worthless. If music was coupled with words, whether in an opera or a *Lied,* it had to be subordinated to the words, and reason must control feeling. In no case must sentiment or passion conquer rationality.

There remains Beethoven, the one musician—indeed, the one creative artist after Mozart's death—who was Goethe's peer in his own time. The first point to insist on is that Beethoven was not a romantic in the sense in which the word has here been used. He did not start from a condescending opposition to the Enlightenment; his art was in no way "neo-German, religious-patriotic"; nor—whatever some effusive critics have said of the "otherworldliness" of his last quartets—did his music represent a flight from the present. He worshiped neither the past nor the future, and certainly not death, fever, or madness. In fact, one would be hard pressed to find any great composer since the days of Handel and of Mozart whose music contains such a joyous affirmation of life. In spite of suffering, Beethoven celebrates life—not pining for another world but exalting the present. For better or for worse, it is characteristic that the *Choral Symphony* ends with an ode to joy, for which the composer used the text of Schiller, Goethe's friend, whom the romantics had derided.

Nor was it Beethoven's intention to drown man in surging sentiment or to abet irrationalism in whatever form. His life-long admiration for Goethe and his lack of sympathy for the romantics are profoundly eloquent. One may also recall how he chided Goethe, who was "deeply moved" when hearing the composer play his own music:

> Ah, sir, I had not expected that from you. . . . Long ago I gave a concert in Berlin. I had worked hard and thought I had done well. I expected a success, but . . . there was not the slightest sign of approval. . . . I soon discovered the clue to this secret: the Berlin public was educated "properly": in token of their appreciation they waved tear-sodden handkerchieves at me. I saw that I had a "romantic" and not an artistic audience. . . . But coming from you, Goethe, I do not like it. When your poems reach my brain . . . I long to climb to the height of your greatness. . . . You must know yourself what it means to gain the applause of those possessed of understanding. If you do not recognize me . . . to what beggarly mob must I play to receive understanding?

Although scarcely used to such rebukes, Goethe called on Beethoven again the next day, still impressed by the man no less than by his music. In a letter to his wife, Goethe recorded his first impression of the composer: "More concentrated, more energetic, more inwardly, I have never yet found any artist." That was not his view of the romantics.

That they did not become friends was more Beethoven's fault than Goethe's. Beethoven continued to find fault with Goethe personally—his little speech to the poet, who insisted on taking a bow when they met the members of the court, has been quoted often—and he even lectured Goethe on his attitude toward a young woman: Bettina. She was then present in Teplitz, where the two men met, but Goethe's house was still closed to her, as it had been ever since her public quarrel with the poet's wife. Goethe had stood by his wife, whom he had married only when their son was sixteen, while Weimar society, which had never accepted her, had sided with Bettina. Bettina was the composer's friend and the first to tell Goethe of his work in glowing terms. Now, with Bettina in town and ignored by Goethe, Beethoven, who called on her, seems to have been so irritated by Goethe's behavior toward her that he was unable to omit all reference to her. By chiding

Goethe about this matter, the composer sealed the impossibility of any friendship, made difficult in any case by Beethoven's
insistence on defying even trivial conventions ostentatiously.
That Goethe was no slave to etiquette is sufficiently attested
by his relation, and eventual marriage, to Christiane.

It is remarkable that Goethe did not permit Beethoven's constant reproaches to deceive him about the man's music. What
prevented friendship was the composer's conduct, not his
work. Goethe clearly distinguished the two when he wrote to
Zelter:

> I have made Beethoven's acquaintance. His talent amazes
> me but, unfortunately, he has no self-control at all. He is,
> no doubt, quite right in finding the world detestable, but
> by behaving as he does he really does not make it any more
> pleasant for himself or for others. We must forgive him a
> great deal, for his hearing is getting very bad; this may in-
> terfere less with his musical than with his social side.

The lack of control is, of course, attributed to Beethoven's
behavior only; and anyone familiar with Goethe's uninhibited
candor in his letters to Zelter, in which he never hesitates to
say the worst he finds in his heart against anybody, will marvel
at the mildness of this letter, which signifies nothing less than
the absence of any real dislike for Beethoven—the more so, seeing how much more negative Zelter's attitude toward Beethoven was at that time. And Goethe always retained a profound
respect for Beethoven's music.

Even so, he was unable to divine the full extent of Beethoven's greatness. But what man in his sixties could apprehend
at a few hearings, without assiduous study, the intricate new
laws of the most recent and revolutionary music? He will find
how old norms to which he was used have been set aside; and
he will be tempted to infer that this implies the absence of
all discipline. Goethe did not succumb to this temptation, but
he certainly did not discover and appreciate the new norms.

Beethoven invites comparison with Michelangelo at a profounder level than that on which Goethe's universal genius is
so often juxtaposed with Leonardo's. Beethoven and Michelangelo were titans who exploded a tradition, left behind its

old restraints, and gave expression to all kinds of aspirations that had never before found embodiment in their respective arts. Previous painting and music are much calmer and appear less troubled; for hitherto art had served either religion or simply delight. Goethe still expressed the feeling that music should merely delight us—nothing else. For Beethoven, however, as for Michelangelo, whom Goethe, characteristically, liked less than Raphael, art became a personal necessity, a vehicle for his despair no less than for his joys—in short, what poetry had always been for Goethe.

In this sense, it is sometimes said that Beethoven "liberated music." But one could also view the matter in a different perspective and insist that what distinguished Beethoven and Michelangelo from their *followers* was their control—the restraint they exercised on the verge of the abyss, the power with which they contained the greatest passion. So considered, they represent a *non plus ultra,* an end rather than a beginning, a fulfillment pregnant with death. For what later generations apprehend is primarily the liberation, the setting aside of laws, the limitless possibilities of subjectivity—what is, at worst, libertinism and license; and, at best, romantic or baroque.

Von Arnim accused Goethe in a letter to Grimm in 1811, speaking the mind of many German romantics at that time: "he fears everything novel in art and all disorder. It is almost laughable." Indeed, that is almost laughable. In 1819, Goethe, at seventy, published the poems of his *West-Eastern Divan,* which were more novel and did more to revolutionize German poetry than did the verse of any German romantic between Hölderlin and Heine. Still later, he completed the second part of *Faust*—a work that displays such an utter contempt for all conventional conceptions of order and that is so novel in design that one despairs of finding any literary parallel: it is almost as if Joyce's *Ulysses* had been published seventy-five years before it did appear.

Decidedly, Goethe did not oppose romanticism because it was novel. He put the matter succinctly to Eckermann (Apr. 2, 1829):

The classical I call the healthy, and the romantic the sick.

. . . Most of the novel things are romantic not because they are novel but because they are weak, sickly, and sick; and the ancient is not classical because it is ancient, but because it is strong, fresh, gay, and healthy.

Goethe detested the cult, or affectation, of melancholy and the pose of pining. That he could master the accents of sadness and longing as well as anyone requires no illustrations: one might even ask whether it was not Goethe who taught his people how such emotions could be expressed poetically.

It is easy to understand how Goethe's poetry helped to inspire not only Beethoven but also Schubert and the later romantic composers. Certainly, Goethe did not oppose expressions of feelings: that was his own métier. What he scorned was the abandonment to feelings, the cultivation of sad emotions, the renunciation of self-discipline and reason, and the subordination of life and character to art. He himself subordinated art to life, cultivated self-control and science, and conquered his emotions—in part, by turning them into works of art.

Beethoven's music is similarly the record of his conquest of suffering; and it is certainly not "weak, sickly, and sick," but "strong, fresh," often "gay," and unconquerably "healthy." Instead of fleeing life, the deaf composer reaffirms it with a vast crescendo that takes him from the *Seventh Symphony* to the *Eighth* and *Ninth*, and then, when it seems as if a whole orchestra could no longer suffice him for his celebration of joy, he concludes his life's work with a series of quartets and is able to say "everything" with a mere four instruments. What better example could there be of Goethe's lines: "In limitation only is the master manifest"—*in der Beschränkung zeigt sich erst der Meister*.

6

Goethe's conception of restraint and limitation was associated with his great admiration for the Greeks and Romans; and this is the sense in which his opposition to romanticism hinged on his own classicism. Yet his paganism tells but half the story and deflects attention from another model that was almost equally important for his work: the Hebrew Bible.

Against the tendency of modern critics to assimilate Homer, Sophocles, and Socrates to Christian norms and to write as if great poetry and high morality were necessarily Christian, one has to insist how relatively isolated a phenomenon Christian culture has been and that even in the West it could be pictured with equal justice as an episode that, with the possible exception of the *Divine Comedy,* produced no literary work to equal either Greek or Hebrew literature, or Shakespeare.

The full story of the impact of the Hebrew Bible on Western thought and art and literature has never yet been told, partly because so much that was Hebrew originally has long been absorbed with such complete success that one no longer thinks of it as having any source at all. Even as hundreds of phrases from the Hebrew Scriptures have become part of the language, whether it be German or English, crucial ideas, too, are commonplaces now and are often falsely considered part of man's natural endowment. Reading the Greeks, some critics simply read these ideas into them: for example, that all men are brothers who, unlike the other animals, are fashioned in the image of the one and only God; that the stranger is essentially like oneself; that war is evil and should be abolished; that one ought to rest one day in seven; and that *every* man ought to make something of himself.

The part of this story that belongs in these reflections on Goethe and romanticism is the impact of the Hebrew sensibility on his style. Nothing could be better to bring out the singularity of the style of the Old Testament than a contrast with most Buddhist scriptures with their endless repetitions. But the very length of these would make quotations in the present context inept, and it may suffice here to refer to section 92 of my *Critique,* where an extended illustration is both quoted and discussed. (Most anthologies of Buddhist scriptures will not do because the repetitions are omitted to accommodate the Western reader, whose conception of style has been formed by the Old Testament, however indirectly.) But another contrast that is more accessible and closer to the point is that between *Fear and Trembling* and the text on which

Kierkegaard's book is based: Genesis 22. To those who have read Kierkegaard without rereading the original, it may come as a shock that Genesis requires only about half a page, although it does not spare us Abraham's emotions.

Kierkegaard is a romantic author, and his model, one might say, are the four Gospels, taken together. Everything has to be told more than once, with variations. His style lacks the austere simplicity of classic Hebrew prose or of a Doric temple and resembles rather more the Gothic with its endless details and complexities, which often are grotesque.

Bible critics have so constantly stressed repetitions in the Old Testament, and have found fault with everything stylistic, that most educated readers have forgotten that—to give an example—in the Revised Standard Version, Genesis requires less than sixty pages for the stories of the Creation, Adam, Eve, the tower, Noah, Abraham, Isaac, Jacob, and Joseph, and the many smaller tales that have been woven into this great sequence. And few who begin to read somewhere in the First Book of Kings will be able to lay down the Bible till they are deep into the Second Book: so laconic is the style, so crowded with momentous figures and events. As much as Sophocles, and ever so much more than Homer, the Old Testament may be viewed as a model for Goethe's dictum: "In limitation only is the master manifest."

The Second Part of *Faust*, which has contributed so much to the idea that its author was at heart a true German romantic, is, of course, not "classical" stylistically and is closer to Gothic art, with its insatiable variety and often grotesque detail. Even so, it is striking how much Goethe's imagination was nourished by the Old Testament—a point he himself made in his memoirs when he discussed his childhood. The self-styled pagan who outdid himself in blaspheming the cross found inspiration without end in the Old Testament.

The prime instance in *Faust* is, of course, furnished by the Prologue in Heaven. Little, if anything, in Part Two equals either that or, for that matter, the remainder of Part One—except the fifth act of Part Two. And that, oddly, abounds in references to the Old Testament. Mephistopheles himself calls attention to the similarity between the moving Philemon and

Baucis episode and the tale of Naboth's vineyard in First
Kings; Goethe adds a reference to Second Samuel after the
first appearance of *Die drei Gewaltigen;* and he took the names
of Habebald and Eilebeute from Isaiah 8:1. Two other echoes
of the Hebrew Scriptures are decisive for the last two great
scenes in which Faust appears.

Although this does not appear to have been noted so far,
Faust's encounter with the specter of Care seems to have been
influenced by Genesis 32:[1] "And Jacob was left alone; and
a man wrestled with him until the breaking of the day. And
when he saw that he did not prevail against him, he touched
the hollow of his thigh; and Jacob's thigh was put out of joint.
. . ." In *Faust,* too, the spirit cannot prevail against the hero
and wounds him when she realizes this, instead of conceding
the battle.

The parallel extends beyond these central features of the
two nightly encounters. In the immediately preceding scene,
Faust, like Jacob, has become guilty in a way that is hideously
unheroic and no longer allows the reader to extend his sympathy to him. The nightly encounter raises the hero's stature
to new dimensions and earns him the reader's renewed respect.

Goethe's treatment of Faust's death was influenced decisively by another model in the Pentateuch: the death of Moses.
The main point is, of course, that Faust, too, dies after envisag-
ing the promised land. A letter Goethe wrote the painter
Friedrich Müller on June 21, 1781, fifty years before he was
to complete the play, illuminates not only this parallel but also
Goethe's sensibility, which was nourished much less by abstract speculations or by philosophical ideas than by his response to a picture and a biblical narrative:

> In the Old Testament it is written that Moses died after the
> Lord had shown him the promised land, and was buried by
> the Lord in a hidden place. This is beautiful. But when,
> especially as you have treated the subject, I behold the man
> who has only just before been shown the grace of the divine
> countenance . . . under the devil's feet, then I am angry

[1] I first called attention to this in *The Germanic Review,* April,
1951.

with the angel who should have hurried there a few moments earlier. . . . If one does want to treat this subject, I think it could not be done in any other way but that the holy man, still full of the vision of the promised land, dies in delight, and angels are engaged in lifting him up in a glory . . . and Satan could, at most, serve as a contrast in a corner in the foreground with his black shoulders, without laying hands on the anointed of the Lord. . . .

In spite of these parallels, Faust is not only not the anointed of the Lord but a man whom the poet views until the very end with a profound ambivalence. To be sure, Faust has a vision of the land in which a future generation is to live in freedom, but, barely before his final speech, we are told by Mephistopheles that the blind hero only *thinks* that he is winning land from the sea for other men to live on. And even if one should mistrust Mephistopheles, which seems unwise, we cannot get around the fact that just before Faust dreams of some future time when he might stand "with free men on free ground" he expresses his delight at hearing "the throng that *slaves* for me"—and Mephistopheles' magical minions whom the blind Faust hears are not at all doing the work of which he speaks but are even then digging his grave.

Scholars have too often overlooked such ambiguities and ironies, partly because they lacked the poet's sense of humor; partly because they were intent on making Faust a hero and a model for humanity—in sum, because they were too moralistic. But Goethe was not telling parables like the New Testament, with the intent of having us guess at the moral. He was telling stories like the Old Testament—stories that often have no moral but present life and human beings as they are.

7

Some of the contrasts in this chapter may have been a little too neat and have perhaps approximated special pleading for Goethe while being too sharply pointed against some of the romantics. If the English romantics had been moved into the foreground, the discussion might have taken a different turn.

But Englishmen who visited the old Goethe noted that he knew nothing of Wordsworth, nor did he speak of Keats; and it seems plain that some of Keats' most famous odes embody the same traits that Goethe disliked in German romanticism, while Wordsworth at his best speaks rather like Goethe's Faust in those outbursts that Goethe's Mephistopheles punctures so cruelly and devastatingly.

Goethe's Faust is a romantic, but Goethe's Mephistopheles is the great antiromantic whose merciless mockery is more sustained than Heine's cutting jibes and possibly more telling than the irony of Joyce and Eliot, a century later. Goethe mastered the romantic accents of vague sentiment, the pose of pining, yearning, fainting, ecstasy, and lofty pantheism quite as well as Keats or Wordsworth; but his perception far exceeded theirs, and, like Shakespeare, he could see enough to recognize the fatal touch of self-deception in this pose. He had the honesty to find it ludicrous and the genius to balance Faust with Mephistopheles. He was the poet not of one pose or one view but of a world in which romanticism, too, could find a place.

Many critics and most of the public have systematically ignored distinctions between Goethe and the chief romantics that had seemed crucial both to him and to them. The resulting misconception of Goethe's significance is of concern not only to Goethe's admirers: it ties in with a similar misunderstanding of Shakespeare, of the whole Western tradition, and of our time and its historic context.

8

Before we take leave of Goethe, let us recall his Shakespearean tolerance once more. As Nietzsche said: *"He does not negate any more."* His attitude was basically affirmative without ever becoming entirely serene, let alone saintly. His Olympian malice was not altogether unlike Einstein's impish playfulness. If there was any resentment in the man it was a resentment of convention, not of individuals, though he later came to use convention as a shield to ward off individuals who threatened to upset his precarious creative economy. He lacked what one might call "the moralistic resentment"—that dissatisfaction with oneself that, instead of creatively enhancing the self, deceives itself about its nature and damns others.

Faust is saved, not because the poet romantically glorifies Faust's ceaseless but profoundly futile striving, which, until the very end, has no respect for other human beings, but because the poet would not consign any man to hell and, secondly, because the poet wants to show his opposition to convention, moralism, and resentment. In a sense, the end of *Faust* is therefore more polemical than has been recognized by the majority of readers.

The title of the penultimate scene, "Entombment," is plainly parodistic, and so are the portable "hell's jaws" that furnish a lighthearted contrast to Dante's awesome portal to the *inferno*. And while Dante, in what Goethe called his "gruesome greatness," had sent Francesca da Rimini to hell, Goethe elevated not only Gretchen but Faust, too, to heaven. While a contemporary usage conditioned by liberal Protestantism would call Goethe's attitude Christian, it is well to remember that he himself considered it deeply anti-Christian.

Like the prophets and the Greek tragedians and like Shakespeare before and Nietzsche after him, he was neither an inane optimist who thought that all men were good and likely to be even better in another hundred years, nor did he believe in original sin and hell. One could do worse than to call the outlook that he shared with such a great tradition *classical*.

7

THE HEGEL MYTH AND
ITS METHOD

Hegel's importance. Hegel was not a pagan like Shakespeare and Goethe but a philosopher who considered himself Christian and tried to do from a Protestant point of view what Aquinas had attempted six hundred years earlier: he sought to fashion a synthesis of Greek philosophy and Christianity, making full use of the labors of his predecessors. Among these he counted not only the great philosophers from Heraclitus and Plato down to Kant, Fichte, and Schelling but also such world-historic individuals as Paul and the men who had made the French Revolution. As he saw it, philosophy did not stand between religion and poetry but above both. Philosophy was, according to him, its age comprehended in thought, and—to exaggerate a little—the philosopher's task was to *comprehend* what the religious person and the poet *feel*.

Hegel's enormous importance becomes clear as soon as we reflect on his historic role. There is, *first,* his direct influence, which appears not only in philosophic idealism, which, at the turn of the last century, dominated British and American philosophy—Bradley, Bosanquet, McTaggart, T. H. Green, and Royce, to give but five examples—but also in almost all subsequent histories of philosophy, beginning with the epoch-making works of Erdmann, Zeller, and Kuno Fischer. It was Hegel who established the history of philosophy as a central academic discipline and as part of the core of any philosophic education. It was also Hegel who established the view that the different philosophic systems that we find in history are to be comprehended in terms of development and that they are gen-

erally one-sided because they owe their origins to a reaction
against what has gone before.

Secondly, most of the more important philosophic movements since his death have been so many reactions against
Hegel's own idealism and cannot be fully understood without
some grasp of his philosophy. The first two great revolts were
those of Kierkegaard and Marx, who swallowed easily as much
of his philosophy as they rejected: notably, his dialectic. Today Marx's dialectic dominates a large part of the total popu-
lation of the globe, while Kierkegaard's has been adapted by
some of the most outstanding thinkers of the free world, notably Heidegger and Tillich, Barth and Niebuhr.

Two later revolts against Hegelianism dominate English and
American philosophy in the twentieth century: pragmatism
and analytic philosophy. William James, though occasionally
he attacked Hegel himself, reconstructed Hegel somewhat in
the image of his Harvard colleague, Royce, who was then the
outstanding American idealist; while Moore, at Cambridge,
who was joined by Russell, led the fight against the influence
of Bradley and McTaggart.

One of the few things on which the analysts, pragmatists,
and existentialists agree with the dialectical theologians is that
Hegel is to be repudiated: their attitude toward Kant, Aristotle, Plato, and the other great philosophers is not at all unani-
mous even within each movement; but opposition to Hegel is
part of the platform of all four, and of the Marxists, too. Oddly,
the man whom all these movements take to be so crucially
important is but little known to most of their adherents; very
few indeed have read as many as two of the four books that
Hegel published.

Hegel is known largely through secondary sources and a few
incriminating slogans and generalizations. The resulting myth,
however, lacked a comprehensive, documented statement till
Karl Popper found a place for it in his widely discussed book,
The Open Society and Its Enemies. After it had gone through
three impressions in England, a revised one-volume edition was
brought out in the United States in 1950, five years after its
original appearance.

2

Critique of a critic. To explode the popular Hegel legend one can hardly do better than to deal in some detail with Popper's Hegel chapter. This involves a temporary departure from religion and poetry, but the development "from Shakespeare to existentialism" cannot be understood without some grasp of Hegel and some discussion of the widely accepted image of Hegel. Moreover, Hegel is so frequently mentioned in contemporary discussions that it is intrinsically worth while to show how wrong many widespread assumptions about him are. Thirdly, our study should include some explicit consideration of questions of method, and especially of common pitfalls. Finally, we shall have occasion, as we develop Hegel's actual views, to call attention to the religious roots of some of his most characteristic notions.

Those who nevertheless prefer to skip this chapter to pick up the thread in the next should at least take note of the author's awareness that gross falsifications of history are not the monopoly of Miniver Cheevy. Forward-looking liberals and even believers in "piecemeal social engineering," like Popper, often distort history, too. And so, alas, did Hegel.

A detailed critique of Popper's sixty-nine pages on Hegel may be prefaced with a motto from Nietzsche's *Ecce Homo:* "I only avail myself of the person as of a strong magnifying glass with which one can render visible a general but creeping calamity which it is otherwise hard to get hold of."

The calamity in our case is twofold. First, Popper's treatment contains more misconceptions about Hegel than any other single essay. Secondly, if one agrees with Popper that "intellectual honesty is fundamental for everything we cherish" (p. 253), one should protest against his methods; for although his hatred of totalitarianism is the inspiration and central motif of his book, his methods are unfortunately similar to those of totalitarian "scholars"—and they are spreading in the free world, too.

3

(_Scholarship_.) Although the mere presence of nineteen pages
of notes suggests that his attack on Hegel is based on careful
scholarship, Popper ignores the most important works on his
subject. This is doubly serious because he is intent on psychologizing the men he attacks: he deals not only with their
arguments but also—if not altogether more—with their alleged
motives. This practice is as dangerous as it is fashionable, but
in some cases there is no outright evidence to the contrary:
one can only say that Popper credits all the men he criticizes,
except Marx, with the worst possible intentions. (Marx he
credits with the best intentions.)

In the case of Hegel, there is voluminous evidence that Popper ignores: beginning with Dilthey's pioneering study of 1906
and the subsequent publication of Hegel's early writings, ample material has been made available concerning the development of his ideas. There is even a two-volume study by Franz
Rosenzweig, the friend of Martin Buber, that specifically treats
the development of those ideas with which Popper is concerned above all: _Hegel und der Staat_.

Furthermore, Popper has relied largely on _Scribner's Hegel
Selections_, a little anthology for students that contains not a
single complete work. Like Gilson in _The Unity of Philosophical Experience_ (p. 246), Popper takes over such a gross mistranslation as "the State is the march of God through the
world," although the original says merely that it is the way of
God with the world that there should be the State, and even
this sentence is lacking in the text published by Hegel and
comes from one of the editor's additions to the posthumous
edition of _The Philosophy of Right_—and the editor admitted
in his Preface that, though these additions were based on lecture notes, "the choice of words" was sometimes his rather
than Hegel's.

Popper also appears to be unaware of crucial passages, if
not entire works, that are not included in these _Selections;_ for
example, the passage on war in Hegel's first book, which shows
that his later conception of war, which is far more moderate,

was not adopted to accommodate the king of Prussia, as Popper maintains. The passage on war in Hegel's *Phenomenology of the Spirit*, in the section on "The Ethical World," was written when Hegel—a Swabian, not a Prussian—admired Napoleon and was published in 1807, a year after Prussia's devastating defeat at Jena. Hegel's views on war will be considered soon (in section 11); but questions of method require our attention first.

4

Quilt quotations. This device, used by other writers, too, has not received the criticism it deserves. Sentences are picked from various contexts, often even out of different books, enclosed by a single set of quotation marks, and separated only by three dots, which are generally taken to indicate no more than the omission of a few words. Plainly, this device can be used to impute to an author views he never held.

Here, for example, is a quilt quotation about war and arson: "Do not think that I have come to bring peace on earth; I have not come to bring peace, but a sword. . . . I came to cast fire upon the earth. . . . Do you think that I have come to give peace on earth? No, I tell you. . . . Let him who has no sword sell his mantle and buy one." This is scarcely the best way to establish Jesus' views of war and arson. In the works of some philosophers, too—notably, Nietzsche—only the context can show whether a word is meant literally.

The writings of Hegel and Plato abound in admittedly one-sided statements that are clearly meant to formulate points of view that are then shown to be inadequate and are countered by another perspective. Thus an impressive quilt quotation could be patched together to convince gullible readers that Hegel was—depending on the "scholar's" plans—either emphatically for or utterly opposed to, say, "equality." But the understanding of Hegel would be advanced ever so much more by citing one of his remarks about equality *in context*, showing how it is a step in an argument that is designed to lead the reader to a better comprehension of equality and not to enlist his emotions either for it or against it.

Even those who would not reduce all philosophy to such
analyses should surely grant the ambiguity of words like equality and freedom, good and God—and also that philosophers
can be of service by distinguishing some of the different meanings of such terms instead of aping politicians by assuring us
that they are heartily in favor of all four. Popper writes like
a district attorney who wants to persuade his audience that
Hegel was against God, freedom, and equality—and uses quilt
quotations to convince us.

The first of these (p. 227) consists of eight fragments of
which every single one is due to one of Hegel's students and
was not published by him. Although Popper scrupulously
marks references to Gans's additions to the *Philosophy of Right*
with an "L" and invariably gives all the references for his quilt
quotations—e.g., "For the eight quotations in this paragraph,
cf. *Selections . . .*"—few readers indeed will recall when they
come to the Notes at the end of the book that "the eight quotations" are the quilt quotations that they took for a single
passage. And Popper advises his readers "first to read without
interruption through the text of a chapter, and then to turn to
the Notes."

Quilt quotations invite comparison with composite photographs. In a campaign for a seat in the U. S. Senate, one such
photograph was used that showed one candidate shaking
hands with the head of the Communist party. It matters little
whether it was labeled in fine print "composite photograph."

To be sure, quotations and photographs that are not patched
together may be grossly unfair, too; and in rare cases, composite ones might not be unfair. But a self-respecting candidate
will not use patched-up photographs of his opponent; and a
scholar should not use a quilt quotation to indict the men he
criticizes.

5

"*Influence.*" No conception is bandied about more unscru-
pulously in the history of ideas than "influence." Popper's notion of it is so utterly unscientific that one should never guess
that he has done important work on logic and on scientific

method. At best, it is reducible to *post hoc, ergo propter hoc.*
Thus he speaks of "the Hegelian Bergson" (p. 256 and n. 66)
and assumes, without giving any evidence whatever, that
Bergson, Smuts, Alexander, and Whitehead were all interested
in Hegel, simply because they were "evolutionists" (p. 225
and n. 6).

What especially concerns Popper—and many another critic
of German thinkers—is the "influence" that the accused had
on the Nazis. His Hegel chapter is studded with quotations
from recent German writers, almost all of which are taken
from *The War Against the West* by Kolnai. In this remarkable book Friedrich Gundolf, Werner Jaeger (Harvard), and
Max Scheler are pictured as "representative of Nazism or at
least its general trend and atmosphere." Kolnai is also under
the impression that the men who contributed most "to the
rise of National Socialism as a creed" were Nietzsche "and
Stefan George, less great but, perhaps because of his homosexuality, more directly instrumental in creating the Third
Reich" (p. 14); that Nietzsche was a "half-Pole" (p. 453);
that the great racist H. S. Chamberlain "was a mellow Eng-
lishman tainted by noxious German influences" (p. 455); and
that Jaspers is a "follower" of Heidegger (p. 207). It would
seem advisable to check the context of any quotations from
Kolnai's book before one uses them, but Kolnai generally gives
no references. Popper writes:

> I am greatly indebted to Kolnai's book, which has made it
> possible for me to quote in the remaining part of this chap-
> ter a considerable number of authors who would otherwise
> have been inaccessible to me. (I have not, however, always
> followed the wording of Kolnai's translations.)

He evidently changed the wording without checking the originals or even the context.

Popper uses quotation after quotation from Kolnai to point
out supposed similarities with Hegel, but never stops to ask
whether the men he cites had read Hegel, what they thought
of him, or where, in fact, they did get their ideas. Thus we
are told that the idea of "fame is revived by Hegel" (p. 266),
for Hegel spoke of fame as a "reward" of the men whose deeds

are recorded in our history books—which would seem a trite enough idea that could also be ascribed to scores of sincere democrats—but Popper goes on: "and Stapel, a propagator of the new paganized Christianity, promptly [i.e., one hundred years later] repeats [*sic*]: 'All great deeds were done for the sake of fame or glory.' " This is surely quite a different idea and not trite but false. Popper himself admits that Stapel "is even more radical than Hegel." Surely, one must question the relevance of the whole section dealing with Stapel and other recent writers; this is not history of ideas but an attempt to establish guilt by association on the same page—in the hope, it seems, that *semper aliquid haeret.*

It is also the height of naïveté. A quick dip into a good dictionary of quotations would have shown Popper a great many closer parallels to Stapel than he found in Hegel. Perhaps the most extreme, and also the most memorable, formulations are found in some poets whose influence would be hard to gauge. Shakespeare writes:

> *Let fame, that all hunt after in their lives,*
> *Live register'd upon our brazen tombs.*

And though these lines occur in one of his comedies, *Love's Labour's Lost,* he certainly did not think meanly of fame. Ben Jonson even went a step further in *Sejanus* (I, ii): "Contempt of fame begets contempt of virtue." And Friedrich Schiller voiced a still more radical view—in a poem that many German school children learn by heart, *Das Siegesfest,* which deals with the Greeks' celebration of their triumph over Troy:

> *Of the goods that man has cherished*
> *Not one is as high as fame;*
> *When the body has long perished*
> *What survives is the great name.*

For every Nazi who knew Hegel's remarks about fame there must have been dozens who knew these lines. Does that prove Schiller a bad man? Or does it show that he was responsible for Nazism?

Besides, Popper often lacks the knowledge of who influenced whom. Thus he speaks of Heidegger and "his master

Hegel" (p. 271) and asserts falsely that Jaspers began as a follower "of the essentialist philosophers Husserl and Scheler" (p. 270). More important, he contrasts the vicious Hegel with superior men "such as Schopenhauer or J. F. Fries" (p. 223), and he constantly makes common cause with Schopenhauer against the allegedly protofascist Hegel, whom he blames even for the Nazis' racism—evidently unaware that Fries and Schopenhauer, unlike the mature Hegel, *were* anti-Semites.

Hegel's earliest essays, which he himself did not publish, show that he started out with violent prejudices against the Jews. These essays will be considered in the next chapter; but they are not represented in *Scribner's Hegel Selections* and hence were not exploited by Popper. Nor have they exerted any perceivable influence. When Hegel later became a man of influence, he insisted that the Jews should be granted equal rights because civic rights belong to man because he is a man and not on account of his ethnic origins or his religion.

Fries, who was Hegel's predecessor at the University of Heidelberg, has often been considered a great liberal, and Hegel has often been condemned for taking a strong stand against him; it is rarely, if ever, mentioned in this context that Fries published a pamphlet in the summer of 1816 in which he called for the "extermination" of Jewry. It appeared simultaneously as a review article in *Heidelbergische Jahrbücher der Litteratur* and as a pamphlet with the title "How the Jews endanger the prosperity and the character of the Germans." According to Fries, the Jews "were and are the bloodsuckers of the people" (p. 243) and "do not at all live and teach according to Mosaic doctrine but according to the Talmud" (p. 251) of which Fries conjures up a frightening picture. "Thus the Jewish caste . . . *should be exterminated completely* [*mit Stumpf und Stiel ausgerottet*] *because it is obviously of all secret and political societies and states within the state the most dangerous*" (p. 256). "Any immigration of Jews should be forbidden, their emigration should be promoted. Their freedom to marry should . . . be limited. . . . It should be forbidden that any Christian be hired by a Jew" (p. 260); and one should again force on them "a special mark on their clothing" (p. 261). In between, Fries protests: "Not against *the*

Jews, our brothers, but against *Jewry* [*der Judenschaft*] we declare war" (p. 248).

This may help us to understand why Hegel, in the Preface to his *Philosophy of Right,* scorned Fries's substitution of "the pap of 'heart, friendship, and enthusiasm'" for moral laws. It would certainly have been unwise of the Jews to rely on Fries's brotherly enthusiasm.

Hegel's often obscure style may have evened the way for later obscurantism, but Fries's and Schopenhauer's flamboyant irrationalism was, stylistically, too, much closer to most Nazi literature. It does not follow that Fries influenced the Nazis. He was soon forgotten, till, in the twentieth century, Leonard Nelson, a Jewish philosopher, founded a neo-Friesian school that had nothing to do with Fries's racial prejudices. The one influential thinker whom Nelson succeeded in leading back to Fries was Rudolf Otto, the Protestant theologian, who is best known for his book on *The Idea of the Holy.* What makes that book so notable is its fine description of the "numinous" experience; but the confused discussion of "The Holy as an A Priori Category" and the romantic notions about "divining" are indebted to Fries.

Popper, though he has written an important book on *Die Logik der Forschung,* "The Logic of Research," does not find it necessary to check his hunches by research when he is concerned with influences in his Hegel chapter. He simply decrees that Hegel "represents the 'missing link,' as it were, between Plato and the modern form of totalitarianism. Most of the modern totalitarians are quite unaware that their ideas can be traced back to Plato. But many know of their indebtedness to Hegel" (p. 226). Seeing that the context indicates a reference to the Nazis and that all the totalitarians cited in this chapter are Fascists, not Communists, Popper only shows his ignorance of this brand of totalitarianism.

Hegel was rarely cited in the Nazi literature, and, when he was referred to, it was usually by way of disapproval. The Nazis' official "philosopher," Alfred Rosenberg, mentioned, and denounced, Hegel twice in his best-selling *Der Mythus des Zwanzigsten Jahrhunderts.* Originally published in 1930, this book had reached an edition of 878,000 copies by 1940. In the same book, a whole chapter is devoted to Popper's be-loved Schopenhauer, whom Rosenberg admired greatly. Ro-senberg also celebrates Plato as "one who wanted in the end to save his people [*Volk*] on a racial basis, through a forci-ble constitution, dictatorial in every detail." Rosenberg also stressed, and excoriated, the "Socratic" elements in Plato.

Plato, unlike Hegel, was widely read in German schools, and special editions were prepared for Greek classes in the *Gym-nasium*, gathering together allegedly fascist passages. In his introduction to one such selection from the *Republic*, pub-lished by Teubner in the series of *Eclogae Graecolatinae*, Dr. Holtorf helpfully listed some of his relevant articles on Plato, including one in the *Völkischer Beobachter*, which was Hitler's own paper. Instead of compiling a list of the many similar con-tributions to the Plato literature, it may suffice to mention that Dr. Hans F. K. Günther, from whom the Nazis admittedly received their racial theories, also devoted a whole book to Plato—not to Hegel—as early as 1928. In 1935, a second edi-tion was published.

Whether Hegel did, or did not, influence the Nazis may not be particularly relevant to Popper's central theses in his book—but then most of his book is not. His often stimulating ideas are amalgamated with a great deal of thoroughly un-sound intellectual history; and Section V of his Hegel chapter (eighteen pages) is representative of the latter. It is also repre-sentative of scores of similar attempts by authors who have less to offer than Karl Popper.

6

Vituperation and allegation of motives. Although Popper, in his introduction, speaks of "the application of the critical and rational methods of science to the problems of the open society" (p. 3), he writes about Hegel in the accents of a prosecutor who addresses a jury. He says of Fichte and Hegel, "such clowns are taken seriously" (p. 249); he demands, "I ask whether it is possible to outdo this despicable perversion of everything that is decent" (p. 244); and he denounces "Hegel's hysterical historicism" (p. 253; cf. p. 269).

Hegel certainly has grievous faults. Among these is his obscure style, but it is dry and unemotional in the extreme. A detailed account of his almost incredibly unemotional style as a lecturer has been given by one of his students, H. G. Hotho, and is quoted in Hermann Glockner's *Hegel* (I, 440 ff.), and in Kuno Fischer's *Hegel*, too. If "hysterical" means, as Webster says, "wildly emotional," Popper deserves this epithet much more than Hegel. For all of Hegel's shortcomings, it seems wildly emotional indeed to say that "he is supreme only in his outstanding lack of originality" and was not even "talented" (p. 227). And "the critical and rational methods of science" could hardly establish Popper's contention that the philosophy of Jaspers is a "gangster" philosophy (p. 272). Nor is this proved by a note on "the gangster philosophy" in the back of the volume, which turns out to furnish us with a quilt quotation (see above) from Ernst von Salomon's book, *The Outlaws*, which bears no perceivable relation to Karl Jaspers—not to speak of Hegel.

Popper's allegation of motives is scarcely distinguishable from vituperation. Hegel is accused of "a perversion . . . of a sincere belief in God" (p. 244), but no evidence whatever is given to substantiate this charge. "Hegel's radical collectivism . . . depends on Frederick William III, king of Prussia" and his "one aim" was "to serve his employer, Frederick William of Prussia" (pp. 227 f.); and it is hinted that Hegel misused philosophy as a means of financial gain (p. 241); but Popper ignores the literature on this question, which includes, in addition to the volumes cited above, T. M. Knox's article on "Hegel and Prussianism" in *Philosophy*, January, 1940, and his discussion with Carritt in the April and July issues.

Hegel, we are told, "wants to stop rational argument; and with it, scientific and intellectual progress" (p. 235), and his dialectics "are very largely designed to pervert the ideas of 1789" (p. 237). When Hegel explicitly comes out in favor of the things that, according to his accuser, he opposed, this is called "lip service" (ns. 11 and 43). Thus Popper claims—like Bäumler in his Nazi version of Nietzsche—that the man whom he professes to interpret did not mean what he clearly said.

Quilt quotations are used to establish a man's views, and his explicit statements are discounted when they are inconvenient.

In the name of "the critical and rational methods of science," one must also protest against such emotional *ad hominem* arguments as that Heidegger's philosophy must be wrong because he became a Nazi later on (p. 271), or that "Haeckel can hardly be taken seriously as a philosopher or scientist. He called himself a free thinker, but his thinking was not sufficiently independent to prevent him from demanding in 1914 'the following fruits of victory . . .'" (n. 65). By the same token, one might seek to discredit Popper's philosophy of science by pointing to his treatment of Hegel, or Newton's physics by calling attention to his absorbing concern with magic, which Lord Keynes has described in his *Essays and Sketches in Biography*.

Popper's occasional references to "the doctrine of the chosen people," which he associates with totalitarianism, show little knowledge of the prophets though a great deal of emotion, and his references to Christianity are also based on sentiment rather than the logic of research. He is "for" Christianity, but means by it something that is utterly at variance with the explicit teachings of Paul, the Catholic Church, Luther, and Calvin.

Hegel's rejection of the adequacy of conscience as a guide in moral questions is countered by Popper's parenthesis, "that is to say, the moralists who refer, for example, to the New Testament" (p. 262)—as if no crimes had ever been committed in the name of the New Testament. Julius Streicher, in his violently anti-Semitic paper, *Der Stürmer*, constantly quoted the Gospel according to St. John.

One of the most important criticisms of Popper's approach, and of the large literature that resembles his attack on Hegel, might be summed up by citing Maritain's epigram from *Scholasticism and Politics* (p. 147): "If books were judged by the bad uses man can put them to, what book has been more misused than the Bible?"

7

Hegel's metaphysics. Two simple points may illustrate how thoroughly Popper misunderstands the whole framework of Hegel's thought. First, he claims that Hegel taught that "self-evidence is the same as truth" (p. 237), although Hegel's first book begins with the denial of this view and Hegel never changed his mind about this.

The second point is more important because Hegel has so often been misunderstood in this way. "Hegel believes, with Aristotle, that the Ideas or essences are *in* the things in flux; or more precisely (as far as we can treat a Hegel with precision), Hegel teaches that they are identical with the things in flux: 'Everything actual is an Idea,' he says" (p. 231). Yet one need not look farther than Royce's helpful article on Hegel's terminology in Baldwin's *Dictionary of Philosophy and Psychology* to find that "actual" is, in Hegel's work, a technical term (as its equivalent was in Plato's and Aristotle's), and that he very emphatically did not claim that Ideas—another technical term—"are identical with the things in flux."

The dictum around which these misinterpretations have been woven most persistently, beginning when Hegel was still alive, occurs in the Preface to his *Philosophy of Right* and reads: "What is rational, is actual; and what is actual, is rational."

This dictum is very similar to Leibniz's idea that this world is the best of all possible worlds. Without sympathizing in the least with either of these two ideas, one should realize that both are rooted in religion. In the third edition of his *Encyclopaedia* (1830; §6) Hegel himself said of his epigram:

These simple sentences have seemed striking to some and have excited hostility—even from people who would not wish to deny some understanding of philosophy, not to speak of religion. . . . When I have spoken of actuality, one might have inquired, without being told to do so, in what sense I use this expression; after all, I have treated actuality in an elaborate *Logic* and there distinguished it precisely not only from the accidental, which, of course, has existence, too, but also, in great detail, from being there, existence, and other concepts.

Alas, this passage was not included in *Scribner's Selections;* hence these distinctions are overlooked by Popper, who reiterates the popular myth that, according to Hegel, "everything that is now real or actual . . . must be reasonable as well as good. And particularly good is, as we shall see, the actually existing Prussian state."

It would prevent some confusion if Hegel's term *wirklich* were translated *actual,* seeing that he opposed it to *potential* rather than to *unreal* or *nonexistent.* An acorn, though certainly real enough in the usual sense of that word, is not, as Hegel uses that term, *wirklich.* Only that is actual in Hegel's sense which fully realizes its own nature or, as Hegel might say, the "idea" of which most existent things fall short. And the Prussian state, though, according to Hegel, more rational than a state that is based on slavery, yet fell short in some respects, as his *Philosophy of Right* makes clear, of the "idea" of the state.

8

The State. When Hegel speaks of "the State" he does not mean every state encountered in experience. Immediately after first offering his epigram about the rational and actual, he himself continued:

What matters is this: to recognize in the semblance of the temporal and transient the substance which is immanent and the eternal which is present in it. For the rational (which is synonymous with the Idea), in its actuality, also embeds itself in external existence and thus manifests itself in an infinite wealth of forms, appearances, and figures, shrouding its core in a multicolored rind. Our consciousness first dwells on this rind, and only after that does philosophic thinking penetrate it to detect the inward pulse and to perceive its beat even in the external forms. The infinitely varied relations, however, which take shape in this externality . . .

this infinite material and its organization are not the subject matter of philosophy.

Thus Hegel would distinguish between the Idea of the State, which he means when he speaks of "the State," and the many states around us. But the Idea, he claims, does not reside in a Platonic heaven, but is present, more or less distorted, in these states. The philosopher should neither immerse himself in the description and detailed analysis of various historical states, nor turn his back on history to behold some inner vision: he should disentangle the rational core from the web of history.

Hegel is not driven to "juridical positivism" and the approbation of every state with which he is confronted, as Popper supposes (p. 252): he can pass judgment. Hegel makes a sharp distinction between such philosophic judgment and the arbitrary criticisms that reflect personal idiosyncrasies and prejudices. This would not involve any difficulty if he were willing to restrict himself to internal criticism, pointing out the multifarious inconsistencies that are so striking in the utterances of most statesmen, in the platforms of most parties, and in the basic convictions of most people. Hegel, however, goes further.

He believes in a rational world order and in his ability to understand it. For him, life is not "a tale told by an idiot"; and history, not merely, although also, a succession of tragedies. There is an ultimate purpose—freedom—and this furnishes a standard of judgment.

A few quotations from the *Philosophy of Right* may illustrate this. "One may be able to show how a law is completely founded in, and consistent with, both circumstances and existing legal institutions, and yet is truly illegitimate and irrational" (§3). Hegel also speaks of *"unalienable"* rights and condemns, without qualification,

> slavery, serfdom, the disqualification from holding property or the prevention of its use or the like, and the deprivation of intelligent rationality, of morality, ethics, and religion, which is encountered in superstition and the concession to others of the authority and full power to determine and prescribe for me what actions I am to perform . . . or what

duties my conscience is to demand from me, or what is to be religious truth for me [§66].

According to the addition of Gans, the editor, Hegel remarked in his lectures in this connection that "the slave has an absolute right to liberate himself" (cf. also §77).

Hegel is not inconsistent when he writes: "the State cannot recognize conscience [Gewissen] in its peculiar form, i.e., as subjective knowledge [Wissen], just as in science, too, subjective opinion, assurance, and the appeal to subjective opinion have no validity" (§137). Conscience is fallible; and, while no government or church has the right to dictate to our conscience, no government can afford to recognize conscience as a legal standard. As several of his interpreters have pointed out, Hegel, when he wrote the Philosophy of Right, was concerned about the recent assassination of the poet Kotzebue by a student who was convinced that the poet was a Russian spy and deserved death.

We are bound to misunderstand Hegel when we apply his remarks about conscience within the framework of the Nazi state. It would be more pertinent if we thought of the German Republic before 1933 and of the conscience of Hitler. For by "the State" Hegel means one in which freedom is realized and "a human being counts because he is a human being, not because he is a Jew, Catholic, Protestant, German, Italian, or the like"—and this "is of infinite importance" (§209; cf. §270 n.). Hegel would consider rational the conscience of an opponent of Hitler who recognized his own absolute right to make himself free and to realize his unalienable rights—but not the conscience of a fanatic impelled by personal motives or perhaps by an equally objectionable ideology.

It is no wonder that the Nazis found small comfort in a book that is based on the conviction that "the hatred of law, of right made determinate by law, is the shibboleth which reveals, and permits us to recognize infallibly, fanaticism, feeble-mindedness, and the hypocrisy of good intentions, however they may disguise themselves" (§258 n.). In his Preface, too, Hegel called the law "the best shibboleth to distinguish the false brothers and friends of the so-called people." One may agree with Herbert Marcuse when he says in *Reason and Revolution: Hegel and the Rise of Social Theory:* "There is no concept less compatible with Fascist ideology than that which founds the state on a universal and rational law that safeguards the interests of every individual, whatever the contingencies of his natural and social status" (pp. 180 f.).

In sum: Popper is mistaken when he says, like many another critic, that, according to Hegel, "the only possible standard of judgment upon the state is the world historical *success* of its actions" (p. 260). Success is not the standard invoked in the *Philosophy of Right* when Hegel speaks of "bad states." "The State" does not refer to one of "the things in flux," but to an Idea and a standard of judgment, to what states would be like if they lived up fully to their *raison d'être*. This reason is to be found partly "in a higher sphere" (§270) for which Hegel himself refers the reader to his system as outlined in his *Encyclopaedia*. The whole realm of Objective Spirit and human institutions that culminates in the State is but the foundation of a higher realm of Absolute Spirit that comprises art, religion, and philosophy.

The discussion of "the State" in the *Philosophy of Right* opens with the pronouncement: "The State is the actuality of the ethical idea." If he were a Platonist, he would mean justice; but Hegel means freedom: not that freedom from all restraints which, at its worst, culminates in anarchy, license, and bestiality, but, rather, man's freedom to develop his humanity and to cultivate art, religion, and philosophy. He considers the State supreme among human institutions because he would subordinate all such institutions to the highest spiritual pursuits and because he believes that these are possible only in "the State." He himself says: "To be sure, all great human beings have formed themselves in solitude—but only by assimilating what had already been created in the State."[1] One might nevertheless insist, as Hegel does not, that conformity should be discouraged beyond the necessary minimum, and one might dwell, as Nietzsche did half a century later, on the dangers of the State.

[1] *Die Vernunft in der Geschichte,* ed. Lasson, p. 92; *Reason in History,* transl. Hartman, p. 51.

It would be absurd to represent Hegel as a radical individualist; but it is equally absurd to claim, as Popper does (p. 258), that Hegel's State is "totalitarian, that is to say, its might must permeate and control the whole life of the people in all its functions: 'The State is therefore the basis and center of all the concrete elements in the life of a people: of Art, Law, Morals, Religion, and Science.'" Popper's claim simply ignores Hegel's emphatic insistence on the sphere of "subjective freedom," which he himself considered a decisive advance over Plato. The quotation from Hegel, of course, does not at all prove the preceding contention: it means—and the context in the lectures on the *Philosophy of History* (Preface) makes this quite clear—that the State alone makes possible the development of art, law, morals, religion, and science. And Hegel's formulation here shows less the influence of Plato, whom Popper represents as a terrible totalitarian, than the impact of Pericles, whom Popper admires. The sentence Popper quotes could almost come from Thucydides' version of Pericles' most famous speech.

Hegel's philosophy is open to many objections, but to confound it with totalitarianism means to misunderstand it. Ernst Cassirer puts the matter very clearly in *The Myth of the State* (1946), a book dealing with much the same material as Popper's, but in a much more scholarly manner. His Hegel chapter ends: "Hegel could extol and glorify the state, he could even apotheosize it. There is, however, a clear and unmistakable difference between his idealization of the power of the state and that sort of idolization that is the characteristic of our modern totalitarian systems."

9

History. Hegel, like Augustine, Lessing, and Kant before him and Comte, Marx, Spengler, and Toynbee after him, believed that history has a pattern and made bold to reveal it. All these attempts are controversial in detail and questionable in principle; but a sound critique of Hegel should also take into account his remarkable restraint: he did not attempt to play the prophet and was content to comprehend the past.

Popper says that his own book could be "described as a collection of marginal notes on the development of certain historicist philosophies" (p. 4); and, as we have seen, he accuses Hegel of "hysterical historicism." But according to Popper's definition, Hegel was no historicist at all: he was not one of those who "believe that they have discovered laws of history which enable them to prophesy the course of historical events." This addiction to predictions is what Popper means by historicism (p. 5).

We are told that Hegel was guilty of

> historical and evolutionary relativism—in the form of the dangerous doctrine that what is believed today is, in fact, true today, and in the equally dangerous corollary that what was true yesterday (*true* and not merely "believed") may be false tomorrow—a doctrine which, surely, is not likely to encourage an appreciation of the significance of tradition [p. 254].

Hegel, of course, excelled in his appreciation of the significance of tradition; in his books and lectures he took for granted its essential rationality, and he condemned as arbitrary any criticism of the past or present that was not accompanied by an appreciation of the significance of tradition.

He did not maintain "that what is believed today is, in fact, true today" but insisted that many of his contemporaries, both philosophers and "men in the street," held many mistaken beliefs. And "what was true yesterday . . . may be false tomorrow" is, in a sense, a commonplace—as when we take such statements as "it is raining" or "the Americans, while saying that all men are endowed by their Creator with certain unalienable rights, including liberty, hold slaves" or "another war might well spread the ideals of the French Revolution, without endangering the future of civilization." The same consideration applies to many a generalization about a nation and about war.

Hegel did not believe that such propositions as "two plus two equals four" were true at one time but not at another; he thought that the truth comes to light gradually and tried to show this in his pioneering lectures on the history of philosophy. He emphasized not how utterly wrong his predecessors had been but how much truth they had seen; yet Plato's and Spinoza's truths were not "all of the truth" but were in need of subsequent qualification and amendment.

Hegel's approach is not amoral. Although he finds the aim of history in its "result" (p. 260) and considers the history of the world the world's court of justice (p. 233 and n. 11), he does not idolize success. His attitude depends on his religious faith that in the long run, somewhere, somehow freedom will and must triumph: *that* is Hegel's "historicism." Those of us who lack his confidence should still note that he does not believe that things are good because they succeed, but that they succeed because they are good. He finds God's revelation in history.

This point is best illustrated by Hegel's polemic against Von Haller in the *Philosophy of Right* (§258). Throughout, he tries to avoid the Scylla of that revolutionary lawlessness that he associates with Fries and the Wartburg festival and the Charybdis of conservative lawlessness that he finds in Von Haller's *Restauration der Staatswissenschaft*. He cites Von Haller (I, 342 ff.): "As in the inorganic world the greater represses the smaller, and the mighty, the weak, etc., thus among the animals, too, and then among human beings, the same law recurs in nobler forms." And Hegel interposes: "Perhaps frequently also in ignoble forms?" He then quotes Von Haller again: "This is thus the eternal, immutable order of God, that the mightier rules, must rule, and always will rule." And Hegel comments: "One sees from this alone, and also from what follows, in what sense might is spoken of here: not the might of the moral and ethical, but the accidental force of nature."

Popper quotes Hegel: "A people can only die a violent death when it has become naturally dead in itself" (p. 263); and Hegel continues, "as e.g. the German Imperial Cities, the German Imperial Constitution" (n. 77). Applied to the collapse of the Holy Roman Empire in 1806, Hegel's remark makes sense, while his bold generalization invites criticism. But one should take into account that Hegel is in agreement with a religious tradition that extends from Isaiah to Toynbee.

Intent on dissociating Hegel from this religious tradition and on associating him with the Nazis instead, Popper fastens on Hegel's conception of world-historical peoples. He quotes (p. 258) Hegel's *Encyclopaedia* (§550) as saying that "the Spirit of the Time invests its Will" in "the self-consciousness of a particular Nation" that "dominates the World." This would seem to be another instance where Popper improved a translation without checking the original (cf. section 5 above). The passage in the *Encyclopaedia* reads: "The self-consciousness of a particular people is the carrier of the current stage of development of the universal spirit as it is present, and the objective actuality into which this spirit lays its will." In *Scribner's Hegel Selections*, this becomes ". . . in which that spirit for a time invests its will." And in Popper, finally, we suddenly encounter "the Spirit of the Time." His profuse capitalization of nouns in his quotations from Hegel is apparently intended to make Hegel look silly.

Hegel goes on to say, though Popper does not quote this, that the spirit "steps onward" and "delivers it over to its chance and doom." His position depends on his assumption that ultimate reality is spiritual and that the spirit reveals itself progressively in history. The stages of this revelation are represented by different peoples, but by only one people at any one time.

This strange notion was adapted by Stefan George and, with the individual prophet in the place of a whole people, became part of the creed of his Circle:

> *In jeder ewe*
> *Ist nur ein gott und einer nur sein künder.*

This idea that "in every epoch, there is but one god, and but one his prophet" is even more obviously false than Hegel's view; and it is doubly ironical because, even in the relatively small field of German poetry, George was no solitary giant but was eclipsed by his contemporary, Rilke.

Hegel's notion was surely suggested to him by the way in which the Romans succeeded the Greeks—and perhaps also the Greeks, the Persians; and the Persians, the Babylonians.

This people is the *dominant* one in world history for this epoch—*and it can be epoch-making in this sense only once.*

Against this absolute right which it has to be the embodiment of the current stage of development of the world spirit, the spirits of the other peoples have no right, and they, even as those whose epoch has passed, do not any longer count in world history.[2]

Above all, Hegel was probably also influenced by the Christian conception of the relation of Christianity to Jew and Greek.

Hegel's conception is dated today: we know more than he did about the history of a great number of civilizations. We can no longer reduce world history to a straight line that leads from the Greeks via the Romans to ourselves; nor can we dispose of ancient Asia as "The Oriental Realm" and understand it simply as the background of the Greeks. We are also aware of ambiguities in the conception of a *Volk* or nation and should not apply such terms to the carriers of Greek or Roman civilization. We understand the flowering of medieval philosophy in terms of the interaction of Jews, Muslims, and Christians against a Greek background, and should not care to say who in that epoch represented the world spirit. Some of us have even lost all belief in a world spirit.

All this does not imply that Hegel's views are wicked or that his basic error is due to his alleged nationalism or tribalism. Toynbee's conception of separate civilizations is open to almost the same objections. (See chapter 19, section 5, below.)

With the exception of entirely isolated communities, no unit can be understood completely without reference to others. But any unit whatever, whether it be Western civilization, France, Athens, or the Burlington Railroad, can be made the object of a historical study. In each instance, one will introduce other units as sparingly as possible and only to throw light on the history of the unit under consideration.

Hegel's whole conception of "world history" is arbitrary and amounts to an attempt to study the development of his own civilization. But here he was at one with almost all of his contemporaries and predecessors who were also under the influence of the Bible. For it is from the Bible that the Western idea that history has a single beginning and moves along a

[2] *Philosophy of Right,* §347.

single track toward a single goal received its impetus and sanction. Today we are apt to be more agnostic about the beginning; we are bound to deny the single track; but we may once again think in another sense of the unity of world history—a unity that is established by the present confluence of hitherto independent streams.

Hegel was not impeded by the recognition that some of the ancestors of his own civilization had made their epoch-making contributions simultaneously. Homer may have been a contemporary of the earliest prophets; Thales and Jeremiah wrote at the same time; and Stoicism flourished while Christianity developed out of Judaism. Elsewhere, Confucius and the Buddha were contemporaries. A pluralistic perspective is needed, as is more respect for individual units. There is no single plan into which all data can be fitted, and Hegel was certainly something of a Procrustes.

Any attempt, however, to read into Hegel's conception of "world domination" an exclusively political or even military sense in order to link him with Hitler is quite illegitimate. It is doubly misleading when one does not emphasize that Hegel was not making predictions or offering suggestions for the future but was scrupulously limiting himself to an attempt to understand the past. Pedagogically, the single-track conception has the virtue of simplicity; and it is still adopted almost universally in the field of Hegel's primary competence—the history of philosophy.

10

Great men and equality. Hegel's conception of world-historical peoples is closely related to his notion of world-historical personalities. Both notions are justifiable up to a point. Some peoples have had little effect on anybody outside themselves, while the Greeks and the Jews, for example, have affected the history of the world out of all proportion to their numbers. Similarly, Socrates and Caesar might well be called world-historical personalities.

It is the rankest emotionalism when Popper writes:

Glory cannot be acquired by everybody; the religion of glory implies antiequalitarianism—it implies a religion of "Great Men." Modern racialism accordingly "knows no equality between souls, no equality between men" (Rosenberg). Thus there are no obstacles to adopting the Leader Principles from the arsenal of the perennial revolt against freedom, or as Hegel calls it, the idea of the World Historical Personality [pp. 266 f.].

Popper implies that we ought to be "for" equalitarianism; but if it involves the belief that no man can achieve anything that cannot be achieved by everybody else, too, it is simply silly. In any sense in which it is at all worth while, equalitarianism is entirely compatible with belief in great men.

According to Popper,

Hegel twists equality into inequality: "That the citizens are equal before the law," Hegel admits, "contains a great truth. But expressed in this way, it is only a tautology; it only states in general that a legal status exists, that the laws rule. But to be more concrete, the citizens . . . are equal before the law only in the points in which they are equal *outside the law* also. *Only that equality which they possess in property, age, . . . etc., can deserve equal treatment before the law.* . . . The laws themselves presuppose unequal conditions. . . . It should be said that it is just the great development and maturity of form in modern states which produces the supreme concrete inequality of individuals in actuality" [p. 239].

The omissions in the Hegel quotation are Popper's, and Popper explains them in the very next sentence:

In this outline of Hegel's twist of the "great truth" of equalitarianism into its opposite, I have radically abbreviated his argument; and I must warn the reader that I shall have to do the same throughout the chapter; for only in this way is it at all possible to present, in a readable manner, his verbosity and the flight of his thoughts (which, I do not doubt, is pathological).

A look at the *Encyclopaedia* (§539) shows that Hegel is not "for" or "against" equality but tries to determine in what sense it can be embodied in the modern state.

> With the appearance of the State, inequality enters; namely, the difference between the governing forces and the governed, authorities, magistrates, directories, etc. The principle of equality, carried out consistently, would repudiate all differences and thus be at odds with any kind of state.

It is in the following discussion that we find the sentence italicized by Popper, and it seems best to quote it without omissions and with Hegel's, rather than Popper's, italics:

> Only that equality which, in whatever way, *happens to exist independently*, regarding wealth, age, physical strength, talents, aptitude, etc., or also crimes, etc., can and should justify an equal treatment of these before the law—in regard to taxes, liability to military service, admission to public office, etc., or punishment, etc.

Hegel's sentence, though hardly elegant, is carefully constructed and exhibits a crucial parallelism. Only those with equal wealth should be taxed equally; age and physical strength should be taken into account by draft boards; talents and aptitudes are relevant qualifications for public service; and so forth. Or should we have equal punishment for all, regardless of whether they have committed equal crimes? Should we induct children into the armed forces and exact equal taxes from the poor and the rich? Is it Hegel that is guilty of a "twist"?

To return to "great men": Hegel said, according to Gans's addition to section 318: "Public opinion contains everything false and everything true, and to find what is true in it is the gift of the great man. Whoever tells his age, and accomplishes, what his age wants and expresses, is the great man of his age." (Popper's "translation" of this passage [p. 267] makes nonsense of it: "In public opinion all is false and true. . . .") Hegel's passage ends, in Popper's translation: "He who does not understand *how to despise public opinion,* as it makes itself heard here and there, will never accomplish anything great." Popper's italics as well as his comments appeal to the reader's prejudice in favor of the supremacy of public opinion, though he previously appealed to the prejudice in favor of the supremacy of conscience. These two standards, however, are very different; and Hegel recognized the fallibility of both because he did not believe, as Popper alleges (p. 237), that "self-evidence is the same as truth." Hegel argued, in the body of section 318, that "to be independent of [public opinion] is the first formal condition of anything great and rational"; and he had the faith that public opinion "will eventually accept it, recognize it, and make it one of its own prejudices."

In the above quotation from Gans's addition, Popper finds an "excellent description of the Leader as a publicist"; and since he has introduced it with a reference to "the Leader principle," one is led to think of the *Führer* and to consider Hegel a proto-Nazi. The quotation, however, is not at odds with a sincere belief in democracy and fits beautifully not only Franklin D. Roosevelt's "interventionism" but also Lincoln's great speeches; for example, "A house divided against itself cannot stand" or "With malice toward none; with charity for all." And it is true of Lincoln, too, when Hegel says of the world-historical personalities, "They were practical, political men. But at the same time they were thinking men, who had an insight into the requirements of the time—into what was ripe for development."

Hegel found that world-historical individuals are always propelled by some passion ("Nothing Great in the World has been accomplished without *passion*") and that their motivation is rarely entirely disinterested. The latter point he expressed in terms of "the cunning of reason." The individual may be motivated not only by profound insights but also by "private interests" and even "self-seeking designs." Alexander was passionately ambitious; but in the long run his private interests furthered Western civilization. The same consideration applies to Caesar and to Franklin D. Roosevelt; in *The American Political Tradition*, Richard Hofstadter has shown how Lincoln, too, was fired by political ambitions until he was elected president.

Popper links Hegel with "the fascist appeal to 'human nature' [which] is to our passions" and proposes that we call this appeal the *"cunning of the revolt against reason"* (p. 268). Yet he himself evidently believes that Napoleon, whose motivation was hardly entirely disinterested and whose methods could scarcely be approved by a devotee of "the open society," was furthering Western civilization to such an extent that the German uprising against him must be labeled "one of these typical tribal reactions against the expansion of a supernational empire" (p. 250).

11

War. Without accepting Hegel's view of war, one should distinguish it clearly from the Fascists'. Three points may suffice here.

First, Hegel looks back, not forward. He is not less interested than Popper in "the furthering of civilization" (p. 268) but finds that our civilization has been furthered by any number of wars in the past; for example, the Greeks' war against the Persians, Alexander's wars of conquest, some of the Romans' wars, and Charlemagne's conquest of the Saxons. Believing that it is the philosopher's task to comprehend "that which is"—to cite the Preface to the *Philosophy of Right*—and not to construct utopias, Hegel speaks of war as one of the factors that have actually furthered civilization.

Second, we should not confuse Hegel's estimate of the wars that had occurred up to his own time with a celebration of war as we know it today or imagine it in the future.

Third, Hegel's attitude is not fully comprehensible when considered apart from its religious roots. He considered all that is finite ephemeral. According to Gans's addition to section 324, he said: "From the pulpits much is preached concerning the insecurity, vanity, and instability of temporal things, and yet everyone . . . thinks that he, at least, will manage to hold on to his possessions." What the preachers fail to get across, "Hussars with drawn sabres" really bring home to us. (Popper writes "glistening sabres" [p. 269]; and the change, though slight, affects the tone of the passage.)

These three points are sufficient to show how Popper misrepresents Hegel's view. "Hegel's theory," we are told, "implies that war is good in itself. 'There is an ethical element in war,' we read" (p. 262). This is a curious notion of implication: from Hegel's contention that "there is an ethical element in war, which should not be considered an absolute evil" (§324), Popper deduces that Hegel considered war "good in itself." Hegel attempted to solve the problem of evil by demonstrating that even evil serves a positive function. He accepted Goethe's conception of "that force which would/Do evil evermore and yet creates the good" (see chapter 5, section 5, above). It is of the very essence of Hegel's dialectical approach to penetrate beyond such assertions as that war is good or evil to a specification of the respects in which it is good and those in which it is evil. Today the evil so far outweighs any conceivable good that we are apt to be impatient with anyone who as much as mentions any good aspects; but in a concrete predicament, the majority still feels that the good outweighs the evil, even if this point is made by speaking of "the lesser evil."

The one passage in which Hegel does consider the question of future wars is not well known and is worth quoting. It is found in his Berlin lectures on aesthetics:

> Suppose that, after having considered the great epics of the past [the *Iliad*, *Cid*, and Tasso's, Ariosto's, and Camoëns' poems], which describe the triumph of the Occident over the Orient, of European measure, of individual beauty, and of self-critical reason over Asiatic splendor, . . . one now wished to think of great epics which might be written in the future: they would only have to represent the victory of the living rationality which may develop in America, over the incarceration into an infinitely progressing measuring and particularizing. For in Europe every people is now limited by another and may not, on its part, begin a war against another European people. If one now wants to go beyond Europe, it can only be to America.[3]

In his lectures on the philosophy of history, Hegel also hailed

[3] *Werke*, ed. Glockner, XIV, 354 f.

the United States as "the land of the future."[4] Plainly, he did
not believe that world history would culminate in Prussia. His
lectures on history do not lead up to a prediction but to the
pronouncement: "To this point consciousness has come."

This may also be the clue to the famous expression of resignation at the end of the Preface to the *Philosophy of Right*—
a passage that, at first glance, seems at odds with the subsequent demand for trial by jury and for a real parliament with
public proceedings, institutions then still lacking in Prussia.
But apparently Hegel did not believe that Prussia, or Europe,
had any real future: "When philosophy paints its grey on grey,
a form of life has grown old, and with grey on grey it cannot
be rejuvenated, but only comprehended. The owl of Minerva
begins its flight only at dusk."

12

Nationalism. On this point Popper's account is particularly
confused. "When nationalism was revived a hundred years
ago [about 1850?], it was in one of the most mixed regions of
Europe, in Germany, and especially in Prussia" (p. 245).
A page later, we hear of "the invasion of German lands by
the first national army, the French army under Napoleon."
Three pages later we are told that Fichte's "windbaggery" gave
"rise to modern nationalism." Fichte died in 1814. Contemptuous of the concept of nationality, Popper maintains that it is
a common belief in democracy, "which forms, one might say,
the uniting factor of multilingual Switzerland" (p. 246). Why,
then, have the Swiss no wish to unite with any democratic
neighbor? Popper's opposition to many features of modern nationalism is well taken; but those who are interested in its development, or who wish to understand it, will do better to
turn to Hans Kohn's *The Idea of Nationalism* (1944) and to
his chapter on "Nationalism and the Open Society" in *The
Twentieth Century* (1949).

One of the major themes of Popper's Hegel chapter is that
"Hegelianism is the renaissance of tribalism" (p. 226). Pop-

[4] *Ibid.,* XI, 128 f.

per's use of "tribalism" and "nationalism" is emotional rather than precise, and he accuses Hegel of both. Even so he must admit that Hegel "sometimes attacked the nationalists" (p. 251). Popper cites Hegel's *Encyclopaedia* where the so-called nation is condemned as rabble:

> And with regard to it, it is the one aim of a state that a nation should *not* come into existence, to power and action, as such an aggregate. Such a condition of a nation is a condition of lawlessness, demoralization, brutishness. In it, the nation would only be a shapeless wild blind force, like that of a stormy elemental sea, which however is not self-destructive, as the nation—a spiritual element—would be.

The Nazis concluded quite correctly that Hegel was unalterably opposed to their conception of the *Volk* and that his idea of the State was its very antithesis.[5]

Popper, on the other hand, is so intent on opposing Hegel that he immediately seeks to enlist the reader's sympathies on the nationalist side when he finds Hegel criticizing it. Thus Popper is not content to point out, quite correctly, that Hegel is referring "to the liberal nationalists" but must add, "whom the king hated like the plague." Hegel's attitude, of course, cannot be understood or reasonably evaluated in terms of the emotional impact of such words as "liberal" and "king." What is wanted is a profile of the movement condemned by Hegel; and that may be found in Herbert Marcuse's *Reason and Revolution* (pp. 179 f.):

> There was much talk of freedom and equality, but it was a freedom that would be the vested privilege of the Teutonic race alone. . . . Hatred of the French went along with hatred of the Jews, Catholics, and "nobles." The movement cried for a truly "German war," so that Germany might unfold "the abundant wealth of her nationality." It demanded a "savior" to achieve German unity, one to whom "the people will forgive all sins." It burned books and yelled woe to the Jews. It believed itself above the law and the

5 Cf., e.g., Rosenberg's *Mythus*, p. 527.

constitution because "there is no law to the just cause." The
state was to be built from "below," through the sheer enthusiasm of the masses, and the "natural" unity of the *Volk*
was to supersede the stratified order of state and society. It
is not difficult to recognize in these "democratic" slogans the
ideology of the Fascist *Volksgemeinschaft*. There is, in point
of fact, a much closer relation between the historical role
of the *Burschenschaften*, with their racism and antirational-
ism, and National Socialism, than there is between Hegel's
position and the latter. Hegel wrote his *Philosophy of Right*
as a defense of the state against this pseudo-democratic
ideology.

The "liberal" Fries called for the extermination of Jewry
(section 5 above), while Hegel denounced the nationalistic
clamor against the extension of civil rights to the Jews, pointing out that this "clamor has overlooked that they are, above
all, human beings" (§270 n.). Are we to condemn Hegel because he agreed with the king, or praise Fries because he
called himself liberal?

13

Racism. Popper's most ridiculous claim—and the last one to
be considered here—is that the Nazis got their racism from
Hegel. In fact, the Nazis did not get their racism from Hegel,
and Hegel was no racist (see section 5 above).

The Nazis did find some support for their racism in Schopenhauer, with whom Popper constantly makes common cause
against Hegel, and in Richard Wagner, who Popper eccentri-
cally insinuates was something of a Hegelian (p. 228) though
he was, of course, a devoted disciple of Schopenhauer. Popper
declares that one W. Schallmeyer, when he wrote a prize essay in 1900, "thus became the grandfather of racial biology"
(p. 256). What, then, is the status of the rather better known
and more influential Gobineau and Chamberlain and any number of other writers who publicized their views before 1900
and were widely read and constantly quoted by the Nazis?

Popper offers us the epigram: "Not 'Hegel + Plato,' but

'Hegel + Haeckel' is the formula of modern racialism" (p. 256). Why Haeckel rather than Bernhard Förster, Julius Langbehn, Hofprediger Stöcker, Chamberlain, Gobineau, or Wagner? Why not Plato, about whose reflections on breeding the Nazis' leading race authority, Dr. Hans F. K. Günther, wrote a whole book—and Günther's tracts on race sold hundreds of thousands of copies in Germany and went through several editions even before 1933? (See section 5 above.) And why Hegel?

Decidedly, Hegel was no racialist; nor does Popper adduce any evidence to prove that he was one. Instead, Popper says: "The transubstantiation of Hegelianism into racialism or of Spirit into Blood does not greatly alter the main tendency of Hegelianism" (p. 256). Perhaps the transubstantiation of God into the *Führer* does not greatly alter Christianity?

One can sympathize with G. R. G. Mure when he says that the increasingly violent and ill-informed attacks on Hegel have reached a point in Popper's Hegel chapter where they become "almost meaninglessly silly."[6] But familiarity with Hegel has waned to the point where reviewers of the original edition of *The Open Society and Its Enemies,* while expressing reservations about the treatment of Plato and Aristotle, have not generally seen fit to protest against the treatment of Hegel; and on the jacket of the English edition Bertrand Russell actually hails the attack on Hegel as "deadly"—for Hegel. Since the publication of the American edition in 1950, John Wild and R. B. Levinson have each published a book to defend Plato against the attacks of Popper and other like-minded critics, and Levinson's *In Defense of Plato* goes a long way toward showing up Popper's methods. But Popper's ten chapters on Plato, although unsound, contain many excellent observations, and his book is so full of interesting discussions that no exposé will relegate it to the limbo of forgotten books. *The Open Society* will be around for a good long while, and that is one reason why its treatment of Hegel deserves a chapter.

What is ultimately important is not the failing of one author but the increasing popularity of the Hegel myth and of the

[6] A *Study of Hegel's Logic,* p. 360.

methods on which it depends. To cite Nietzsche's *Ecce Homo* once more: "I only avail myself of the person as a magnifying glass with which one can render visible a general but creeping calamity which it is otherwise hard to get hold of."

Popper should be allowed the last word. And any critic of his work could do worse than to cite in his own behalf what Popper says to justify his own critique of Toynbee:

> I consider this a most remarkable and interesting book. . . . He has much to say that is most stimulating and challenging. . . . I also agree with many of the political tendencies expressed in his work, and most emphatically with his attack upon modern nationalism and the tribalist and "archaist," i.e., culturally reactionary tendencies, which are connected with it. The reason why, in spite of this, I single out . . . [this] work in order to charge it with irrationality, is that only when we see the effects of this poison in a work of such merit do we fully appreciate its danger [pp. 435 f.].

8

THE YOUNG HEGEL
AND RELIGION

How to approach Hegel. To find an approach to Hegel's later philosophy is extremely difficult. Taking their cue from him, some of the best Hegel scholars have attempted a historical approach. Richard Kroner, for example, wrote two volumes on the development *Von Kant bis Hegel,* while G. R. G. Mure devoted the first half of his *Introduction to Hegel* to Aristotle. Both procedures are illuminating, but we could also begin with Plato, Proclus, or Spinoza. The crucial question remains: How did Hegel come to relate his own philosophy so closely to that of his predecessors? How did he arrive at his unique conception of the close relation of systematic philosophy to the history of philosophy? What led him—the hyperbolic expression is almost justified—to the discovery of the history of philosophy, a discipline that he established with his lectures on that subject that were published by his students in three volumes after he had died?

Many studies, of course, have bypassed any historical approach and have plunged immediately into the *Logic*—the center of attention in the English literature—or, more judiciously, into the *Phenomenology,* which has more and more become the favorite of Continental scholars, not only in Germany. When we are thus confronted with Hegel's full-fledged philosophy, however, we find Hegel constantly reminding us that it is very difficult to make a beginning: wherever he begins, all the rest is presupposed. He keeps comparing his philosophy to a circle and says in effect with T. S. Eliot: "In my beginning is my end" and "Every phrase and every sentence is an end and a beginning."

He insists on having a system but denies that it is based on assumptions he could fairly state at the outset—or anywhere. Hegel is unintentionally obscurantist at this point. His central assumption is indeed different from a mathematician's axioms, or even from Spinoza's: he takes for granted the essential truth of all the great philosophies of the past. Heraclitus and Parmenides, Plato and Aristotle, Descartes, Spinoza, and Kant had all seen the truth, but not all of the truth: their insights were partial. What is needed is the crowning integration of their visions, a synthesis of all that has gone before. Thus, Hegel's beginning, by presupposing his vision of the whole history of philosophy from the pre-Socratics to Schelling, presupposes his subsequent exposition.

It is only in Hegel's early essays that we encounter him without any such premise. In fact, at first his attitude was just the opposite of this. He himself did not publish these essays. It was only in 1906 that Dilthey called attention to them in his *Jugendgeschichte Hegels;* and, in the following year, this material was made available in a separate volume, admirably edited by one of Dilthey's students, Hermann Nohl. Unfortunately, Nohl gave the book a very misleading title: *Hegels theologische Jugendschriften.*

Just as interest in Hegel was thus being revived in Germany after a long lapse, Hegel went into eclipse in England and in the United States; it took forty-two years before two of these essays appeared in an English translation by T. M. Knox as Hegel's *Early Theological Writings.* What distinguishes these writings from Hegel's later works is, in part, that they are anti-theological. A new reading of these antitheological essays furnishes the best introduction to Hegel's later works; it leads to a new conception of his intellectual development; and it helps to correct a far-reaching and fateful falsification of German cultural history.

2

The antitheological essays. It will be best to consider the four titles in the German volume one by one. The first two are omitted from the English edition, which features a sixty-six-page introduction by Richard Kroner. This is as scholarly as one would expect it to be in view of his earlier two-volume work—but equally subjective. Even as the title of the larger work suggested simultaneously Kroner's own development "from Kant to Hegel," the Introduction to the *Early Theological Writings* intimates Kroner's subsequent development into a mystic and a theologian. Hegel is now envisaged as "a Christian mystic" (p. 8) and a "Romanticist" (p. 14).

Are these early papers really theological? Only insofar as Webster defines one meaning of theology as "the critical, historical, and psychological study of religion and religious ideas." By the same token, Gibbon's *Decline and Fall*, Nietzsche's *Antichrist*, and Freud's *Future of an Illusion* could also be called "theological writings"—which would certainly be most misleading.

Hegel's essays are not antireligious but consistently depreciate theology in any customary sense of that word. We shall begin by considering five fragments that the German editor printed under the title *Folk Religion and Christianity*. Like the other so-called theological writings, they were not intended for publication by Hegel himself but are more interesting than many things he did publish. The next four sections deal with these earliest fragments, which are not available in English, under systematic headings.

3

Subjective and objective religion. Hegel begins with this contrast.

> Objective religion is *fides quae creditur*, . . . can be systematized, presented in a book or a lecture; subjective religion expresses itself only in feelings and acts [p. 6]. Subjective religion is all that matters. . . . Let the theologians quarrel about dogmas, about that which belongs to objective religion [p. 8]. Subjective religion is pretty much the same in all good human beings, while their objective religion can have almost any color whatever [p. 10].

In support, Hegel cites Lessing's *Nathan*, the greatest drama

of the German Enlightenment. It has three heroes, a Christian,
a Muslim, and a Jew, Nathan, who is modeled after Lessing's
friend, Moses Mendelssohn. The moral of the play is stated in
Nathan's version of the fable of the three rings: we cannot
know which religion is true, we should respect other religions,
and, above all, we should be moral. This is the work cited most
often in these so-called theological writings—invariably with
approval. And Hegel says expressly: "the most venerable human beings are assuredly not always those who have specu-
lated most about religion and who very often transform their
religion into theology" (p. 10).

Hegel goes on to denounce "the self-important conceit that
characterizes the sectarian spirit which deems itself wiser than
all human beings of other parties," finds an example in Tertul-
lian, and expresses his admiration for Socrates. Of his more
sarcastic remarks, one example may suffice:

> What a bald and forced remark it is when the good Gellert
> says somewhere that today any small child knows more
> about God than the wisest pagan—just like Tertullian. . . .
> As if the compendium of morals in my closet there, which
> I can use at will to wrap a stinking cheese, had more value
> than the, perhaps at times unjust, heart of Frederick II. For
> the difference between Tertullian's *opifex* [artisan] or Gel-
> lert's child, into whom the theological leaven has been
> beaten with the catechism, and the paper on which morals
> have been printed, is after all none too great in this respect:
> any consciousness gained through experience is lacking al-
> most equally in all three cases [pp. 11 f.].

4

Hegel's difference with Kant. In his antitheological attitude,
Hegel is at one with Lessing and other protagonists of the Enlightenment, and his insistence on the sole importance of subjective religion may remind us of Kant's dictum about the sole
intrinsic value of the good will. Yet Hegel differed with Kant
in some important respects, even in these earliest fragments.

The understanding serves only objective religion. By purifying principles and by representing them in their purity, the understanding has produced splendid fruit, such as Lessing's *Nathan*, and it deserves the eulogies heaped on it. But the understanding can never transform principles into practice. The understanding is a courtier who obeys his master's moods and knows how to provide justifications for any passion and for any enterprise.

Here we are reminded of David Hume's famous formulation in his *Treatise* (Book II, Part III, §3): "Reason is . . . the slave of the passions." The understanding can rationalize any kind of conduct. "Enlightenment of the understanding makes more clever but not better" (p. 12).

What is needed to bring about moral conduct is, at least for the mass of the people, something in man's passional nature; and "love, though it is a pathological principle of action, is unselfish" (p. 18). The word "pathological" refers to Kant's usage: according to Kant, conduct motivated by love rather than by sheer respect for reason is not moral because its motivation is not rational but pathological, by which he means that it is grounded in the passions.

Moral teachings, says Hegel, must indeed be "authorized by the universal reason of man"; but they must also be "so human that they correspond to that stage of morality which a people has attained" (p. 21). Kant's ethics thus seems unrealistic. Mere respect for the moral law will not do; nor, Hegel thinks, will Christianity.

5

Hegel's vitriolic treatment of Christianity. In these fragments Hegel's hostility was not confined to Christian *theology;* and his sarcastic jibes about Christianity invite comparison with Voltaire, with Kierkegaard's *Attack on Christendom,* and with Nietzsche. Stylistically, too, he is much closer to these powerful polemicists than to the intricate and frequently obscure prose of his later years.

What distinguishes him from Voltaire and Kierkegaard,

though not from Nietzsche, is the recurrence of sardonic contrasts of Christianity with ancient Greece.

> Not only does one train the Christian mob from childhood on to pray constantly; one also tries continually to persuade them of the supreme necessity of prayer by promising its sure fulfillment. And one has piled up such a heap of reasons for comfort in misfortune . . . that we might be sorry in the end that we cannot lose a father or a mother once a week. . . . It might be very interesting to compare all this with the faith of the Greeks. . . . For them, misfortune was misfortune, pain was pain . . . [pp. 22 f.].

> The popular feasts of the Greeks were all religious feasts. . . . Everything, even the excesses of the bacchanals, was sacred to some god. . . . At our greatest public feast, one approaches the enjoyment of the holy host in the color of mourning, with downcast eyes. At the very feast which ought to be the feast of universal brotherhood, many are afraid that through the brotherly goblet they might be infected with a venereal disease by someone who drank from it before. And lest one's mind remain attentive, God forbid, wrapt in a holy feeling, one must reach into one's pocket in the midst of things and put one's offering on a plate—whereas the Greeks, with the friendly gifts of nature, wreathed with flowers, clothed in the colors of joy . . . [pp. 26 f.].

This is the friend of Hölderlin, the hymnic poet who loved Greece and found the modern world a desert—a Hegel unknown to the mass of those who write about him. Nor did the young Hegel spare Christ, whom he contrasts cuttingly with Socrates, of whom he says:

> Of course, one did not hear him deliver sermons on a platform or a mount: How could it even have occurred to Socrates, in Greece, to deliver sermons? He aimed to enlighten [!] men. . . . The number of his closer friends was indeterminate: the thirteenth, fourteenth, and the rest were as welcome as the preceding ones. . . . Socrates did not live in them and was not the head from which they, as the mem-

bers, received the juice of life. He had no mold into which he wished to pour his characters and no rule according to which he might have desired to even out their differences: for that only small spirits would have been at his disposal; and he cared for these, too, but they certainly did not become his closest friends. He had no mind to polish for himself a small corps that might be his bodyguard, with the same uniform, drill, passwords—a corps that would have one spirit and bear his name forever. . . . Each one of his students was himself a master: many founded schools of their own; several were great generals, statesmen, heroes of all kinds . . . not heroes in martyrdom and suffering, but in action and in life. Besides, whoever was a fisherman, remained a fisherman; nobody was to leave his home; with each he started with his handicraft and thus led him from the hand to the spirit. . . . He developed concepts out of the soul of man, where they had been all along and needed nothing but a midwife. He gave nobody cause to say: How now? Is not this the son of Sophroniscus? Where did he attain such wisdom that he dares to teach us? He did not offend anyone by swaggering self-importance or by using high-flown and mysterious phrases of the sort that impress only the ignorant and credulous [pp. 33 f.].

Later, Hegel cites Montesquieu's *Esprit des loix* to the effect that one should not enumerate the evils that religion has produced without admitting that it has had good effects, too; and he tries to look at Jesus' teachings in a more positive way. Even so, he considers them impossible as social norms, and irony wins the upper hand again:

One has never yet heard that a man whose coat was stolen, but who was able to save his vest and pants, was reproached by a Christian teacher for not giving these up, too. And in the case of oaths, where the clergy must surely know of Christ's explicit prohibition, this very clergy has to play the most solemn part. What was it that excited more than anything else the hatred of the scribes and the counsels of the Jews against Christ? Was it not his individualistic way both of acting himself and of judging the actions of others when they conflicted not only with sacred customs but also with civil laws? When it was a matter of judging a case in accordance with the law of the courts, Christ attacked the administrators of these laws. But even if they had been the most irreproachable of men and quite of his own mind, they still would have had to judge irrespective of that, in accordance with the laws. The judge must often speak differently from the human being and condemn what as a human being he might pardon. From all this it should be clear that the teachings and the principles of Jesus were really suitable only for the education of single human beings, and intended only for this [p. 41].

Jesus' command to the young man to distribute his wealth to the poor would lead

to consequences far too absurd than that one could ever think of extending it to a large people. And if a group constitutes itself among another people, like the early Christians, under a law of this sort, holding all possessions in common, then the spirit of such a command disappears precisely at the moment when such institutions are established: not only does it awaken, by introducing compulsion, the desire for concealing something, as it did in Ananias, but it also restricts the benefit of this renunciation to the members of the group . . . and thus it stands opposed to the spirit of love that pours out its blessings on the circumcised and the uncircumcised [this sounds like Paul, but Hegel goes on], on the baptized and the unbaptized [pp. 41 f.].

Although Hegel finds something in Jesus' teachings that he can admire and respect, he is opposed not only to theology but also to all Christian institutions—not only to the Catholic Church, for which he never developed any sympathy, but also to the Reformers. He excoriates "the presumption to try the reins and heart and to judge and punish consciences" and finds its seeds "in the first origins of Christianity, since that which is possible only in a small family was falsely extended to civil society"; and he denounces "confession, church ban, penance, and the whole series of such debasing monuments of human degradation."

"The Reformers," too, are reproached for their establishment of "Christian police institutions. . . . The establishment of church power as the champion of the freedom of conscience against the power of the princes never occurred to them: they subjected Christianity to worldly power." They never rose above

> the concept of the church as a kind of state within the state, as a visible homogeneous community and a union in a common rite. How far Luther, for example, was from any idea of the worship of God in spirit and truth, is apparent in his sorry quarrels with Zwingli, Oecolampadius, and the rest. He took from the clergy the power to rule by force, over men's purses, too, but he himself still wanted to rule over their opinions [p. 42].

Hegel condemns Protestantism for substituting "theological prejudices concerning an innate corruption of human nature" for "a real knowledge of the human heart"; and he says of "theological compendia" that "one must be ashamed that all this art and scholarship has been devoted to a matter which mere common sense grasps in a quarter of an hour." The seeds of all later ills he finds "already in the first undeveloped draft" for a "Christian society." These seeds were nursed and utilized "by the lust for domination and hypocrisy" (pp. 43 f.).

Hegel concludes that Christianity cannot raise the masses to a higher level of morality any more than Kantian respect for reason.

> Institutions and laws of a small society, where each citizen retains the freedom to be, or not to be, a member, are in no way admissible when extended to a large civil society and cannot coexist with civil liberty. . . . Nothing is more intolerable than publicly employed guardians of morals. Whoever acts with a pure heart is always the first to be misunderstood by the people with the moral and religious yardstick [pp. 44 f.].

6

Folk religion. What is needed, according to the young
Hegel, is not Christianity or mere reason but a folk religion.
This conception, influenced by Hegel's idealized picture of
classical Greece and perhaps also by Herder, differs from contemporary romanticism by insisting on the primacy of morals
and the sovereignty of reason. "The highest end of man is morality, and among his dispositions for promoting this end, his
disposition for religion is one of the most outstanding" (p. 48).
"We consider it a necessary requirement for a folk religion
that it does not force its teachings upon anyone, nor does violence to any human conscience." Its doctrines "must not contain anything that universal human reason does not recognize
—no certain or dogmatic claims which transcend the limits of
reason, even if their sanction had its origin in heaven itself"
(p. 50). Incomprehensible doctrines and mysteries, though
backed by the most venerable traditions, "reason must repudiate; in its demands for moral goodness it cannot compromise"
(p. 52).

Hegel also expressly rejects any doctrines that are said to
"transcend reason without contradicting reason." Perhaps "the
doctrines as such do not contradict reason, but it contradicts
reason to believe them" (pp. 53 f.).

Some of this is even more rigoristic than Kant. What is less
rigoristic, however, is Hegel's concern with "the education of
mankind"—to cite the title of one of Lessing's essays—and the
concern with the whole human being, including the imagination. While the appeal to art and what Schiller called "aesthetic education" was the most characteristic solution of the
seventeen-nineties, Hegel looked to religion. But it is hardly
surprising that he could not give us any concrete picture of
such a purely rational folk religion and was hence unable to
complete any of the drafts considered here.

7

Hegel's "romanticism." It is important to recognize the full
extent of Hegel's early affinity with, and debt to, the Enlighten-

ment, both to gain a better understanding of his intellectual development and to bridge the great cultural gap between Germany on the one hand and the English-speaking peoples on the other. Most modern German writers depreciate the Enlightenment as shallow and un-German and mistakenly read their own antipathy into their heroes. Yet most of the greatest Germans were sympathetic toward the Enlightenment. This is true not only of Leibniz and Frederick the Great, of Lessing and Kant, but also of Goethe and Schiller, Fichte and Hegel, and, as I have tried to show in my book on him, of Nietzsche.

Seen in this perspective, it is doubly regrettable that Kroner should claim in his long Introduction to these essays that the fragments just reported on, but omitted in his edition, show how Hegel opposed Christianity "as the religion of the Enlightenment dominated by reason" (p. 3). As we have seen, Hegel subjects Christianity to vitriolic strictures, in large part because he took it to be utterly at odds with the ideals of the Enlightenment.

The romanticized picture of the young Hegel can be traced back to Dilthey. It was his interest in the early German romantics—he wrote celebrated essays on Novalis and Schleiermacher—that led him to the early Hegel. We can still be grateful to him for calling attention to Hegel's first essays, but we must give up the misconception that these writings are theological and that, to cite Kroner once more, "during Hegel's young manhood he was an enthusiastic Romanticist" (p. 14).

It is with this claim that Kroner's section on "Romanticism" begins, and this sentence sums up the whole section. Even so, Kroner admits rightly that Hegel "was realistic enough to see the weaknesses of past civilizations, and he was anti-Romantic in glorifying the present as the fruitful moment or the *kairos* given to his generation" (p. 16). One may also safely agree that "Hegel was called upon to transcend the horizon of the Romanticists, to reconcile their revolutionary message with the more sober views of Enlightenment. . . . He was called upon to intellectualize Romanticism and to spiritualize Enlightenment" (pp. 20 ff.). But perhaps this is truer of Hegel's later intentions than it is of his actual achievement.

Whether the young Hegel was a romantic or not depends,

of course, on the meaning one attaches to "romanticism"; that term has been considered in some detail in chapter 6 above. Kroner maintains, like a great many other scholars, that the "philhellenic affection is in itself a Romantic trait" (p. 16). This popular view overlooks the crucial difference between the peculiar "classicism" of Goethe and Schiller, of which Goethe's *Iphigenia* (1790) is the outstanding example, and the romanticism of the Schlegels, Tieck, and Novalis, who coined the word "romanticism" in its modern sense and who, before the end of the century, abandoned "philhellenism" for Germanic models, especially of the medieval period.

Hegel never aligned himself with the romantics against Goethe and Schiller. The formative influences on the young Hegel were Goethe and Schiller and, besides Kant, above all Lessing. The philhellenism of his panegyric on Socrates with its many blasphemies against Christ is surely anything but romantic. And least of all is it theological.

8

The Life of Jesus. This is the title of Hegel's second effort, written in 1795 and never translated into English. It begins with the singularly untheological and unromantic declaration, reminiscent of Robespierre: "Pure reason, incapable of any limitation, is the deity itself." Jesus' "parents were Joseph and Mary" (p. 75); and the account closes, pointedly, with Jesus' burial (p. 136). In between we find—as Knox says in accounting for his omission of the essay—"little more than a forced attempt to depict Jesus as a teacher of . . . Kant's ethics" (p. v).

Thus the young Hegel lets Jesus say:

> What you can will to be a universal law among men, valid also against yourselves, according to that maxim act—this is the basic law of ethics, the content of all legislation and of the sacred books of all peoples [p. 87].

> What I teach I do not offer as my ideas or property. I do not demand that anyone should accept it on my authority. . . . I subject it to the judgment of universal reason [p. 89].

This inner law is a law of freedom to which, as given by himself, man subjects himself voluntarily: it is eternal, and in it we find the feeling of immortality [p. 98].

Oh, that men had stopped there and never added to the duties imposed by reason a lot of other burdens to bedevil poor humanity [p. 102].

Thus many . . . who worshipped Zeus, or Brahma, or Wotan, will find grace before the judge of the world [p. 107].

Hegel's Jesus knows no authority but that of reason, rejects faith, and demands only "the service of reason and virtue" (p. 122). While there are no references to Kant in the footnotes, it is significant, as will be seen later (in section 13), that the authorities cited include, besides the Gospels, not only Lessing's *Nathan* (p. 100) but also Goethe's *Iphigenia* (p. 98).

What is the motivation of this tour de force? Surely, this is Hegel's attempt to write the scripture of his folk religion. Moral demands are strengthened psychologically by the thoroughly humanized figure and story of Jesus. The strange result should be compared not only with the Gospels but also with Kant, who is here made readable and palatable for the people. Theology is still rejected, and Jesus is employed to propagate Kant's ethics.

9

The Positivity of the Christian Religion. This essay was also written in 1795. Hegel says at the outset that it is his basic assumption "that the end and essence of all true religion, and of our religion, too, is the morality of man" (p. 153). Again he makes common cause with Kant and the Enlightenment against romanticism and theology. "Positive" he defines as meaning "founded on authority and placing the worth of man not at all, or at least not only, in morality" (p. 155). He has in mind a contrast that is very similar to that which Erich Fromm has developed between "humanistic" and "authoritarian" religion in his Terry Lectures on *Psychoanalysis and Religion.*[1]

Kroner claims that "obviously, Hegel was fighting especially against the Roman Catholic church"; and in support of this false contention he quotes Hegel: "Great men have claimed that the fundamental meaning of 'Protestant' is a man or a church which has not bound itself to certain unalterable standards of faith but which protests against all authority in matters of belief" (p. 8). But Kroner does not mention that Hegel immediately goes on to disagree with these great men by insisting that the Protestant churches have, as a matter of fact, not lived up to any such "negative determination" (p. 199).

Not only does Hegel include Protestantism in his indictment, but he aims to show that the seeds of positivity, or authoritarianism, must be found in the teachings and the conduct of Jesus himself. Here Hegel goes far beyond Fromm, who pictures not only Jesus but also "early Christianity" as a prime example of humanistic, nonauthoritarian religion. The charges against Jesus are pressed in considerable detail and amount to a formidable indictment; yet Hegel does not blame Jesus, but his contemporary audience, the Jews, who, according to Hegel, were impervious to any other approach.

After Jesus, Hegel considers the church. Before long, he includes Protestantism in his indictment and says, for example, that "the Protestant church is a state as much as the Catholic one, regardless of the fact that it dislikes that name" (p. 181).

> In some Protestant states a so-called Act Concerning Confirmation has been introduced, and the child renews the baptismal bond; i.e., in its fourteenth or fifteenth year it enters voluntarily into a contract with the church and does solemnly what the witnesses at the baptism could only promise—only, the church has carefully arranged things to ensure that the child will not have become acquainted with anything but the faith of its church, and the church . . . accepts the child's babbling of the formulas of faith, which is generally not informed by any real understanding, as if

[1] 1950. For a detailed criticism of Fromm's contrast, see my *Critique,* §77.

it were an expression of the free choice of the understanding [p. 182].

Hegel goes into considerably more detail, but this example may suffice to show that his strictures are neither directed at Catholicism alone nor only against the Lutheranism of his own time. He is concerned with "the positivity of the Christian religion" and not merely with occasional lapses from grace.

Some German scholars have tried to square the facts with their antipathy against the Enlightenment by seeking to connect Hegel's essays with all sorts of spiritualistic, and even theosophic, elements that, they say, were still alive at Tübingen when Hegel attended the theological seminary. However that may be, it deserves emphasis how very close to the spirit of the Enlightenment the young Hegel was. Hegel expressly regrets that "In almost all Catholic as well as Protestant countries the church state with its right has prevailed over the civil state" (p. 184), and he draws this contrast: "the state demands it as a duty that the rights of men of other faiths must be respected," while "the officials of the tolerating church (including the Protestants) always speak of kindness, of pity, and of love which should be extended to those who err—of inclinations which cannot be commanded as duties but which ought to be shown voluntarily" (p. 185). Surely, his stand here is not that of the sectarians but that of a protagonist of the Enlightenment.

The same is possibly still more obvious three and four pages later. "Every man brings into the world not only the right to a mere animal existence but also the right to develop his capacities, to become a human being." The state, however, has abdicated its responsibilities in these matters to the church.

> But if the church by its education should have got to the point where it has either totally suppressed understanding and reason in matters of religious reflection or at least filled the imagination with such terror that reason and understanding cannot and may not dare to become conscious of their freedom . . . then the church would have . . . violated the natural right of the children to a free development

of their capacities, and it would have educated slaves instead of free citizens.

In the next sentence the hypothetical phrasing is dropped, and
Hegel concludes that "the state, for all its good intentions, has
become a traitor to the rights of children" (pp. 186 f.).

It is quite extraordinary how far the reluctance to admit
plain facts can go even among highly competent scholars. After
quoting Lessing's *Nathan* once again, Hegel says on the following page:

> There is much more hope that a man who has been accus-
> tomed from his childhood to the duty of believing may later
> be converted to the faith of another church, than that a
> man whose imagination is free of its images and whose un-
> derstanding is free of its fetters may ever be brought to such
> faith and such obedience to opinions as a church requires.

Now consider the most detailed treatment of the early Hegel:
Theodor Haering's *Hegel, Sein Wollen und Sein Werk*, a
chronological history of Hegel's development up to his first
book, in two volumes of 785 and 525 pages, published in 1929
and 1938. Here is Haering's paraphrase of the second part of
the sentence quoted: ". . . than to convert a man who has
been brought up without any religion to a faith without which,
after all, according to Hegel's opinion, a real member of a people can never be and persist" (p. 241). The young Hegel's
sarcastic opposition to "obedience to opinions" and to the "fet-
ters" of faith is transmuted into its opposite.

Such misunderstandings have been facilitated by the fact
that Hegel's bitterly ironical and often picturesque criticisms
are not accompanied by any positive proposals. He does not
proceed, for example, to recommend that children should be
brought up without any knowledge of religion. He writes as a
historian with a special interest in all kinds of ironies. He has
no platform of his own but is following the historical development in search of one. This distinguishes him even now from
many exponents of the Enlightenment; but he himself is preoccupied with his differences with all churches.

Each church claims that nothing is

as easy as finding the truth: one only has to memorize one
of its catechisms. And it does not accept [Schiller's verse,
from "Das Ideal und Das Leben":]

> Only seriousness paled by no toil
> Finds the deeply hidden fount of truth.

The church holds open market with it: the river of churchly
truth roars noisily through every street, and everybody can
fill his brains with its water [p. 204].

Some German writers would, no doubt, prefer to level a similar criticism against the Enlightenment; but Hegel attacked
the churches, and his criticism also applies to spiritualistic sectarians who claimed some sort of inspiration. Later, Hegel developed this theme, first in his critique of the romantic cult of
intuition, in the preface to his *Phenomenology,* and then, in
the *Philosophy of Right,* in his polemics against Fries' philosophy of feeling.

In his early essay, Hegel specifically deplores the effect of
"the spread of Christianity" on ethics:

> In the moral system of the church it is crucial that morals
> are based on religion and on our dependence on the deity:
> the foundation on which morality is here developed is not a
> fact of our spirit, not a proposition which could be devel-
> oped out of our consciousness, but something that is learnt.

In other words, ethics "is not founded on freedom, not on
autonomy of the will" (p. 205). This sounds Kantian, but it
also points in the direction of Hegel's *Phenomenology:* here
is a hint of his later program to begin with a fact of man's
spirit and then to develop out of our consciousness what the
church teaches from outside.

10

Moses Mendelssohn. Ultimately Hegel finds in Christianity
the loss of the very gain that Jesus represented to begin with:
man is again subjected to a form of heteronomy: "the state
of mind of the Christian is prescribed to him in detail," much

as conduct was prescribed in detail to the Jews. When Hegel goes on to say that "in the Christian church there is also the contradictory addition that feelings are commanded, while in Judaism it was after all only actions," and that "the necessary consequence" of this had to be "self-deception" (p. 209), he shows the influence of Moses Mendelssohn, who had found the superiority of Judaism in its freedom from all dogma.

Hegel's relation to Mendelssohn is curious. Lessing's friend was the one great Jewish representative of the German Enlightenment and had tried to show that Judaism, which left the mind free and unfettered, was especially enlightened. Hegel, however, took an exceptionally dim view of Judaism and blamed the Jews' unenlightened attitude for the fateful "positivity," or authoritarianism, of Jesus. Even so, the German editor informs us in a note that Hegel's discussions of the relation of church and state in his essay on *The Positivity of the Christian Religion* "are based primarily on Mendelssohn's *Jerusalem";* and Haering shows in detail how Mendelssohn's influence on Hegel was probably "the greatest stimulus which he received from the outside during this time" (p. 158).

The state must not allow any dominant church. "The fundamental error which lies at the bottom of the whole system of a church is its failure to recognize the rights of every capacity of the human spirit, and especially the first among these —reason." Hence "the system of the church can be nothing but a system of contempt for human beings" (p. 211).

> And if it is counter to the right of reason in every human being that he should be subjected to such a foreign code, then the whole power of the church is unrightful. The right to give his law to himself . . . no human being can renounce; for with such a renunciation he would cease to be a human being [p. 212].

This same conception of inalienable rights is still encountered a quarter of a century later in Hegel's *Philosophy of Right*.

11

Christianity as a misfortune. In an addition to his essay on *The Positivity of the Christian Religion,* Hegel attacks Christianity in still more general terms.

> Christianity has depopulated Walhalla, chopped down the holy groves, and eradicated the popular imagination as so much shameful superstition and devilish poison. Instead it has given us the imagination of a people whose climate, legislation, culture, and interests are foreign to us, and whose history is quite unrelated to us [p. 215].

Shakespeare, says Hegel, has given his people "its own sphere of imaginative representations" (p. 216); but the Germans have neither a religion of their own nor a Shakespeare.

At the same time, Hegel specifically repudiates the course to which the romantics were soon to resort and which Richard Wagner later pursued to its climax: "To reconstruct the lost imagination of a nation has always been to no avail" (p. 217). Toward the end of his career, in his Berlin lectures on aesthetics, he made the same point even more emphatically, coupled with an explicit polemic against the work done meanwhile by the German romantics (III, 348 f.).

Instead of finding some special greatness in the German past, Hegel, like Goethe, tried to encompass the best the world could offer, notably including the offerings of the Greeks, and then to add to this great heritage in turn, hoping that his own contribution might be worthy of its predecessors and deserve attention outside his own country. He did not pine for a lost past or wish he might have been allowed to live in a brighter future: he accepted the present as his opportunity to accomplish work that he vastly preferred to anything he could have done in any other age.

In his early writings, however, Hegel does accuse Christianity of having destroyed what is now, unfortunately, lost. And he adds a section on "The Difference Between the Greek Religion of Imagination and the Christian Positive Religion" in which he sarcastically repudiates the customary contrast between the Christians' alleged "happiness and science with the unhappiness and gloom of the pagans" (p. 219). How, then, were the pagans converted?

"The customary answer" seems absurd to Hegel:

> That the attention of these peoples was called to the wretchedness and misery of their religion, that their understanding came to see the absurdity and ridiculousness of the fables of their mythology . . . and that they accepted Christianity as a religion that satisfies all the needs of man's spirit and heart, that answers all questions of the human reason adequately, and that proved its divine origins by means of miracles.

In fact, these pagans "are our models today in all that is great, beautiful, noble, and free." Clearly, "the spread of the Christian religion was accomplished by anything rather than reason and understanding." Rather, "the Greek and Roman religion was only a religion for free peoples, and with the loss of freedom . . . its adequacy for human beings had to be lost, too" (p. 221).

Like Nietzsche almost a century later, Hegel considers Christianity a religion adequate for slaves:

> The despotism of the Roman princes had hounded the spirit of man from the face of the earth. Deprived of freedom, man was forced to let that in him which was eternal, his absolute, flee into the deity; and the spread of misery forced him to seek and expect blessedness in heaven. The objectification of the deity went hand in hand with the corruption and slavery of man and is really only a revelation and manifestation of this spirit of the age [pp. 227 f.].

12

Hegel, Marx, and Lukács. The last quotation may bring to mind not only Nietzsche but Marx, too. Spiritual developments are here explained in terms of sociological and economic developments: the spread of Christianity was based on the spread of misery and slavery. Yet Hegel is concerned, even in this early essay, with the human spirit only, and political and economic conditions interest him only from this point of view. If his interest is "practical" in the Kantian sense, it is wholly impractical from the Marxian point of view: Hegel's indictment of Christianity is based on moral considerations. What concerns him is not the standard of living to which the mass of men have been reduced but the heteronomy that, partly under Kantian influence, he views as a form of spiritual slavery.

These differences between the young Hegel and Marx are underestimated by Georg Lukács in his work of over 700 pages on *Der junge Hegel* (1948). Like most of Lukács' many books, this study is most erudite but constantly cites Marx, Engels, and Lenin as authoritative dogma. The author realizes that Hegel's early theological phase is a fiction, but in his polemics he substitutes invective for demonstration and supplants this legend with a myth of his own when he claims, for example, that the conception of Hegel's early theological period is "a historic legend circulated by reactionary apologists of imperialism" (p. 45).

Six years later, in 1954, a few months after I had first voiced this criticism of Lukács in *The Philosophical Review,* he published a book on the destruction of reason (*Die Zerstörung der Vernunft*), in which I, too, am classified in similar fashion. Referring to my book on Nietzsche, Lukács explains its purpose thus: "After Nietzsche has come to seem compromised by the enthusiasm of the Hitlerites, he is to be 'denazified' for the purposes of American imperialism, together with Hjalmar Schacht and General Guderian" (p. 273). Such ingenious parallels are Lukács' forte:

Even as Truman or Eisenhower do not want to appear in public as the heirs of Hitler, but rather as the men who are continuing the lifework of Washington or Lincoln, so the direct apologetics of our time, though at heart irrationalistic, has a preference for finding its ancestors in the Enlightenment. . . . It is no different in philosophy. Kaufmann, for example, wants to turn Nietzsche into a worthy successor of the great men of the Enlightenment, and it is extraordinarily characteristic that this contemporary "renaissance of the Enlightenment" has brought us as a great discovery and revaluation, a revival of the Marquis de Sade, etc., etc. [p. 619].

Truman, Eisenhower, and the Marquis de Sade are not mentioned in my *Nietzsche;* but what *is* said in support of my interpretation of Nietzsche is ignored by Lukács. He attempts to establish guilt by association, and he appeals to prejudice and to authority, not to evidence.

Indeed, Lukács does not hesitate to base his criticisms on outright falsifications of the facts.

In the interpretation of a contemporary American, like Kaufmann, Nietzsche's agreement with Christianity outweighs the differences [p. 290]. Here is the social basis for the fact that Elisabeth Förster-Nietzsche and Jaspers and Kaufmann are all so zealously concerned to find threads that link Nietzsche with Christianity and the Christian church. Socially, they are quite justified because the ethic of Nietzsche, as we [G.L.] have sketched it, agrees completely with the political practice of the pope, of Cardinal Spellman, etc. [p. 291].

In fact, no previous study of Nietzsche's thought had presented such a thorough indictment of Nietzsche's sister Elisabeth, or differed with Jaspers' reading in such detail (see also chapter 15 below), or given such a fully documented analysis of Nietzsche's critique of Christianity, as my own. The reader may judge for himself to what extent the argument of the present volume, or of my *Critique,* is dictated by agreement with the pope or Cardinal Spellman.

Lukács is probably the leading Marxist luminary in the whole field of intellectual history since World War II, and his prolific productions are printed and reprinted in huge editions, and respected for their erudition by many non-Marxists, too. Of course, Karl Marx was a man of incomparably greater originality than Lukács and did not toe any party line or pay periodic homage to canonical scriptures; yet in his polemics Marx, like Lukács, relied on vituperation and prejudice, and this whole tradition of which Lukács is a relatively high-level representative is by no means as enlightened and as scientific as it claims to be. The weaknesses here claimed are not only found in the writings of the hacks who crowd the lower echelons.

Marx's and Engels' essays in the *Deutsche Ideologie* are all but unreadable because they systematically preferred invective to reasons and substituted outright profanity for argument. Although they certainly did not want to stop "scientific and intellectual progress," as Popper claims of Hegel, Marx did write much of the time like a man who "wants to stop rational argument" (p. 235). To this extent at least, one may find the seeds of the positivity of the Marxist religion in the person and the teachings of the founder—in line with Hegel's parallel treatment of Christianity.

In his attack on Hegel, Karl Popper uses methods very similar to Lukács', as was shown in chapter 7; but Popper's critique of Marx is extraordinarily sympathetic—especially if one compares it with his unfair treatment of Plato, Aristotle, and Hegel. But his Marx, too, differs from the real Marx. A single crucial illustration may suffice.

Popper devotes an important and long chapter to his thesis that Marx's greatness lies in part in his refusal to rely on a view of human nature and in his discovery of "The Autonomy of Sociology." What Popper has to say in this connection is interesting, but the fact remains that Marx made crucial predictions that have been proved wrong by the event—and that they have proved wrong in part because they depended on a false view of human nature.

Marx believed man's nature to be such that, under the strains of a capitalistic system, he is bound to act in accordance with the most myopic notion of his own self-interest. Like Freud in the next century, he developed a theory of human nature of which he himself was in some ways a living refutation.[2]

According to Marx, nonindustrial Russia and China should not have turned Communist when they did; but such highly industrialized countries as the United States, England, and those of western Europe ought to have developed increasingly

[2] Cf. my *Critique*, section 97, for Freud.

large and desperate proletariats that, long before now, should have had no other recourse but a revolution, followed by the dictatorship of the proletariat. In fact, Marx's writings helped to arouse a widespread humanitarian concern with the plight of the working class; and in some men this concern was coupled with the insight that, as it were, charity is the best policy.

In time, many members of the best families of England and the United States followed the example set by Marx and Engels to the modest extent of becoming "traitors to their class"; and, without a revolution, peaceful reforms were effected that have raised the standard of living of the working classes in the United States, for example, to a level of which Marx had scarcely dreamed.

When we try to understand Marx's mistaken view of man, we are less helped by economic facts than we are by knowing Hegel, against whom Marx was revolting. A knowledge of Hegel helps us in two ways. First, because Hegel taught us to understand the history of ideas in terms of a dialectical development in which men react against the views held by their predecessors and correct any one-sidedness in these views by going to the opposite extreme that, alas, is equally one-sided. Secondly, because it was against Hegel's one-sided emphasis on spiritual factors that Karl Marx rebelled with his materialism.

Hegel's philosophy of history illuminates Marx's philosophy of history far better than does Marx's own. The reason: Hegel's philosophy of history is at its best when applied to philosophies and things spiritual but is hardly helpful for economic analysis, while Marx's philosophy of history is at its worst when it is used—as it often is—to deal with philosophy, religion, art, and literature. To cover up its failure at that point, Marx and the Marxists since his time resort to name-calling and allegations of fantastic motives.

There is one further factor that should not be underestimated: Lukács, like hundreds of lesser Marxists, simply cannot conceive any more of scholarship that is oblivious of the politics of the hour. It would be a mistake to assume that his thirty-five books represent a tireless translation into print of his spontaneous stream of class consciousness. In a serialized

"Intellectual Biography" of Lukács, Morris Watnick has shown that in 1923 Lukács' deviationist Hegelianism made him the target of a Communist campaign of "personal vilification" that had "established something of a record for calculated ferocity," and Communists had been warned against "the dangers of studying Hegel." So Lukács learned that his arguments must be "disingenuously brought into line with the structure of orthodox doctrine to make them less obtrusive." After Hitler came to power and he sought refuge in the Soviet Union, he performed "one of the most abject acts of self-degradation on record," and he filled his books with "unfailing panegyrics to Stalinism." Finally, in *Der junge Hegel*, he tried to redeem his early deviation by showing that the young Hegel had really been a good Marxist and "by appealing *ad nauseam* to the authority of Lenin's post-1914 Hegelianism, even to the point of falsifying the record where his own work was involved. But all to no avail, judging by the orthodox Communist reaction." In *Die Zerstörung der Vernunft* (1954), Watnick finds Lukács troubled by "recalling that he shared the same teachers with many of the spokesmen for Nazism, and by a frantic compulsion, therefore, to disavow them." Lukács cannot afford—and cannot understand any more how anybody else can afford—to ignore slight changes in the political weather. And it is a tribute to his astuteness, though it makes ridiculous his scientific pretensions, that he has survived all kinds of changes. Although he participated in the Nagy government in Hungary and was subsequently deported to Rumania, "where he spent some four months under house arrest . . . five months after the suppression of the Hungarian uprising he was back in Budapest, seemingly none the worse off for the experience and, at that, appointed co-editor of a new philosophical journal. . . . Of those who figured prominently in the uprising, then, he is apparently the only leader thus far to have made his peace with the Kadar regime and to resume something of his former work." This is the man whom Herbert Read and Thomas Mann have called, quite rightly, too, "the most intelligent Marxist critic of our times." Here the Twentieth Century has produced realities beyond Hegel's and Marx's imagination, and when it comes to tracing such developments, neither Hegel's nor Marx's philosophy of history provides any adequate framework of explanation.

13

The Spirit of Christianity and Its Fate. This longish piece is the last of Hegel's so-called theological essays. It was probably written in 1799, and here we encounter the first major turning point in his development; but even here he becomes neither theological nor romantic.

He begins with an account of what he considers the spirit of Judaism, and the ridiculous anti-Semitism of these pages makes it doubly remarkable that the mature Hegel, in the *Philosophy of Right,* used his considerable influence on behalf of equal rights for the Jews. Both an incredibly distorted picture of Judaism and the belief in inalienable human rights were common at the time and are found conjoined in some of the most celebrated men of the Enlightenment, including even Jefferson. Neither the young Hegel nor the mature Jefferson published his anti-Semitic remarks; and they played no part in the vast Nazi literature about the Jews.

It is in his discussion of Jesus that Hegel turns against Kant and enters a new phase.

> A man who wished to restore the human being again in his totality could not possibly choose such a path [as Kant's] which only adds a rigid conceit to the human being's division against himself. Acting in the spirit of the laws could not mean for him acting from respect for duty and in contradiction to the inclinations; for in that case both parts of the spirit (of this division of the mind against itself one cannot speak in any other way) would no longer act *in* the spirit of the laws but against it . . . [p. 266].

Kant's dichotomy of reason and inclination characterizes merely one phase in man's development. Kant was a man divided against himself, and for him morality consisted in obedience to law. According to Hegel, the Jewish religion represents the same type, though less nobly so. But any such division within the spirit makes man a slave of the law, even if it is a law he gives to himself.

To give an example, not found in Hegel: The man who must interrupt this and cannot do that because it would interfere with his self-imposed regimen is a slave of his schedule even though there is no outside authority to hold him to it. Any morality that resembles such a pattern corresponds to a stage of the spirit that must be surpassed. "Jesus' spirit, which was sublimely above morality, shows itself turned directly against the law in the Sermon on the Mount" (p. 266). What Hegel turns against, however, is not all morality but only one type of morality. Both here and in his later works, Hegel calls the type that he repudiates *Moralität*, while he calls the higher type, represented by Jesus in the present essay, *Sittlichkeit*.

Kroner thinks that Hegel here becomes "a Christian mystic" and that "it is of profound significance that he discovered his own soul by discovering the soul of Jesus" (pp. 8 f.). In fact, Hegel, who had previously put Kant's *Moralität* into the mouth of Jesus, now makes Jesus the prophet of the *Sittlichkeit* represented by Goethe's Iphigenia.

It is to German classicism, not to the romantic protest against it, that Hegel here owes his greatest debt. While Hölderlin, his close friend, pined away with longing for ancient Greece, Hegel found in Goethe a present embodiment of what he admired in the past. Goethe saved him from Kant and presented him, in the flesh as well as in his works, with the superior type of humanity that Hegel now exalts above *Moralität*. Here was the whole man whom Nietzsche still celebrated almost a century later: "Goethe— . . . what he wanted was *totality;* he fought the mutual extraneousness of reason, sense, feeling, and will (preached . . . by Kant, the antipodes of Goethe)."

What Hegel now calls *Sittlichkeit* is close to Aristotle's ethics. According to Aristotle, only boors must overcome temptation while the civilized man acts in accordance with his civilized inclinations. Nothing could be more at variance with his ethics, or with Hegel's *Sittlichkeit*, than Jesus' counsel. "If your hand causes you to sin, cut it off; it is better for you to enter life maimed than with two hands to go to hell, to the unquenchable fire" (Mark 9:43; cf. Sermon on the Mount, Matt. 5:30).

Hegel returns to Aristotle rather than to Jesus when he writes, in his discussion of the Sermon on the Mount: "The agreement of inclination with the law is of such a nature that law and inclination are no longer different; and the expression 'agreement of inclination and law' therefore becomes quite unsuitable" (p. 268).[3]

When Hegel calls the state of mind that characterizes the undivided man "love," it is easy to see how this would remind a theologian of Jesus, Paul, and mysticism. But Hegel has no place at all in his scheme for a transcendent faith. He speaks of faith, to be sure, but is yet much closer to Goethe than he is to any church. In those who had faith, Jesus "recognized kindred spirits"; for "with such complete trust in another human being, with such devotion to him, with such love which holds back nothing, only a pure or purified soul can throw itself into the arms of one equally pure." And again: "Faith is the spirit's recognition of spirit; and only equal spirits can recognize and understand each other" (p. 289).

Hegel understands faith, not as the recognition of one's own impotence, not as the response to the wholly other, not as throwing oneself on the mercy of an omnipotent God whom one cannot hope to please by any works, but—and it would be hard to stray farther from Luther and Calvin, Barth and Niebuhr, not to speak of Catholicism—as the love and trust between two free spirits. He voices the essentially humanistic faith of Goethe's *Iphigenia*. Indeed, the quotations in the last paragraph describe exactly Iphigenia's attitude toward the King of Tauris, which lifts the curse of Tantalus. Hegel is also close to Goethe's later poem, *Wär' nicht das Auge sonnenhaft:*

> *Were not the eye so like the sun,*
> *It never could behold the sun:*
> *If the god's own power did not lie in us,*
> *How could that which is godlike delight us?*

[3] My own views of the ethics of the New Testament may be found in my *Critique.*

In Hegel's words: "Faith in what is godlike is possible only because the person who has faith contains in himself what is godlike—what recognizes in that in which it has faith, itself, its very own nature" (p. 313).

These positive statements are best rounded out by a reference to what Hegel repudiates:

> Miracles represent what is least godlike because they are least natural and contain the harshest opposition of spirit and body in its full and overwhelming brutality. Godlike activity is the re-establishment and representation of unity; miracles represent the deepest rent [p. 339].

From here Hegel proceeds to a final unfavorable contrast of Christianity with classical Greece, and on the last page he once more names both the Catholic and the Protestant church as falling below his standard: "It is their destiny that church and state, divine service and life, piety and virtue, spiritual and mundane activity can never be fused into one." That is how the essay ends.

Much of the last part of the essay deals rather opaquely with fate and its conciliation through love; it is strikingly similar to certain sections in the *Phenomenology* and seems an elaboration of the motto that Goethe later gave his *Iphigenia:*

> *Every failing that is human*
> *Pure humanity atones.*

For the central theme of Goethe's drama is that Orestes can be reconciled with fate and liberated from the furies of his conscience without any divine intervention, simply by the pure humanity of his sister.

Goethe's *Iphigenia* is also an important source for Hegel's extraordinary exaltation, in the *Phenomenology,* of the relationship between brother and sister. Commentators have long noted that Hegel was alluding to Sophocles' *Antigone;* but Hegel's whole development was decisively determined by the fact that in his own time he found a drama of comparable stature, and a poet and human being like Goethe.

14

Revolt against the Enlightenment. In the end, Hegel turns
against the Enlightenment in one important respect. Consider
these lines from his discussion of the spirit of Judaism—surely
applicable to the writers of the Enlightenment, too: "An image
of a god was for them mere stone or wood: it does not see nor
hear, etc. With this litany they consider themselves marvel-
ously wise . . . and have no conception of the deification of
such images in the vision of love and the enjoyment of beauty"
(p. 250).

Does it not follow that any approach to history that depicts
it merely as the record of superstition and stupidity is superficial, and that one ought to penetrate the state of mind that
finds expression in each stage? This is precisely the consequence that Hegel drew a year later when, in 1800, he tried
to rewrite his essay on *The Positivity of the Christian Religion.*
He did not get beyond writing a new introduction, which is
utterly at odds with the essay as he left it:

> The following essay does not have the purpose of inquiring
> whether there are positive doctrines and commandments in
> the Christian religion. . . . The horrible blabbering in this
> vein with its endless extent and inward emptiness has be-
> come too boring and has altogether lost interest—so much
> so that it would rather be a need of our time to hear the
> proof of the opposite of this enlightening application of uni-
> versal concepts. Of course, the proof of the opposite must
> not be conducted with the principles and methods with
> which the education of the times favored the old dogmatics.
> Rather, one would have to deduce this now repudiated dog-
> matics out of what we now consider the needs of human
> nature and thus show its naturalness and its necessity [!].
> Such an attempt would presuppose the faith that the con-
> victions of many centuries, that which the millions who,
> during these centuries, lived by them and died for them
> considered their duty and holy truth—that this was not bare
> nonsense or immorality . . . [p. 143].

In this fragment of 1800 we see Hegel coming around to his later attitude toward history, and at this point we can understand it. We may still feel that a historian should expose the superstitions and the evil deeds of men and institutions canonized today. But Hegel did not begin with the perverse determination to ignore all crimes and follies. Gradually he became convinced of the blindness and futility involved in seeing nothing but this. Like Goethe and Schiller, he was not long satisfied with any purely negative endeavor. He did not want to remain at the level of negation. Nor was he satisfied to leave his own standards outside the flux of history, unrelated to the past.

15

Two fateful errors. As he moved from this fragment to the *Phenomenology*, Hegel took two most unfortunate steps. The first concerns a confusion about "necessity" (see the last long quotation) and mars not only the *Phenomenology* but Hegel's later system, too. He used "necessary" as a synonym of "natural" and an antonym of "arbitrary" or "utterly capricious." Hegel failed to distinguish between giving some reasons for a development and demonstrating its necessity.

The pervasive chronological confusion of the illustrations in the *Phenomenology*, which exasperates most readers, is due to the fact that in Hegel's mind Kant's attitude toward the moral law harks back to the Jews' morality; and Goethe is close to Sophocles. This would not introduce any difficulty into an ordinary typology; but Hegel's types correspond to various levels of maturity and are represented by him as developing out of each other. Because some of the ancients were more mature than most moderns, he frequently selects his illustrations without regard for the actual historical sequence. This is surely legitimate and in keeping with the earliest fragments: the "child into whom the theological leaven has been beaten with the catechism" is not superior to Socrates; for "any consciousness gained through experience is lacking" (see section 3 above).

It is Goethe who leads us to think of Storm and Stress,

classicism, and romanticism not as so many alternatives but
as so many stages in a single development toward maturity.
And Goethe's development probably helped to suggest to Hegel the interesting, but surely untenable, idea that *all* styles,
outlooks, religions, and philosophies can be arranged in a single
sequence of increasing maturity (cf. chapter 4, sections 2 and
6). This was the second great error which affects not only the
Phenomenology but also the later works.

16

The logic of passion. A quotation from Goethe's *Wilhelm
Meister* (VII, 9), published in 1796, gives us another clue for
the understanding of the *Phenomenology.*

> Not to keep from error, is the duty of the educator of men,
> but to guide the erring one, even to let him swill his error
> out of full cups—that is the wisdom of teachers. Whoever
> merely tastes of his error, will keep house with it for a long
> time . . . but whoever drains it completely will have to get
> to know it unless he be insane.

Those who merely nibble at a philosophic position may
never get beyond it, while those who take it even more seriously than its creator did and push it to its final consequences
will get to know it and pass through it to a more mature
position, propelled higher and higher by their very seriousness.
This is the sense in which the dialectic of Hegel's *Phenomenology* is a *logic of passion.*

Far from pitting reason against passion, or academic pedantry against deep experience, Hegel charges the romantics,
whom he attacks in the Preface of his *Phenomenology,* with
a lack of seriousness. As Goethe did, too, he considered them
essentially weak spirits who tried to hide their lack of disciplined strength in a mist of emotion—or perhaps nibbling
connoisseurs.

Hegel's own development illustrates the logic of passion. He
embraced his puzzling faith in the essential rationality of tradition and his assumption that the great philosophies of the
past are all partially true only after he had gone through the

very opposite attitude and, in Goethe's phrase, swilled it out of full cups.

Hegel always remained faithful to some elements of the Enlightenment, such as the belief in inalienable human rights and the faith in reason, but he reacted violently against other aspects. Where he had previously condemned Christianity for its irrationality, he later celebrated Christian dogmas as ultimate philosophic truths in religious form.

Instead of achieving a crowning synthesis, he unwittingly illustrated his own dialectic by overreacting against the views of his youth and by going to the opposite extreme. Yet he did not atone for his early opposition to Christianity by submitting to it, as some of the romantics did. Though the tone of his later remarks about Christianity is approving, he approves of Christianity only as an admirable but inadequate anticipation of his own philosophy, at a subphilosophic level. Although many Protestants were grateful, Kierkegaard never tired of denouncing the blasphemous presumption of any such step "beyond" obedient faith.

Hegel always remained the heir of the Enlightenment, opposed to romanticisms and theology alike, insofar as he maintained until the end that there is one pursuit that is far superior even to art and religion: philosophy.

9

HEGEL: CONTRIBUTION
AND CALAMITY

Benedetto Croce wrote a book on *What is Living and
What is Dead in the Philosophy of Hegel.* He agreed with the
mature Hegel that what survives is what is of lasting value.
But the unfortunate survival of this notion really illustrates
Nietzsche's profound observation that the "debauches and
vices of the philosopher are always accepted first and made
matters of belief."[1] Not only are they accepted first, but they
prevail and are successful with large masses of people. This is
evident in the case of Nietzsche himself. It is scarcely less obvious regarding Hegel's influence.

An attempt to show this briefly may round out the account
of Hegel in the two preceding chapters. After a defense of
Hegel against the usual charges that he was a proto-Nazi,
and after a detailed analysis of his early writings, some critical
estimate of his mature philosophy is needed. To do justice to
Hegel without writing a whole book on him, it will be best
to relate the dangers of his thought to his outstanding merits
and to try to show how closely related contributions and calamity can be.

2

The first thing that meets the eye when one attempts to
study Hegel is the uncommon difficulty of his style. It is
plainly a function of his way of thinking. One cannot help asking oneself whether Hegel is really profound or merely opaque.

[1] *Gay Science,* §99.

It is therefore interesting that Goethe and Schiller esteemed
him highly and regretted that so eminent a mind should find
it so hard to communicate. On November 27, 1803, Goethe
wrote Schiller:

> In connection with Hegel I have been wondering whether
> one could not secure a great advantage for him if one could
> teach him something about the technique of speaking. He
> is a truly excellent human being; but his utterances are open
> to too many objections. [Es ist ein ganz vortrefflicher
> Mensch; aber es steht seinen Äusserungen gar zu viel ent-
> gegen.]

Three days later, Schiller replied:

> Your letter shows that you are cheerful, and I am delighted
> that you are getting better acquainted with Hegel. What
> he lacks, one will scarcely be able to give him; but this
> want of the facility for presentation is altogether the na-
> tional flaw of the Germans, and, at least for a German au-
> dience, it is compensated by the German virtue of thor-
> oughness and honest seriousness. You should try to bring
> Hegel and Fernow together; I should think that it must be
> possible to help each through the other. Confronted with
> Fernow, Hegel must think up some teaching method to
> make his Idealism comprehensible for Fernow; and Fernow
> would be forced to rise above his shallowness.

Goethe accepted this suggestion; but Schiller's stratagem
does not seem to have helped Hegel, to judge by his later
works. In Hoffmeister's critical edition of Hegel's correspondence, in German, we find that the University of Berlin wrote to
Hegel to ask him frankly, before extending a definite call to
him, whether his oral presentation of his thoughts was not too
exacting for students. He was requested to examine himself
in this regard; and he did not resent this inquiry but was
grateful for such candor (II, 112, 123, 398 ff.).

Today few German philosophers would even think of criticizing Hegel for his obscurity; he was a philosopher, and only
a Philistine would expect him to be easier to read. It is precisely this widespread attitude that shows how calamitous

Hegel's influence has been. After all, Goethe and Schiller were no Philistines and did not lack profundity. But Hegel has become the prototype of the German philosopher, and his necessity has gradually become a virtue that is quite deliberately emulated.

Hegel's outstanding merit that was in his case closely connected with this failing was clearly perceived by Schiller. Hegel was a true "knight against death and devil"—to cite the title of one of Dürer's best-known engravings: undeterred by any difficulty, he tackled problems that easier authors generally leave alone; and he often illuminated such problems and said interesting and important things about them. This has been overlooked by his critics, from Fries and Schopenhauer to Russell and Popper.

This does not alter the fact that his obscurity is a serious fault whenever that which he says darkly and opaquely could have been thought and said more clearly. This criticism might well have been acknowledged by Hegel himself, and it could be supported with quotations from his Preface to the *Phenomenology*. This fault is worth exposing because the vices of a thinker are more influential than his merits.

There is a passage in one of Schiller's plays, *Wallensteins Lager*, that makes this point definitively:

> *Wie er räuspert und wie er spuckt,*
> *Das habt ihr ihm glücklich abgeguckt.*
>
> *How he coughs and how he spits*
> *Is quickly aped by lesser wits.*

In the case at hand, this observation applies not only to scores of philosophy professors but also to Kierkegaard—and, of course, to *his* minions.

3

Hegel's second great fault consists in the pseudoprecision of his dialectic. Nobody who has taken pains to follow Hegel step by step will be able to deny that his imposing deductions are not compelling, even though one may be able to rethink them with a little trouble. For Hegel failed to distinguish between giving some reasons for a development and demonstrating its necessity (see chapter 8, section 15: "Two fateful errors").

At this point, Hegel's contribution consists in his transformation of Fichte's and Schelling's arid dialectic into a logic of passion (cf. chapter 8, section 16)—a stroke of genius, though the transformation was unfortunately only half accomplished by him and was not completed by any of his successors. Under the influence of Goethe and of his own development, Hegel developed something, especially in the *Phenomenology,* that is worlds removed from the *Panlogismus* of which he has often been accused. Not only does he anticipate some of Kierkegaard's central ideas, but occasionally he expresses them far better than Kierkegaard and his successors.

In spite of this, Hegel never renounced the spurious discipline and fake precision of Fichte's pseudoscientific dialectic. Indeed, not only did he preserve this ostentation but he helped it to exert an influence that it had never had in Fichte's or in Schelling's hands.

Here we encounter a decisive limitation of Hegel's stature, a flaw that mars every one of his books, and a fateful danger of his mode of thought, even though he succeeded again and again in formulating thoughts of lasting value in terms of this dialectic. The most important charge that can be leveled against Hegel is this: not only Marx and Kierkegaard but their modern successors, too, albeit indirectly, have learned the art of pseudodemonstration from the work of Hegel.

Both Marx and Kierkegaard, however, did Hegel a grave injustice when they misrepresented his dialectic as a tireless three-step, moving mechanically from theses to antitheses and hence to syntheses. The triad of thesis, antithesis, and synthesis is encountered in Kant, Fichte, and Schelling, but mentioned only once in the twenty volumes of Hegel's works (ed. Glockner)—not approvingly but at the end of his critique of Kant, in the lectures on the history of philosophy. A similar disapproval of this "triplicity" is found earlier in the preface to the *Phenomenology.*

The question remains whether Hegel did not constantly em-

ploy this scheme, even if he did not use the terms falsely ascribed to him. He did not. To be sure, even a cursory glance at
his tables of contents shows that he liked to divide things
into three parts—but it also shows that these are rarely reducible to thesis, antithesis, and synthesis. In the *Logic*, for
example, only the first triad (being, nothing, and becoming) invites this reduction, while most of the sequel is impervious to it. In his philosophy of history, Hegel divides history into three epochs: in the first (the ancient Orient), *one*
is free (the ruler); in the second (Greece and Rome), *some*
are free; while in the modern world, *all* are acknowledged to
be free, at least in principle. Clearly, this triad cannot be con-
strued as thesis, antithesis, and synthesis, and Hegel's disparagement of the attempt to impose such a scheme on everything ought to be taken seriously. (Cf. G. E. Mueller's "The
Hegel Legend of 'Thesis-Antithesis-Synthesis.'")

The quality of both the secondary literature and most translations represents a serious obstacle at this point. To give a
single example, Robert S. Hartman has produced a popular
translation of the introductory portion of Hegel's lectures on
the philosophy of history, entitled *Reason in History;* and in
his long editorial introduction he offers us a chart, explicitly
construing Hegel's thought in terms of thesis and antithesis
and synthesis. In the immediately following sentence we are
told: "It is seen that the philosophy of history is the culmination of the Hegelian system." In fact, Hegel found a place for
his philosophy of history at the end of his *Philosophy of Right*
—in other words, at the end of his discussion of "Objective
Spirit"—and above that there is still the whole realm of "Absolute Spirit," comprising art, religion, and philosophy. If we
insist on speaking of a "culmination," instead of accepting
Hegel's frequently repeated metaphor of the circle, it is clearly
the lectures on the history of philosophy that represent the
culmination of his system.

When we move from Hartman's introduction to his translation, the text seems to bear him out on one point: we do
find Hegel using the term "antithesis" over and over on page
32. But if we go back to the original German text, we find that
in one place the translator has supplied the word in a paren-

thesis, by way of assimilating Hegel to his preconceptions; twice he has used the word to render *Gegensatz* (opposite), and three times in place of "other."

4

Hegel's traditionalism poses the third great danger. He educated men to try to understand—to the exclusion of criticism. The contribution with which this fault was associated meets the eye; deliberately, Hegel turned against the hypercritical approach of the Enlightenment, which he himself had shared in his early antitheological essays, and tried, as perhaps no man before him, to do justice to the past. Going far beyond the relatively few and insignificant beginnings that existed even then he established the history of philosophy.

Under Hegel's influence, empathy flourished in Germany and developed an imposing virtuosity, while critical thinking wasted away in the humanities. Lessing and Kant, with their critical bent, had certainly not been shallow; but gradually it came to be considered sheer naïveté if one as much as asked whether a great philosopher might possibly be guilty of a fallacy and whether some of his central ideas might be untenable. This lack of critical acumen has been fatal politically, too.

The three dangers detailed here are closely connected. The obscurity that gradually helps to make respectable a certain degree of incomprehensibility, until eventually whatever is comprehensible is *eo ipso* considered relatively shallow; fake precision and pseudodemonstrations; and, finally, the demand for empathy and rethinking without criticism—that is the quintessence of the authoritarian obscurantism that Kafka represented satirically-prophetically in *The Castle*. In the twentieth century, Germany has lived through this nightmare—and philosophically it has not yet left it behind entirely.

If Hegel's work contained nothing but darkness, pseudo-precision, and uncritical empathy, then he would not be a great philosopher but merely a calamity. But one can concede the dangers of Hegel's thought without denying his greatness: distinction and danger are twins.

5

A philosopher's work, scarcely less than an artist's, must also be experienced entirely apart from its influence. For the work is an autonomous world—a creation whose rank cannot be increased or diminished by any successor. The stupidity of ardent admirers does not debase the work any more than the lack of any succession. The frescoes on the ceiling of the Sistine Chapel do not owe their greatness to what influence they may have exerted on Tintoretto; and the sculptures of Tell-el-Amarna would not lose their greatness if they should have had no influence at all. Rembrandt's stature is out of all proportion to his influence on other painters; and the same is true, the other way around, of Picasso.

In philosophy the situation is complicated by the common supposition that philosophers discover truths much as Columbus discovered America. This misunderstanding is a major reason for the fact that the influence of a philosopher is generally bad when it is great.

Nietzsche's catastrophic "influence" is known only too well. Actually, what is much more exceptional is his immense impact, within less than thirty years after his death, on men like Rilke, Hesse, Thomas Mann, Gide, and Malraux, not to mention a host of controversial thinkers. What made possible this *good* influence was, not least of all, Nietzsche's refusal to impose an idiosyncratic terminology; truly great and independent spirits found it possible to learn from him without renouncing their own originality.

Many a great philosopher buries posterity under his work: it becomes a prison for the spirit, not a spur to new creation. The obvious analogy between his categories and a work of poetry is overlooked, and highly personal modes of expression become a strait jacket for subsequent thought. His insights are not grasped, but the words in which he clothed them meet the eye; and although they never were entirely adequate they become the basis of endless discussions. Terminology supplants thought; exegesis, vision.

Is a philosopher to be blamed for that? Schiller once wrote a distich on "Kant and his Interpreters":

One who is opulent offers   legions of famishing beggars
food. When the kings construct, carters find plenty of work.

The beggars wait for the rich and depend on them. In a note, published posthumously in *The Will to Power* (§916), Nietzsche remarks that most modern scholars can "think *re-actively* only: that is, they must read before they can think." It is by preference that they seek out dark thinkers with a difficult terminology: they provide more work.

The creator of a thought-labyrinth generally tried to give expression to experiences and insights. But the hosts who settle down in his labyrinth to earn their living as interior decorators represent the triumph of professionalism. The quality of these interior decorators does not prove anything against a philosopher's work, and their quantity is no argument in its favor. What matters in the last analysis is the substance of the work: what new experiences and thoughts it formulates.

This applies to Hegel no less than to Heidegger or Wittgenstein. Yet the substance of Hegel's work has rarely been investigated in this sense. Most readers have followed one of three courses. Some are charmed by his terminology and try to think the way he thought, as if true thinking did not always require spontaneity. Others, more numerous by far, are put off by his terminology, repudiate him, and are blind to his achievement. Still others, including Marx and Kierkegaard as well as many of our own contemporaries, think that they repudiate him but yet take over a great many things, though some become untenable once they are severed from the core of Hegel's thought.

The dialectic makes sense in the context of a spiritual development in which genuine contradictions are possible. One can move from a proposition to its denial. Transposed into a materialistic framework, the dialectic loses all precision; there is no longer any contradiction, only conflict. In this sense, dialectical materialism is a contradiction in terms; and least of all is it scientific, though "dialectical materialism" and "scientific materialism" are widely used as synonyms. What remains after such a transposition of the dialectic is at best a dramatic form of presentation but, the vociferous claims of Marxist writers notwithstanding, no method of inquiry.

Hegel moves back and forth between the logic of passion and a precise motion from propositions to their denial; and he uses the conception of a dialectic to bring order into vast historical developments. Although his claims for his dialectic are extravagant and cannot be maintained, he makes us aware of peculiarities of concepts, of relations that obtain between them, of historical connections, and of states of mind that go with various outlooks. In the hands of many dialectical materialists and dialectical theologians, however, the dialectic has become a mere jugglery of big words—a lack of insight that pretends to be profound and frequently deceives the writer into thinking that his prose is deep merely because it is abysmal.

6

Hegel has influenced posterity as very few philosophers. German thought through the nineteenth century and Anglo-American idealism around the turn of the century are un-thinkable without him, and the philosophy of the twentieth century is to a large extent a multifarious revolt against his influence; but pragmatism, positivism, and existentialism are closer to Hegel than to his epigoni against whom they turned in the first place. William James's attacks on Hegel, for example, sometimes almost champion Hegel against Royce, though James falsely assumes that everything he found objectionable in his Harvard colleague came from Hegel.

Nineteenth-century literary criticism and aesthetics are also dominated by Hegel, while the so-called new criticism, with its one-sided, antihistoric emphasis on formal elements represents a revolt against Hegelian and Marxist writers. Again, the opposition to the epigoni is clear, while the substance of Hegel's own aesthetics has not received the attention it deserves.

The time has come to study Hegel not merely historically, because intellectual history during the past 150 years cannot be understood apart from him, but to ask about the substance

of his thought. Instead of tracing history *Von Kant bis Hegel,*
like Kroner, or *Von Hegel zu Nietzsche,* like Löwith, thus re-
maining within the framework of Hegel's own historical approach, Hegel should be studied from an altogether different
point of view that might be called, using a Nietzschean term,
"supra-historical." One might read Hegel as we read Plato—
chiefly to expose oneself to his outlook and to learn from his insights. Instead of reflecting, like Heidegger, on "Hegel's Concept of Experience," one should penetrate to Hegel's own experience. But that may be safely left to others.

7

One final reflection may pave the way for the chapters on
Kierkegaard and Nietzsche. The three great faults discussed in
the present chapter are, without exception, absent from the
antitheological essays considered in the last chapter. It is only
in the last of these essays, "The Spirit of Christianity and Its
Fate," that they begin to emerge. Was Schiller possibly wrong
after all when he wrote Goethe that Hegel's obscurity was
probably incurable and nothing less than "the national flaw of
the Germans"? Evidently, the obscurity was acquired in Hegel's case and not innate, and it appeared together with the
fake precision of his dialectic and the traditionalist effort to
discover the epitome of reason in his Christian heritage and
to find his own philosophy implicit in the ancient dogmas.

Although the American public goes further than the German public in assuming that philosophy is, to say the least,
continuous with theology, not one of the really outstanding
English-speaking philosophers since the Reformation was a
Christian, except Bishop Berkeley in the early eighteenth century. Bacon, Hobbes, Locke, Hume, Bentham, Mill, James,
Dewey, Moore, and Russell represent an amazing continuity
both in this respect and in their lucid prose, which is not
tainted by the three flaws that we found in Hegel.

In Germany, Hegel could not look back upon any long
philosophical tradition. Leibniz had written French and Latin.
More recently, there were two different traditions. One was
represented by Lessing's antitheological polemics, by some of

Kant's essays, and by Schiller. The other one took its inspiration from Kant's major works and was represented by Fichte and Schelling who, although not Christians—Fichte was dismissed on a charge of atheism, and Schelling became a Christian only late in life—tried to blend Kant with a mysticism that had roots in Boehme and Cusanus and Eckhart. It had a religious tone, though the coloring was pantheistic, and it was romantic. Instead of being antitheological, it began to develop a new kind of theology.

Hegel began his work in the first tradition, as a follower of Lessing and Schiller; but by 1800 he had turned to the other tradition and resolved to formulate his own position as an advance over the philosophy of Fichte. At first he thought of making common cause with Schelling; but, by the time he published his first book, he was resolved to proceed alone—beyond Schelling, too.

Once we view Hegel's development in this perspective, we can hardly help wondering what might have happened if he had remained more faithful to the first tradition. We can grant that his later works are rich and comprehensive far beyond his early essays, and still ask whether Hegel's later scope and depth would not have been compatible with Lessing's style or Schiller's; or with Kierkegaard's, where it is not corrupted by the fateful influence of Hegel's later works; or with Nietzsche's.

Kierkegaard and Nietzsche prove beyond a doubt that the most impassioned seriousness is quite compatible with graceful prose and that lucidity does not preclude profundity or first-hand knowledge of art and religion. But both men lack the discipline, sobriety, and many-sided erudition that would have distinguished Hegel even if he should have followed in the steps of Lessing, of Kant's essays, and of Schiller. The whole history of philosophy would have taken a different course. There would have been no need for the excesses of the existentialist revolt, or for the extremes to which the positivists went.

Ben Jonson felt that Shakespeare might have made improvements here and there by blotting lines, but on the whole one would not want Shakespeare different from the way he was. The same is true of Mozart and of Goethe. Even with some lesser men one has the feeling that they got out of themselves whatever they had to offer, that they spent themselves completely, that they did what they could.

Hegel, though great, makes us feel that he might have been much greater. He was a man of genius who, early in life, made a wrong choice. And we are the poorer for it.

I O

KIERKEGAARD

That Kierkegaard with his prolific contempt for parsons and professors should at long last have been translated into English largely by a parson and a professor is ironical but not ultimately serious. But that a man who wanted to "create difficulties everywhere" and be an offense should be praised and buried in academic appreciations without offending anybody is tragic.[1] With other writers one may begin with an appreciative exposition and end with a criticism or two; with Kierkegaard one should first be offended. We should work our way through initial objections.

Because these objections reflect the vexation and offense of what Kierkegaard might have called an existing individual and because eventually they give way to another attitude and are qualified, it would be misleading to state them either impersonally as assured results or personally as convictions. What else remains? One can follow Kierkegaard's example and invent a pseudonym to produce in short order and without judicious qualifications the offense that must precede appropriation. Let us borrow a chapter heading from Kierkegaard's own *Fear and Trembling* and begin with

"A PRELIMINARY EXPECTORATION"
By Brother Brash

Kierkegaard may be considered in at least four ways: as a

[1] *Postscript*, p. 166. The abbreviations of most titles should be self-explanatory. "Lowrie" means *A Short Life of Kierkegaard;* "Thomte," *Kierkegaard's Philosophy of Religion;* "Bretall," *A Kierkegaard Anthology;* and *Adler* means *On Authority and Revelation: The Book on Adler.*

stylist, a religious writer, a psychologist, and a philosopher. In
all four respects he is remarkable but, to use one of his favorite
words from Paul, a *skandalon*.

As a *stylist* he is most imaginative but is verbose and repeti-
tious; his theoretical prose is often needlessly involved; and in
his attempts at philosophy he out-Hegels Hegel. Occasionally
he writes sentences of which his many commentators and
translators are unable to make any sense. If, as some of them
plead, his intention in such cases was humorous and he was
trying to satirize Hegel, he would seem to have failed in an
endeavor in which success should have been relatively easy to
attain. Another translator, Emanuel Hirsch, claims in his version of Kierkegaard's *Die Schriften über sich selbst* (p. 121)
that "Kierkegaard often deliberately strained for an involved
and difficult syntax to force the reader to proceed slowly" and
admits that this attempt results in a "twisted and intricate
style." That he might have been a sloppy writer who published as many as four books a year without taking the time
to prune his prose and that his literary and intellectual conscience was perhaps lax even for a religious writer—such possibilities are scarcely considered by his admirers, who have almost monopolized the literature about him. But what is most
distressing is Kierkegaard's inimitable blend of existential urgency and epic digressions—and his highly imitable and fateful fusion of this urgency with verbal acrobatics, which at
times defy analysis and at other times clothe trivialities in
pomp.

2

As a *religious writer*, Kierkegaard is, first of all, one of the
foremost recent spokesmen of authoritarian religion. Consider
a dictum from his voluminous *Journals*, dated 1847:

They would have us believe that objections against Christianity come from doubt. This is always a misunderstanding. Objections against Christianity come from insubordination, unwillingness to obey, rebellion against all authority.

Therefore they have hitherto been beating the air against objectors, because they have fought intellectually with doubt, instead of fighting ethically with rebellion [Lowrie, p. 122; *Journals*, §630].

Any attempt to defend Christianity only undermines its authority, and Kierkegaard argues that "he who first invented the notion of defending Christianity in Christendom is *de facto* Judas No. 2; he also betrays with a kiss." Kierkegaard exhorts his reader "to become a believer—*nota bene!* by adoringly humbling himself under the extraordinary." It is in "the absurd" that "Christianity begins—and the offense"; and we must believe without any possibility of comprehension (*Sickness*, pp. 217 f., 229 f.). It is blind obedience that Kierkegaard demands; and it is noteworthy that his authoritarianism extends beyond religion. Thus he writes in 1847, in his Preface to *The Confusion of the Present Age*, posing, as he often does, as the mere editor of a book that, in fact, he has written himself: "For the misfortune of our age—in the political as well as in the religious sphere, and in all things—is disobedience, unwillingness to obey. And one deceives oneself and others by wishing to make us imagine that it is doubt. No, it is insubordination." A year later, after the revolutions of 1848, Kierkegaard reaffirmed this position (*Adler*, pp. xviii ff.).

The ethical import of this authoritarianism is expounded in *Fear and Trembling*, which Kierkegaard himself considered one of his best books—an estimate in which most of his admirers concur. Here Abraham is celebrated for the faith he showed in being willing to sacrifice Isaac. The book deals less with Abraham than with the meaning of faith, and the central sentence is this: "If faith does not make it a holy act to be willing to murder one's son, then let the same condemnation be pronounced upon Abraham as upon every other man" (p. 41).

Abraham is "the knight of faith" because his faith did not shrink from the absurd. But here Kierkegaard is guilty of two anachronisms. First, he attributes to Abraham a rigid distinction between the religious and the ethical order. Some inkling of such a distinction may indeed be found in an earlier chapter (Genesis 18) where Abraham pleads with God that he must not destroy Sodom if there be just men in it. But this wonderful story, which is utterly incompatible with Kierkegaard's authoritarian reading of Genesis, certainly does not justify him when he attributes to Abraham a full-fledged ethical code entirely apart from his relation to God. On this anachronism, however, Kierkegaard's book depends.

The second and crucial anachronism is this: If a man today proposed to act as Abraham did, I should not, like Kierkegaard, "saddle my horse and ride with him" (p. 43); for I should not believe the man that it was God who had asked him to sacrifice his son. Kierkegaard places the intuitive certainty that we are confronted with God's will above all critical reflection. For him faith is "everything" (p. 42). In Genesis it is assumed that Abraham knows God well, that there is no doubt whatever that it is God who speaks to him, and above all that in fact—ex hypothesi—it is God. In this last respect the situation may be compared with that of Job who—ex hypothesi —has never done anything evil. These conditions cannot simply be taken over. Indeed, it might well be argued that one of the major lessons of the story in Genesis is precisely this: If any man hereafter should feel called upon to sacrifice his son, he may be sure that God does *not* want him to do it.

The "knight of faith" whom Kierkegaard extols and would like to equal is best characterized in two words: He is the incarnation of *sancta simplicitas*, to cite the words that Hus is said to have uttered on the stake in 1415 when he noted with what zeal some poor benighted soul added a piece of wood to the pile on which he was being burnt to death. However holy such naïveté may consider itself, it is hardly fair to adorn it with the name of Abraham by way of persuading men that it is truly sacred. Far from being unfortunately rare in our time, such blind fanaticism is one of the scourges of humanity. There are too many men, not too few, who are willing to believe that it is their sacred duty to sacrifice others.

This critique of Kierkegaard is far truer to his spirit than any effusion about the aesthetic merits of his book. His existential pathos consists in his demand that we should not read with the detachment of the spectator who is not himself involved. "If faith does not make it a holy act to be willing to murder," then, according to Kierkegaard, Abraham must be condemned—and Kierkegaard's essay must be criticized. The issue is as clear as that.

Either you saddle your horse and become a fellow traveler of those who go forth with the simple faith that they are called upon to kill men, or you do not. That is the question Kierkegaard poses. But his admirers would rather not answer it and prefer to obscure the issue with rhapsodies about Kierkegaard's fine qualities.

There is a story in the Talmud in which some rabbis have an argument about a point of law. One of them performs various miracles to persuade the others that he is right, and when all else fails he exclaims: "If the law is as I think, they shall tell us from heaven." And a loud voice is heard: "What have you against Rabbi Eliezer, for the law is as he says." But the rabbis decide: "We no longer pay attention to voices, for on Mount Sinai already thou hast written into the Torah to decide according to the majority." Later, one of them meets Elijah and asks him what God did in that hour, and Elijah replies: "God smiled and said: My children have won against me, my children have won."[2]

In this story God is the father; but not all fathers are stern, humorless authoritarians like Kierkegaard's father. God is pictured like the proverbial Jewish father: it is as if he had taught his sons to play chess and was delighted and proud that one of them had beaten him for the first time. He has given his children priceless gifts and is pleased when they grow up and learn to use them independently.

Kierkegaard's conception of God and of the proper relationship between father and son is utterly different and authoritarian through and through. Consider his own words:

> In case a son were to say, "I obey my father, not because he is my father but because . . . his commands are always profound and clever"—then . . . the son accentuates some-

2 Baba Mezia 59b. The story, together with its interesting conclusion, which has been omitted here, is analyzed in my *Critique*, §77.

thing which is entirely beside the point . . . [and] undermines obedience. And this, too, is affectation when there is
so much about accepting Christianity and believing in
Christ on account of the profundity. . . . The whole of
modern Speculation is therefore "affected" by reason of having done away with *obedience* . . . and authority [*Adler*,
pp. 166 f.].

Most modern Protestants, including Kierkegaard's most enthusiastic admirers, are not authoritarian in his sense and
would be included in his condemnation. Thus he continues:

A clergyman who is entirely correct in his eloquence must
speak thus in introducing a word of Christ: "This word was
spoken by him to whom, according to his own statement,
all power hath been given in heaven and in earth. Now,
thou, my hearer, must consider by thyself whether thou
wilt bow to this authority or no. But if thou wilt not do so,
then for heaven's sake do not go off and accept the word
because it is clever and profound or wondrously beautiful,
for this is blasphemy, it is wanting to treat God like an
aesthetic critic."

Any suggestion that we must examine the content to determine whether a saying or a command is indeed from God is
emphatically rejected by Kierkegaard:

The apostle says he is from God. The others answer, "Well
then, let us see whether the content of the doctrine is divine,
for in that case we will accept it along with the claim that
it was revealed to thee." In that way both God and the
apostle are mocked. . . . And meanwhile the apostle and
God must presumably wait at the door or in the porter's
lodge until the case has been decided by the wise men in
the *bel étage*. The elect man should according to God's
ordinance assert his divine authority to chase away all impertinent people who will not obey him but argue [*Adler*,
pp. 109 f.].

If the label of authoritarianism is amply justified by Kierkegaard's repeated insistence on "authority" and by his equation

of critical thinking with insubordination and blasphemy, it is yet plain that he himself refused to submit to the authority of any man or institution. While firmly believing in the necessity of authority and blind obedience, he placed the blame for the lack of both in the nineteenth century at least in part on those representatives of Christianity who had forfeited their authority and did not deserve obedience.

What, then, are the criteria of genuine authority? What may we ask short of blasphemy before we submit humbly to any man who claims authority? In the whole work that Kierkegaard devoted to the problems of *Authority and Revelation* we find only two criteria, repeated a number of times: "An apostle has no other proof but his own assertation, and at the most by his willingness to suffer everything for the sake of the doctrine" (pp. 117 f.). It would be an understatement to say that no safeguard whatever remains against fanaticism: fanaticism and the lack of a sensitive intellectual conscience are made the proof of authority, and Kierkegaard wistfully deplores his own intelligence.

Those who favor an authoritarian faith may not consider these reflections a critique of Kierkegaard as a religious writer. If so, they should remember that the problem has an ancient history and should ask themselves what Kierkegaard has contributed to its clarification. The Catholic Church, of course, has always employed other criteria, and the willingness of scores of heretics to suffer the stake has never persuaded the church that they were true apostles. Nor did Calvin change his mind about the Trinity after he had burnt Servetus, the Unitarian. Luther, to be sure, began by claiming the supremacy of conscience but soon found that he had invited anarchy by sanctioning all kinds of doctrines and actions that he could not but condemn as utterly outrageous. And since he had begun by ruling reason out of court, as he considered reason a whore whom a Christian must reject before he can enter the kingdom of heaven, nothing remained to him but to set up another authoritarian church. Those who thrill to the young Luther who made the Reformation and repudiate the "old" Luther who, only a very few years later, became an authoritarian, should ask whether Luther had not staked his Reformation on an unsound issue when he postulated a spurious alternative between the authority of the Catholic Church and the supremacy of the individual conscience that has thrown reason to the winds.

Many Protestants still thrill to Luther's insistence that he would not recant unless refuted from Scripture. Have they forgotten how soon he repudiated the Epistle of James, the brother of Jesus, as "an epistle of utter straw"? Or how easily the Catholic Church, or any other denomination, not to speak of the devil, could cite Scripture against Luther? Or how difficult it is to reach agreement about the teaching of Scripture? The Pharisees knew that; the rabbis in our Talmudic story knew it; and the church found it out and gradually developed an elaborate machinery of arbitration. Luther himself, who began by assuming that Scripture was on his side, while the Catholic Church simply ignored Scripture, soon found that he could not agree about Scripture with Zwingli, nor with Calvin, nor with the Anabaptists, nor with any number of others who were no less sincere, and occasionally more scrupulous, than he was.

Looking back on this history, what does Kierkegaard contribute? A single-minded insistence on authority and obedience, a superior contempt for doubt and "insubordination"—but no clarification of the genuine difficulties that have beset religious men and women for centuries. Of course, he is right that reason cannot conclusively settle some of life's central questions, but he is fatally wrong when he minimizes, or altogether ignores, the all-important difference between a thoughtful and a fanatical decision, between a choice that is responsible and one that is not; and what calls for censure above all else is his deliberate disparagement of critical scrutiny as blasphemy, impertinence, and insubordination.

Nor is this all that needs to be said against Kierkegaard as a religious writer. His stature is further limited by the fact that he has no understanding whatever of any religious attitude other than his own—the two between which he himself is torn. He has no inkling of the religiosity of Genesis, or of later Jewish or Buddhistic or Hindu or Confucian piety, no remote grasp of Congregationalist or Unitarian religiousness, and, as

Lowrie remarks, "he ignored the Calvinistic branch of Protestantism as completely as if it did not exist" (p. 219).

The point is not that he does not mention these religions but that he ignores them when, for example, he defines religiosity. Kierkegaard maintains

> that religiosity is inwardness, that inwardness is the relationship of the individual to himself before God, his reflection into himself, and that it is precisely from this that the suffering derives, this also being the ground of its essential pertinence to the religious life, so that the absence of it [suffering] signifies the absence of religiosity [*Postscript*, p. 391].

This passage is doubly self-centered. Most religious people are less preoccupied with themselves and their own relationship to themselves; and we may therefore say in the first place that Kierkegaard's religiosity is unusually self-centered. And, secondly, he writes as if his own self-centered religiosity were the only one.

This self-centeredness and this addiction to self-projection are Kierkegaard's most central faults. They limit his stature not only as a religious writer but also as a human being. He becomes embarrassing when he enthuses about "the religious genius" and offers us an oblique self-portrait (*Dread*, pp. 96 ff.); when he pictures himself, again obliquely, as "the most eminent poet-existence" (*Sickness*, p. 208); or when he decides not to publish *The Point of View for My Work as an Author* in his lifetime because he is not sure "whether a man has a right to let people know how good he is" (Lowrie, p. 212).

Even those who relish the sarcasm of Socrates' *Apology* and the impudence of Nietzsche's *Ecce Homo* may well find parts of the Introduction to *The Point of View* and ever so much else in Kierkegaard's books and *Journals* sanctimonious. He writes: "But however much I have suffered from misunderstanding, I cannot but thank God for what is of infinite importance to me, that He has granted me understanding of the truth." And elsewhere: "I have never fought in such a way as to say: I am the true Christian, others are not Christians. No, my contention has been this: *I know what Christianity is,* my imperfection as a Christian I myself fully recognize—but I know what Christianity is" (*Point,* pp. 8 f., 159).

Unlike the Hebrew prophets, Kierkegaard is charged with self-importance. He does not disappear in his message like Amos; nor does his life become a mere parable of his message —of no interest in itself—like Hosea's: Kierkegaard's individuality is always with us—a tormented individuality like that of a character in Dostoevsky, without the open horizon of Nietzsche, Goethe, or Kant—a limited, poor, infinitely pathetic and upsetting individuality. It would be absurd to censure him for not writing a comparative history of religion; but his studied ignorance of all other forms of religion amounts to nothing less than a deliberate blindness to human possibilities.

3

It is Kierkegaard's *psychology* that suffers most seriously from his peculiar self-centeredness. Some of his books, notably *The Concept of Dread* and *The Sickness Unto Death,* have subtitles that characterize them as "psychological"; and Kierkegaard himself admits that his psychology is based on introspection (*Dread,* pp. 46, 70 f.). He certainly offers some shrewd flashes of psychological insight, but as soon as one tries to make a list of them one is disappointed to find how few of them there are. He does not develop a comprehensive theory like Freud, or even like Nietzsche with his conceptions of the will to power, sublimation, and resentment. Kierkegaard offers only sundry observations, and even these suffer from two crucial defects.

The first of these is self-projection coupled with a range of experience that is far too narrow to permit significant generalizations. He shows no understanding of Abraham in *Fear and Trembling,* none of Antigone in *Either/Or,* none of Solomon in *Stage's on Life's Way:* he always writes about himself. His brilliant sketch of "Stoic" defiance in *The Sickness Unto Death* is such that Kierkegaard himself is driven to admit that "this sort of despair is seldom seen in the world" (p. 206). When he adds, "Nevertheless such a despairer is to be met with also in real life," we are served notice that he projects himself, as if that did not go without saying. His strange Stoic does not doubt God, has no qualms about the meaning of "God," but out of sheer pride refuses obedience. It is, Kierkegaard says, as if a "clerical error would revolt against the author, out of hatred for him were to forbid him to correct it, and were to say, 'No, I will not be erased, I will stand as a witness against thee, that thou art a very poor writer.'" Being physically deformed, Kierkegaard knew the temptation of flinging himself into the face of God with words like these; and for him obedience to God meant humble acceptance of the absurd.

If this interpretation should seem unduly personal, consider the deeply moving pages in *Fear and Trembling* that deal ostensibly with Shakespeare's Richard III. Kierkegaard considers the famous monologue in the first scene "worth more than all the moral systems which have no inkling of the terrors of existence" and quotes from it:

> *I, that am rudely stamp'd and want love's majesty*
> *To strut before a wanton ambling nymph;*
> *I that am curtail'd of this fair proportion,*
> *Cheated of feature by dissembling nature,*
> *Deform'd, unfinish'd, sent before my time*
> *Into this breathing world, scarce half made up,*
> *And that so lamely and unfashionable*
> *That dogs bark at me as I halt by them.*

These lines, of course, are pathetically applicable to Kierkegaard, who comments: "Essentially such natures . . . are either lost in the demoniacal paradox [like Richard] or saved in the divine [as Kierkegaard hoped to be]" (pp. 114 f.). As so often, the generalization does not at all stand up; such passages demand to be read as fragments of the soul's dialogue with itself.

In his *Journals* Kierkegaard noted with characteristic coyness:

> After my death no one will find in my papers (this is my comfort) a single explanation of what it was that really filled my life, the secret writing in my inmost parts which

explains everything and often transforms what the world
would call bagatelles into events of prodigious importance
for me, which I too regard as insignificant apart from the
secret gloss which explains them [Lowrie, p. 70; *Journals*,
§431].

This note should be compared with Nietzsche's observation:

The worst readers of aphorisms are the writer's friends if
they are intent on guessing back from the general to the
particular instance to which the aphorism owes its origin:
for with this pot-peeking they reduce the author's whole
effort to nothing, and thus they only deserve it when, instead of a philosophic outlook or instruction, they gain
nothing but—at best, or at worst—the satisfaction of a vulgar
curiosity [*Human*, II, 129].

For Nietzsche his own experience is the mere occasion for
more general insights that are meant to have objective validity:
he develops theories, offers analyses, and is a psychologist and
a philosopher. Kierkegaard, on the other hand, considers all
such enterprises frivolous as long as his salvation is at stake.
While Nietzsche says, "Of all that is written I love only what
a man has written with his blood," he does not equal Kierkegaard's subjectivity.

I have said that Kierkegaard's range of experience was narrow; and yet his life was certainly no less interesting than
Freud's or Nietzsche's. The point is rather that he was so
largely preoccupied with four experiences that he projects end-
lessly: his father's sin in cursing God when he was a poor boy,
long before Kierkegaard was born; his father's dissoluteness,
particularly his probable seduction of Kierkegaard's mother
when she was a maid in his house; his own dissoluteness after
he first found out about his father's; and the way he broke his
engagement, pretending that he was a frivolous person, unworthy of Regine. In *The Concept of Dread*, for example,
where he deals psychologically with original sin and admits
that his psychology is based on his own case, he is preoccupied
with the relation of his own sin to his father's; and he probably
wondered whether his own deformity was not a punishment for
his father's sins. We should also recall his remark about his

father: "I learnt from him what father-love is, and thereby I got a conception of the divine father-love" (*Journals*, §335). Much more important, his own love of his father, whom he probably considered not only sinful but responsible for his own misfortune, but to whom he dedicated book after book, became for him the paradigm of how he should love God: without reason, overriding moral scruples, humbling himself lovingly before the utterly absurd.

If the uncritical projection and generalization of a very few unusual experiences constitutes the first major defect of Kierkegaard's psychology, the second defect is self-deception. *Fear and Trembling*, for example, was clearly prompted by his own broken engagement, to which it alludes constantly (cf. *Journals*, §965). But Kierkegaard does not only project his own problems into Abraham and into so many others whom he introduces in endless digressions; he also deceives himself about his own motivation by sanctimoniously celebrating himself as a "knight of resignation" who acted as he did because God himself had told him to do so. And he congratulates himself on his humility in not applying to himself the highest title, that of the "knight of faith." Whoever compares Kierkegaard's endless pseudo-explanations of his broken engagement, now in terms of three stages and now in terms of a "teleological suspension of the ethical," with Kafka's treatment of his own profoundly similar experience in *The Judgment* and, above all, in his magnificently honest and humane *Letter to the Father*, can hardly help asking himself whether Kierkegaard's cant has ever been equaled by a writer of equal rank.

How naïve is Kierkegaard psychologically when he reiterates, "If he does not love like Abraham, then every thought of offering Isaac would not be a trial but a base temptation" and "that I loved him with all my soul is the presumption apart from which the whole thing becomes a crime" (pp. 42, 46). He is trying to justify himself, but surely the agent's suffering and anguish can no more establish that God demands an act than absurdity can prove that God wants us to believe something. And why should God be such a good Kantian that when he overrides our ethical duty he always overrides our inclination too? If he commands the absurd, why should he not

for once side with our inclination against our duty? To cite
Max Brod: "Is it impossible after all that God might give the
command to kill his son not to an Abraham who loves his son
but to an Abraham who hates his son . . . ?" (*Heidentum,
Christentum, Judentum,* I, 315.)

It may seem impertinent to psychologize Kierkegaard; but
his discussions are so pointedly subjective and incomplete, so
close to special pleading, and so full of allusions to his life that
it seems convenient not to list all the omissions, oversights, and
fallacies, but to say once and for all that his psychology is
vitiated by uncritical self-projection and sanctimonious self-
deception.

Kierkegaard's failure to search his heart whether he was not
also afraid of marriage, at least in part for all too human reasons, and his insistence on explaining his behavior religiously
in terms of faith bring to mind Nietzsche's malicious but profound epigram: " 'Faith' means not *wanting* to know what is
true" (*Antichrist,* §52).

Let me summarize my case so far by briefly comparing Kierkegaard's *Attack on Christendom* with Nietzsche's *Antichrist.*
Each comes at the end of the author's career; neither of them
is the author's greatest work; both inveigh against hypocrisy.
But in all three respects so far considered Nietzsche's work is
more substantial. However we may disagree with him, his style
is powerful where Kierkegaard's is enfeebled by his repetitious-
ness; Nietzsche deals with a great variety of religious attitudes
where Kierkegaard merely contrasts purity and impurity,
black and white; and as a psychologist Nietzsche offers not
merely sundry flashes but a budding psychology of *Weltanschauungen,* including a provocative "psychology of 'faith' "
(§§50 ff.) in which he calls attention to all sorts of problems
that Kierkegaard consistently avoids. Obviously, Nietzsche's
attack is open to scores of criticisms, but it is far meatier than
Kierkegaard's. For Nietzsche is a philosopher and a psychologist while Kierkegaard, to cite his own words once more, is
"fighting ethically with rebellion." Kierkegaard is essentially a
moralist who diverts and dazzles us with stories and psychological tidbits.

4

So much for the stylist, the religious writer, and the psychologist. But what of Kierkegaard as a *philosopher?* Let me enter four charges against him—or rather against those who would turn him into a philosopher. First and most important, Kierkegaard neither was nor wanted to be a philosopher. Hegel's dictum, in the Preface to his *Phenomenology*, "Philosophy, however, must beware of wishing to be edifying," only embittered Kierkegaard (*Journals*, §320). To be sure, the really great philosophers, including Hegel, *are* edifying and say to us among other things: "You must change your life." But the decisive difference between their challenge and that of religious teachers and preachers is that the philosophers' demand is a paraphrase of Socrates' dictum in the *Apology*, that the unexamined life is not worth living. It is a call to become critical, to place convention on the rack. Kierkegaard on the other hand, says: "The important thing is to understand what I am destined for, to perceive what the Deity wants *me* to do; the point is to find the truth which is truth *for me*, to find *that idea for which I am ready to live and die*" (Lowrie, pp. 82 f.; *Journals*, §22). Philosophy, to be sure, will never give him this idea, but it might well safeguard a man against some ideas for which he might better not live or die. Kierkegaard admits that "philosophy cannot and should not give faith"; but he adds that it should "take nothing away, and least of all should fool people out of something as if it were nothing" (*Fear*, p. 44). But a training in philosophy must fool people out of many childhood beliefs, religious and nonreligious, not by attacking them specifically, but incidentally by developing our critical powers. In violently objecting to this, Kierkegaard is deeply and essentially opposed to philosophy.

The second charge is merely a minor variant of the first. Reversing the whole trend of modern philosophy, he goes back to the authority of Scripture and cites verses and even single words to establish points; and he dogmatizes, for example, about original sin, like a theologian rather than a philosopher. His psychological observations add spice, no more—as when he psychologizes God and, projecting his own broken engagement, explains God's predicament thus: "Not to reveal oneself is the death of love, to reveal oneself is the death of the beloved" (*Fragments,* p. 23).

The third charge is that Kierkegaard accepts Christian and Hegelian categories and modes of thinking without examining them and juggles around such phrases as dialectical, spirit, the eternal, nothing, infinite reflection, potentiate, the posited sin, self, freedom, and many others without seeking clarity about their meaning. His discussion of God's existence, proofs, and the Unknown, in the *Fragments,* is on the level of sleight-of-hand apologetics, as are such entirely representative statements as these: "If he has no God, neither has he a self" and "we can demonstrate the eternal in man from the fact that despair cannot consume his self" (*Sickness,* pp. 173, 153). Those who know Kierkegaard will easily recall dozens of more intricate passages that are less easily found out.

The fourth and final charge against Kierkegaard as a philosopher is that the kind of dialectic in which he excels could be used to "prove" anything. Although he constantly invokes Socrates, he fails to understand the central point of Socrates' mission: the relentless questioning of convention, prompted by the evident conviction that even holy and respectable ends do not justify unanalyzed concepts, murky arguments, and the lack of a sensitive intellectual conscience. The pious ruse that a man is too serious to concern himself with anything as frivolous as mere concepts cannot allay the suspicion that he is not serious enough. And if he insists that he is not a philosopher, why should we contradict him?

That Kierkegaard does not offer any philosophic theory is a far less serious matter, although a suggestive theory might go far toward balancing some of the aforementioned defects. The closest thing to a theory that we find is Kierkegaard's notion of the three stages, and next to that his dictum that "truth is subjectivity." Neither of these can stand scrutiny. To wind up my critique, I shall try to show this.

To begin with the aesthetic, ethical, and religious stage, these are clearly not exhaustive but are mere projections of what were for Kierkegaard himself live options. When he discusses the religious stage he speaks of what tempts him, not of Calvinism, Catholicism, or Judaism. When he speaks of the ethical stage, he does not speak of Spinoza or the Stoics but of possibilities that mean a great deal to himself.

If a man decides to set himself a task—for example, to create works of art as Goethe did, or Sartre's hero at the end of *La Nausée*—does he leave the aesthetic stage and enter the ethical, seeing that the life of pleasure gives way to a committed life? Kierkegaard has no answer: he pontificates about marriage and suggests that the ethical stage is marriage. Again, to respect another person as another person and not merely as a character in one's own biography might be one important meaning of being an ethical person. But Kierkegaard fails to clarify the relation of this attitude to the phenomenon of commitment. In fact, he does not understand this attitude at all. For him the suffering of others is of concern only in so far as he himself is responsible for it or somehow the protagonist. He is that strange phenomenon, a solipsistic moralist.

Thus Kierkegaard can say of Abraham: "This is his comfort, for he says: 'But yet this will not come to pass, or, if it does come to pass, then the Lord will give me a new Isaac, by virtue viz. of the absurd'" (*Fear*, p. 124). Isaac is not recognized as an independent person. "What Kierkegaard overlooks completely is that Abraham might have prayed for Isaac; he might have seen this as Isaac's cause, as well as his own."[3] Similarly, the Regine for whom Kierkegaard wrote so many of his books was not the real Regine who actually read them—out loud to her husband. The real Regine had signally failed to play the role assigned to her: she had not allowed herself to be sacrificed but had promptly married another. And Kierkegaard did not rejoice in her happiness, as Kafka did in much the same situation; he felt hurt. In book after book he tried to explain himself and to pour gall into her happiness. She, however, used his accomplishments to impress her husband and to enjoy his respectful love that much more.

Agreeing with such other interpreters as Hirsch, Geismar, and Lowrie, Thomte maintains that "Kierkegaard presents only

[3] Marvin Fox, "Kierkegaard and Rabbinic Judaism," in *Judaism*, Apr., 1953.

one great choice: *Either* the aesthetic mode of life, whether it
be a life of pleasure, despair, or religious and metaphysical
contemplation, *or* the ethical mode of life . . . culminating in
Christianity" (p. 104). Or to cite Kierkegaard's own note "On
my literary work as a whole": "In one sense it is a question
put to the age, about a choice: they must choose either to make
aesthetics everything and so explain everything in that way,
or religion" (*Journals*, §991).

Kierkegaard constantly uses the word "aesthetics" when he
does not really mean aesthetics but a variety of other things,
including both art and an aesthetic, or a hedonistic, attitude
toward life. As for the content of the choice he poses: this
happens to be *his* problem; so he infers that it is *the* problem.

To evaluaté Kierkegaard's three stages we must go back to
Hegel's *Phenomenology of the Spirit*. In *The Mind of Kierkegaard* James Collins, a very scholarly and sympathetic Thomist
historian, remarks:

> The reader is liable to overlook the anti-Hegelian signifi-
> cance of certain points of agreement between the esthetic
> and ethical spokesmen [in Kierkegaard's works]. . . .
> They jointly satirize the marvelous objectivity of systematiz-
> ers, who are so concerned with the plight of others that
> they forget their own, who can dismiss the "unhappy con-
> sciousness" [in Hegel's *Phenomenology*] in a couple of dis-
> interested paragraphs and then pass on, just as unconcern-
> edly, to a disquisition on other equally impersonal topics
> [p. 113].

Actually, Hegel devotes to the "unhappy consciousness" more
than a dozen closely printed penetrating pages. He tries to
show that *Weltanschauungen* are not so many theories in
books on library shelves but correlates of the states of mind
of individuals. He considers them not contemporaneous but
stages in the development of the spirit like the Romanesque,
Gothic, Renaissance, and Baroque styles, or Storm and Stress,
Classicism, and Romanticism. Most individuals know only one
stage, while a Goethe traverses many as his passion impels him
to push each to its extreme and thus to discover its limitations
and go beyond it. The dialectic of Hegel's *Phenomenology* is

the logic of passion. And what Collins calls "the marvelous
objectivity of systematizers who are so concerned with the
plight of others that they forget their own" is in fact the attitude of a man who wants to transcend the provincialism of his
own immediate environment, who tries to educate his mind by
immersing it successively in different states of mind, and who
believes that this is an essential part of a training in philosophy.
A man so educated would hardly project himself into Isaac's
father, Abraham, and make so much of his suffering, without
ever giving a thought to the effect of his sacrifice on the boy's
mother.

Kierkegaard, on the other hand, is so concerned with his
own plight that he is willing to forget that of others. He accepts
Hegel's correlation of *Weltanschauungen* with states of mind
but gives up the conception of the many stages. He selects
three in terms of which he can discuss his own plight—roughly,
the "unhappy consciousness," one of the several ethical sections, and what Hegel calls "the spiritual animal kingdom"—
and embellishes them, alternating between urgency and anecdotes. The result is interesting but not a philosophical theory.

5

The one other point, finally, at which some would find a
philosophical theory is Kierkegaard's dictum, "truth is subjectivity" (*Postscript,* pp. 169 ff.). Yet this is not a theory but
a multiple confusion. Kierkegaard has in mind several different ideas.

His first and main point is that what makes a man a true
Christian is not so much correct belief as sincerity and devoutness. But even about this Kierkegaard is far from clear. In
places he approximates a broadly tolerant, nondogmatic, even
nondenominational attitude. But he is by no means prepared
to press his passing contrast between the insincere Christian
and the passionate pagan (pp. 179 f.). The only contrast he is
prepared to press is that between sincere and insincere Christians. This contrast involves no theory of truth at all. While
Kierkegaard thinks he is engaging the Hegelians on their own

plain, what he says is utterly incommensurate with Hegel's teaching. Hegel is a philosopher who tries to clarify concepts —but sometimes obfuscates them—while Kierkegaard wants to go to heaven and dogmatizes about the conditions one must meet to get there. He tells us in so many words that Hegel and the parsons and professors and most of his readers are excluded from the kingdom of heaven, which he himself hopes to enter (p. 20).

He presupposes the truth of Christianity and says in effect: we all believe these propositions to be true; the question is merely what attitude we should adopt toward them. Philosophy is entirely out of the picture: the choice is between sincerity and hypocrisy, black and white.

The second point that Kierkegaard injects into this discussion is an occasional confusion between subjective certainty and objective truth. "When one man investigates objectively the problem of immortality, and another embraces the uncertainty with the passion of the infinite: where is there most truth, and who has the greater certainty?" Kierkegaard further compounds this confusion by introducing Socrates and claiming—against both the *Phaedo* and the *Apology,* simply ignoring both—that Socrates neither offered proofs of the immortality of the soul nor was agnostic but staked his whole life on his faith in immortality. With a passionate disregard for objectivity Kierkegaard rewrites history in accordance with the requirements of his own inwardness. But even if he were right about Socrates, a martyr does not establish the truth of a proposition by dying for it. Yet Kierkegaard concludes: "Is any better proof capable of being given for the immortality of the soul?"

The third point with which Kierkegaard confuses the issue is a psychological observation that diverts the uncritical reader and gives him the feeling that here at last is a thinker worth reading:

A young girl may enjoy all the sweetness of love on the basis of what is merely a weak hope that she is beloved, because she rests everything on this weak hope; but many a wedded matron, more than once subjected to the strongest expres-

sions of love, has insofar indeed had proofs, but strangely
enough has not enjoyed *quod erat demonstrandum.*

Surely, the relative bliss of the two women does not tell us
which of them is really loved. The moral of the story is not
that "truth is subjectivity" but that, as Nietzsche says, for
some people—not for Nietzsche himself—

> it is a matter of complete indifference whether something is
> true, while it is of the utmost importance whether it is be-
> lieved to be true. Truth and *faith* that something is true:
> two completely separate realms of interest—almost diametri-
> cally opposite realms—they are reached by utterly different
> paths [*Antichrist*, §23].

The fourth point that Kierkegaard seems to have in mind is
brought out by James Collins when he says that Kierkegaard's
position is "an indirect protest against the Hegelian pretensions
to serve up all truth in an objective, cut-and-dried way. He
contended strongly that truth is no finished product, which
can be handed over the counter of philosophy, quite impersonally and effortlessly" (p. 39). This alleged protest against
Hegel comes straight out of Hegel, who says in the Preface to
the *Phenomenology:* "Truth is not a minted coin that can be
handed over and accepted as a finished thing." And Hegel specifically castigates that "dogmatism" which insists "that truth
consists in a sentence which represents a fixed result." And in
an early essay, Hegel remarks sarcastically that every church
claims that nothing is

> as easy as finding the truth; one only has to memorize one
> of its catechisms. And it does not accept that
>
> > Only seriousness paled by no toil
> > Finds the deeply hidden fount of truth.

The church holds open market with it; the river of churchly
truth roars noisily through every street, and everybody can
fill his brains with its water [cf. chapter 8 above, section 9].

What does Kierkegaard add to this? Only confusion. He accepts Hegel's point that simple propositions are not enough.

But where Hegel adds that what is wanted is analysis, or what he sometimes calls differentiation or mediation or comprehension, Kierkegaard calls for passion. "What our age lacks," he says, "is not reflection but passion." That certainly is not true today; and even in the nineteenth century Nietzsche was surely far more right in calling for more passion and more reflection too. He avoided the egregious blunder of Kierkegaard, who wrote: "The conclusions of passion are the only reliable ones, that is, the only convincing conclusions" (*Fear*, pp. 53, 109).

Confronted with belief in a proposition, Hegel, as a philosopher, asks: what does it mean? Kierkegaard, as a moralist, asks: are you willing to die for it? And he adds misleadingly that if you are the proposition is subjectively true; sometimes he even leaves out the word "subjectively" and gives the impression that passion is a proof of propositional truth. In fact, however, my attitude proves nothing about my proposition, only something about me.

In this connection it should be noted that Hegel's formulation that "truth is not a minted coin" comes from Lessing's *Nathan* (Act III, scene 6), the work most frequently cited by the young Hegel. Early in his *Postscript* Kierkegaard devotes two enthusiastic chapters to another of Lessing's remarks about truth and assumes that in Lessing he has found the antipodes of Hegel, though in fact Hegel had absorbed the lessons of Lessing.

Indeed, in his early essays Hegel expressly rated "subjective religion" above "objective religion" (cf. chapter 8, section 3, above). Later, to be sure, he recognized three realms of the spirit—in this order: Subjective, Objective, and Absolute Spirit.

It is noteworthy that Lessing's position, like Hegel's, was free of Kierkegaard's confusions and, of course, was by no means anticritical. On the contrary. Lessing had written in the preface to *Wie die Alten den Tod gebildet:* "It may be that the truth has never yet been determined through a dispute: nevertheless, the truth has gained from every dispute. The dispute has nourished the spirit of examination." And directly before saying that if he had to choose between all the truth in God's right hand and the ever live striving for truth, coupled

with eternal error, in God's left, he would choose the latter
—the dictum Kierkegaard so admired—Lessing explained very
clearly indeed:

> Not the truth in whose possession any man is, or thinks he
> is, but the honest effort he has made to find out the truth,
> is what constitutes the worth of man. For it is not through
> the possession but through the inquiry after truth that his
> powers expand, and in this alone consists his ever growing
> perfection [*Duplik*].

Lessing distinguished very sharply between what constitutes
the truth of a proposition and what constitutes the worth of a
human being; he believed that a man could be wrong about
many things and yet a worthier man than another who was
right; and he realized that this attitude was incompatible
with any Christian orthodoxy, let alone Kierkegaard's belief
that doubt is really insubordination, and critical thinking
blasphemy.

As Kierkegaard's argument progresses, the confusion mounts.
To show that truth is subjectivity he distinguishes *what* is said
from *how* it is said, and then proceeds:

> At its maximum this inward "how" is the passion of the in-
> finite, and the passion of the infinite is the truth. [Surely,
> this is wrong and begs the question.] But the passion of the
> infinite is precisely subjectivity, and thus subjectivity be-
> comes the truth. Objectively there is no infinite decisiveness,
> and hence it is objectively in order to annul the difference
> between good and evil, together with the principle of con-
> tradiction [why?], and therewith also the infinite difference
> between the true and the false. [Why?] Only in subjectivity
> is there decisiveness, to seek objectivity is to be in error.
> [Why?] It is the passion of the infinite that is the decisive
> factor and not its content, for its content is precisely itself.
> [??] In this manner subjectivity and the subjective "how"
> constitute the truth [p. 181].

Confronted with this dazzling demonstration, the general
reader will perhaps assume that his intelligence is at fault,
while at least one apologist has explained a similar passage

thus: "Here we have S.K., almost with tongue in cheek, expressing himself with great precision in the terminology of that Hegelianism which he hated above all else" (Bretall, p. 340). Hegel is certainly often very difficult, but I think every serious student of Hegel would admit that he did not write this kind of thing. It may be more to the point to remember that Kierkegaard was then thirty-two years old—and made no secret of his contempt for philosophy.

In the passage cited Kierkegaard argues that the content of the infinite passion is "precisely itself." He requires eight more pages to show that "the absurd is the object of faith, and the only object that can be believed," and another five pages to establish that the dogmas of Christianity are so absurd that they alone can be believed: "That God has existed in human form, has been born, grown up, and so forth, is surely the paradox *sensu strictissimo*, the absolute paradox."

Kierkegaard argues that Christianity must be believed because (1) nothing could be more absurd and (2) the greatest passion and sincerity can be developed in believing what one knows to be absurd. The second premise is obviously false, at least as far as sincerity is concerned; and, as for the first, the suggestion that Nero was God incarnate seems much more absurd than the same claim regarding Jesus; some portions of the Koran are perhaps more absurd than at least some Christian beliefs; and so forth.

Kierkegaard here invites comparison with William James at his worst, in the famous essay on "The Will to Believe" where James argues with great rhetorical skill that a man who gives up his childhood beliefs because they might be wrong is like "a general informing his soldiers that it is better to keep out of battle forever than to risk a single wound," while the man who accepts a belief that tempts him is heroic because he takes a risk. But Kierkegaard, of course, was conscious of the humor in his claim that nothing could be more absurd than what one has always believed—and that precisely for this reason nothing could be believed with greater passion.

I have argued against Kierkegaard as a stylist, a religious writer, a psychologist, and a philosopher. Neither does he compare with the great masters of satire, and his humor, finally,

is the indecisive humor of the romantic who is not quite sure
of himself (remember his many pseudonyms, too) and, to permit himself a saving ambiguity, writes, to cite Bretall's happy
phrase once more, "almost with tongue in cheek."

Thus spoke Brother Brash.

Brother Brash's "expectoration" is indeed emphatically "preliminary" in at least two ways. First, as suggested at the outset, it reflects the vexation that should precede appropriation.
To "appreciate" Kierkegaard is to betray him. He wants to be
confronted, existing individual against existing individual. And
secondly, Brother Brash may be considered the devil's advocate. The devil's advocate, of course, was originally an official
appointed by the church to marshal all relevant objections
before a person was canonized. Today many would canonize
Kierkegaard as a philosopher. It is in the face of these attempts that Brother Brash has done his job. The prosecution
rests.

Brother Brash must be answered. But if even the objections
had to be presented in a somewhat abrupt condensation, how
much more does the same consideration apply to any possible
defense, seeing that criticism is always easier! Hence the reply,
too, ought to be entrusted to a pseudonym; for it cannot get
beyond a point of view; it cannot be formulated as an assured
result, at least not short of a vastly more comprehensive discussion.

"KIERKEGAARD'S SIGNIFICANCE"
By Brother Brief

Brother Brash may upset many of Kierkegaard's admirers,
but Kierkegaard himself might well have been far more dis-
turbed by those who disagree with Brash. The right defense
should not rebut the strictures here assembled but should accept them and insist that they tell only half the story. However Kierkegaard overestimated his achievements as a stylist, a
religious writer in the sense discussed by Brother Brash, a psychologist, and a philosopher, it was clearly not his primary
ambition to win fame in any of these categories, let alone to
earn a place in histories of philosophy. His central category

was that of the individual—as a category that cracks all other categories. "If I were to desire an inscription for my tombstone, I should desire none other than 'That Individual'" (*Point*, p. 131). And an individual he certainly was like scarcely any other writer in world literature.

Here lies his first achievement. Outstanding stylists, after all, are far more common than outstanding individuals who represent a new kind of humanity, like Socrates or Goethe (see chapter 4 above). Such men are easy to admire from a distance, but their contemporaries are rarely comfortable in their presence. As soon as we come close enough, we, too, are apt to feel this discomfort. We are confronted with disturbing possibilities—and usually withdraw into an attitude of cultured appreciation. Without equaling the stature of Socrates or Goethe, Kierkegaard belongs with this small group of men who do not readily fit into our schemes of classification because they explode traditional norms. Lacking the safe barrier of centuries, most readers try to gain a comfortable distance by focusing attention on his style or theories in order to lose sight, if possible, of *him*.

Those who are willing to concentrate on the individual usually try to get away from his individuality by treating the person as a case, psychologically. One can go much further in that direction than Brother Brash. A single long passage from Kierkegaard's *Journals* (§413), will at once suggest what possibilities there are, for the story is clearly autobiographical:

His home did not offer many diversions, and as he almost never went out, he early grew accustomed to occupying himself with his own thoughts. His father was a very severe man, apparently dry and prosaic, but under his frieze coat he concealed a glowing imagination which even old age could not dim. When occasionally Johannes asked his permission to go out, he generally refused to give it, though once in a while he proposed instead that Johannes should take his hand and walk up and down the room. . . . It was left entirely to Johannes to determine where they should go. So they went out of doors to a nearby castle in Spain, or out to the seashore, or about the streets, wherever Johannes

wished to go, for his father was equal to anything. While
they went up and down the room his father described all
that they saw; they greeted passers-by, carriages rattled past
them and drowned his father's voice. . . . He described so
accurately, so vividly, so explicitly even to the last details
. . . that after half an hour of such a walk with his father
he was as much overwhelmed and fatigued as if he had
been a whole day out of doors. Johannes soon learned from
his father how to exercise this magic power. . . . The father's almighty imagination was capable of shaping everything. . . . To Johannes it seemed as if the world were
coming into existence during the conversation, as if his father were our Lord and he were his favourite. . . . While
thus there was being developed in him an almost vegetative
tendency to drowse in imagination, which was in part
aesthetic, in part more intellectual, another side of his soul
was being strongly shaped, namely, his sense for the sudden,
the surprising. . . . His father combined an irresistible dialectic with an almighty imagination. . . . When Johannes
grew older he had no toys to lay aside, for he had learned
to play with that which was to be the serious business of
his life. . . .

This one passage throws more light than most articles on
Kierkegaard's personality and style, his relation to his father
and his notion of God, his dread of marriage and his inability
to understand Genesis, and his insistence on treating Regine
and the clergy, Abraham and Antigone as so many figures in
his own biography. Those who want to talk or write about
Fear and Trembling without ever exposing themselves to its
challenge should find ample material here.

Suppose, however, we ask for once not what we can do with
Kierkegaard but, rather, what he might do to us. As soon as
we consider his style, his religious writings, his psychology, and
his philosophic efforts from the point of view of that which
mattered most to Kierkegaard himself, Brother Brash's objections are seen to be of limited relevance.

In spite of his many pseudonyms, Kierkegaard never disappears behind his work like Plato, Shakespeare, or Hegel. But

any such self-effacing attitude appears immoral to Kierkegaard. He may not have understood the seriousness of which
this attitude may be born, and it was certainly presumptuous,
if not sanctimonious, of him to arrogate such terms as "ethical"
and "religious" almost as if they were his monopoly. But from
his own point of view, his preoccupation with himself was not
an all too human failing but the one thing needful.

His style, however aggravating, is a splendid medium for
his purpose. With its epic digressions and its urgency, and
even with its philosophic acrobatics, dancing on the tightrope
between seriousness and satire, Kierkegaard's prose never permits us to lose ourselves in a story or an argument: we are
constantly confronted with the author's individuality—and are
made to think about our own.

His psychology is a vortex psychology that draws us into
self-reflection against our will and never permits us to rest content with impersonal results. He makes us aware not of facts
but of decisions that we have made and that we might make.
He forces on us not answers but questions. He abolishes the
untenable analogy of the self with an object or a brute fact
that is given and solid and replaces it with an awareness of
possibilities.

His relation to philosophy is best expressed by changing one
small word in Marx's famous dictum: "The philosophers have
merely interpreted the world differently, but what matters is
to change"—not "it," as Marx said, but ourselves.

His central idea is that Christendom has forgotten the core
of Christianity—to change our hearts—and that philosophy, by
no means only Hegel's, has aided and abetted Christendom in
this betrayal. Brother Brash's critique does not eliminate the
possibility that Kierkegaard came closer to the heart of original
Christianity than Hegel and Aquinas, Schleiermacher and
Harnack, and the whole of liberal Protestantism. Perhaps Kierkegaard understood the differentia of Christianity better than
those who have given up almost everything that originally,
and for centuries, distinguished Christianity, while assimilating
their religion to the outlook of non-Christians.

If liberal Protestantism were right about "the essence of
Christianity"—to use Harnack's phrase—then the evangelists

betrayed Jesus and Christianity almost as much as Paul, and Luther and Calvin no less than the Roman Catholic and Greek Orthodox churches. Indeed, some of the most outstanding liberal Protestant scholars, notably Albert Schweitzer, find the conclusion inescapable that Jesus himself failed to represent the essentials of Christianity—that is, of what Schweitzer and others take to be the essentials. In effect, they find the essence of Christianity in the moral teachings of the Hebrew prophets and their passionate concern with social justice, which Schweitzer and others wistfully admit is absent from the New Testament and formed no part of Jesus' teaching. Even those who prefer Schweitzer's dedication to his social and ethical conception of the kingdom to Kierkegaard's preoccupation with himself cannot brush aside the question whether Schweitzer is not closer to the outlook of the prophets while Kierkegaard is closer to the spirit of the New Testament. More than any other writer, Kierkegaard confronts us with the question: what does it mean to be a Christian? And he does not permit us any permanent escape into history or philology. He presses us for a decision, one way or the other.

At this point his significance is not restricted to Christianity. He sees that religion without intensity is almost a contradiction in terms. Perhaps one might wish that he himself had said this more clearly; but an epigram would be a foothold in the vortex of his prose and might help us to escape from his demands. As it is, his challenge to his readers, especially to those who claim to be religious, is unmistakable.

Essentially, then, Kierkegaard is a moralist with a rare power to upset—a moralist in a perfectly recognizable sense, though one would be at a loss to find anyone else in quite the same genre. One can hardly be satisfied with him or pleased; but his greatest value may well be that he does not allow us to be satisfied or pleased with ourselves.

His philosophic significance is less clear. Brother Brash compared Kierkegaard with Hegel, very much to Hegel's advantage. But do different outlooks really correspond to different stages of maturity, as Hegel argued? Surely, Hegel's dialectical "deductions" of these outlooks often lack all plausibility, and we cannot write off the religions of ancient Asia as Christianity in embryo. Kierkegaard insists that we cannot escape a decision between contemporaneous possibilities. He flies in the face of all attempts to establish Christianity as the end product of a world-wide development or progressive revelation. He challenges every endeavor to establish the Christian ethic, or more likely one's own—whether one parades it under this name or not—on the basis of any form whatever of intuitionism, Kantianism, or utilitarianism. It is the necessity of decision—the central theme of Deuteronomy and the prophets that was rediscovered by Milton in his *Areopagitica* as the great antithesis of every form of Platonism—that Kierkegaard, another anti-Plato, calls to the attention of philosophers.

Perhaps Nietzsche sometimes made the same point even clearer. I recall Zarathustra's words "On Those Who Are Sublime": "You tell me, friends, that there is no disputing of tastes and tasting? But all of life is a dispute over tastes and tasting." But where Hegel had sought to reduce basic differences to different degrees of maturity, Nietzsche correlated them with more or less power; this solution of the problem of decision distracts from the problem itself: indeed, most readers do not understand Nietzsche's solution because they do not see the problem.

I am ready to summarize Kierkegaard's possible importance for philosophy in terms of a few closely related points. First, his vortex psychology with its radical revision of the popular conception of the self has led, and may yet lead, to new ways of understanding man. Secondly, Christianity has so profoundly influenced Western philosophy, especially ethics and metaphysics, that a man who changes previously accepted notions of Christianity is almost bound to affect philosophical discussion, particularly in these two fields. The works of Jaspers, Heidegger, and Sartre bear witness to both points; but Kierkegaard's impulse may yet lead other philosophers into different directions. Thirdly, Kierkegaard, together with Nietzsche, confronts us with the problem of decision, which has been consistently avoided in almost every ethic, not to speak of metaphysics, throughout the history of Western philosophy. That both men are forerunners of existentialism is well known; that Kierkegaard, like Nietzsche, is at this point close to modern positivism, too, is hardly ever recognized: if it were, there might be more hope of some *rapprochement* between these two great revolts against traditional philosophy.

Hegel needs to be defended against his detractors; Kierkegaard, against his admirers. Many of those who praise Kierkegaard are much closer to Hegel than to him.

Hegel was no totalitarian. Like most American secondary school teachers, he did not define freedom as nonconformity but taught his students that their society was the freest in history. He acknowledged that world-historic individuals come into conflict with the morality of their day, but emphasized that they succeed in changing the morality of later ages. Kierkegaard was wrong in saying, as he often did, that Hegel's system has no moral implications. It does: we ought to absorb the ethic of our society, conform, and find our station and fulfill its duties. Hegel admits that history is not a tale of happiness but "the slaughterhouse in which the happiness of nations, the wisdom of states, and the virtue of individuals have been sacrificed"; but he trusts that such great sacrifices serve a purpose, that there is more freedom in the modern world than in the past, and that freedom cannot fail to grow.

Kierkegaard takes no pride in the progress of freedom or science. Modern man's achievements, far from solving our basic problems, are distractions. All men, except true Christians—if there be any—are in despair. Kierkegaard comes nowhere near substantiating his claim that only Christian faith can save us from despair. To meet the further objection that it makes no sense to say that a man is in despair but does not know it, one can redefine despair, as Kierkegaard does, to mean a wrong relationship to God. At that point, Kierkegaard's thesis will cease to be interesting to most readers. But there is another suggestion in *The Sickness unto Death:* despair is also defined as a wrong relation to oneself. Kierkegaard claims that almost all men try to escape from themselves. And our station and its duties, science and philosophy, social activities and the churches, too, help us to run away from ourselves.

In philosophy we discuss all kinds of problems, except our personal problems. And the churches, far from preaching solitude and urging men to stand alone, promote community activities, togetherness, and all sorts of diversions. The increase in church attendance after World War II and the so-called revival of religion would have sickened Kierkegaard no less than the Hebrew prophets.

He was authoritarian. He reminds us that almost all of the great Christians were authoritarian. But he was also a voice crying in the wilderness, telling each of us to leave father and mother, instead of saying like the false prophets: "The family that prays together stays together."

Those who would credit Kierkegaard with a theory or partial, but imperfect, formulations of ideas that were better formulated by Aquinas may well underestimate their man. Against all such endeavors, and many more, Brother Brash's critique may stand; but it does not do justice to Søren Kierkegaard, "that individual."

Thus spoke Brother Brief.

I I

HOW NIETZSCHE
REVOLUTIONIZED ETHICS

In the development from Shakespeare to existentialism no figure is more important than Nietzsche. Compared with him, Kierkegaard seems narrow for all his intensity, and few other writers of any age equal his fusion of scope and passion, of range and depth. In this respect there is something Shakespearean about Nietzsche, although his often strident polemical tone leaves no doubt about the differences between the two men.

More often than most great writers, Nietzsche has been seen in the perspective of his relation to some specific man or movement: at one time it was evolutionism; at another, Nazism; and, after the defeat of Hitler, existentialism. But no one approach of this kind is at all adequate to bring out that experience of the world on which Nietzsche's philosophy was based. To that end, it would be more fruitful to juxtapose Nietzsche with a great poet—and this will be done in the next two chapters. The danger of that approach is that it may be too aesthetic and may fail to do justice to the bite of Nietzsche's thought. Before we develop Nietzsche's continuity with a great tradition, we ought to ask ourselves in what way he revolutionized thought. And if a single field must be chosen to give at least some idea of the break that Nietzsche brought about, ethics is the best choice. Indirectly, this discussion should also illuminate his relation to the Nazis and the existentialists.

Nietzsche's ideas about ethics are far less well known than some of his striking coinages: immoralist, overman, master morality, slave morality, beyond good and evil, will to power, revaluation of all values, and philosophizing with a hammer. These are indeed among his key conceptions, but they can be understood correctly only in context. This is true of philosophic terms generally: Plato's ideas or forms, Spinoza's God, Berkeley's ideas, and Kant's intuition all do not mean what they would mean in a nonphilosophic context; but scarcely anybody supposes that they do. In Nietzsche's case, however, this mistake is a commonplace—surely because few other philosophers, if any, have equaled the brilliance and suggestiveness of his formulations. His phrases, once heard, are never forgotten; they stand up by themselves, without requiring the support of any context; and so they have come to live independently of their sire's intentions. In this chapter an attempt will be made to sketch the context from which Nietzsche's central conceptions derive their meaning.

2

Nietzsche revolutionized ethics by asking new questions. As he saw it, his predecessors had simply taken for granted that they knew what was good and what was evil. Moral judgments had been accepted as incontrovertible facts, and the philosophers had considered it their task to find reasons for them. In other words, traditional moral philosophers made it their business to rationalize the moral idiosyncrasies of their environment. What F. H. Bradley was to say of metaphysics in his Preface to *Appearance and Reality* (1891) is what Nietzsche said in effect of traditional ethics: it is "the finding of bad reasons for what we believe on instinct." But Nietzsche would not have added like Bradley that "to find these reasons is no less an instinct." Nor, indeed, did he consider moral idiosyncrasies instinctive in any literal sense. Far from construing them as part of our biological make-up, Nietzsche was struck by the great variety of moral views in different times and places.

To cite Nietzsche's *Zarathustra* ("On Old and New Tablets," §2): "When I came to men I found them sitting on an old conceit: the conceit that they have long known what is good and evil for man. All talk of virtue seemed an old and weary matter to man; and whoever wanted to sleep well still talked of good and evil before going to sleep." With Nietzsche, our common moral valuations are suddenly considered questionable, and ethics, instead of being a matter of inconsequential rationalizations, becomes a critique of culture, a vivisection of modern man.

In *Beyond Good and Evil* (§186) Nietzsche presents the other side of the coin: in a sense, his undertaking is more modest than that of his predecessors.

One should own up in all strictness what is still necessary here for a long time to come, what alone is justified so far: to collect material, to conceptualize and arrange a vast realm of subtle feelings of value and differences of value which are alive, grow, beget, and perish—and perhaps attempts to present vividly some of the more frequent and recurring forms of such living crystallizations—all to prepare a *typology* of morals. To be sure: so far one has not been so modest. With a stiff seriousness that inspires laughter, all our philosophers demanded something far more exalted, presumptuous, and solemn from themselves as soon as they approached the study of morality: they wanted to supply a *rational foundation* for morals; and every philosopher so far has believed that he has provided such a foundation. Morality itself, however, was accepted as "given." How remote from their coarse pride was that task which they considered insignificant and left in dust and dirt—the task of description, although the subtlest fingers and senses can scarcely be subtle enough for it. Because our moral philosophers knew the facts of morality only very approximately in arbitrary extracts or in accidental epitomes—for example, as the morality of their environment, their class, their church, their time, their climate and part of the world—because they were poorly informed and not even very curious about different peoples, ages, and the past, they never laid eyes on the real problems of morality; for these emerge only when we compare *many* moralities. In all previous studies of morality one thing was lacking, strange as that may sound: the problem of morality itself; what was lacking was the suspicion that there was anything at all problematic here. What the philosophers called "a rational foundation for morality" and tried to supply was, properly considered, only a scholarly variation of a common *faith* in the prevalent morality; a new means of *expression* of this faith; in short, itself simply another feature of, or rather another fact within, a particular morality; indeed, in the last analysis, a kind of denial that this morality might ever be considered problematic—certainly the very opposite of an examination, analysis, questioning, and vivisection of this very faith.

Nietzsche is prepared to press two new questions. How does our prevalent morality compare with other moralities? And what can be said about morality in general? To begin with the first question, the morality of his society does not strike Nietzsche as divine or as supremely venerable; and he has no wish, any more than Freud a quarter of a century later, to defend its surpassing wisdom. On the contrary, he finds it far from admirable in many respects and in some ways quite contemptible in comparison with other moralities, developed elsewhere.

We have quoted Nietzsche's demand for "attempts to present vividly some of the more frequent and recurring forms . . . to prepare a *typology* of morals." Later, in *Beyond Good and Evil* (§260), he suggests two types:

Wandering through the many subtler and coarser moralities which have so far been prevalent on earth, or still are prevalent, I found that certain features recurred regularly together and were closely associated—until I finally discovered two basic types and one basic difference. There is *master morality* and *slave morality.* I add immediately that in all the higher and more mixed cultures there also appear attempts at mediation between these two moralities, and yet more often the interpenetration and mutual misunderstanding of both, and at times they occur directly alongside of each other—even in the same human being, within a single soul. The moral discrimination of values has originated either among a ruling group whose consciousness of their difference from the ruled group was accompanied by delight—or among the ruled group, the slaves and the dependent of all degrees. In the first case, when the ruling group determines what is "good," the exalted, proud states of the soul are experienced as conferring distinction and determining the order of rank. The noble man separates from himself those in whom the opposite of such exalted, proud states finds expression: he despises them. It should be noted immediately that in this first type of morality the opposition of "good" and "*bad*" means about the same as "noble" and "contemptible." (The opposition of "good" and "*evil*" has a different origin.) One feels contempt for the cowardly, the anxious, the petty, those who are intent on narrow utility; also for the mistrustful with their unfree glances, those who humble themselves, the doglike people who allow themselves to be maltreated, the begging flatterers, above all the liars: it is part of the fundamental faith of all aristocrats that the common people lie. "We truthful ones"—thus the nobility in ancient Greece referred to itself. It is plain that moral designations were everywhere first applied to *human beings* and only later, derivatively, to actions. Therefore it is a gross mistake when historians of morality start out from such questions as: why was the compassionate action praised? The noble kind of man experiences *itself* as determining values. . . . Such a morality is self-glorification. In the foreground there is the feeling of fullness, of power that wants to overflow, the happiness of high tension, the consciousness of wealth which would give and bestow. The noble man, too, helps the unfortunate, but not, or almost not, out of pity, but more prompted by an urge which is begotten by the excess of power. The noble man honors himself as one who is powerful—also one who has power over himself, who knows how to speak and be silent, who delights in being severe and hard with himself and respects all severity and hardness.

This contrast of the two types is elaborated in the first of the three inquiries that constitute Nietzsche's next book, *Toward a Genealogy of Morals*. The first chapter is entitled "Good and Evil versus Good and Bad." Here Nietzsche attempts a detailed portrait of slave morality, which contrasts

not good and bad but good and evil. Slave morality, he suggests (§10), is created by

> the *ressentiment* of those who are denied the real reaction,
> that of the deed, and who compensate with an imaginary
> revenge. Whereas all noble morality grows out of a trium-
> phant affirmation of oneself, slave morality immediately says
> No to what comes from outside, to what is different, to
> what is not oneself: and this No is its creative deed. This
> reversal of the value-positing glance—this *necessary* direc-
> tion outward instead of back to oneself—is of the nature of
> *ressentiment:* to come into being, slave morality requires an
> outside world, a counterworld.

The noble morality begins with self-affirmation, "and its
negative concept, 'base,' 'mean,' 'bad,' is only an after-born,
pale, contrasting image." Slave morality, on the other hand,
begins with a negation; and its positive ideals are afterthoughts, contrasts to what is hated.

Misconceptions about Nietzsche's two types are legion, and
they shall not be catalogued here. But another passage from
the section just cited may dispel some of them: nobility precludes resentment.

> To be unable to take one's own enemies, accidents, and mis-
> deeds seriously for long—that is the sign of strong and rich
> natures. . . . Such a man simply shakes off with one shrug
> much vermin that would have buried itself deep in others;
> here alone it is also possible—assuming that it is possible at
> all on earth—that there be real *"love* of one's enemies." How
> much respect has a noble person for his enemies! And such
> respect is already a bridge to love. After all, he demands
> his enemy for himself, as his distinction; he can stand no
> enemy but one in whom there is nothing to be despised and
> *much* to be honored. Conversely, imagine "the enemy" as
> conceived by a man of *ressentiment*—and here precisely is
> his deed, his creation: he has conceived "the evil enemy,"
> *"the evil one"*—and indeed as the fundamental concept from
> which he then derives, as an afterimage and counterinstance,
> a "good one"—himself.

We are now ready to understand the phrase "beyond good and evil." The first chapter of the *Genealogy* ends: "*Beyond Good and Evil*—at least this does *not* mean 'Beyond Good and Bad.'" Nietzsche associates the contrast of good and *evil* with the morality of resentment; and the suggestion that we might go "beyond good and evil" invites comparison with Zarathustra's challenge in the chapter "On the Virtuous": "you are too *pure* for the filth of the words: revenge, punishment, reward, retribution." The same chapter contains a typology of different conceptions of virtue with vivisectional intent. The conception of resentment as the source of many moral judgments is one of Nietzsche's central themes. A powerful early statement will be found in *The Dawn* (§202); and in *Zarathustra* the theme is developed in the chapters "On the Adder's Bite," "On the Pitying," "On the Tarantulas" ("For *that man be delivered from revenge*, that is for me the bridge to the highest hope"), and "On Redemption."

Nietzsche presents master and slave morality as two types without claiming that every morality must represent either one or the other; and least of all does he claim, as is often supposed, that every man is either a master or a slave. When he speaks of these two types, he uses the words master and slave in a fairly literal manner to suggest that moral judgments will differ, depending on whether they were developed among men who ruled or men who were oppressed. And immediately after first introducing the terms he adds, as we have seen, "that in all the higher and more mixed cultures" the two types interpenetrate, and moral views derived from both strains may be encountered in the same person. Here he is of course referring to our own culture. And he devoted much effort to pointing up the inconsistencies in our moral judgments; and particularly he sought to uncover the ways in which the Christian virtues were molded by the resentment of the oppressed classes among which Christianity first made headway.

What Nietzsche opposed in Christian morality was not, as is often claimed, a humane attitude. On the contrary, what he opposed were such features as these: resentment, an antagonism against excellence, a predisposition in favor of mediocrity or even downright baseness, a leveling tendency, the conviction that sex is sinful, a devaluation of both body and intellect in favor of the soul, and the devaluation of this whole world in favor of another. In the end, he suggests that all these traits are rooted in resentment.

3

"How one philosophizes with a hammer" is the subtitle of one of Nietzsche's last works, *The Twilight of the Idols,* and he explains in the preface what he means: he speaks of idols "which are here touched with a hammer as with a tuning fork"; and instead of crushing the idols he speaks of hearing "as a reply that famous hollow sound which speaks of bloated entrails." The book was originally to bear the title "A Psychologist's Idleness," and Nietzsche's instrument is clearly the little hammer of the psychologist, not a sledge.

It is similar with the "revaluation of all values." Nietzsche does not arbitrarily invert our traditional valuations but tries to show, by an act of internal criticism, how the moral judgments of Christianity are born of resentment and how Christian morality, being profoundly hateful, must be condemned by its own professed standards.

Beyond that, Nietzsche pictures Christianity as the "revaluation of all the values of antiquity" (*Beyond Good and Evil,* §46). He claims that the Christians turned the embodiment of classical morality into the prototype of evil. He has in mind not only the Christian revaluation of pride, physical excellence, and sex but also such passages as this one from the first chapter of Paul's First Epistle to the Corinthians, which Nietzsche cites in his *Antichrist* (§45): "God hath chosen the foolish things of the world to ruin the wise; and God hath chosen the weak things of the world to ruin what is strong; and base things of the world, and things which are despised, hath God chosen, yea, and what is nothing, to bring to nought what is something." Far from seeing himself as a wayward iconoclast who turns upside down the whole Western tradition in morals, Nietzsche claims that Christianity stood classical morality on its head.

While the epithets "master morality" and "slave morality"

are intended, first of all, to be descriptive and to refer to origins, Nietzsche's contrast is, of course, hortatory too. He wants
to wean us from those elements in our moral heritage that are
characteristic of slave morality. But two points should be
noted. First, Nietzsche's analyses do not stand or fall with his
preferences, any more than his preferences stand or fall with
his analyses. And, secondly, his typology does not by any
means commit him to any unreserved acceptance, let alone
glorification, of master morality. In the chapter on "The 'Im-
provers' of Mankind" in *Twilight of the Idols,* Nietzsche discusses the Indian "law of Manu" as an example of master morality and leaves no doubt whatever about his own reaction
to Manu's inhumane treatment of the outcastes, the chandalas:
"These regulations are instructive enough: here we encounter
for once *Aryan* humanity, quite pure, quite primordial—we
learn that the concept of 'pure blood' is the opposite of a harm-
less concept."

4

This brief account may give some indication of Nietzsche's
answer to his own question of how our prevalent morality compares with other moralities. There remains the question: What
can be said about morality in general? If we do not accept
morality as simply given, and if we acknowledge that there
are many different moralities, what can we make of this whole
phenomenon of morality? There are two sections in *Beyond
Good and Evil* (188 and 198) that offer interesting suggestions in answer to this question.

Every morality is, as opposed to *laisser aller,* a bit of tyranny
against "nature"; also against "reason"; but this in itself is
no objection, as long as we do not have some other morality
which permits us to decree that every kind of tyranny and
unreason is impermissible. What is essential and inestima-
ble in every morality is that it constitutes a long compulsion:
to understand Stoicism or Port Royal or Puritanism, one
should recall the compulsion under which every language

so far has achieved strength and freedom—the metrical compulsion of rhyme and rhythm.

Nietzsche goes on to point out how all "freedom, subtlety,
boldness" require discipline; and without discipline we should
not have the achievements "for whose sake life on earth is
worthwhile; for example, virtue, art, music, dance, reason,
spirituality." Nietzsche concludes this section (188):

> "Thou shalt obey someone, and for a long time; else thou
> wilt perish and lose the last respect for yourself"—this ap-
> pears to me to be the moral imperative of nature which,
> however, is neither "categorical" as the old Kant would have
> it (hence the "else") nor addressed to the individual (what
> do individuals matter?), but to peoples, races, ages, classes
> —but above all to the human animal, to *man*.

In the other section (198) it is suggested that every morality that addresses itself to the individual is really a prescription for living with one's passions. Nietzsche tries to show
this in the cases of Stoicism, Spinoza, Aristotle, and Goethe,
and claims that these moralities are "without exception baroque and unreasonable in form—because they are addressed
to 'all' and generalize where generalizations are impermissible." Interpreted conditionally and taken with a grain of salt,
they contain a good deal of wisdom, but no moral code can
be unconditionally applied to all men.

5

The type that Nietzsche himself most admires is by no
means his own invention. He resembles Socrates and the great-
souled man of Aristotle's *Nicomachean Ethics* (IV, 3) as well
as Shakespeare's ninety-fourth sonnet and these lines from
Measure for Measure: "O, it is excellent/To have a giant's
strength; but it is tyrannous/To use it like a giant." To cite
Zarathustra ("On Those Who Are Sublime"): "There is nobody from whom I want beauty as much as from you who are
powerful: let your kindness be your final self-conquest. Of all
evil I deem you capable: therefore I want the good from you.

Verily, I have often laughed at the weaklings who thought themselves good because they had no claws" (cf. chapter 1 above).

The highest type, to Nietzsche's mind, is the passionate man who is the master of his passions, able to employ them creatively without having to resort to asceticism for fear that his passions might conquer him. But not everybody is capable of this achievement, and Nietzsche does not believe in the possibility of a universal morality. He prefers self-control and sublimation to both license and asceticism, but concedes that for some asceticism may be necessary. Those who require such a radical prescription strike him as weaker, less powerful types than men like Goethe, for example.

The will to power is, according to Nietzsche, a universal drive, found in all men. It prompts the slave who dreams of a heaven from which he hopes to behold his master in hell no less than it prompts the master. Both resentment and brutality, both sadism and asceticism are expressions of it. Indeed, Nietzsche thinks that all human behavior is reducible to this single basic force. He does not endorse the will to power any more than Freud endorses sexual desire; but he thinks we shall be better off if we face the facts and understand ourselves than if we condemn others hypocritically, without understanding.

The overman, finally, is not what Nietzsche expects from the evolutionary process (he himself rejected this misinterpretation unequivocally) but the image and incarnation of the accomplishment of man's striving. Instead of placing perfection either above the clouds or in the past, nineteen centuries ago, and instead of asking man to adore a perfection of which he is constitutionally incapable, Nietzsche places it before man as an object of will and purpose: here is what man should make of himself. In the words of Zarathustra's first speech to the people: *"I teach you the overman.* Man is something that shall be overcome. What have you done to overcome him?"

Every morality is a recipe for a certain type of man, an explication of a vision of what man might be. Nietzsche suggests that we examine every morality with this in mind, and ask ourselves what we think of this vision—or that. And he offers us a vision of his own.

NIETZSCHE AND RILKE

This study of Nietzsche and Rilke, and particularly of what they have in common, is meant to throw light on both and also on the relation of philosophy and poetry. There are, of course, obvious differences between the two men; but it is unlikely that an extended contrast would prove illuminating. Some reflection on what they have in common, on the other hand, may help us to understand the relation of poetry to philosophy more than the customary juxtaposition of Dante and Aquinas—as atypical a pair as one is likely to find: Aquinas, with his dogmatic commitments, is utterly unlike any Greek or modern philosopher; the *Divine Comedy* is unlike any other poem; and Dante's relation to Aquinas is unlike that of any other major poet and philosopher. Nietzsche and Rilke, on the other hand, furnish a nearly ideal pair. Probably they are, respectively, the greatest German philosopher and poet of the last hundred years: they wrote in the same language and belong roughly to the same age.

Two further facts make it strange that comparisons have not become a commonplace long ago, especially in view of the vast literature that has accumulated around both men. First, Nietzsche's influence is very apparent, if as yet very ill digested, in some of Rilke's *juvenilia*. And secondly, both men loved the same woman—probably more than any other. Nietzsche loved Lou Salomé in 1882 when she was barely over twenty, and she listened to his innermost ideas without quite reciprocating his feelings. Their relation was short-lived but intense, and their break and Nietzsche's subsequent solitude precipitated his first attempt to develop his whole philosophy

in a single major work, his *Zarathustra*. When Rilke met her
fifteen years later, in 1897, Nietzsche was slowly dying; he
was known the world over; Lou herself had recently published
a book about him; and she was mature while Rilke, at twenty-
two, was not. She was married to Professor Andreas but became Rilke's mistress, traveled with him, and their love was
complete.

There is no need, however, for making a juxtaposition biographical: the only data required will be found in the work of
the two men, and the emphasis will fall on Rilke's poems.
Nietzsche will be introduced only insofar as that which Rilke's
poems express happens to be very close to the spirit of Nietzsche's work. The question of influence shall not detain us.

My approach differs almost equally from the distinctive critical methods of the nineteenth and the twentieth century. If
nineteenth-century literary criticism has concerned itself too
much with historical and biographical considerations that lead
beyond the work of art, the "new" criticism, which has studied
works without external reference, has rarely got beyond formal considerations. I propose to focus attention on the *contents*
of Rilke's poems, on the experiences that they communicate,
but without trivializing them biographically.

2

Rilke's earlier poems are often underestimated by those who
admire his *Duino Elegies* and *Sonnets to Orpheus,* especially
by those intent on finding a philosophy in these often obscure
later works. But much can be said in favor of beginning with
three pre-Duino poems, which are short enough to be quoted
without omission and simple enough to require no commentary. Moreover, they are among Rilke's best.

The Song of the Idiot

They do not hinder me. They let me go.
They say, nothing could happen even so.
How good.
Nothing can happen. Everything revolves engrossed
always around the Holy Ghost,

around a certain ghost (you know)—
how good.

No, one should really not suppose
that there is any danger in those.
There's of course the blood.
The blood is the hardest thing. The blood is a chore,
sometimes I think I can't any more.
(How good.)

Look at that ball, isn't it fair—
red and round as an everywhere.
Good you created the ball.
Whether it comes when we call?

How oddly all things seem to humor some whim,
they flock together, apart they swim,
friendly and just a little dim;
how good.

This poem, from *Das Buch der Bilder*, certainly does not communicate any philosophy nor even any belief. It does not develop any argument but proceeds largely by free associations that are frequently suggested by rhymes; and unrhymed translations are therefore particularly inadequate. The poet projects himself into the mind of an idiot and recreates an irrational stream of consciousness. And yet little is needed to transform this poem into a philosophic position: merely the claim that the world really is as it appears to the idiot. This, of course, Rilke neither says nor implies; and the poem is part of a sequence of similar projections into sane, if invariably sad, states of mind.

Even so the inclusion of this theme and Rilke's success with it invite the reflection that perhaps he does not feel too sure of the rationality of the world, and that a poet with a firm belief in a purposive world order would have been very much less likely to write such a poem. Surely, the same might be said of Faulkner's *The Sound and the Fury*. But what is true of the novelist who forces us to see the world from the point of view of a castrated idiot is perhaps less applicable to a lyric poet who depends on different moods almost as much as a dramatist.

The next poem comes from the first part of *Neue Gedichte* and is one of Rilke's most perfect.

The Panther

In the Jardin des Plantes, Paris

His glance, worn by the passing of the bars,
has grown so weary it has lost its hold.
It seems to him, there are a thousand bars,
and then behind a thousand bars no world.

The soft gait of the supple, forceful paces
revolving in a circle almost nil,
is like a dance of power that embraces
a core containing, dazed, a mighty will.

Rarely the pupil's curtain, soundlessly,
is raised—and then an image enters him,
goes through the silent tension of the limbs—
and in his heart ceases to be.

Again, nothing is asserted: no belief, no truth, no philosophy. And again it takes only a single additional line to transform a perfect poem into a doubtful philosophy; namely: this is a portrait of the human condition. Rilke's historical and geographical proximity to Kafka may suggest that this addition would be entirely in his spirit, but this is exceedingly doubtful. Why should not the poet who projects himself into an orphan, the Buddha, a prisoner, a woman's fate, Orpheus, Euridice, and Hermes (all three in turn), the birth of Venus, Leda, and countless others, project himself also into the mood of those who feel more or less perpetually like Kafka?

A poem can illustrate a philosophy insofar as the philosophy itself is a metaphysical projection of an experience, a mood, an attitude. The poet may know this mood as one among many or as the dominant experience of his own life; he may enter into it as a virtuoso or be trapped in it; he may illustrate the same philosophy over and over again or bring to life many, whether as a tour de force or as an unwitting record of his

own range of experience; and he may be quite unaware of
the fact that others have converted such experiences into
philosophies.

The third poem, from the second part of *Neue Gedichte*,
is more direct than the other two. The poet no longer projects
himself into an idiot or an animal but, as in most of his later
works, seems to speak for himself.

Archaic Torso of Apollo

We did not know his high, unheard of head
where his eyes' apples ripened. Yet his torso has
retained their glowing as
a candelabrum where his vision, not yet dead,

only turned low, still shines. For else the breast
could not blind you, nor could we still discern
the smile that wanders in the loins' faint turn
to that core which once carried manhood's crest.

Else would this stone, disfigured and too small,
stand mute under the shoulders' lucid fall
and not gleam like a great cat's skin, and not

burst out of all its contours, bright
as a great star: there is no spot
that does not see you. You must change your life.

If one considers this sonnet as an illustration of a philosophy,
it must be a very different philosophy from that of the two
earlier poems: no longer Kafka but Sartre, no longer nihilism
but a call for a decision. Both philosophies, however, can be
found in the work of Nietzsche, too, and in the same sequence
as in Rilke.

The nihilism illustrated by "The Panther" is, after all, qualified by the suggestion that life is justified only as an aesthetic
phenomenon—and this is one of the key sentences of Nietzsche's first book, *The Birth of Tragedy*. It would surely be
false to say that all of Rilke's early poems illustrate this attitude, but enough of the best of them do to warrant the
claim that the feeling about the world that Nietzsche formu-

lated in this way was one that Rilke knew, too, firsthand, without any special feat of imagination.

In the "Archaic Torso of Apollo" this early aestheticism is transcended, but the achievement of the Greeks is experienced nevertheless in a characteristically Nietzschean manner. The mere contrast between classical antiquity and our own paltriness is, of course, too common to establish any strong parallel: to mention a single outstanding example, it is one of the central motifs of Joyce's *Ulysses*. But Rilke, like Nietzsche, does not react with resignation, irony, or humor, let alone romantic nostalgia. To him the archaic torso is a work of art and a human achievement rather than a symbol of an irretrievable past; and therefore he experiences it, not only as a reproach, but also as a challenge and a promise. His attitude is that of Nietzsche in his third book, *On the Advantage and Disadvantage of History for Life,* where it is urged that besides the outlook of the antiquarian and that of the critic of the past there is, thirdly, the "monumentalistic" attitude. Rilke's poem may be taken as an illustration of this attitude, which, as it happens, neither he nor Nietzsche ever relinquished.

We have no right, to be sure, to infer from "Archaic Torso of Apollo" that Rilke maintained a particular position or identified himself permanently with certain ideas. What the sonnet, taken by itself, shows is only that Rilke knew a certain experience that some other people, notably Nietzsche, have had, too. But what I shall try to show next is that Rilke communicated in his poetry quite a number of experiences that are far from common and that are rarely encountered in the work of other poets or philosophers—except Nietzsche. I shall begin with four interrelated motifs that are equally characteristic of, and central in, the work of both men. Here are certain fundamental experiences that inspired both a philosopher and a poet, to be transmuted by each in accordance with his distinctive genius.

3

What Rilke has in common with Nietzsche is, *first* of all, his experience of his own historical situation. In his seventh elegy he formulates it in terms no less applicable to Nietzsche than to himself:

Every brute inversion of the world knows the disinherited
to whom the past no longer belongs, and not yet the future.

For most men their historical situation poses no problem; they are not even aware of it. It did not occur to Aristotle that the world of the Greek city states was disappearing forever under his very eyes. Aquinas built confidently for all eternity. Kant hoped that his *Critique of Pure Reason* would enable men at long last to find the real truth within two decades. Hegel was the first great philosopher with any keen sense of his historical position, and he saw himself as the heir of three thousand years. He felt secure in his possession of the past, and his refusal to speculate about the future went hand in hand with the feeling that the past and the present were sufficient for him. Goethe's attitude was similar.

In the course of the nineteenth century some writers found their relation to the past almost as troubled as their situation in the present. Marx is an outstanding example; but, denied the romantics' escape into the past, he fled into an equally imaginary future that he thought he could foresee and that he believed belonged to him. He still had a faith in a world order and even in a kind of moral providence.

Kierkegaard, for all his profoundly critical attitude toward past and present, was a man of faith; and so was Dostoevsky, though his psychological insight was unclouded by any illusion. Rilke's two lines apply to Nietzsche as to no other equally outstanding figure before him.

Exactly the same is true of the following four lines from *Stundenbuch*, which suggest the *second* great common motif and could be inscribed over Nietzsche's work no less than Rilke's:

I believe in everything unsaid still.
My most pious feelings I want to set free.
What no man has yet dared to will
shall one day be instinctive with me.

For those "to whom the past no longer belongs, and not yet
the future," piety cannot mean what it once meant. The peculiar piety of Nietzsche and Rilke does not consist in any reverent
acceptance of some tradition, but rather in a rejection of all
that has hardened into stereotypes and in the resolve to be
open and ready for their own individual call. Without believing in any god, they feel that if only they will be entirely
receptive they will be addressed personally and experience a
necessity, a duty, a destiny that will be just theirs and nobody else's, but no less their duty than any categorical imperative.

What Nietzsche and Rilke want is a new honesty, and the
sin against the spirit is for them the essentially insincere escape
into traditional values and clichés. What is old cannot be altogether adequate now, for me, in an unprecedented situation.
It is honesty that demands what is still unsaid. Honesty is the
new piety.

Rilke speaks for Nietzsche, too, when he says in his first
elegy "that we are not very reliably at home in the interpreted
world." Most men, of course, are; and William James frankly
insisted on the importance of feeling at home in the universe.
But what is for James a legitimate approach to piety is ruled
out for Nietzsche and Rilke precisely by their piety: their new
honesty does not permit any such security; their new piety
involves an openness for experiences that explode our customary interpretations. They refuse to reduce an experience or insight to fit it into a preconceived scheme of things.

What is involved in this disdain for security is stated beautifully in one of Rilke's letters (April 12, 1923); and what
he here describes as the central inspiration of his elegies and
sonnets may be considered the *third* great common motif of
his work and Nietzsche's.

> Whoever does not affirm at some time or other with a defi-
> nite resolve—yes, jubilate at—the terribleness of life, never

takes possession of the unutterable powers of our existence; he merely walks at the edge; and when the decision is made eventually, he will have been neither one of the living nor one of the dead. To show the *identity* of terribleness and bliss, these two faces of the same divine head—indeed, of this *single* face that merely looks this way or that, depending on the distance from which, or the mood in which, we perceive it—that is the essential meaning and concept of my two books.

Here the poet does what Goethe scornfully refused to do: he states the "idea" of what he himself considers his greatest poetic work. But if we reflect on Goethe's words to Eckermann (cited above in chapter 4, section 3) there is no real disagreement: Rilke's "essential meaning and concept" could hardly be called "the meagre thread of a single idea," nor is it anything "abstract." It is his "vision and impression" of life. In his experience the terribleness and bliss of life are as a single face that merely looks this way or that depending on his distance from it or his mood. It is only by walking at the edge and seeking shelter that he can escape the terror of existence; but that means inevitably that no bliss is left either, only the balance of mediocrity. On the other hand, when he plunges into life, exposing himself to the slings and arrows of outrageous fortune, the very intensity of his suffering fills him with ecstasy.

From this point of view, the Christian martyrs deserve admiration as men who did not walk at the edge. The young Nietzsche considered artist, saint, and philosopher the highest types of humanity and always retained some feeling for the ascetic. He might well have agreed with Rilke's statement, in the letter already cited:

I have often said to myself that this was the urge or (if it is permitted to say so) the holy cunning of the martyrs that they craved to put behind themselves pain, the most terrible pain, the excess of all pain—that which otherwise distributes itself unforeseeably over a whole life and mingles with its moments in small or larger doses of physical and spiritual sufferings—to evoke this whole possibility of suffering *at once*, to conjure it up so that afterwards, after one has weathered it, there might be only bliss.

Although he does not walk at the edge, the martyr, too, seeks security. Far from choosing the precarious life that Nietzsche and Rilke elect, he throws away life to buy safety beyond. What separates Nietzsche and Rilke from the martyrs is ultimately—and this is the *fourth* great common motif—their complete repudiation of otherworldliness.

This is not only of the essence of Rilke's poetry but also the main theme of his last major prose work, "The Letter of the Young Workingman," written in February, 1922, during the very days when he also wrote the elegies and sonnets. The fourteen pages of this protest against Christianity do not only breathe Nietzsche's spirit but echo particular passages in his books. It is hard to believe that Rilke should not have been conscious of this; but, whether he recognized them or not, it is interesting that such passages should have come to his mind while he wrote the elegies and sonnets.

"Do not forever compel us to fall back into the distress and melancholy that it cost him, as you say, to 'redeem' us. Let us at long last be redeemed." Compare this with Zarathustra's discourse "On Priests": ". . . Melancholy. They would have to sing better songs for me to have faith in their Redeemer: and his disciples would have to look more redeemed!" And the famous passage on Cesare Borgia near the end of Nietzsche's *Antichrist* is certainly the model for this contrast:

> Even within the church, indeed in its very crown, *this* world exacted its abundance and its native overflow. Why is the church not praised for having been so sturdy that it did not collapse under the weight of the vitality of certain popes whose thrones were heavy with bastard children, courtesans, and murders? Was there not more Christianity in them than in the arid restorers of the Gospels—namely, something living, inexorable, transmuted?

I recall the culmination of Nietzsche's passage: "But life! But the triumph of life! But the great Yes to all high, beautiful, audacious things! And Luther *restored the church:* he attacked it."

Some other parallels may be fully accounted for by the basically similar attitude of both men; for example, the preference for the Old Testament over the New and the great indictment of the Christian attitude toward sex. What is most significant in any case is not the number of variations on the theme but the central motif of radical opposition to otherworldliness. This is stated in "The Letter of the Young Workingman," not only in the spirit, but even in the style of Zarathustra's discourse "On the Afterworldly":

> What madness, to distract us to a beyond, when we are surrounded right here by tasks and expectations and futures! What fraud, to purloin images of earthly rapture to sell them to heaven behind our backs! Oh, it is high time for the impoverished earth to claim back all those loans which have been raised on her bliss to furnish some over-future!

Rilke accepts Zarathustra's challenge to remain faithful to the earth; and his earth, like Nietzsche's, is not that of literary naturalism or realism any more than the Victorian or romantic world or the universe of science or religion. It is an ecstatically experienced world alive with all the glory of the mystics' God. In a letter (February 22, 1923), Rilke recalls how he once used to speak of God and adds: "Now you would hardly ever hear me refer to him. . . . His attributes are taken away from God, the no longer utterable, and return to the creation."

4

If ever there was Dionysian poetry in Nietzsche's sense— poetry that celebrates life with all its agony, verse that praises suffering as part of the passion of existence—it is found in the *Duino Elegies* and the *Sonnets to Orpheus.* For that matter, Rilke knew, of course, that the features of Orpheus and Dionysus blend even in Greek legend; and the myth of Dionysus' martyrdom and rebirth, which is crucial for Nietzsche's conception, is related of Orpheus as well.

Dionysus versus "the Crucified One": there you have the
contrast. It is not martyrdom that constitutes the difference
—only here it has two different senses. . . . The problem is
that of the meaning of suffering: whether a Christian meaning or a tragic meaning. In the first case, it is supposed to
be the path to a sacred existence; in the second case, *existence is considered sacred enough* to justify even a tremendous amount of suffering. . . . The god on the cross is
a curse on life, a pointer to seek redemption from it; Dionysus cut to pieces is a promise of life: it is eternally reborn
and comes back from destruction.

In this aphorism (§1052) from *The Will to Power*, we can
substitute "Orpheus" for "Dionysus" without the least change
in meaning.

Nietzsche thought that this joyous affirmation of life with
all its pain could be found in Greek tragedy. Certainly, for all
the influence of the Greeks on classical German poetry, it could
not be found in Goethe or Schiller. In Faust, to be sure, Goethe
portrayed a man who craves the agony and bliss of the whole
race, preferring the totality of experience, if there were such
a thing, to the drab dust of a merely academic existence; but
any love of the present moment, any boundless affirmation of
it, any wish to hold on to it, is precisely what Faust cannot
understand. In fact, he cannot distinguish it from Philistine
sloth. Even in his final speech he tells the moment to abide
only because he enjoys his anticipation of an imaginary future
that is, moreover—and the poet takes pains to underscore this
—utterly at odds with reality.

Goethe, unlike his Faust, knew a completely un-Philistine
appreciation of the moment, especially in his old age; but although Nietzsche, near the end of *The Twilight of the Idols*,
celebrated Goethe's attitude as the incarnation of a "Dionysian" faith, the affirmation of Goethe's "It be as it may, It was,
oh, so fair" seems serene rather than ecstatic. Here is resignation rather than rapture, peace rather than passion, even a
touch of weariness.

Nietzsche fuses Goethe's radical this-worldliness with the

genuine joy of Schiller's famous hymn that looks forward to
another world:

> *Suffer bravely, myriads!*
> *Suffer for the better world!*
> *Up above the firmament*
> *A great God will give rewards.*

Generally, Schiller's attitude was not one of otherworldliness
but of heroic defiance of suffering. The Dionysian affirmation
of Zarathustra's "Drunken Song" strikes a new note:

Have you ever said Yes to a single joy? O my friends, then
you have said Yes, too, to *all* woe. All things are entangled,
ensnared, enamored; if ever you wanted one thing twice, if
ever you said, "You please me, happiness! Abide, moment!"
then you wanted *all* back. All anew, all eternally, all entangled, ensnared, enamored—oh, then you *loved* the world.
Eternal ones, love it eternally and evermore; and to woe,
too, you say: go, but return! *For all joy wants—eternity.*
. . . *What* does joy not want? It is thirstier, more cordial,
hungrier, more terrible, more secret than all woe; it wants
itself, it bites into *itself*, the ring's will strives in it; it wants
love, it wants hatred, it is overrich, gives, throws away, begs
that one might take it, thanks the taker, it would like to be
hated; so rich is joy that it thirsts for woe, for hell, for hatred, for disgrace, for the cripple, for *world*—this world, oh,
you know it!

This feeling is significantly different from the romantics' occasional celebration of the lust of suffering and the voluptuous
delight of agony. Novalis, for example, celebrates pain as a
foretaste of death because he hates life. Altogether, the romantics' praise of suffering is, most typically, a repudiation of
the present, akin to their escape into the past or the future:
it is, at bottom, praise of another world or of a brief ecstasy
that, while it lasts, lifts the poet out of this world. Nietzsche's
attitude is not found in German literature before him; but it is
the central mood of Rilke's elegies and sonnets.

In this mood the four motifs that we have stated separately
are fused into a single experience: Nietzsche and Rilke, "to

whom the past no longer belongs, and not yet the future," develop a new piety that denies them the security of any tradition as well as any escape from the terror of life, including even the ancient hope for bliss in another life; but their radical affirmation of this world with all its agony becomes an experience of ecstatic bliss.

5

A glance at one elegy and one sonnet may show how some apparently striking differences between Nietzsche and Rilke are merely superficial. "Why," Rilke asks at the beginning of his ninth elegy, "have to be human?" And he answers: "because being here is much" and then explains:

>   *Once*
> everything, only *once. Once* and no more. And we, too,
> *once.* Never again. But having
> been this *once*, even though only *once:*
> having been on *earth* does not seem revokable.

On the face of it, this is the very opposite of Nietzsche's doctrine of the eternal recurrence of the same events. But if we understand this doctrine as the metaphysical projection of the feeling expressed in the words we have quoted from "The Drunken Song," we see that the central experience of Nietzsche and Rilke is the same. What Rilke's emphatic "once" is meant to rule out is not an eternal recurrence but a beyond; and what he, like Nietzsche, affirms rapturously is this world. A few lines later, Rilke exclaims—and this is surely the epitome of "The Drunken Song"—"Would love to hold on to all forever."

One can, of course, pose philosophical puzzles about the eternal recurrence, and it is perfectly fair to subject the theoretical explication of a mood to theoretical scrutiny and criticism. Some objections, however, rest on a psychological misunderstanding, a failure to grasp the central experience. Interpreters have paid insufficient attention to Zarathustra's opening discourse "On The Three Metamorphoses" in which

the highest stage in the development of the spirit is represented by the child. One possible and particularly important
attitude toward the eternal recurrence of the same events is
neither moralistic nor speculative but, rather, like a child's delight in a merry-go-round—or a child's wish to have a story
it likes repeated again and again and again.

The other great apparent difference between Nietzsche and
Rilke is suggested by the many references to angels in the
elegies. Instead of examining all these passages in an effort to
understand what exactly Rilke may have meant, it will suffice
to cite a letter Rilke wrote during the last year of his life, on
November 13, 1925. It was written to his Polish translator and
was plainly intended by the poet as a major document. He
explains how he wants to be understood: *"Not in the Christian
sense* (from which I move away more and more passionately)
but in a purely earthly, deeply earthly, blissfully earthly"
sense. And again:

> By making the mistake of applying *Catholic* conceptions
> of death, of the beyond, and of eternity to the elegies or
> sonnets, one moves away completely from their point of de-
> parture and becomes involved in an ever more thorough
> misunderstanding. The "angel" of the elegies has nothing to
> do with the angel of the Christian heaven (sooner with the
> angelic figures of Islam). The angel of the *elegies* is the
> creature in whom that transformation of the visible into the
> invisible at which we work appears completed.

In other words, he is the image or incarnation of the accomplishment of our striving, and his features thus merge with
those of Nietzsche's *Übermensch.*

In his discourse "On Poets" Zarathustra says: "All gods are
poets' parables, poets' prevarications. Verily, it always lifts us
higher—specifically, to the realm of the clouds: upon these we
place our motley bastards and call them gods and overmen."
In Rilke, gods and angels are indeed mere poets' parables and
are actually used interchangeably. In the third sonnet to
Orpheus, for example, a god appears where the elegies would
have introduced an angel, and Nietzsche the overman:

A god can do it. But how can one follow,
mere man, oh, tell me, through the narrow art?
Man's sense is discord. Where ways of the heart
are crossing stands no temple for Apollo.

Song, as you teach it, does not reach nor yearn,
nor does it woo what is at last attained;
song is existence. For the god, unstrained.
But when do we exist? When will he turn,

to help us to exist, the earth and sky?
It is not this, youth, that you love, although
your voice then opens up your lips—oh, try

forgetting that you ever sang. That flees.
Singing in truth is breath that does not flow.
An aimless breath. Flight in the god. A breeze.

In some translations the last word is rendered as "gale." But
what Rilke exalts here is precisely the absence of any storm;
and even if it is granted that god, angel, overman, Orpheus,
and Dionysus become indistinguishable at this point, this lack
of strain may seem to establish a marked difference with
Nietzsche, who is generally held to have conceived a more
ferocious ideal. In fact, however, Zarathustra follows up his
discourse "On Self-Overcoming" with one "On Those Who
Are Sublime"; and this is strikingly similar in content to Rilke's
sonnet:

I do not like these tense souls. . . . If he grew tired of his
sublimity, this sublime one, only then would his beauty
commence. . . . His deed itself still lies on him as a shadow:
the hand still darkens the doer. As yet he has not overcome
his deed. Though I love the bull's neck on him, I also want
to see the eyes of the angel. He must still discard his heroic
will; he shall be elevated, not merely sublime: the ether itself should elevate him, the will-less one.

Surely, this is the theme of the third sonnet to Orpheus.

6

Let us now consider three more late poems, all short enough
to be cited without omission, to illustrate specific parallels to
Nietzsche's thought. I am not implying that all the later poems
are so Nietzschean nor, for that matter, that all are so clear or
so good. Here, to begin with, is the ninth poem from the second part of *Sonnets to Orpheus*:

Jubilate not when you judge that no rack is required,
men's necks no longer stretched in metallic splendor.
None is enhanced, no man's heart, because a desired
spasm of mildness makes your contortion more tender.

What they received through the ages, the rack and the rod,
scaffolds surrender as children the toys of their previous
birthday. Into the pure, the high, the undevious,
opened-up heart—thus does not enter the god

of genuine mildness. He would come with might and expand
radiantly as but the godlike will.
More than a wind for huge ships that are safe near the land.

Neither less than the secret, silent vibration
conquering us from within like a still
playing child of unlimited copulation.

This is the heart of Nietzsche's critique of modern man, the
point of his insistent question, "*whether we have become more
moral.*" In the section of *The Twilight of the Idols* that bears
this title, Nietzsche protests against a reviewer who "went so
far that he 'understood' the meaning of my work—not without
expressing his respect for my courage and daring—to be a demand for the abolition of all decent feelings. Thank you! In
reply, I take the liberty of raising the question whether we
have really become more moral." The "tenderness" of bourgeois morality seemed a mockery to Nietzsche and Rilke; and
the poet evidently agreed with these sentences in the chapter
"On Those Who Are Sublime":

Gracefulness is part of the graciousness of the great-souled.

. . . When power becomes gracious and descends into the visible—such descent I call beauty. And there is nobody from whom I want beauty as much as from you who are powerful: let your kindness be your final self-conquest. Of all evil I deem you capable: therefore I want the good from you. Verily, I have often laughed at the weaklings who thought themselves good because they had no claws.

A similar experience is formulated near the beginning of Rilke's first elegy:

> *The beautiful is nothing*
> *but the beginning of the terrible that we still barely endure,*
> *and we admire it so because it serenely disdains*
> *to destroy us.*

The twelfth sonnet of Part Two concerns itself with the images of fire and change that are frequently encountered in Nietzsche's work, but the parallel extends far beyond the imagery.

Choose to be changed. Oh experience the rapture of fire
in which a life is concealed, exulting in change as it burns;
and the projecting spirit who is master of the entire
earth, loves the figure's flight less than the point where it turns.

That which would lock itself up—already is frozen.
Does it feel safe in the shadow of colorless grey?
Wait, what is hardest will warn from afar what has chosen
hardness: a hammer will shatter its prey.

He that squanders himself as a well is cognized by cognition
and it leads him rejoicing through the serene creation
which often ceases to start and begins with the end.

Every span of delight is the child or grandchild of division
which they traverse in wonder. And Daphne, since her trans-
> *formation*
into a baytree, desires that you choose to be changed into
> *wind.*

This sonnet invites comparison with Nietzsche's dictum: *Nur wer sich wandelt, bleibt mit mir verwandt* (only those who

continue to change remain related to me)[1]—and with his little poem:

> *Yes, I know from where I came!*
> *Ever hungry like a flame*
> *I consume myself and glow.*
> *Light grows all that I conceive,*
> *ashes everything I leave:*
> *Flame I am assuredly.*

While the first three lines of Rilke's sestet are certainly very
obscure—and, I think, inferior to the rest of the poem—the
octave is really deceptively clear. The meaning of the words is
so easily seen that one is apt to overlook that what is meant is
anything but easy. Everybody wants to lock himself up after
having undergone a few transformations in adolescence and
perhaps for a few years after that; everybody chooses some
state of being, usually without even realizing that he chooses
it, and says, more or less explicitly: that is the way I am, or
happen to be. Or: I have always said that. . . . Or: I am the
kind who. . . . Or one takes refuge in heredity and environment. Or, if one has read some of the psychoanalysts, one
blames one's parents' mistakes: it is all their fault: "Choose to
be changed" is not only a call for continual growth; it is an
implicit denunciation of all these myths and of any security
that may be found in a tradition or expected from a single
conversion; it is an invitation to the most precarious life
imaginable.

The last of the three poems to be cited here may have been
Rilke's last German poem. (Many of his last poems were
French—reminding us of Nietzsche's occasional wish that he
might have been able to write some of his books in French
rather than in German.)

> *Dove that remained outside,   outside the dovecote,*
> *back in its sphere and home,   one with the day and night,*
> *it knows the secrecy   when the most remote*
> *terror is fused into   deeply felt flight.*

[1] From the poem concluding *Beyond Good and Evil*. The standard English translation misses the point completely: "None but new
kith are native of my land."

Of all the doves the   always most protected,
never endangered most,   does not know tenderness;
richest of all hearts is   the resurrected:
turning back liberates,   freedom rejoices.

Over the nowhere   arches the everywhere.
Oh, the ball that is   thrown, that we dare,
does it not fill our hands   differently than before?
By the weight of return   it is more.

The theme of this poem can be traced back beyond the
prodigal son; but Rilke is not trying to lend a voice to some
ancient wisdom but is recording his own experience, which
is free of all otherworldly or doctrinaire overtones. And his
"purely earthly, deeply earthly, blissfully earthly" feeling is
no longer an illustration of the biblical dictum that there is
more joy in heaven over one repentant sinner than over ninety-
nine just men—for the conception of sin is no longer meaning-
ful here—but a variation in a minor key of aphorism 283 in
Nietzsche's *Gay Science:* "Believe me, the secret of the greatest fruitfulness and the greatest enjoyment of existence is: to
live dangerously!"

The image of the ball conjoined with the substantival use
of the everywhere takes us back to the first poem we cited,
"The Song of the Idiot," which also features both. In that
poem "everything revolves engrossed/always around the Holy
Ghost." In "The Panther" the image of revolving is maintained,
but in the center there is, "dazed, a mighty will." Still, life
makes no sense. But if this will were awakened? In "Archaic
Torso of Apollo" the senseless circular motion is given up, and
the human organ of reproduction has become the center—the
symbol of creativity. Now there is a possibility of meaning:
"You must change your life." But how? "A god can do it. But
how can one follow?" In the sonnets the answer is given again
and again with the image of the wind. Singing in truth is a
wind. "And Daphne, since her transformation into a baytree,
desires that you choose to be changed into wind." The wind
is that which never locks itself up in any form, which never
seeks or finds shelter, the symbol of the utterly abandoned
and exposed life that is yet unstrained. In the ball the image

of the wind, of flight, merges with the older image of spherical revolution. Moving in circles is the epitome of senselessness, and so, in a way, is the child's throwing of the ball or the aimless blowing of the wind. There is nothing that gives our lives meaning and, viewed from the outside, life, which ends in death, is senseless. There is no meaning outside, but Rilke and Nietzsche proclaim that a certain kind of life is its own reward, that a certain mode of experience makes life infinitely worth while, and that "the secret of the greatest fruitfulness and the greatest enjoyment of existence is: to *live dangerously!*"

13
ART, TRADITION, AND TRUTH

Both Nietzsche and Rilke have sometimes been criticized for their supposed inversion of "the tradition." Nietzsche in particular has been linked with Marx and Kierkegaard, and Marx has been cited again and again as having admitted that he wanted to stand Hegel on his head. Here one finds a welcome image for what is supposed to be wrong with all these men. As it happens, however, Marx has been misquoted, and the charge against all of these men should be dismissed. Alluding to one of Hegel's images, in the Preface to the *Phenomenology*, Marx held that Hegel had stood man on his head —as if the spirit were basic—and Marx proposed to put man on his feet again. Similarly, Kierkegaard believed that the church had turned Christianity upside down, and Nietzsche thought that Christianity had turned almost everything upside down, a proposition with which Rilke agreed at least in part. Each was opposed to some particular tradition and—this is especially true of Nietzsche and Rilke—also to any attempt to seek security in a tradition. But there is no such thing as "the" tradition, except in an inclusive sense in which Nietzsche and Rilke are part of it—the sense in which "the tradition" is the universe of discourse in which we place and try to understand them.

It may throw some light not only on Nietzsche and Rilke but on philosophy and poetry generally if we consider some specific criticisms and see, as we refute them, how the practice of these two men is really representative of great philosophers and poets generally. Above all we should be able in this way to illuminate the relation of art to tradition and truth.

Lest we set up a strawman, let us consider some strictures actually suggested by a critic—as it happens, the only one in the vast literature on Nietzsche and on Rilke who has attempted any detailed comparison: Erich Heller, who has included an essay on "Rilke and Nietzsche, With a Discourse on Thought, Belief, and Poetry" in his book, *The Disinherited Mind* (1952). On most points I agree with Heller, and I have learned from his essay. What I am interested in is not criticism of another critic but a better understanding of some really important problems that have rarely been posed so well. Some of Heller's brilliantly formulated criticisms shall here be used as points of departure.

"In the great poetry of the European tradition," Heller says, "the emotions do not interpret; they respond to the interpreted world. In Rilke's mature poetry the emotions do the interpreting and then respond to their own interpretation" (p. 136). At this point one is apt to think of Faulkner: often he does not first give us the interpreted course of events and then the emotional response of his characters, but he lets their emotions do the interpreting, and many readers find it very difficult to determine what has occurred. Heller continues: "All great art (and, for that matter, every human order stabilized by tradition) rests on a fundamentally fixed correspondence between the impact of external experience on man and man's articulate answers."

Is this an acceptable characterization of great art or, for that matter, great philosophy? To begin with the latter, some of the great philosophers have done a good deal of rationalizing, but that for which they are remembered is their refusal to accept the traditional order. We do not continue to read Descartes because his proofs of God's existence or the immortality of the soul command our respect, but because he resolved to doubt everything. We study Berkeley not because he was a bishop but because he questioned the existence of matter. It is not his traditional life but his radical skepticism that establishes Hume's claim to greatness. And Kant's stature is not a function of his postulates of God, freedom, and immortality, which few philosophers have taken seriously, but of his *Critique of Pure Reason,* which sought to annihilate the very basis of traditional metaphysics and theology.

In this respect the great poets are at one with the great philosophers. Most of the famous names can be disregarded here because great poets who have written more than half a dozen fine poems without real scope are exceedingly rare. The few that remain are described splendidly, if quite unintentionally, by Heller's strictures of Rilke:

> Rilke, however, is the poet of a world, the philosopher of which is Nietzsche. Its formations evade all traditional systems of cartography. Doubt has dislodged all certainties. The unnameable is christened and the unsayable uttered. It is a world in which the order of correspondences is violently disturbed. We can no longer be sure that we love the lovable and abhor the detestable. Good does no good and evil no harm [p. 137].

This might as well have been written about Shakespeare, whose art it is to win our hearts for men from whom our judgment would recoil. Coriolanus may seem an extreme example. But what of Lear? Macbeth? Or even Hamlet? Does Hamlet's callous attitude after he has dispatched Polonius warrant the affection that almost every reader feels for him? Or is his calculated and unmerciful destruction of Rosencrantz and Guildenstern so lovable? Or his behavior toward Ophelia? Or anything at all he does? Or is it not a fact that in Shakespeare's plays our emotions do *not* "respond to the interpreted world" but instead "do the interpreting and then respond to their own interpretation"?

No other English poet even approximates the scope of Shakespeare. But Milton and Blake, who have at least tried to create worlds of their own, are certainly no less open to Heller's objections than Rilke. "We can no longer be sure that we love the lovable and abhor the detestable." Is not this the very heart of *Paradise Lost?* Or *The Marriage of Heaven and Hell?* Or Goethe's *Faust?* Or Dostoevsky's work?

The piety of the poet consists in a reverence not for tradition but for experience. The great poet is not a mellifluous liar but a man too honest to be able to accept what is stabilized and fixed. Impressed with the lack of correspondence between his own experience and the customary interpretations, he refuses to sacrifice his perception to the stereotyped idols of society. He is, like the great philosopher, a revolutionary. In Nietzsche's words: the creator breaks the old tablets. What Heller considers an objection is really nothing less than a criterion of great poetry: "The unnameable is christened and the unsayable uttered."

To be sure, there are differences of degree; also of emphasis. Shakespeare's very success blinds us to his radical divergence from our customary valuations. Kant was content to bury some of the force of his radicalism in the obscurity of involved pedantry. And Plato offered some of his most revolutionary suggestions in the tone of urbane conversation. So, for that matter, did Hume. Not every philosopher challenges society to put him to death for subverting "the tradition" like Socrates.

The point is not that men like Nietzsche and Rilke were not so revolutionary after all. Rather, all great poetry and philosophy is deeply subversive—a fact appreciated by Plato and other advocates of censorship but overlooked by the cultured Philistine who admires the great art of the past and condemns that of the present, without recapturing the experience behind either.

The common suggestion that Nietzsche or Rilke, or any number of others, falls outside "the tradition" or inverts it is probably reducible to one of two positions: either we must reject, by the same token, all the great philosophers and poets, modern as well as Greek, or we are confronted with the truism that Nietzsche and Rilke are very different from Aquinas and Dante. More likely than not, Aquinas is viewed out of his historical context, and Dante's revolutionary innovations are disregarded. More important, Shakespeare, Milton, and Blake, Descartes, Hume, and Kant are all considered as so many stages of decline. This may be *one* way of seeing history; but the suggestion that Nietzsche and Rilke and other moderns stand apart as men who invert the European tradition is a sheer perversion of fact.

Consider just one of these supposed inversions to which Hel-

ler alludes (p. 137): "Lovers seek separation, not union." He
has in mind Rilke's only "Love Song":

> How could I keep my soul so that it might
> not touch on yours? How could I elevate
> it over you to reach to other things?
> Oh, I would like to hide it out of sight
> with something lost in endless darkenings,
> in some remote, still place, so desolate
> it does not sing whenever your depth sings.
> Yet all that touches us, myself and you,
> takes us together like a violin bow
> that draws a single voice out of two strings.
> Upon what instrument have we been strung?
> And who is playing with us in his hand?
> Sweet is the song.

This poem does not reflect either a deliberately contrived or a
historically accomplished inversion of the world. What it does
reveal is the honesty of a perception that was not blinded by
traditional preconceptions, stereotypes, or clichés.

Do lovers always and only seek union? If the experience
recorded in Rilke's poem is new, it is new in the same way
in which the Impressionists' experience of light and shadow
and color or Giotto's experience of perspective was new. In
each case, convention impeded perception, and the achievement of the artist was a triumph of honesty.

Of course, lovers do not always seek separation, any more
than love always makes us more lonely, or, for that matter,
less lonely. There is a wealth of experiences that are not dreamt
of in the poetry we have—no less, in fact, than are dreamt of
only in poetry.

The experience that Rilke communicates depends on an excessive sensitivity to the feelings of others, or at least one other
human being, and a penchant for analysis—traits that occur
separately more often than together—and perhaps also a purpose in life beyond loving and being loved. Without exception,
these were traits of Nietzsche too, and they help to explain
his dictum, "my greatest dangers lie in pity." He himself comments on it in a letter (September 14, 1884): "This is the

mistake which I seem to make eternally, that I imagine the
sufferings of others as far greater than they really are."

Nietzsche's "revaluation" of pity was prompted in part by
his honest perception of various experiences of pity, which for
him was not a mere word but a cross. I do not mean to dissolve a philosophic position by deriving it from psychological
accidents; on the contrary, any philosophic discussion of pity
should be based on an understanding of the experience of pitying and being pitied. Nor did Nietzsche here invert "the tradition." As he himself insisted, his critique of pity is in the
tradition of Plato, Aristotle, the Stoics, Spinoza, La Roche-
foucauld, and Kant. Surely, many of those who make much
of tradition do not really know it well at all, and "the tradition"
is, more often than not, an honorific name for the critic's own
prejudices or, to be more polite, values. And belief in "the
tradition" is so popular partly because it makes a virtue of
security from deep and disturbing experiences.

Dante's *Vita Nuova* is sufficient testimony that he did not
seek such security. We have few comparable records of self-
exposure in both senses—meaning, first of all, exposure to profound distraction. In this experience and in the act of creation
in which it issues, the received order is always "violently dis-
turbed" and "the unsayable uttered." In this respect, the work
of Nietzsche and Rilke is at one with that of other great philosophers and poets, and they are closer to Dante than are
the traditionalists. Tradition is what comes afterwards.

2

Let us return to Heller for another major criticism:

Neither Rilke nor Nietzsche praises the praiseworthy. They
praise. They do not believe the unbelievable. They believe.
And it is their praising and believing itself that becomes
praiseworthy and believable in the act of worship. Theirs is
a *religio intransitiva*. Future anthropologists may see in it
the distinctive religious achievement of modern Europe, the
theological equivalent of *l'art pour l'art* [p. 136].

This is a seductive interpretation, almost equally close to

some Thomists and to Jaspers' reading of Nietzsche, but it is utterly unfair to both Nietzsche and Rilke. Their intense celebration of intensity may occasionally appear in this light, and the attitude Heller describes is certainly not entirely imaginary. In fact, this outlook has been given expression in one of the finest works of recent German prose, Hermann Hesse's *Klingsors letzter Sommer*, in which Klingsor says:

> The sensuous is not worth one hair more than the spirit—as little as the other way around. It is all one, it is all equally good. Whether you embrace a woman or make a poem is the same. If only the main thing is there, the love, the burning, being seized, then it makes no difference whether you are a monk on Mount Athos or an epicurean in Paris.

In their mature phase, both Nietzsche and Rilke refused to praise either the monk or the epicurean. Far from merely praising or believing in belief, both believed in, and praised, a particular kind of man and way of life. Both were inspired by their vision of "a *new* greatness of man." And in section 212 of *Beyond Good and Evil* Nietzsche argued that every great philosopher has been inspired by such a vision.

He "has always found himself, and always had to find himself, in opposition to his today." The great philosophers have always been "the bad conscience of their time." Inspired by their vision of "a *new* greatness of man," they have applied "the knife vivisectionally to the very virtues of the time" and uncovered "how much hypocrisy" and "how many lies were concealed under the most honored type of their contemporary morality, how much virtue was outlived." Nietzsche's own profuse criticisms, too, were inspired by a positive conception: "Today the concept of 'greatness' entails being noble, wanting to be by oneself, being capable of being different, standing alone, and having to live independently." Or as he says toward the end of this passage: "Precisely this should be called greatness: to be capable of being as manifold as whole, as wide as full."

Clearly, Nietzsche is not praising indiscriminately for the sake of praising. One must empty his extremely concrete conceptions of their wealth of psychological detail before one can claim that they are hollow abstractions. In the process of doing this—and Jaspers, for example, has done this in his two books on Nietzsche—one is bound to lose sight of the intimate connection, so accurately stressed by Nietzsche himself, between his positive conceptions and his trenchant criticisms of modern man. That his strictures are misunderstood when they are divorced from the vision that inspires them is the theme of the chapter "On Passing By" in which Zarathustra distinguishes himself from his ape by insisting: "Out of love alone shall my despising and my warning bird fly up, not out of the swamp." Zarathustra's comment on "The Despisers of the Body" is no less applicable to Nietzsche and the philosophers whom he admires: "It is their respect that begets their contempt."

The man whom Nietzsche praises is neither an epicurean nor a monk, however burning and however seized, but he combines sensuousness and spirituality, profound feeling and a penetrating intellect. He is the man of reflective passion and passionate reflection. All of Nietzsche's heroes, from Heraclitus and Socrates to Caesar, Leonardo, and Goethe are models and anticipations of such a type, "as manifold as whole, as wide as full."

What Rilke has in common with Nietzsche is not praise for the sake of praising but, rather, that he praised the same kind of life and, again like Nietzsche, praised it not merely implicitly but with all his power and consciousness. It is this that distinguishes Nietzsche and Rilke from most philosophers and poets of the past. Moreover, it is from Nietzsche above all others that one learns to ask about every philosophy and every religion, and about great poets and artists, too: What is it that they praise?

Once we ask this question, we cannot fail to see how much closer Nietzsche is to Plato, Aristotle, and Shakespeare than are most of the defenders of "the tradition," let alone those who believe in the modern trinity of Christianity, science, and democracy. One invokes the awesome name of Aristotle but ignores his striking portrait of the great-souled man. One cannot but admit Shakespeare's greatness but does not ask what kind of man and life he praised; one ignores, or tries to explain away, his ninety-fourth sonnet instead of comparing it with his plays or such lines as these from *Measure for Measure:*

> *O, it is excellent*
> *To have a giant's strength; but it is tyrannous*
> *To use it like a giant.*

Surely, this is Nietzsche in a nutshell (cf. chapter 1 above). Nietzsche's praise is neither intransitive nor does it invert "the tradition"; rather, the man he envisages invites comparison with the visions of Plato, Aristotle, and Shakespeare.

3

The one major charge that is still lacking in this orthodox indictment of Nietzsche and Rilke is their abandonment of something that is usually called, rather vaguely, "realism." Heller does not require this cliché and spells out the charge in some detail. For Nietzsche and Rilke, he says,

> the separation between art and reality appears to be complete. Reality is the death of the spirit and art its salvation. Where does truth reside? Is it in the deadly real world or in the saving vision of the artist? The question lingers on the all but imperceptible border-line between delusion and lunacy, between Nietzsche's madness and Rilke's prophetic pose, tenaciously maintained even beyond the confines of poetic inspiration. Nietzsche, believing that truth was insufferable and that poetry was an illusion, continually suspected that at least some of his thought was merely poetry. Rilke, on the other hand, succeeded most of the time in convincing himself that the thought behind his poetry was the mind of truth [p. 139].

Rilke's facile belief that his elegies and sonnets were gifts of inscrutable inspiration undoubtedly reflects a lack of strength and a sense of his own inability to effect any improvements. There are lines in the elegies that appear to be the mere padding of pathos, and many passages in the sonnets make little sense. Again and again the mood and the verve must sustain the lines, and the lines fail to sustain the mood. Here the poet's appeal to inspiration cannot hide the failure of inspiration.

Rilke's elegies sometimes share the fault of Whitman's long poems, though Rilke's obscurity makes it harder to find him out. Most of the sonnets, too, are marred by a lack of sufficient insight or perception to fill fourteen lines. But the same is surely true of Shakespeare's sonnets, and even some of Shakespeare's best achieve excellence only in the opening lines and end rather lamely. The above-mentioned ninety-fourth sonnet is one of the most notable exceptions. Many weaknesses of Rilke's *Sonnets to Orpheus* are explained by his boast that the first twenty-six sonnets were written between the second and the fifth of February, 1922, and that he never altered a word. We recall Ben Jonson's retort to those who praised Shakespeare for never blotting a line: wish he had blotted a thousand! While some of Rilke's commentators have been too worshipful, and obscurity, though not necessarily a fault, is no proof of profundity either, all this does not set Rilke apart or prove him a minor poet. The fact remains that few poets of any age have written as many superb poems as Rilke.

To come to Nietzsche. When he contrasted truth and beauty, he had in mind a particular conception of beauty: a prettification of reality. He opposed those who argued that something must be true because it would be beautiful if it were, or that something could not be true because it was not at all pretty. Like everything admitted about Rilke, this is very far indeed from supporting any complete "separation between art and reality." So is Nietzsche's fear in "The Song of Melancholy" in *Zarathustra* that he might be "only poet." As he says in the same poem, he means that he might be "only speaking colorfully, . . . climbing around on mendacious word bridges." Although he considered *Zarathustra* the gift of inspiration, as he tells us in *Ecce Homo*, Nietzsche did not stop writing afterward and consider his life sufficiently justified, as Rilke did more or less after having completed his elegies and sonnets. In spite of his exceedingly poor health, Nietzsche sought further clarity in half a dozen further books in which he is clearly not "only speaking colorfully."

Here is some basis for contrasting Nietzsche and Rilke. In section 146 of *Human, All-too-Human,* Nietzsche says: "Regarding truths, the artist has a weaker morality than the thinker." But Rilke's lack of perfect sincerity goes beyond any necessity of his art; and the "prophetic pose" that disturbs Heller in some of the letters also mars some of the elegies and sonnets. This lack of ultimate honesty with himself is one reason for ranking Rilke below Nietzsche in over-all stature. Besides, Nietzsche's scope far exceeds Rilke's. But the question of the separation of art and reality cannot be settled in these terms; it raises a much more general issue.

The dualism of art and reality has been denied by almost all artists. If "reality" is monopolized by convention and mediocrity, and all intense experience and keen perception are banished from it, then, of course, the artist is cut off from it. But one can surely question the preconceptions in which men hide from the risks of powerful experience. Nietzsche and Rilke did not exalt prettification above sordid reality; they rejected bloodless stereotypes for a vision of magnificent terror.

Consider such diverse painters as Rembrandt, Rubens, and Van Gogh. Rembrandt did not shut his eyes to reality to escape into a realm of agreeable fancy: he saw the aged, the beggars, and the outcasts of society as they had not been seen before. He penetrated all kinds of traditional prejudices to see the beauty of reality. Well might a contemporary have objected, as Heller does to Rilke and Nietzsche: "We can no longer be sure that we love the lovable and abhor the detestable." Precisely this revaluation is a measure of Rembrandt's greatness.

A critic brought up on the values of Raphael, Giorgione, or even Titian might have voiced Heller's protest when confronted with Rubens' nudes. But Rubens did not escape from reality into art: he saw beauty where previous painters had failed to see it; he was in Nietzsche's sense a Dionysian artist. And so was Van Gogh. His world may be a realm of madness; his flowers, cypresses, and starry skies do not look like snapshots. But he did not fly into fancy; he did not retreat from a tragic world to find refuge among comfortable creatures of the mind. Rather, he seems to be saying: even in madness there is beauty, even in fever and torment there is glory, even in despair there is power.

In the end all three criticisms of Nietzsche and Rilke come down to this: they were different from Aquinas; they did not

praise what Aquinas praised or believe what he believed; and
their conception of reality was not his. The norm need not be
Aquinas, though it often is he even when he is not named; the
norm could be merely the anonymous "one"—what Heidegger
calls *Das Man*. What matters is that the critic thinks he knows
what is praiseworthy and what is real, instead of considering
the possibility that men like Nietzsche and Rilke, Plato and
Shakespeare, Rembrandt and Rubens can teach us something
about these matters by changing our perception. If it were not
for that, I fail to see why they should merit our sustained
attention.

4

The fashionable attempt to understand great thinkers or artists in terms of their historical situation leads to as much misunderstanding as understanding. Neither shortcomings nor
tragedy should be blamed on "the time." One should first consider whether other ages—and here one should not think solely
of the Middle Ages of which, moreover, one usually does not
know too much—were entirely different. Nor should one rush
into psychological explanations without asking whether writers of a different psychological constitution fare very differently. Nietzsche's and Rilke's profound solitude, broken only
briefly by the philosopher's friendship with Wagner and the
poet's with Rodin, and the encounter of both, fifteen years
apart, with Lou Salomé, seems to have affected their work
and invites psychological and historical explanations. I shall
give the merest suggestion of each kind of approach.

In personal life both men were exceedingly shy and retiring.
Their passion was set free only when they wrote. The world
has gained because they poured all·their feelings into their
books; but the histrionics that others vent casually on their
friends have here become part of the work. Solitude, while
greatly increasing the intensity of feeling, diminishes the powers of self-criticism.

Or: it was the age that condemned these men to utter lone-
liness. And that very lack of ordinary communication that
keeps the writer's experience undefiled by common precon-

ceptions also makes for a lack of disciplined scrutiny. We find
the same faults in the last two great books of James Joyce and
already in the second part of *Faust,* which Goethe kept secret
until his death. At the beginning of the nineteenth century the
artist loses contact with his audience and as a result becomes
undisciplined. By way of contrast, Aeschylus and Sophocles
contended against each other before an interested public,
which they were educating in the process. Nietzsche and Rilke
stood alone without rivals or audience, and what little adula-
tion each received only made matters worse.

Such explanations do not go deep enough. Shakespeare had
an audience and wrote with the immediate aim of having his
plays performed, and there was no lack of rivals except insofar
as his greatness precludes our giving them that name. Yet
what striking lack of disciplined scrutiny! And what incredible
histrionics have here become part of the work! The same is
true of Plato's dialogues. Rilke is vastly different from Shakespeare, and Nietzsche from Plato; yet they all face the same
problem. It is rooted in the poetic impulse that is as eager to
express as it is reluctant to exclude. Most philosophers do not
know this plight; but that is because, unlike Plato and Nietzsche, they are no poets.

5

The relation of great poetry to "the time" and to truth deserves further reflection. Comparing Shakespeare with Dante,
T. S. Eliot says: "It is *equally* great poetry, though the philosophy behind it is not great." Eliot is another critic who
knows what is real and praiseworthy and true, without the
benefit of any reading of Shakespeare. As if Shakespeare might
not affect one's notions of great philosophy. In this instance,
however, Shakespeare receives a dispensation: "It was his
business to express the greatest emotional intensity of his time,
based on whatever his time happened to think." It is one of
the central themes of Eliot's essay on "Shakespeare and the
Stoicism of Seneca," which we have quoted, that critics should
not read themselves into Shakespeare; but surely Eliot is thinking of himself when he suggests that the shortcomings of the

poet must be blamed on his time. As if "his time" thought
anything in particular. Shakespeare's, like ours, abounded in
ideas.

Nevertheless I agree that the truth of beliefs is not relevant
to the greatness of poetry. Once more I shall use Heller as a
foil. He argues that Rilke's poetry expresses beliefs, that these
beliefs happen to be false (as Eliot would say: "the philosophy
behind it is not great"), and that (as Eliot would not say)
Rilke's poetry is worse for that. Rilke expressed Nietzsche's
philosophy in verse, and this may well have been as great a
philosophy as "his time" offered him; but if Rilke's beliefs had
been Christian—this standard is suggested throughout Heller's
book—his poetry would be that much better.

The argument that to Heller's mind "finally proves" the relevance of the truth of beliefs to the greatness of poetry is this:

> There are ideas and beliefs so prosaic, outlandish or perverse
> in their innermost structure that no great or good poetry
> can come from them; for instance Hitler's racialism. . . .
> If there were no relation, there would be no reason either
> why the most perverse or idiotic beliefs should not be con-
> vertible into *great* poetry. They are not [p. 126].

That some ideas are too prosaic is, of course, quite irrelevant.
Probably no great or good poetry will ever give an exposition
of Goedel's theorem, but not because it is untrue. And as for
Hitler's racialism, Germany did not produce any great poetry
at all under Hitler's regime; and the reasons are obvious. Moreover, biological, or pseudo-biological, theories rarely form the
subject matter of great serious poetry.

Perhaps dramatic poetry is the genre in which beliefs are
most frequently expressed. Does it bear out Heller's view? On
the contrary: the great tragic poets excel precisely at presenting attitudes that one would generally consider "outlandish or
perverse" with such poetic power that we experience them
from the inside. In epic poetry, the attitudes of Homer's heroes,
or the poet's for that matter, are scarcely closer to Christianity
than Rilke's elegies. Great poetry does not fit moralistic preconceptions. It was because he recognized this that Plato pro-

posed to expurgate Homer and expel the dramatic poets from his ideal city.

We should ask, not only Heller but also Eliot, whether there is any major work of great and good poetry that does not abound in "outlandish or perverse" ideas, whether even one is "Christian" in the somewhat laudatory sense that determines contemporary English usage. Dante reached the heights of his poetic power in his *Inferno*, and his beliefs about hell might well strike modern readers as "outlandish or perverse." And the hero of the greatest Protestant epic is Satan.

The traditionalist critics take for granted that we know the truth of beliefs quite independently of poetry and that the greatness of a *philosopher* is unquestionably determined by the truth of his beliefs. Both these assumptions are false. If the question were raised whether J. S. Mill was a greater philosopher than Plato, would the issue depend on how many beliefs of each were true and how many false? The traditionalists do not understand the function of beliefs either in philosophy or in poetry.

6

The most concise and suggestive formulation of the function of beliefs in poetry is T. S. Eliot's: "The poet who 'thinks' is merely the poet who can express the emotional equivalent of thought. But he is not necessarily interested in the thought itself." I think this is very wrong.

Consider once more Rilke's poem, "Archaic Torso of Apollo," quoted in section 2 of the last chapter. Surely, Rilke did not have a thought before he looked for a suitable emotional equivalent, found a torso, and decided that this might do. What he records is his experience of the statue—an experience in which various perceptions, thoughts, and emotions interpenetrate, as they do in the poem. The poem expresses several thoughts, not merely their emotional equivalents. It presents the thoughts themselves in their emotional context, as parts of an experience.

The thought apart from any experience, torn out of its living context and examined under the intellectual microscope

like a piece of dead tissue, does not concern the poet, qua
poet. It may interest him insofar as he is also philosophically
inclined. So far, Eliot is right; but I should not call the piece
of dead tissue "the thought itself."

Eliot's notion of thinking is altogether inadequate: "In truth
neither Shakespeare nor Dante did any real thinking—that was
not their job." Whatever "real" thinking may be, it certainly
is no job. Shakespeare did not really think, says Eliot, because
there is no evidence "that he thought to any purpose; that he
had any coherent view of life, or that he recommended any
procedure to follow." These are very strange criteria of thinking, at variance not only with our ordinary use of the term
but also with the practice of many outstanding philosophers.
When Eliot denies that Shakespeare thought, but then speaks
of "whatever his time happened to think," he comes close to
implying that there are really only two kinds of thinking: the
"good" thinking accepted by Dante, and the "bad" thinking
of the times in which poets less fortunate than Dante are condemned to live and write.

The separation of thought from experience, however, which
Eliot makes the criterion of "real" thinking, has its dark side.
Religious beliefs, for example, though originally prompted by
some experience, often become a substitute for religious experience or prevent the believer from savoring the full range
of his own inimitable experience. The thought that "you must
change your life" is a relatively common thought, present not
only in Rilke's time but in all ages. What distinguishes the poet
is not that he found a striking emotional equivalent for it, but
that he did not let the thought get in the way of the experience; what Rilke has in common with Nietzsche is not beliefs
so much as experiences—and the determination to let no belief dehydrate them.

The dichotomy of thought and emotion on which Eliot depends is quite modern and particularly characteristic, *pace*
Eliot, of logical positivism, especially in its first and crudest
phase. It was largely alien to Greek philosophy. Plato juxtaposed reason and the senses without confining emotion to either
realm: he knew the passion of thinking too well. Among the
earliest pre-Socratics there is no evidence of any division of

man into disjointed faculties; this is one main reason why Heidegger rejects the whole Western tradition that begins with Plato, why he goes back to the pre-Socratics, and why he has occupied himself so largely with Hölderlin and Rilke. He seeks a mode of perception that leaves behind the disunity of modern man. And Rilke, like Nietzsche, is an outstanding representative of a nonpositivistic sensibility in which thought and emotion interpenetrate.

In sum: I cannot agree that the philosopher is interested "in the thought itself" while the poet is not. Many philosophers are altogether too exclusively concerned with the relation of a thought to other thoughts, and too little with the thought itself. They are interested in its consistency with other ideas and in the adequacy of arguments in which it appears either as a link or as a conclusion; but they are "not necessarily interested in the thought itself"—often much less so than the poet. Most men, including many philosophers, discuss the truth of beliefs without any clear notion of their meaning—of their many possible meanings. What the poet, however, is supremely interested in and can teach the philosopher is the meaning of thoughts; and where this is ignored, any discussion of truth is likely to degenerate into the most arid scholasticism. The relation between philosopher and poet is not a one-way affair, and least of all does the poet give polished expression to the ideas of the philosopher. As we have seen, no philosopher influenced Goethe half as much as he influenced subsequent philosophy (cf. chapters 4 and 8).

7

What does the great poet do? I have rejected the traditionalists' account of the relation of poetry to tradition, reality, and truth: they fail to recognize the essential autonomy of poetry that subverts stereotypes hallowed by tradition, changes our perception of reality, and makes accepted truths questionable by making us aware of the concrete meanings of ideas.

The poet does not imitate reality. This Greek conception, which was originally suggested by epic and dramatic poetry, does not do justice to Homer and Sophocles any more than to

Shakespeare. The great poet is the enemy of our everyday reality: he makes that which we have seen with our own eyes appear as a mere shadow of that reality which we encounter in *Oedipus, Lear,* or *The Brothers Karamazov.* He shows us that we live blindly on the surface and says in Rilke's words: "you must change your life."

In drama and epic, novel and lyrical poem, the poet records individual experiences in their unmitigated subjectivity and thus expands our subjectivity and cracks our horizons. The poet is not bound by any man's thoughts; he records experience with its emotionally colored thoughts and his thoughts about emotions. He neither imitates an archaic torso of Apollo nor sets down in rhyme thoughts about it that someone else has had before him. He gives us the experience of a man who is unusually sensitive and thoughtful.

Rilke's "Archaic Torso of Apollo" is admittedly quite different from a clinical recording of a stream of consciousness. But how can one communicate an emotion, or for that matter any experience, seeing that emotion has part in all of them? General labels like "admire" or "beautiful" or "love" conceal a multitude of thoughts, sensations, and perceptions, if they do not altogether supplant the dazzling texture of experience. A phrase like "shoulders' lucid fall" is not the emotional equivalent of a thought—what thought?—but the thoughtful equivalent of an emotional experience.

In the child's consciousness, thought and emotion are not yet dissociated, and many words that later lose their color have a powerful emotional impact. Gradually we learn to some extent to disentangle thoughts from emotions, not only in mathematics and science generally but whenever we are asked to tell simply and briefly "what happened." Eventually, the emotions shrivel until they become weak enough to be confined by a small vocabulary and content merely to accompany that which really matters. The great artist liberates the emotions and recreates the sheer wonder of childhood without surrendering the development of the intellect.

Like a child, the great artist is less confined by convention than most adults: he experiences things in a profoundly individual manner, more intensely and honestly, less swayed by reputations and authorities. Aware of this, Nietzsche and Rilke occasionally made the child the symbol of the creator, but neither shared the anti-intellectualism of some of the romantics or wanted to return to childhood or "nature." Nietzsche in particular recognized that the greatest artists were men of surpassing intellectual power, men like Leonardo and Michelangelo, Dante and Goethe; and he wanted the same freedom for the intellect as for the emotions. Neither he nor Rilke would consider following the precedent of some of the romantics by fleeing back into the arms of authority.

Feeling the impact of Rodin and Cézanne—he wrote on both —Rilke thought at times that it was the poet's task

> *just to say: house,*
> *bridge, well, gate, jug, fruit tree, window—*
> *at most: column, tower—but to say it, understand,*
> *oh, to say it as the things themselves never*
> *thought of existing intensely.*

Seeing how a painter can take a jug or an apple and restore to it the intensity that it had lost in ordinary adult perception; seeing how a sculptor can take the apparently unmysterious shape of a human body and show us passion, longing, despair, grace, agony, and beauty, Rilke thought that the poet might take the everyday words and restore their poetry to them.

One can re-experience this thought and understand it; but if we examine it instead of abandoning ourselves to the rhythms of Rilke's ninth elegy, we find that this aestheticism borders on the absurd: "Are we perhaps *here* just to say: house"? Rilke himself might have admitted that we are here for no purpose at all, but can give our life a purpose; and "just to say: house" is an absurd purpose.

The poet is not condemned merely to revitalize words; and any mystery that one can ultimately find in the words, "house, bridge, well" is a paltry and bloodless thing compared to Rodin's *Tête de la douleur* or *La Martyre*—the mute hopelessness that the sculptor has forced to utter not merely a blessing (like Balaam who had intended to pronounce a curse) but the comfort of complete achievement—that fusion of the passion of life with the repose of death which is accomplished only in the rarest moments and endures only in great art.

The great poet revitalizes words only incidentally. To brook comparison with Rodin he must achieve with words what Rodin does in bronze or marble. He does not imitate reality but realizes that our everyday world is not merely a brute reality but also a human creation that is no longer recognized as such, because the mass of men have lost the perception of those more poetic, more creative, more childlike men who originally fashioned words and values as a mirror of the mysteries they felt. But the poet does not restore the life that was there in the beginning, in childhood or in the childhood of the race: he creates new life, more than life—that for which human life is a reach and aspiration.

Rilke suggests, later in the ninth elegy, that the artist transforms the earth:

> *Earth, is not this what you want: to arise in us*
> invisible?—*Is it not your dream*
> *to be invisible once?—Earth! Invisible!*
> *What if not transformation is your urgent command?*

Here man's aspiration is projected into the earth, and the poet receives his call from the earth as the Hebrew prophets received theirs from God.

John Stuart Mill once defined matter as "the permanent possibility of sensation." For Rilke reality is a call to perceive—but to perceive as has never been perceived before—and to transform, to create our own world, which is essentially new. The world is the raw material of the creator. It is not what a divine creator has in the beginning wrought out of chaos; we are still confronted by the chaos out of which we must create a world.

Not only the traditionalists have shrunk from this prospect; Plato did, too. He thought that what passes in time is merely an imperfect explication of what is eternal. Time, he said, is the moving image of eternity. Such otherworldliness slights the power of man. Art is the eternal image of the moving. The flux is sound and fury signifying nothing, but human art has fashioned works of such perfection that men have thought the world must be a copy of what are in fact human creations. For man's deepest superstition demands that excellence must have priority in time, too. Nothing has ever prevailed against it in the popular mind except the more recent superstition that excellence must always appear late. But excellence, like ecstasy, is always possible. And it is a fallacy to mistake our oblivion of time for an experience of something transcendent and eternal. In truth, it is only in some works of art that ecstasy endures.

I4

PHILOSOPHY VERSUS POETRY

A writer with a style of his own has the power to be present on the printed page. His personality prevails over distance and death, and his sentences have their characteristic bearing and peculiar intonation even when they are not spoken. Impersonal conventions lose their force: language is no longer dominated by the stern demands of ritual tradition and asserts her sovereignty, changing and inventing and alluding at her pleasure. But when language, freed from bondage, defies the restraints of custom, she sometimes gains mastery over the man who had hoped to use her—Nietzsche, for example, as he wrote his *Zarathustra*.

It is as if, intoxicated with a sense of her own possibilities, she seduced the master to make merry with her. He revels in beauty and even in genuine insights, by no means entirely deluded in his sense that he has gained unprecedented heights, but mercifully unaware of the cost of his Pyrrhic triumph. Never before, perhaps, has language attained such brilliancy, and few writers have framed such penetrating perspectives in prose. The stale molds of generations of artists are abandoned, their models are transcended, and we are stunned by an authentic and incomparable record of experiences of which the raw material may be known to us, while the revolutionary form uncovers unsuspected potentialities and opens up new areas for man's self-understanding.

The price, however—not only for the writer but for us, too—may be sheer calamity. If it comes to a few years of his life that he might have spent with a little more quiet contentment, but less knowledge of life for all that; or if it be his sanity, burned out in the flare of his revelations or perhaps slowly corroded by an infection that, however, heightened his perception and permitted him to see through what had been opaque to others—this cost, though made up of endless nights like those in which he fashioned his work, is nevertheless a pittance compared to the real catastrophe. For the very work for which he sacrificed comfort, life, and sanity may become a monument to all he fought against, insuring its immortality in the museum of world literature—indeed, the very voice with which his opponents speak with fiery tongues to a posterity that—ultimate irony—believes itself to be listening to the poet himself.

But is this tragedy not purely personal, and immaterial to mankind, unless we make a point of projecting ourselves fictitiously, and somewhat sentimentally, into the artist's consciousness, which is mercifully blotted out by death or madness?

Suppose the poet was also a great thinker whose reason, as a rapier, slashed through the cobwebs of our inherited darkness, severed the blinds of superstition, and let in light and air and a promise of freedom—and then he suddenly became aware of the surpassing beauty of language and of the life he might spend cultivating her, teaching her his own ways, and begetting his art with her. Suppose the rare case of such a mind, made for greatness, able to lead us into the light, and burning to do nothing less. He is hoping to make language serve this end by enticing and bewitching us into listening to him. He wants to charm and overpower us until we leave the fleshpots of our ignorance and the myths of father and mother. And then language conquers him and lures him back into primeval fantasies. Word pictures merge with dreams. Insights, tentatively garbed in myths, draw us back into long abandoned spheres of mythical barbarism, and the poet's childish nightmares become our realities. His earliest experiences, long outgrown at the conscious level and transcended in the magnificent constructions of his mature reason, now not only emerge in occasional dreams or in metaphors and parables that might enhance his message but gain independent life and enter history.

This is itself an image and a parable, but something like this has happened more than once. Two of the most interesting

philosophers of all time are cases in point: men of an almost
unique intensity and depth and at the same time of a scope
that, as it were, always includes horizons beyond every horizon; men in whom range and profundity do not exclude each
other, and at the same time fascinating poets to whom we owe
some of the most perceptive insights: Plato, the myth-intoxicated protagonist of reason, and Nietzsche, the Dionysian Voltaire. Both were heirs of Socrates, whom they loved, and yet
both betrayed him, even if not consciously. Socrates was their
love, but poetry even more than Socrates. They reviled the
poets for the greater glory of reason and struggled against the
snares of language—and yet created myths more powerful than
those of their opponents.

2

Plato considered the visions of the poets dangerous because
they are apt to overwhelm reason and arouse unreasonable
thoughts and feelings. In this, he esteemed the power of poetry
more highly than most thinkers. And yet this fear betrays a
certain inhumanity that is in evidence elsewhere in the *Republic* and in the *Laws*, too. For what Plato holds against poetry
is precisely its power to enlarge men's sympathies.

Moreover, possibly no other poet from Homer to Euripides
has used his poetry as much as Plato to overpower reason. No
doubt, Plato's contemporaries sometimes cited Homer as authoritative, almost as men of later centuries have cited Scripture or, less often, Plato. Yet the visions of these poets that
Plato feared do not menace our reason now. We still love and
admire them, but only as magnificent poetry. They still liberate
and form the youthful imagination and crack all too narrow
horizons, though unfortunately they reach less and less young
people every year. But they scarcely touch belief and what
men might consider true. In rational reflection we may use
Homeric episodes as illustrations or a Sophoclean situation as
a point of departure; and beyond that the poets point to possibilities that we might otherwise ignore, and they teach us to
understand what we might well shrug off too easily if it were
not for them; but their visions do not mold our thoughts des-

potically and never compel reason to submit to their imagery.

Plato's visions, on the other hand—for example, that of a state from which most of the poets must be exiled lest they should lead men astray—have dominated the thought of posterity more than any tyrant. To be sure, Plato began his career by burning the poems of his youth and by penning a song of songs on free inquiry in his wonderful *Apology*. And later, too, he celebrated Socrates, whose unreserved devotion to critical thinking had led him to martyrdom, charged with impiety and with corrupting youth. And yet Plato used this same man in the *Republic* to expound the vision of a society in which censorship was to prevent impiety and in which youth was to be kept from any contact with philosophy. Still later, in the *Laws*, he fashioned the blueprint of the Inquisition: it was Plato who gave us the concepts of dogma and heresy and contrived a system of spying and punishments, including death for second offenders.

What has this departure from the spirit of the Socratic *Apology* to do with love of language and the witchery of words? There must have been many motives for his change, but the poet's impulse was among them: the delight in—no, the utter possession by—visions, the domineering urge to commit them to language, to shape them in adequate prose, to modulate the last detail. In the architect of the ideal city we recognize the artist who is so jealous of the poets: he is their rival—their successful rival—not only in his comprehensive visions and in the over-all design of many dialogues, but also in the continual abandonment of any pretense of rational inquiry for the sake of what is frankly admitted to be myth. Whether these myths draw freely on ancient lore or are invented on the spur of the moment, it was surely not reason that fashioned them, nor the lust for truth, but the poetic impulse.

That Socrates had not been similarly possessed is attested by all reports of him. His medium was not poetry but his character, which impressed other men directly—not only Plato but also Alcibiades and Xenophon, Aristippus and Antisthenes. In his thoughts he was less concerned with visions—even his ethical ideal had become flesh in him—than with criticism. And he did not require the written word.

Plato could not but write, and usually wrote with beguiling beauty. And when he chose another style for once, as in the second part of his *Parmenides,* he himself had furnished ample precedent for the lavishly un-Socratic, mythical interpretations of the Neoplatonists. His fusion of rational inquiry and myth, which so often means the submission of Socratic questioning to myth, became the pattern for Philo and Augustine, the archetype of Neoplatonism, of scholasticism, and of almost all theology. In modern times, finally, most imitators did not have the stature of a Schelling, and recent history reminds us of the dangers of a mode of thinking that stops before myths or even serves them. Does totalitarianism begin where reason abdicates? And did Plato, albeit involuntarily, give reason a good conscience in its self-betrayal?

It may be objected that the highest truths are suprarational and hence must be accepted piously whether from tradition, from authority, or poetry. Was it not Plato's very wisdom to recognize the limits of inquiry and to complement his reasoning with myths? And did he not scrupulously distinguish myth and philosophy? There is always the temptation of bowing to tradition by suspending our critical faculties—for example, by making our peace with Plato and exonerating him: his greatness precludes criticism; his stature makes our analysis irreverent—and Plato himself, in the *Laws,* might even have turned us over to the Nocturnal Council for eventual execution.

We must ask if the vision of the Nocturnal Council or of the ideal city, the myth of the creation in the *Timaeus,* the parable (or "noble lie") of the three metals with its conception of the radical inequality of men, or the parable of the cave, or any of the other myths, set forth ultimate truths in the most adequate manner possible. And how are we to tell if we accept them because piety requires it, or tradition, or authority? Whether reason had really reached its limits in any particular instance where it suddenly gives way to myth is a question that cannot be decided by appeal to myths but only by rational examination. Quite generally, the limits of reason can be discovered only by reason itself. And if a myth should represent those limits correctly, only reason can establish this.

Plato's myths, like many less charming myths of the twen-

tieth century, do not by any means always represent ultimate
truths, nor do they appear only when further inquiry has become impossible. Also, there are in his work, as in our time,
many mythical elements that are not marked as such; and
apparently rational arguments are often subservient to a vision.
But the visions themselves—*and this is the only objection to
them*—are not examined conscientiously but are accepted as
oracles.

For philosophy, as for the sciences, vision and intuition are
indispensable, but we cannot welcome their gifts indiscriminately without inviting superstition and random stupidity. The
genius of a poet is not sufficient warrant against such dangers.
Plato, for example, with his impassioned denunciations of the
poets, has lulled reason—his own no less than that of his readers—into a trance in which it has the sensation of vigorous
exertion even while it merely witnesses a procession of dream
images, summoned partly from tradition, partly from the poet's
past. For Plato recognized the dangers of poetry—but only in
others.

Neither the wrath of Achilles nor the sufferings of Odysseus
enslaves reason as Plato does when he compels us, from generation to generation, to return to the cave of his imagination
to view the world that even now surrounded us in splendor
and bright beauty, as if it were mere shadows on a wall of
rock, and as if even the greatest paintings and sculptures were
shadows of shadows. The power of this vision transcends all
arguments and, like a fiery speaker, is not deterred by objections. The image outlasts all reasons, and—perhaps partly because he realizes this—the philosopher permits himself all but
incredible liberties in his argumentation. He does not shrink
from almost laughable fallacies and exuberant leaps of thought
to utterly unproved positions that are yet presented as if they
were implied by what has gone before. And alleged refutations
of opponents often lack all cogency. Yet the intent does not
seem demagogical. Possibly, Plato wants to offer students op-
portunities to analyze his arguments and faults of reasoning.
But even if this should have been one of the uses of the texts
—and even that is doubtful—the same impulse is at work that

leads Plato to impute views and arguments to various Sophists whom he introduces in his dialogues, though they would have been quick to disown what he attributes to them. He invites comparison with Aristophanes, who treated Socrates in the same way in a comedy. And from Plato's *Symposium* it would seem that Plato did not hold this against the comedian, seeing that Plato puts one of his finest myths into the mouth of Aristophanes. But we must judge a philosopher according to far stricter standards than we should apply to a dramatist.

We must also recall Plato's fateful dream of a society consisting of rulers, soldiers, and mob, with the right of deception reserved for the rulers, with censorship of all the arts, all poetry, all thought, and with a rigidly specified education, assuring a continual supply of the right wisdom. Here, too, it is important to note that the charm of this idea is quite independent of the arguments adduced in its behalf, which are far less well known. The picture casts its spell without the aid of reason.

In the light of recent history and of the use to which Plato was put by Nazi educators, we cannot shut our eyes to the great danger of philosophies that thus address themselves to man's irrationality while paralyzing his critical spirit, half mockingly, half playfully. If mockery is needed now it is Socratic mockery: irony at the expense of unreason and uncritical thinking.

3

Surely, this is an utterly one-sided picture of Plato in which his totalitarianism—meaning the belief that the government has the right to regulate all phases of men's lives—is emphasized out of proportion while some other sides of Plato's thought have been ignored. After all, we know the irony of Socrates mainly from Plato's dialogues. Even in the *Republic,* not to speak of other dialogues, he arouses reason by awakening it to ever novel problems. Utterly at variance with his own ideas about education, he never refuses to see something new. In many men Plato has kindled the desire to pursue problems wherever inquiry may lead, defying all attempts at censorship. This greatest thinker of all time was not a wicked foe of freedom but a man who was in many ways at odds with himself.

The historian of ideas may point to the conflicting influences of, first, Socrates and, later, some of the Pythagoreans. The *Apology* was probably almost purely Socratic while the *Republic* and *Phaedo* show how Plato came under the spell of the Pythagoreans. Yet the split between the poetic and the rational impulse preceded such divergent influences; and the dualism of Plato's character cannot be fully explained in terms of two conflicting heritages, any more than the complexities of Paul's epistles are reducible to the clash of Greek and Hebrew elements. The overwhelmingly critical attitude of Socrates did not permanently satisfy the mind of Plato. His bent was too mystical and speculative or, in one word, too poetical.

Karl Popper, whose caricature of Hegel has been considered in chapter 7, has pictured Plato as Socrates' Judas. For all his attempts at psychological explanations, Popper vastly underestimates the profound complexity of the soul that finds expression in the dialogues. If in effect Plato did betray his master, whom he surely loved, it was probably more in the way in which Paul, according to some critics, betrayed Jesus: the personal tragedy lies in the man's devotion to his master; and the historical calamity, in the price that we have had to pay for this unwitting betrayal. For Plato attained immortality in part by lending an immortal voice to those whom at first he attacked. If it was Plato who, in the *Apology*, lavished such eloquence on Socrates that his accusers seemed silenced forever, it was also Plato who later, in the *Republic* and the *Laws* —without, it seems, realizing this tragic irony—invented a reply that still plagues us.

Socrates, who wanted to awaken reason in the men with whom he talked, had pictured himself as the very embodiment of criticism, as a gadfly on the neck of men. Plato, however, with his beautiful images, often puts the critical sense to sleep. Reacting against the Greek enlightenment, he gave an unprecedented stimulus to speculation.

4

Plato's poetry is not the sugar-coating on a pill, a mere device, as Lucretius said of his own verse, to make his philosophy more palatable. True poetry cannot be used as a mere surface; it is something that possesses a man's soul. Socrates had said ironically that the poets do not understand their own verse; but Plato occasionally celebrated the poetic frenzy with an evidently un-Socratic enthusiasm and, it would seem, with first-hand knowledge. He feared poetry because he knew its power; and yet it outwitted him, and he supposed that he could use it as a mere means, subjected to the censorship of reason, as he suggests in the *Republic*. But poets who submit to censorship and employ language with its images and rhythms only to sugar-coat ideas that were clear to them before cease to be poets. Poetry is an expression of the love of language; and when the once beloved is used as a mere means, love has ceased.

When the poet uses language he also allows language to use him; and what he writes is constantly suggested to him by the images and sounds, the rhymes and rhythms, the allusions and alliterations of the language. He finds his inspiration partly in his slowly growing work, proceeds in unforeseen directions, and at times finds fitting places for a phrase, an image, or a vision, without asking every time if reason, as a censor, would approve of every word—or of every suggestion and insinuation. Yet sometimes he himself follows such suggestions and pursues the implications of his way of putting things. And a vision, if it is majestic or suggestive, is not readily suppressed for other reasons. Surely, Plato did not tell beautiful stories only—as many critics assume—when he had first considered conscientiously whether he might not, with some trouble, make the same point less enchantingly. And visions did not come only when reason had come to a dead end.

Plato was, and always remained, a true poet, and it was precisely the wealth of his visions and his myths that prompted him to *write* in spite of Socrates' example. But if the stories and the parables, the visions and the myths often preceded the context in which he presents them or flashed into his mind as he was writing, then Plato's doctrines are at crucial points based on his poetry. Philosophy—not only Plato's—is at times reflection on a piece of poetry and follows out its implications and suggestions.

If the sugar—or, as the German proverb puts it, *gold*—is primary, one might well reproach the poet for not keeping his pills to himself. Why should he encumber us with doctrines that are partly all too literal interpretations of fine myths and metaphors? Certainly, not all poetic inspiration comes from higher regions, and a lot of it is rooted in our childhood or in the infancy of our culture. We must never accept inspiration as an oracle. We can receive it on a nonphilosophic level and enjoy it without seeking a true doctrine in it. But if we do accept it on the level of philosophy, we must submit it to the full rigor of reason and, with the impassioned hardness of the thinker, test it in the fire of unsentimental criticism.

This view is not popular and never has been. Socrates' unromantic criticism of the poets did not endear him to the Athenian public and did much to earn him that hostility which led to his trial. It made him almost as many enemies as his exposure of the politicians. Why? Because men have always sought a royal road to truth. At this point many motives come together: above all, sloth and the yearning for security. The claim of the great religions, and the small religions, and the little sects, that they provide a safe and easy short-cut to the truth always finds eager ears and often is backed up by powerful organizations and rewards and threats, both in this world and after. Those who outgrow such claims are often not prepared to give up every hope of finding truth wrapped in a handy text: some turn to natural or social science, while others think that "beauty is truth, truth beauty," and revere poetic inspiration. But the greatest scientists and poets have no such illusions.

Goethe made a remark to Eckermann (January 18, 1825) that is worth volumes about truth and poetry: "Lord Byron is great only as a poet; as soon as he reflects he is a child." This epigram says briefly and convincingly what Plato often said much more emphatically: in matters of philosophy, poets are suspect, and it is foolish to suppose that a great poet must be, or is probably, a great philosopher or thinker. On the contrary, it is inherently unlikely.

Shakespeare's vision of the universe and of man's lot may have been more profound than Descartes' or Aquinas', Reinhold Niebuhr's or John Dewey's; but the beauty of a line or passage is no warrant of the truth of its assertion. To the question whether any view is true, the sensuous perfection of the statement is irrelevant. And Shakespeare's poetry is most profound and true in speeches in which he does not "reflect," to use Goethe's word. Some of his bald assertions, born of his almost unequaled disillusionment, are much truer than the painstaking ratiocinations of the so-called philosophic poets. But to show which of his assertions are true requires argument and critical reflection.

It so happens in Shakespeare's case that the passages that conform to conventional religious sentiments are often poor poetically because they lack all spontaneity and inspiration while the speeches that explode convention and give form to Shakespeare's own experience elevate us to an altogether different plane. Prospero's most poetic speech almost cracks the context as it reaches out beyond all requirements of the plot to say that "the great globe itself" will "leave not a rack behind" and that "our little life is rounded with a sleep." His Epilogue with its conventional religious imagery is charming in spite of its doggerel but does not compare as poetry or in sheer power with the earlier speech. Similarly, Portia's famous sermon on "the quality of mercy" is incredibly prosy and does not brook comparison in strength of utterance with Timon's indictments of man. Nor does it have the fluency and bold force of conviction that marks Macbeth's lines on "a tale told by an idiot."

To some readers this may be sufficient proof that beauty and truth are far from inseparable. But even if it were a fact in Shakespeare's case that some of his most perfect lines are also true—insofar as they are statements of general import and not, like some of Lady Macbeth's glorious speeches, incantations—we should still require critical reflection to decide in every instance whether what sounds beautiful is also true.

5

The great philosopher who is also a poet does not prove either that philosophy and poetry are at bottom one. We must approach him with suspicion unless we are ready to insult him by considering him merely as a poet or—worse—as a stylist. When we study his philosophy we must ask whether it is influenced, indeed infected, by its intimate relation with poetry. Poetry is like a panther: it delights the eye; but against any attempt to enslave it, it may wreak revenge.

Nietzsche was the sworn enemy of all pseudoscience, whether romantic or theological; the archenemy of German nationalism, the opponent of the myth-intoxicated, anti-Semitic Wagner; a professed good European and admirer of the French Enlightenment. He wanted to found the enthusiasm about reason that had been characteristic of the Enlightenment upon a more profound understanding of man, thus raising the erratic intuitions of some of the romantics to the level of unsentimental science. He wanted to do justice to the irrational, but not by way of a cult of feeling: he sought psychological understanding. The Enlightenment was to be deepened by romanticism; and romanticism, to be harnessed by the Enlightenment. That was the intent of Nietzsche's philosophy of self-overcoming, of his psychology of the will to power, and of his affirmation of the passions as the necessary raw material of creative sublimation. The powerful man in Nietzsche's sense is the passionate man who is the master of his passions: Goethe, for example. Or Leonardo. Or Julius Caesar—not as the master of the Roman Empire but as the master of himself; for this involved possession of a singularly rich, complex, and subtle nature.

Nietzsche's central concern was thus with man's humanity. Beginning with his early essays, the *Untimely Meditations*, he wanted to counter Darwin's doctrine of the continuity of man and beast with a new image of humanity that must be based on an empirical, a psychological, foundation. Thus he sought what in man might be "not only animal," that which might give man an exceptional position in the cosmos—not brutal qualities but those which differentiate man and elevate him. And he found man's artistic and man's philosophic efforts, but above all else the gift of organizing the chaos of his passions and desires—the power to "give style" to one's own character.

Alas, the philosopher fell in love with language. He no longer could resist a daring play on words, a witty epigram, or an elegant polemic, merely because they might lead to profuse misunderstanding. When coinages occurred to him—like the will to power, the blond beast, master morality, and overman—he did not suppress them or immediately define them carefully: he enjoyed them, loved them, played with them, and hoped against his judgment that it might suffice if now and then he castigated misconceptions with sardonic malice, worthy of a Socrates, and if he told his readers that he must be read with caution and attention to what goes before and to what follows.

Definitions would scarcely have helped. One cannot coin a good phrase or create a splendid image and expect that readers—and the far more numerous nonreaders who eventually hear of it, too—will employ it in their own thoughts only in the context that it had in the writer's mind. Soon fantastic notions are read into the philosopher; and many people who know little but some of his coinages and metaphors assume there *is* no context and the man was no philosopher, ascribing their own lack of effort to the writer.

Much misunderstanding is due to bad reading and to poor and frequently unscrupulous interpreters. But Nietzsche abetted such developments when he succumbed to language. Certainly, his philosophy was no mere over-compensation of his own faults, and his conceptions of the overman and the will to power represent major achievements, since they are inseparable from his notion of sublimation. But the images to which Nietzsche gave poetic license came up from that inner realm of shadows in which that which the philosopher and human being had long overcome continued its timeless and fleshless being. And in the associations that are kindled by these images, against Nietzsche's own unequivocally expressed desire, we discern the poison of the serpent whom the thinker vanquished. He bruised the serpent's head, but the serpent bruised his heel.

What is at stake here is not merely a small number of misinterpretations. The whole heritage of the Enlightenment and all relations to Gibbon, Hume, Voltaire, and to the origins of modern democratic thought have been ignored or denied persistently. The first-rate achievements of the Enlightenment in Germany were soon inundated by the romantic flood of what Goethe called "neo-German, religious-patriotic art." Lessing's critique of theology and his enlightened ideas were soon forgotten; one was content to point to his restless personality and possibly also to his literary criticism. Kant was seen as the precursor of idealism; his *Idea for a Universal History with Cosmopolitan Intent* with its conception of a League of Nations and his essay *Toward Eternal Peace* received little attention. It became an axiom that the Enlightenment had been ridiculously shallow; and one took no chances on this score and claimed, contrary to the facts, that its chief German representative had been a Berlin book dealer, named Nicolai. The young Hegel was interpreted as a mystic; Heine and Freud were either seen as romantics or repudiated as un-German; and Nietzsche became a "late son of romanticism."

Nietzsche himself, to be sure, had repeatedly indicted romanticism and nationalism with all the vehemence that is so typical of long delayed reactions; he had stressed his roots in the French Enlightenment, and some of his analyses invite comparison with Hume's. But all this was discounted as proof of his pitiful self-laceration. In this way bridge upon bridge to humanity and international understanding was burned.

The last phase of this development is by far the most radical. In his essay on "Nietzsche's Word 'God is Dead'" Heidegger is not content to spirit away out of Nietzsche's thought the central appeal to humanity: by means of highly arbitrary methods that show no regard for context he construes Nietzsche's philosophy as the tombstone of the whole European tradition. What might be a bridge becomes a breach between

Germany and Europe. And this break is sealed by the fact that philosophy, which spoke in European accents in the works of Nietzsche, now parades in a purely national and untranslatable language.

It is not always by means of poetry that language overwhelms philosophers. A thinker who has a style of his own without being a poet may immerse himself thoroughly in words and what he takes to be their etymologies, and the sensational glare of his analyses that attracts wide attention may at times be a mere paper fire. He thinks that unlike all previous thinkers since the early Greeks he is on the traces of Being itself, but it is language that has her sport with him. And in the end the love of language leads the philosopher to poetry after all, and he demands that we give up the whole conception of prosaic truth and instead listen to the voice of the pre-Socratic poet-philosophers or find ultimate revelations in Hölderlin's final madness.

We do not slight Hölderlin and Rilke if we question their philosophical eminence. It is because we do not demand philosophical excellence from poets that we can find great poetry in the splendid rhythms that mirror Hölderlin's insanity. The popularity in postwar Germany of Heidegger's attempts to gain a new standpoint in *Interpretations of Hölderlin's Poetry* almost makes one wonder whether large masses of people have become so used to bowing before madness and illogic, accepting the intuitions of a madman as authoritative revelations, that the demise of one such authority has set them looking frantically, like dope addicts, to find another source.

The recovery of sanity and humanity demands the disciplined repudiation of narcotics. Reason is needed, not the intoxication of the sometimes splendid madness of Nietzsche's prose nor the romantic cult of sentiment. The great German philosophers—Kant, Fichte, Hegel, and Nietzsche no less than Leibniz—tried without exception to absorb the riches of the European Enlightenment instead of simply rejecting it as shallow; and the great poets, emphatically including those of Germany, also point the way toward humanity.

6

Poets are not philosophical oracles. Yet they have not only the gift of lending expression to single feelings and attitudes but also the power to create characters, enabling the reader to gain experiences for which any possibility would otherwise be lacking in a single human life. Poetry makes possible a vast expansion of our world, an extension of sympathy, and a profounder understanding not only of human possibilities but also of human realities.

To fulfill this mission, poetry need not become didactic. A lyric poem can awaken longing; a novel, sympathy with Raskolnikov and thus a better understanding not only of other men but of ourselves, too. Similarly, the greatness of *Faust* lies, not least of all, in Goethe's characters. Whoever has really experienced Faust and shared his world for once will become different even if he has not consciously reflected at great length on the ideas that might be implicit in the play. Mephistopheles and Gretchen, too, have their effect on our character; and so do, even if to a lesser extent, Lieschen and Valentin, who come to life in a single scene each.

Poetry can supplement philosophy best when it quite renounces the attempt to offer mystic truths and instead confronts us with what reason can never fully comprehend: above all, with man's inexhaustible possibilities and with that aspect of experience which language can never fully grasp so long as it does not make use of all its resources.

Man's possibilities and our own potentialities are limited. There is a breaking point—but one man in a million reaches it. The rest seek refuge in mediocrity. T. E. Hulme once compared the romantic view that sees man as a well with the classical view that denies man's infinite perfectibility, asserts his limitations, and, in effect, sees him as a bucket. The contrast is academic: most men stay so near the surface and do not spend more of themselves than a few miserly drops. Man is neither a well nor a bucket but a lake. And poetry describes some of the images he mirrors and some of the weird creatures he harbors. Poetry reveals man to himself.

At its best, poetry does not sugar-coat philosophies but, rather, makes philosophy seem two-dimensional by showing us what depths there are that most philosophies leave unexplored. But poetry is not essentially polemical: it is older than philosophy and at its best rarely concerned with it.

Eliot supposes that philosophy comes first and furnishes the poet with his *Weltanschauung;* but great poetry comes into being long before philosophy is born, and the great poets usually require no philosophy. Eliot writes as if Shakespeare had been an exception in this respect when in fact this was one of the few ways in which he was not an exception. It was Dante whose use of Aquinas was exceptional: Homer and Hesiod, Aeschylus and Sophocles, Euripides and Aristophanes, Vergil, Shakespeare, and Goethe were neither philosophers nor used another man's philosophy.

Philosophy does not just happen to develop after poetry: it begins as critical reflection on the offerings of the poets, and it rarely betrays its origins completely. One of its central tasks is always to show up the illicit pretensions of the poets and the would-be poets who mistake their fantasies for truth. There is a sense in which poetry comes close to being a sweet poison, and philosophy hurts. The philosopher is the gadfly who will not allow men to drowse languidly in the dusk of murky sentiment and comfortable prejudice: he wakes them up and casts a glaring shaft of light into the twilight of imagination.

Philosophy cannot illuminate everything at once. Whenever it makes clear a few things, much else remains in semidarkness —and it is the poet who reminds us of this, drawing freely on the riches of the vast periphery of shadows. If we had poetry only and no philosophy at all, we could either remain satisfied with fancy and more than a little childish or, worse, we might seek in poetry a substitute for knowledge and accept the judgments and assumptions of some honey-tongued master of language without any power of discrimination.

Discrimination is so odious and onerous that many a philosopher since Plato's time would sooner not be quite so critical. To be a hierophant or mystagogue seems much more dignified, significant, and edifying than the lowly task of the poor gadfly. Again and again, philosophers have preferred to comprehend and explicate great poetry according to their lights instead of criticizing it. If they have done it without any critical discrimination, they have obviously betrayed their calling. But more often they have picked out what they liked, left out what they did not like, and used quotations in place of arguments. In its extreme form, this is called theology, and the method might be called, using a political term: gerrymandering (cf. my *Critique*, section 56).

That is one way of fusing philosophy and poetry. It is not the only one. It is also possible, as we have seen, for a philosopher to fuse both genres by writing dialogues, like Plato, or *Thus Spoke Zarathustra*, like Nietzsche. Yet another possibility has been well represented by Jean-Paul Sartre and Albert Camus: instead of fusing philosophy and poetry in the same work, they have fashioned stories, plays, and novels—and then, in their philosophical works, expounded the ideas that had been implicit in their literary pieces.

Treated merely as an exposition of their more artistic works, the philosophic writings of Camus and Sartre can claim more authority than any of the exegeses theologians offer us of Scriptures that they have not written themselves and that, therefore, they are not in such a privileged position to expound with unique understanding. But if we treat Sartre's and Camus's more philosophic works not as mere interpretations of their literary labors but as offering theories that claim to have more general application—and this is clearly how both men desire to be read—we find that their generalizations are often untenable.

Sartre's story on "The Childhood of a Leader" is magnificent, but his "Portrait of the Antisemite," although probably one of his best essays and emphatically worth reading, overgeneralizes by treating the dubious hero of his own short story as *the* anti-Semite par excellence. Sartre's short story, "The Wall," is magnificent, but his philosophy of man's condition abounds in overgeneralizations: extremely interesting but arbitrary for all that.[1]

[1] "Portrait of the Antisemite" and "The Wall" are both reprinted in my *Existentialism from Dostoevsky to Sartre,* along with Sartre's famous lecture "Existentialism is a Humanism" and the chapter on

The same fault is even more in evidence in Camus's philosophic efforts. *The Stranger* is a little masterpiece; but the attempt to squeeze out of this novel a philosophy of the absurd —not merely as an explication of the text but as a theory about the world and life—is once again unsound. His philosophical efforts are altogether beneath comparison with his fiction.[2]

Camus was a nightingale who thought he was an owl. He brings to mind once more Goethe's comment that "Byron is great only as a poet; as soon as he reflects he is a child." But millions took Camus's reflections seriously, because his views were so attractive, because he wrote so well, and because he took himself so seriously. Alas, he deceived himself and thought he was what he was not. The same flaw mars some of his fiction: "the stranger" is not what the author thinks he is—incarnate apathy. "The stranger" tells us that he is indifferent and that he paid no attention to the tedious goings-on in court during his trial, but the few details he did observe and his skill in describing them prove that, far from embodying the state of mind about which Camus wants to tell a parable, "the stranger" has the sensitivity and the intelligence of a good poet. Socrates claimed that the Athenian poets, who did not pose as philosophers, could not give accurate accounts of their own work. Camus is open to the same charge—perhaps more so.

Sartre, whom one would not think of likening to a nightingale because he lacks Camus's great charm, excels Camus both in imaginative power and in philosophic penetration. He does not write parables but envisages a living situation, concrete even if it should be mythical—and the analysis comes later. His philosophy is full of stimulating insights, and some good interpreters deny that all, or even most, of these come from

"Self-Deception" from *L'être et le néant*. All four are discussed *ibid.*, pp. 40 ff.

[2] See my essay on "Existentialism and Death" (B.10 in the Bibliography below). For a very different view of Sartre and Camus see Hazel E. Barnes, "Walter Kaufmann's New Piety" in *Chicago Review*, Autumn 1959, and her book, *The Literature of Possibility: A Study in Humanistic Existentialism*, The University of Nebraska Press, 1959.

reflection on his more imaginative writings. Be that as it may.

For a philosopher it will not do to confine himself, even if only in the main, to some one scripture, whether it be the Bible, the Upanishads, or his own fiction. Nor will it do for him to be content, even if only very largely, to expound, to explicate, and to interpret. He must cultivate critical thinking. If he does not, who will?

One can criticize the fictions that have come to be accepted widely. One can make a habit of examining all dreams and fancies that purport to be more than dreams and fancies—very much including one's own.

Philosophy that does not shrink from this Socratic heritage leaves ample room for poetry and finds no need, like Plato, to expel the poets. What is important is that there should not be one scripture only, but many poets. Philosophy learns more from the best of them than it can learn from almost anyone else: poetry liberates us from the egocentric predicament and teaches us how others feel and think and judge.

It is when we begin to ask how we ourselves should judge, it is when our views have become problematic to us in the light of what the poets have told us of other possibilities that philosophy is born.

Confronted with philosophy and poetry, extolling one at the other's expense would be madness. To try to make one disappear in the other is bound to be fatal. We need both; and here, for once, it is easy to make a joy of necessity.

JASPERS' RELATION
TO NIETZSCHE

Nietzsche's influence on contemporary thought has been extremely widespread, and revealing references to him are scattered through the works of Freud and Sartre, Jung and Spengler, Gide and Malraux, Scheler and Nicolai Hartmann, Shaw, and a great many others. Thomas Mann and Martin Heidegger, Simmel and Vaihinger, Stefan Zweig and Ludwig Klages, Paul Elmer More and H. L. Mencken, Leo Schestow and Josiah Royce are among those who have devoted whole essays or books to him. Karl Jaspers is one of the few to have written two whole books as well as several essays on Nietzsche; and in many of Jaspers' other writings, too, his preoccupation with Nietzsche is striking.

As we leave Nietzsche to consider existentialism, some reflections on Jaspers' relation to Nietzsche furnish an ideal approach. It should throw light on both men and on the development of German thought over a period of approximately three-quarters of a century.

Both men, though of German background, came to hold professorships at Basel, Switzerland: Nietzsche, as a classical philologist; Jaspers, though he studied medicine and later specialized in psychopathology, as a philosopher. Nietzsche's "Untimely Meditation" on history, published after the Franco-Prussian War in 1874, and Jaspers' book *The Origin and Goal of History*—longer but less meaty—published after World War II in 1949, frame an epoch.

From the Western point of view it seems as if Germany had withdrawn from the West: Jaspers' style, though not as obscure as Heidegger's, is less European than Nietzsche's or even

Kant's. But from the German point of view, English-speaking philosophy is no part of the great European tradition that extends from the Greeks through the Middle Ages to Descartes, Spinoza, Leibniz, Kant, Hegel, Nietzsche, and existentialism; there is something barren about Hume, Mill, and Dewey, too; and it generally takes England and the United States about half a century to catch up with German philosophy. Kant arrived in the English-speaking world only after he had long been overshadowed by Hegel in his native country, and Hegelianism became dominant in England and America after Hegel had long gone into eclipse in Germany. From this point of view the time seems ripe now for the reception of Nietzsche, while Jaspers and Heidegger will be appreciated only about 2000 A.D. or, if anything, a little later. The only ray of light in this gloomy prospect is that, according to this analogy, existentialism will by then be out of fashion in Germany.

Those who suspect that existentialism may be right in some sense and that it is surely superior to analytic philosophy, hardly need encouragement to have a closer look. And those who are inclined to think that it would be a misfortune if existentialism made headway in the English-speaking world should realize that if they simply shut their eyes to it and concentrate more than ever on linguistic or logical analysis they will thereby help to insure the very development they hate to contemplate. For the potential audience for the existentialists consists of those who feel that, when they ask for bread, the most competent English-speaking philosophers offer them a stone. What Jaspers and Heidegger have to offer is less clear, partly owing to the language barrier, but mainly owning to the obscurity of their writings. Many Anglo-American philosophers suspect that the writings of the existentialists are not stones but nuts—hollow nuts. There is only one way to find out: to crack the forbidding shell and see what, if anything, it hides.

2

Jaspers' attitude toward Nietzsche—and Kant. In his essay "On My Philosophy," Jaspers has summed up his relation to

Nietzsche in one sentence: "Kant became *the* philosopher for me and has remained so. . . . Nietzsche gained importance for me only late as the magnificent revelation of nihilism and the task of overcoming it (in my youth I had avoided him, repelled by the extremes, the rapture, and the diversity)" (*E.*, p. 137).[1] Nietzsche serves an essentially negative function in Jaspers' work: he is the best guide to the realm beyond which one encounters Kant. Nietzsche's philosophy becomes a mere handmaiden of Kant's postulational theology.

In his famous lecture on "Existentialism," Sartre has called Jaspers a professed Catholic, though his background is in fact Protestant and his religious outlook quite nondenominational. The monumental, but exceedingly fallible, *Oxford Dictionary of the Christian Church* wrongly classifies him as a "Christian" existentialist. Jaspers' faith is distinctly Kantian and not at all centered in Christ. In his philosophy of history, too, he does not find the "axis" of history in the Incarnation but in the age of the Hebrew prophets, the Greek philosophers, Confucius, Lao-tzu, and the Buddha.

Jaspers is too often seen as the heir of Nietzsche and Kierkegaard to whom he is in many ways less close than to Kant. The neo-Kantians, to be sure, he finds uncongenial, and he likes to denounce "professors' philosophy"; but the Kantian antinomies and Kant's concern with the realm of decision, freedom, and faith have become exemplary for Jaspers. And even as Kant "had to do away with knowledge to make room for faith," Jaspers values Nietzsche in large measure because he thinks that Nietzsche did away with knowledge, thus making room for Jaspers' "philosophic faith"—not just for Jaspers' book *Der Philosophische Glaube* (translated as *The Perennial Scope of*

---

[1] A complete translation of this essay may be found in my *Existentialism from Dostoevsky to Sartre*, which also contains Jaspers' essay on "Kierkegaard and Nietzsche." In subsequent references, this volume is cited as *E.*; Jaspers' book, *Nietzsche und das Christentum*, as *Christentum;* his *Einführung in die Philosophie* (translated as *The Way to Wisdom*), as *Einführung;* and my own *Nietzsche* (rev. ed., Meridian Books), as *N.* A detailed comparison of my *Nietzsche* with the interpretations of Jaspers and Heidegger appeared in Sartre's journal, *Les Temps Modernes*, May, 1951: "Nietzsche aujourd'hui" by J. Vuillemin.

Philosophy) but for Jaspers' philosophic stance, which he
himself characterizes as a kind of hovering or suspension
(*Schwebe*).

This diagnosis implies that Jaspers' conception of Nietzsche
is an integral part of Jaspers' philosophy. But it also means
that Nietzsche's philosophy is accepted only as an antecham-
ber. Would Nietzsche have been happy with this approach?
Of course, he fancied himself as a Socrates who exhorted his
pupils to go beyond him, creating their own philosophies:
"One repays a teacher badly, if one always remains a pupil
only" (*Zarathustra*). Even so, it would undoubtedly have
struck him as a preposterous irony, had he seen his thought
reduced to a labyrinth that one enters only to become convinced that there is no way out except Kant's Indian rope
trick. For Kant throws his postulates of practical reason into
the air and uses them to climb out of sight into the transcendent realm, to God, while most of the onlookers rub their eyes,
incapable of explaining how the feat was performed, and wondering, perhaps, whether it was a matter of hypnotic suggestion—a trick protected by Kant's unique prestige.

Nietzsche saw himself as a "herald and precursor" of the
"philosophers of the future" (*Beyond Good and Evil*)—not of
Kant's postulates of God, freedom, and immortality. In fact,
just this "practical philosophy" was what he could not forgive
Kant and what he never tired of deriding.

> I bear the Germans a grudge for having made such a mis-
> take about *Kant* and his "backdoor philosophy," as I call it
> —for that was not the type of intellectual integrity [*Twilight*,
> ix, §16].

> All these great enthusiasts and prodigies behave like our
> little females: they consider "beautiful sentiments" adequate
> arguments, regard a heaving bosom as the bellows of the
> deity, and conviction a *criterion* of truth. In the end, Kant
> tried, with "German" innocence, to give this corruption, this
> lack of any intellectual conscience, scientific status with his
> notion of "practical reason": he invented a special kind of
> reason for cases in which one need not bother about reason.
> . . . When we consider that among almost all peoples the

philosopher is merely the next development of the priestly
type, then this legacy of the priest, this self-deceiving coun-
terfeit, ceases to be surprising [*Antichrist*, §12].

And in the immediately preceding section, Nietzsche even
writes: "Kant became an idiot."

Jaspers has criticized Nietzsche for lacking respect for greatness and cited his outbursts against Kant. Yet Nietzsche often
expressed his respect for Kant. What enraged him was mainly
that Kant followed up his first *Critique* with the second: the
"invention," as he put it in *The Will to Power* (§578), of "the
transcendent world." How would he have felt about Jaspers'
suggestion that it is Nietzsche's great value to prepare us for
the necessity of a Kantian faith?

The Kantianism of Jaspers' "philosophic faith" is well expressed at the beginning of the chapter on "Faith and Enlightenment" in *Einführung in die Philosophie:*

> We have pronounced principles of philosophic faith: God
> is; there is the unconditional demand. . . . Not one of these
> five principles is provable like finite knowledge of objects in
> the world. . . . They are not valid as something professed
> but remain, in spite of the strength of being believed, in
> the suspension of that which is not known.

Here the similarity to Kant could hardly be greater. Even
so, Jaspers' debt to Kant has been slightly exaggerated in this
section; and his relation to Nietzsche, rather oversimplified.
A much more detailed account is required to do justice to the
complexity of these relations. It will be best to begin with
Jaspers' *Psychologie der Weltanschauungen* (1919), which is
more Nietzschean, and less Kantian, than his later work.

3

Psychologie der Weltanschauungen. This book deals with a
fascinating but little explored topic. Where one would usually
raise questions of truth and falsity, it is the psychological background of different outlooks that is probed here: "psychology"
in Nietzsche's sense. Even more crucial is the precedent set by

Nietzsche in offering descriptive analyses that are simultaneously appeals to the reader: a type is depicted in such a manner that we should recognize some of its features in ourselves
and either renounce them with indignant disgust or develop a
burning aspiration to realize them more fully. This kind of
psychology wants to implant, or strengthen, a deep dissatisfaction with our present state of being. It aims to pierce the
soul as an "arrow of longing" (*Zarathustra*).

Jaspers himself seems to have become fully conscious of this
only at a much later date. Thus he writes in 1941, in his essay
"On my Philosophy":

> In *Psychologie der Weltanschauungen* . . . I believed that
> I let pass in pure contemplation what occurs; yet, as a mat-
> ter of fact, I projected the one truth of human existence
> which was peculiarly mine . . . and everywhere I showed
> the current of that which falls off from, empties of content,
> or perverts this norm. It was hidden philosophy which here
> misunderstood itself as objectively descriptive psychology
> [*E.*, pp. 155 f.].

In the same paragraph, Jaspers calls the book "an overbearing work of youth, whose contents, indeed, I still recognize as
mine, but whose form was inadequate." But did Jaspers later
find a more adequate form, when he moved away from psychology to straightforward philosophy? Is his subsequent
Existenzerhellung (1932) a more satisfactory mode of illuminating possibilities of human existence? To point out that his
later efforts are thinner, because lacking in the wealth of concrete illustrations, does not answer this question. But perhaps
it was wrong in principle for Jaspers, who had started as a
psychiatrist and first published *Allgemeine Psychopathologie*
(1913), to renounce psychology more and more, moving gradually from Nietzsche's psychologically penetrating philosophy
to Kant's. For all his greatness, Kant is open to attack precisely
for his sweeping disregard of psychology and his pointedly
unempirical approach to the human mind. To throw light on
human potentialities and to fashion an arrow of longing, Nietzsche's example might have served Jaspers far better—not to
speak of Nietzsche's style.

Even *Psychologie der Weltanschauungen* culminates in an "Appendix: Kant's Doctrine of Ideas" and is, of course, much less "overbearing" than Nietzsche's psychological etchings with their bold, sharply defined lines. Those, however, who consider it mainly a progeny of Dilthey's psychologizing overlook the central call to the reader: the work does not want merely to add to our information; it wants to change us. What it leads toward is not the Christianity of Kierkegaard, who occasionally attempted something similar, but a state of being that is, no less than the method employed, very close to the spirit of Nietzsche.

Beyond all this, the book abounds in important parallels to Nietzsche. Right at the outset, for example, there is a distinction that comes straight out of Nietzsche:

> Philosophers have not only been calm, irresponsible contemplators, but movers and shapers of the world. This philosophy we call *prophetic philosophy*. It confronts universal contemplation as something essentially different because it *gives* Weltanschauung, shows sense and meaning, and sets up tables of values as norms, as valid. This philosophy alone would deserve the name of philosophy, if the name were to retain its noble, powerful ring [p. 2].

This recalls *Beyond Good and Evil* (§211), which culminates in the claim: "The philosophers, properly, however, are commanders and legislators." Even Jaspers' subsequent complaint that "today there is no longer any prophetic philosophy" can be found in Nietzsche's aphorism; only Nietzsche is still more resigned and questions whether any philosopher has ever perfectly represented the prophetic type: "Are there such philosophers today? Have there been such philosophers yet? *Must* there not be such philosophers?"

As a second parallel, take Jaspers' use of Nietzsche's psychology of the will to power and of his conception of *ressentiment*:

> Principles are made to serve for an apology, *ex post facto*, for something which originated from quite different sources. Among the oppressed, such an apology employs the doctrines of *ressentiment* which, by a revaluation, change the

weak and bad into the stronger and better. Among dominant
types, it employs the legitimistic doctrines of race, history,
and superior ability to gain recognition for their power and
their exercise of force as something that is right, and to
permit themselves to experience it as right. These processes
have as their ultimate source some drive for power which
can appropriate any contents of any Weltanschauung in
quite different ways, too, to win out, as the case may be,
through *esprit,* profundity, or dialectical superiority. Thus
all contents of the spirit are, as it were, a mere arsenal of
arms to give oneself significance [p. 37].

This is surely straight Nietzsche, and the absence of any express acknowledgment is probably motivated by the feeling
that the debt is obvious enough to render specific references
overly pedantic: words like *Ressentiment, Umwertung,* and
Macht automatically remind the German reader of Nietzsche.

A sweeping acknowledgment to Nietzsche may serve as our
third example. At the beginning of the section on "Types of
Philosophic Thinking" Jaspers writes:

The psychologically significant directions of thinking could,
of course, be made evident with reference to any thinking
whatever. We choose the pre-Socratics on account of their
relative simplicity, on account of their greatness, and above
all on account of Nietzsche's example; for he used them to
demonstrate the types of philosophic personalities [p. 204].

And in a footnote on the next page: "The following account
rests chiefly on the following sources: Diels, *Fragmente der
Vorsokratiker,* and Nietzsche, *Die Philosophie im tragischen
Zeitalter der Griechen.*" In other words, the account is based
"chiefly" on the fragments themselves and on Nietzsche's interpretations. Of the following ten pages, which cover Greek
philosophy from Thales to Aristotle, four pages are devoted to
Heraclitus, and Jaspers' intense admiration for him is even
more obvious than Nietzsche's.

Jaspers' view of Aristotle is no less striking. It is as negative
as a popular misconception pictures Nietzsche's. Actually, it
recalls Nietzsche's jibes at later Alexandrian erudition. Jaspers

finds Aristotle "without original, creative vision" and merely "the eternal type of the great scholar." And the chapter ends: "Jacob Burckhardt had a contempt for Aristotle." There is, to put it mildly, no indication that Jaspers differs with Burckhardt. Nor has he changed his mind since. In his *Einführung in die Philosophie* (1950), we encounter an eloquent omission of Aristotle's name. Jaspers enumerates the world-historical contributions of the Greeks during the period from 800 B.C. to 200 B.C.: "Greece saw Homer; the philosophers, Parmenides, Heraclitus, Plato; the tragedians; Thucydides and Archimedes" (p. 96). Later in the same volume (p. 147), Jaspers concedes: "From Aristotle one learns the categories which dominate all occidental thinking since. He has determined the language (the terminology) of philosophizing"; but Jaspers adds significantly: "whether one thinks with him, or against him, or in such a manner that one overcomes this whole plane of philosophizing." Here Jaspers suggests clearly that he is breaking with the main stream of Western philosophy, although he himself may consider it a "falling off" from, or a "perversion" of, the true line that leads from Heraclitus and Plato to Kierkegaard and Nietzsche. But the view of Plato and Nietzsche implicit in this conception is open to question; and we shall try to show later how Nietzsche is really much more in the tradition from which Jaspers would dissociate him.

In the next section of *Psychologie der Weltanschauungen*, the very title, at least in German, at once brings to mind Nietzsche: "Valuations and Tables of Values." So does the discussion in which Nietzsche is soon mentioned explicitly. Again, the descriptive account is heavy with valuational overtones that further strengthen the association with Nietzsche. Thus the four cardinal virtues are traced from Plato, via Cicero, to Christianity, until the knowledge of God becomes "conditional upon grace and at the same time, in its contents, unfree and churchly. . . . The width and freedom of Plato is replaced by a narrow otherworldliness; Plato's integration of everything, by suppression and elimination of drives and of what is worldly" (p. 223). A page later, we hear "how Aristotle already had shallowed the conception of measure into that of a mean between two extremes." Then "the doctrine that happiness is the highest good" is depicted—from Nietzsche's, rather than Kant's, point of view—as "a doctrine to renounce enthusiasm, to affirm mere existence [*Dasein*], while undercutting life as a process; everything is to remain as it is" (p. 227). We are thus urged to reject this view, not because it is incompatible with sheer respect for duty, but because it is said to lead to a Stoic acceptance of the *status quo* and is hence considered incompatible with the desire to raise one's state of being. Kant, as a matter of fact, is specifically commended here—but for rather Nietzschean reasons.

As the final instance from this section, consider Jaspers' characterization of a type with which he clearly identifies himself: "He does not crawl off into the shell [*Gehäuse*] of a determinate value hierarchy" (p. 228). The conception of the shell is one of the key ideas of the book, and the phrase quoted leaves little doubt concerning Jaspers' opinion of those who, unlike Nietzsche, make their home in such a construct.

Next, let us consider two contrasts that closely parallel Nietzschean suggestions. Jaspers introduces his section on "Skepticism and Nihilism" with the declaration: "The first and the very last question concerning Weltanschauung is whether one says Yes or No to life as a whole" (p. 285). Nietzsche's name is encountered only a page later, but this dichotomy runs through his entire philosophy, from his first book to his last. Thus he contends in *The Birth of Tragedy* that the ancient Greeks, confronted with "the dreadful destructive turmoil of so-called world history as well as . . . the cruelty of nature," did not have recourse to "a Buddhistic negation of the will," but with their tragedies said Yes to life as a whole with all its agonies. Later, Nietzsche came to denounce Christianity as saying No to life, and his last work, *Ecce Homo*, ends: "Dionysus versus the Crucified." If a brief commentary is wanted, one may turn to *The Will to Power* (§401): "Why has there been no philosophy which said *Yes*, no religion which said *Yes?* . . . Dionysus versus the 'Crucified.'" Dionysus, to Nietzsche, stands for the exuberant affirmation of life, for the creative employment of the instincts as opposed to the allegedly Christian doctrine of their abnegation; for this-worldliness as opposed to all otherworldliness. In another note in *The Will to Power* (§1041), Nietzsche explains:

> Such an *experimental philosophy* as I live it anticipates experimentally even the possibilities of thorough nihilism. But this does not mean that it remains a negation, a No, a will to a No. Rather it wants to get through to the opposite— to a *Dionysian saying Yes* to the world as it is, without subtraction, exception, and selection.

What distinguishes this Dionysian affirmation from the Stoics' acceptance of the world is that Nietzsche's enthusiastic Yes embraces all the extremes of joy and suffering, while the Stoic would minimize both; and Nietzsche further ridicules the Stoic notion of living "according to nature" by claiming that life is "the very will to be otherwise than . . . nature"— a perpetual self-overcoming, a ceaseless aspiration for a higher state of being (*Gay Science*, §2, and *Beyond*, §9).

Another contrast in Jaspers' book that echoes Nietzsche is that of the "chaotic" and the "demonic" man (pp. 345 ff.). This recalls Nietzsche's juxtaposition of the "romantic" and the "Dionysian" type (cf. *N.*, pp. 321–27, 398–400; also pp. 116 ff. and 131). "Romantic" became as much of an opprobrium for Nietzsche as "chaotic" is for Jaspers, and the final flight to the authority of the Church is one of the features emphasized by both men. Jaspers also speaks of "*die chaotische Romantik*" and uses Nietzsche as one of his models for the description of the "demonic" type.

Later on, the "demonic" type is broken down into three subtypes, the demonic realist, the demonic romantic, and the saint, and Nietzsche—certainly no realist or saint—is understood as a "demonic romantic." This is quite consistent with an earlier passage in the book (p. 13) where Jaspers says of Kierkegaard and Nietzsche: "Both are romantics in their inner movement; yet both are passionately anti-romantic because the actual representatives of that which has been called romanticism have almost always been lacking in seriousness, arty, epicurean, or unfree—" in short, "chaotic" types. In the later characterization of the "demonic romantic" no names are mentioned, but such phrases as "here is the genesis of the great

original psychologist" and "in the form of aphorisms and fragments" point in Nietzsche's direction. The following passage
apparently presents what was Jaspers' conception of Nietzsche
in 1919:

> The torrent of overcharged life, which melts down all it
> creates, leaves behind as something objective only this tre-
> mendous pile of ruins to bear witness of the wealth of his
> genius. Every whole, whether a work of systematic thought
> or poetry, remains uncompleted and is in its very disposition
> a fragment, a great aphorism. In action, in love, and in
> friendship it is the same: the most tremendous enhancement
> of the moment, the utmost deepening, yet the incapacity for
> holding on, for giving final form, or for shaping into a whole.
> The onrushing torrent of the demonic drives to new domi-
> nant destinies and experiences. All this romanticism is some-
> how meteoric [p. 437].

In essentials, Jaspers' picture of Nietzsche has never changed.
He still envisages him very much like this in his late works.
We shall see later that this interpretation can be traced back
to the poet, Stefan George—and that it is highly questionable.

To conclude these reflections on Jaspers' *Psychologie der
Weltanschauungen*, let us cite another instance of Jaspers'
evaluations:

> We do not yet have a Weltanschauung when we can con-
> template and comprehend all the forms of the spirit—which
> is what we are trying to do here—nor do we have it when
> we direct our affirmative intention toward types which we
> call "life"; we have it only when we actually exist in a type
> or—insofar as a rare human being has been elected for a life
> in the demonic sense—when this life creates forms and
> shapes in action, in the conduct of life, in works of art, or
> finally in prophetic philosophy [p. 373].

Thus the early Jaspers "directed his affirmative intention" toward Nietzsche, whom he considered one of the "elect." Nietzsche was one of his "educators" in the specific sense that Nietzsche himself associated with that term when he wrote on
"Schopenhauer as Educator."

Yet it would be a mistake to make out even the early Jaspers as a follower of Nietzsche or as a Nietzschean. He is surely speaking of himself when he writes: "Personalities like Socrates, Kant, Kierkegaard, and Nietzsche give him the strongest impetus; heads like Hegel, the richest education" (p. 379). In a general way, the influence of Hegel's *Phenomenology* on Jaspers' *Psychologie der Weltanschauungen* is quite obvious; in detail, it is discussed by Jaspers himself in the latter work (pp. 364–79). The impetus he received from Socrates and Kierkegaard is similar to that from Nietzsche: the attempt to live one's philosophy, the effort to raise oneself to a higher state of being, and to help others to do likewise. In some ways, Jaspers is closer to Nietzsche than to Kierkegaard: he recognizes no theological framework nor any commitment at all to a particular religious tradition. Beyond that, many specific parallels have been adduced above. Even so, there was always one philosopher whom Jaspers revered at least as much, probably more: Kant.

4

Jaspers' Nietzsche and the George Circle's. In 1912, Jaspers attended an exhibition in Cologne. Ten years later, in a study of *Strindberg und Van Gogh,* he wrote up some of the ideas that had occurred to him on this occasion and remarked with a rare flash of humor:

> In Cologne at this exhibition in 1912, where the wonderful Van Goghs were surrounded by expressionist art from all over Europe in queer monotony, I sometimes had a feeling as if Van Gogh were the sublime and only case of one mad against his will among so many who want to be mad but are only too healthy [p. 182].

This certainly does not sound romantic, but consider Jaspers' judgment of Van Gogh:

> His works, taken in isolation, would probably stand very far beneath the great creations of art in the last five hundred years; yet the *Existenz* taken as a whole—which, however,

would never be clear without the works of art and expresses itself clearly above all in these works—this is of unique stature [p. 157].

This sentence might serve equally well as the motto of Jaspers' *Nietzsche*.

An almost perfect parallel to this approach can be found in Friedrich Schlegel's view of Lessing, the greatest literary exponent of the German Enlightenment: "He himself was worth more than all his talents. In his individuality [Jaspers might say, *Existenz*] lay his greatness" (cf. *N.*, pp. 116 ff., 378). Schlegel, as guiding spirit of the original romantic movement, had no use for Lessing's enlightened views, but admired his restless, searching mind. It was similar with the German romantics' attitude toward Goethe: admiration for his Protean development, coupled with either neglect of, or outright opposition to, his professed views (cf. *N.*, pp. 131, 380 f.). Kierkegaard's attitude toward Lessing was the same: enthusiasm for the man who had preferred the way to the goal, but a lack of interest in his ideas. Stefan George, finally, adopted the same attitude toward Nietzsche and, through the members of the George Circle, influenced the Nietzsche picture of a generation of German writers, including Jaspers.

George's apostrophe of Nietzsche, on the occasion of the philosopher's death in 1900, creates the picture later elaborated by Jaspers:

> *Didst thou create gods but to overthrow them,*
> *Never enjoying rest or what thou built?*
> *Thou hast destroyed what in thyself was closest*
> *To tremble after it with new desire*
> *And to cry out in pain of solitude.*[2]

First, Bertram, one of George's lesser minions, propagated this view in his *Nietzsche: Attempt at a Mythology* (1918): what made the philosopher so remarkable was not his philosophy, which Bertram all but ignores; it was his heroic, yet aimless,

[2] For a translation of more of George's "Nietzsche" from *Der Siebente Ring* and for the discussion and quotations in this paragraph, cf. the "Prologue" of my *Nietzsche*.

self-laceration. Then the rest of the George Circle took up the cry. Ernst Gundolf, for example, relying on the master's intuition and on "the most perfect instruction" of "Bertram's brilliant book" rather than on any solid knowledge of Nietzsche's work, produces this picture of Nietzsche, in *Nietzsche als Richter unserer Zeit* (1923): "He followed his law and his fatality: to sit in judgment over all that existed, to move the goal beyond all that had been achieved into the unachievable, and to strive for the infinite out of a finitude which he could not bear any more" (pp. 31 f.).

It is a fundamentally similar conception of Nietzsche that Jaspers expresses fifteen years later in his monograph on *Nietzsche and Christianity:* "Out of every position one may have adopted, i.e. out of every finitude we are expelled; we are set *whirling*" (p. 71).

Nietzsche is thus envisaged as a thinker who proudly refused to seek refuge in the confinement of any shell (*Gehäuse*); but, while Jaspers agrees with the George Circle up to this point, his evaluation differs sharply. For George's disciples pitied the poor philosopher: the poet had called him "most unblessed" and his followers outdid each other in patronizing expressions of sympathy; for they had found refuge in their master's shell. In fact, they were so blinded by their authoritarian worship of George that the relatively greatest Nietzsche scholar among them, Kurt Hildebrandt, who wrote four books on Nietzsche, could offer this explanation for Nietzsche's allegedly endless dissatisfaction—also in *Nietzsche als Richter unserer Zeit* (p. 102): "Only George *is* what Nietzsche convulsively coveted to be."

Jaspers' judgment has never been clouded by adherence to any party line or by prostration of his critical faculties before a human oracle. He values Nietzsche's alleged explosion of every finite position, not as the best that was possible before Stefan George was given to us, but as the proper function of philosophical reason—as opposed to philosophical faith. In Kantian terms, this is the best that pure theoretical reason can do; but practical reason is another matter.

Jaspers' agreement with the George Circle is, however, far-reaching. He accepts their judgment that Nietzsche's doctrine of the eternal recurrence of the same events is a "deceptively mocking mystery of delusion"—to cite Bertram's *Nietzsche* (p. 12)—and that his other conclusions, too, are—to cite Jaspers himself—"a pile of absurdities and vacuities" (*Christentum*, p. 71). The conception of the overman is arbitrarily emptied of its rich psychological content and is written off as a symbol of the unachievable; the eternal recurrence is misunderstood as a religious myth; the idea of the will to power is marked off as a dead end street; and the conception of sublimation, which links the will to power with the overman, is all but ignored. One need not agree with Nietzsche to realize that his central ideas are neither empty nor absurd. Yet elsewhere, too, Jaspers gives us this same picture: "*Nietzsche*: endless reflection, sounding out and questioning everything, digging without reaching a new foundation, except in new absurdities" (*Einführung*, p. 155). Surely, this is George's and Bertram's conception over again.

To this over-all continuity, one may add at least one more specific link: Bertram, who later defended the Nazis' suppression of free speech in a popular volume, *Von der Freiheit des Wortes* (Inselbücherei), under the motto, "The most genuine freedom is a holy imprisonment of the heart," proposed in his *Nietzsche* to understand Nietzsche as "the typically ambiguous one" (p. 8). Surely, this is an instance of self-projection—unfortunate because Bertram so little resembled Nietzsche, and because he was unimpeded by any scholarly conscience in "finding" ambiguities. Yet while Jaspers, in his *Nietzsche* (p. 5), justly criticized Bertram for ignoring the context of Nietzsche's ideas and the process of his thinking, Jaspers himself developed this theme, and "ambiguity" is one of the key conceptions of his *Nietzsche*, too.

Students of Nietzsche are apt to take this for a corroboration of Bertram's very unscholarly thesis—unless they know Jaspers well enough to realize that "ambiguity" is one of the central terms in his philosophy, no less than in Sartre's and Simone de Beauvoir's. Thus, while the notion of Nietzsche's ambiguity links Jaspers' interpretation closely with Bertram's, Jaspers employs the term to designate Nietzsche's profundity, not to criticize him. The assumption is that truth actually is "ambiguous," i.e., irreducible to any set of propositions.

The concrete examples that Jaspers gives of Nietzsche's ambiguity are very questionable. Let us here consider "the example which exhibits *in concreto* the most extreme reversal possible: Nietzsche's attitude toward Jesus. We recall how Nietzsche envisaged Jesus with respect for the honesty of this way of life, yet at the same time with rejection of the type of decadence which finds expression in this way of life" (*Christentum*, p. 71). So far, of course, there is no ambiguity or reversal at all. One can reject a position without questioning its honesty, and one can respect a type one considers decadent. Nietzsche—though Jaspers and other interpreters have failed to note this—pictured Jesus in the image of Prince Myshkin in Dostoevsky's *The Idiot;* and the attitude here under consideration is presumably that of most readers toward Myshkin (cf. *N.*, pp. 289 ff. and 396).

Jaspers' next point is that, according to Nietzsche, Jesus was psychologically incapable of resistance (like Myshkin) and no hero; yet Nietzsche says in *Ecce Homo* that he himself is also a type sharply distinguished from the heroic. The wording in both passages is similar and seems to Jaspers proof of "self-identification with the opponent." This conclusion, too, is unwarranted: two types can differ from the heroic without being identical; Myshkin and Goethe can agree in lacking any passion for seeking out obstacles or for changing the world and can still be quite different from each other. And it is with Goethe and Socrates rather than with Myshkin and Jesus that Nietzsche seeks to link himself in the hyperboles of *Ecce Homo.*

The same considerations apply to Jaspers' other points: Nietzsche's claim that Jesus (again like Myshkin) represented spontaneity of action, and was thus in a sense opposed to morality with its rigid prescriptions, is no proof of self-identification with Jesus any more than Nietzsche's belief that Jesus experienced blessedness as present in his heart. Jaspers' failure or refusal to examine Nietzsche's psychological conceptions of Jesus, and of such approximations of the overman as Socrates or Goethe, bars him from understanding Nietzsche's quite unambiguous position. Nietzsche's pictures are neither absurd nor vacuous, though he was surely mistaken about the historical Jesus. The vacuity is a function of Jaspers' approach that empties valid conceptions of their empirical content; and the absurdity is due to an interpretation that plays off these hollow symbols against each other.

The section on "self-identification with the opponent" begins: "This ambiguous attitude toward Jesus—once fighting against him, then identifying himself with him; once negating him, then affirming him—is itself only an example of an occurrence which is universal in Nietzsche." On the contrary: the method of interpretation that leads to this false result is an example of an occurrence that is universal in Jaspers' discussions of Nietzsche.

The section just quoted ends:

One finds in Nietzsche the most amazing attempts to bring together again into a higher unity what he has first separated and opposed to each other. The most extreme case is again the manner of his affirmation of Jesus. Nietzsche imagines—without any power of vision and unrealizable— the synthesis of the ultimate opposition. . . . "the Roman Caesar with Christ's soul."

Yet this phrase from *The Will to Power* (§983) does not represent a convulsive attempt at synthesizing two symbols that exclude each other by definition, no conceptual jugglery that defies imagination, but the very heart of Nietzsche's vision of the overman. Being capable of both sympathy and hardness, of loving and ruling, not using claws though having them, and creating out of an overflow and a superabundance: that is Nietzsche's ideal and norm by which he judges both the Roman Caesars and Jesus. The idea is not unattainable but historically represented, to Nietzsche's mind, in varying degrees of perfection by Socrates and Julius Caesar, Frederick II of Hohenstauffen, Leonardo, and Goethe (cf. chapters 1, 11, and 12 above).

The two sections from *Nietzsche und das Christentum* that have been quoted here are preceded by, and supply the evidence for, a section entitled: "The Failure of All Positions and the Whirl." It is in this section that we find the previously cited dictum: "Out of every position one may have adopted, i.e. out of every finitude we are expelled; we are set whirling." We now see that this is false as a characterization of "Nietzsche's New Philosophy" (the name of the chapter containing these sections) and true only of Jaspers' moving, but methodologically untenable, interpretation—which here echoes Bertram's.

Among Jaspers' differences with the Nietzsche picture of Stefan George and his Circle, one of the most decisive has already been suggested. George's disciples not only accepted the master's whims as dogma but set a preposterous precedent by writing history to order. Even the most gifted among them, Friedrich Gundolf, in his three volumes on Shakespeare—one specifically devoted to *Shakespeare und der deutsche Geist*—is not content to tell us that he disapproves of Count Baudissin's versions of thirteen of Shakespeare's plays in the famous so-called Schlegel-Tieck translation but reads the poor man out of history by not deigning to mention him. It is surely one of the great merits of Jaspers' *Nietzsche* that he gives due emphasis to Nietzsche's radical antiauthoritarianism. And Jaspers has consistently followed Nietzsche in rejecting the master-disciple relationship and in teaching independence.

Where George had considered Nietzsche his own precursor, Jaspers takes him for a precursor of *Existenzphilosophie*. But while George's conception of himself—tirelessly echoed by his adulators—lacked all sense of proportion and bordered on the pathological, Jaspers is not at all like the wren who soared above the clouds on an eagle's wings, unnoticed by him, and then flew up another ten feet, boasting that he could fly higher than the eagle. Jaspers is no wren, nor claims to be an eagle. Certainly, he does not, like George, consider Nietzsche his own personal John the Baptist. A sense of modesty, even diffidence, is the very basis of his decision to teach philosophy:

> As the realization overcame me that, at the time, there was no true philosophy at the universities, I thought that facing such a vacuum even he, who was too weak to create his own philosophy, had the right to hold forth about philosophy, to declare what it once was and what it could be. Only then,

approaching my fortieth birthday, I made philosophy my
life's work [*E.*, p. 133].

Such modesty and candor offer a stark contrast indeed with
the pomp and self-congratulation of the Stefan George cult.
Even so, Jaspers agrees with the *George Kreis* in discounting
Nietzsche's philosophy. This disregard is quite intentional and
is expressly announced in the subtitle of Jaspers' *Nietzsche:
Einführung in das Verständnis seines Philosophierens* (*Introduction to an Understanding of his Philosophizing*). Jaspers
is interested, and sees Nietzsche's historic significance, in what
he considers Nietzsche's way of philosophizing, not in his philosophy. This is clear throughout the book; it is equally unmistakable in Jaspers' subsequent smaller study, *Nietzsche und
das Christentum;* and he restated this point in 1951 in a discussion of "Nietzsche's Importance in the History of Philosophy":

> One must know what it means to be concerned with Nietz-
> sche, and how this concern leads to no conclusion. For
> Nietzsche leads into realms of philosophizing which still lie
> this side of clear conceptualization, but press toward it. . . .
> Nietzsche is interpreted in two ways. One interpretation
> finds his importance is an achievement he completed. He
> becomes the founder of a philosophy . . . the philosophy
> of the will to power, the eternal recurrence, the Dionysian
> grasp of life. For quite another interpretation, which we
> profess, Nietzsche's importance lies in his loosening func-
> tion. His exciting force, which leads the human being to the
> authentic problems and to himself, does not instruct the
> reader, but awakens him.[8]

There is certainly much truth in this; and yet such phrases
as "leads to no conclusion" and "this side of clear conceptu-
alization" are stunning when one recalls Nietzsche's acid clarity, his uniquely vivid concepts, and his often violent con-

[8] "Zu Nietzsche's Bedeutung in der Geschichte der Philosophie,"
first published in *Die Neue Rundschau,* and then in two different
English translations in *The Hibbert Journal,* April, 1951, and in
Partisan Review, January, 1952. The above translation is my own.

clusions. In view of Jaspers' own relative vagueness and inconclusiveness, one is tempted to sarcasm: is this merely another wearisome instance of an interpreter's reading himself into Nietzsche?

Jaspers says: "The procedure in understanding texts is a simile for all comprehension of being" (*Einführung*, p. 74). May we not conclude that Jaspers' interpretation of Nietzsche reflects Jaspers' general philosophy? And when Jaspers tells us that concern with Nietzsche "leads to no conclusion," is not this because Jaspers is concerned with Nietzsche as a means of *Existenzerhellung* (illumination of existence)—and *"Existenzerhellung* leads . . . to no result," as he himself admits in *Die Geistige Situation der Zeit* (p. 147). Or consider the following discussion of "all true philosophizing." Nietzsche is not mentioned at all, but the phrases used are the very same ones that Jaspers employs elsewhere when he characterizes Nietzsche—an association that is still further strengthened by the use of the masculine pronoun, *"er,"* he, where an English translation must say, "it."

> It loosens us from the fetters of determinate thinking, not by abandoning such thinking, but by pushing it to its limits. . . . It forces us to return out of every dead end rigidity. . . . The loss of the absoluteness of things and of the epistemology of things is called nihilism by those who thus lose their footing. . . . Our philosophic thinking passes through this nihilism which is really the liberation for true being. . . . The plunge from the rigidities which were deceptive after all, turns into the ability to stay in suspense; what seemed abyss becomes the space of freedom—the seeming nothing turns into that from which true being speaks to us [*Einführung*, pp. 36 f.].

One recalls Jaspers' declaration, cited at the beginning of this essay, that Kant is for him "the philosopher *par excellence"* and Nietzsche only "the magnificent revelation of nihilism and of the task of going beyond nihilism." We have also seen that for Nietzsche himself "nihilism" was something to pass through to a Dionysian affirmation, while Jaspers simply discounts Nietzsche's positive conclusions as "absurdities" and thus reduces him to a labyrinth that one enters only to become convinced that there is no way out except Kant's Indian rope trick. Or to vary the metaphor, we go to Nietzsche to be set whirling, to be forced to plunge—that the angels of Kantianism may then come to our rescue and keep us suspended in mid-air.

Martin Luther declared that "the commandments" of all sorts of good works in Scripture "were ordained solely that man might thus realize his incapacity for good and learn to despair in himself" (Walch ed., XIX, 992). As a preacher of grace and salvation through faith alone, Luther boldly interpreted all biblical demands to do good as demands to realize that we cannot do good. Similarly, Jaspers understands Nietzsche's challenging conclusions as demonstrations that no conclusions are possible and that "philosophic faith" is needed. Such interpretations are less helpful for those who would gain an understanding of the Bible or of Nietzsche than for students of Luther's thought or Jaspers'.

Sarcasm, however, would be utterly out of place in an examination of Jaspers' *Nietzsche:* Jaspers' stature is sufficient, and his philosophy important enough in its own right, to command respect; and, seen in its historical setting, his *Nietzsche* was an act of courage, whatever its connection may have been with the fact that the Nazis suspended the author as a university professor within a year of its publication.

5

Jaspers' Nietzsche versus the Nazis'. At a time when such self-styled Nietzscheans as Richard Oehler at the Nietzsche-Archiv and Alfred Bäumler at the University of Berlin were loudly proclaiming Nietzsche as a proto-Nazi; when Bertram, the author of the most influential pre-Nazi interpretation, had aligned himself with the party, while Klages, who had written perhaps the most brilliant monograph, was carrying irrationalism and anti-Semitism to such extremes that, at that time, even the Nazis would not follow him—the appearance of this new Nietzsche book by a widely respected Heidelberg professor was eloquent indeed. Here was a solid study that presented Nietzsche as not having been a Nazi. Seen in this historical perspective, the section entitled "Nietzsche wants no believers" (pp. 19 f.) takes on a new significance; and the end of the long Introduction appears as a protest: "The task is to become oneself as one appropriates Nietzsche. Instead of yielding to the seduction of accepting doctrines and laws in their apparent univocality as something universally valid, it is his challenge to produce the [highest] possible rank of one's own character." In Germany, in 1936, these words were a slap, not only at the prevalent Nietzsche picture, but also at Nazi education generally. Even more outspoken is a later passage: "Nietzsche can be used by all the powers which he fought: he can serve . . . the violence which mistakes the idea of the will to power as an order of rank for a justification of any brutality" (p. 391). But to Jaspers' catalogue of such misinterpretations one might well add his own attempt to use Nietzsche to lead us back to Jaspers' "philosophic faith."

Jaspers' *Nietzsche*, although not improvised as a political polemic, but the kind of interpretation Jaspers might have written in any event, was the antithesis of Bäumler's Nazi version of Nietzsche. Where Bäumler and his followers saw Nietzsche as a metaphysician with a system, who wrote "as one having authority," Jaspers extolled the lonely seeker after truth, the great challenger not only of all authority but even of his own ideas, the dialectician who can—and this is where Jaspers goes too far—always be cited in contradiction to himself.

Of course, Nietzsche can always be cited as contradicting the views the Nazis found in him; so—as long as one does not question that Nietzsche *also* maintained these Nazistic tenets—it follows that he always contradicted himself. Yet it would be superficial to assume that Jaspers merely could not, at the time, say outright that Nietzsche never held the views ascribed to him by Bäumler. Like other existentialists, too, Jaspers is deeply impressed with the puzzling character of all existence and by its confounding irreducibility to any one set of principles; and when he tells us at the outset of his *Nietzsche* (p. 8) never to be satisfied, when reading Nietzsche, until we have *also* found the contradiction," he is not casting aspersions on Nietzsche but is describing Nietzsche's greatest value: he sets us whirling. And Jaspers himself goes on to say that we should "experience these contradictions in their necessity."

Jaspers could have written his *Nietzsche* independently of any Nazi provocation, though the time of its publication makes the book even more remarkable. Jaspers read himself into Nietzsche; but since he has stature, his Nietzsche does, too. What is tragic, however, is that this courageous interpretation by a penetrating philosopher should have helped unwittingly to mute a singularly unambiguous message to Germany. In the whole history of German letters no other voice has spoken out with such prophetic vigor and withering sarcasm against the very forces that culminated in National Socialism; neither Lessing and Schiller nor Goethe and Heine approximated Nietzsche's brilliant indignation or the sustained wit of his scorn of nationalism and state idolatry, anti-Semitism, militarism, and cultural barbarism, and all the other festering vices to which he opposed his ideal of the Good European.

To be sure, no German could have made his interpretation the vehicle for such a message in 1936. But why not in 1926? Why did the German Republic's attempt to link itself with Weimar remain such a feeble, ineffective gesture? Was it not in part because the writers and scholars of Germany failed to show how much of the great German cultural tradition pointed toward the ideal of the Good European? Was it not tragic that they let the rightist opposition spread the utterly mendacious myth that all the great Germans had been rightists and nationalists? Lessing's enlightened ideas were ignored, as if he had been nothing but a restless seeker and a brilliant literary critic. Kant's vision of a League of Nations and of eternal peace and his insistence on never reducing a human being to a mere means was ignored, while his insistence on "duty" was perverted into a sanction for blind obedience to authorities, as if the autonomy of the rational person were not the core of his ethic. Schiller, who had celebrated the striving for liberty and equality in drama after drama, from *Don Carlos'* "Sir, grant liberty of thought" to Wilhelm Tell's tyrannicide, was brazenly claimed as a German nationalist, although not one of his major dramas was set in Germany, unless one wants to count his first effort, *The Robbers*. The rich heritage of the Enlightenment in Fichte and Hegel, Mozart and Beethoven was ignored, while Fichte's later nationalism and Hegel's glorification of "the State" were emphasized out of context and out of all proportion. This was surely one of the most preposterous and fateful falsifications of history ever perpetrated.

Nietzsche's thunderbolts might perhaps have penetrated this miasma and cleared the air. His flashes might have exposed the rot and corruption. The shower of his questions, punctuated by the thunder of his denunciations might have purged the intellectual filth in which Nazism was breeding. Yet Nietzsche himself was partly responsible for not getting his message across. Seduced by the beauty of the language, by suggestive phrases and bewitching metaphors, he had often written in a manner that invited misunderstanding. He had tried to counteract such misapprehensions by the most scathing denunciations elsewhere and knew that, if not the immediate context, certainly his work taken as a whole showed his views to be quite unequivocal. Yet the beauty of the language attracted an unforeseen host of readers, and the words and parables that had intoxicated Nietzsche soon intoxicated other, lesser minds as well. Zarathustra's apes—to use an appropriate Nietzschean phrase—had no mind to consider flamboyant passages in context or to ponder their relation to the author's earlier and later works; and they still had some of Nietzsche's phrases on their lips when, like the monkey hordes in Kipling's *Junglebook*, they were dancing, hypnotized, to the tune of the great snake.

Nietzsche's fault here is a tragic function of his personality, a chapter in the long saga of the relation of philosophy and poetry (cf. chapter 14 above). But it is no less tragic that not a single German interpreter of stature should have liberated Nietzsche's timely, sorely needed message from the iridescent webs of myth and metaphor, that not one should have mastered his abandoned bow to drive his well-fashioned arrows into the unworthy suitors of his people. It is tragic that even Jaspers should not have risen above the conception of "ambiguity," which, while certainly at odds with Nazi versions, could scarcely become a rallying point of any opposition, nor do justice to Nietzsche.

This criticism may appear to be reducible to a mere difference of opinion between Jaspers and his critic. In that case, it could lead at best to an intellectual duel, apt to prove just as little as any other duel. I reject his Nietzsche, he mine. If the reader has sufficient imagination, he may well reject both. And some will suggest: everybody is entitled to his own Nietzsche. But the question here is not one of one interpretation versus another: the charge—which will be discussed further later on —is that Jaspers' *method* is indefensible.

This is a serious criticism, but great philosophers have rarely been disinterested guides to the thought of their predecessors. One would hardly gather from Plato how close some of the Sophists had come to many facets of modern democratic thought; Aristotle's portrait of Plato, in turn, is a fine instance of partiality; and Nietzsche himself excelled in aphoristic caricatures with pedagogical intent. Today, there are Santayana's and Russell's often uninformed distortions, especially of German philosophy since Kant. So viewed, Jaspers' *Nietzsche* appears highly distinguished: Jaspers is exceedingly well informed; unlike Aristotle, he is beyond the very suspicion of envy; and unlike Plato, he is not using great names as foils, or to prevail in a historic contest by eternalizing his opponent's name in infamy.

It is thus the very excellence of Jaspers' book that makes its faults important. He does not claim the poetic license of the architect of dialogues or sculptor of aphorisms but presents us with a wonderfully learned full-length study and offers more direct quotations per page than any previous Nietzsche interpreter, invariably giving the page references, too. Use of an illicit method in such a superior work is doubly serious.

Finally, it adds to the historical momentum of the charge against Jaspers, although it is morally an extenuating circumstance, that previous German interpretations had almost entirely ignored the whole heritage of the Enlightenment in Nietzsche, and indeed that whole aspect of his philosophy which might conceivably have given German history a turn for the better. Jaspers' failure here is clearly not due to any lack of courage but to lack of vision.

6

Jaspers contra Freud. It may be revealing that the same oversight, even blindness, occurs where Jaspers is confronted with the man who is probably the greatest among Nietzsche's heirs, a man who followed in the footsteps of Goethe, Heine, and Nietzsche by attempting to deepen and enrich the attitudes of the Enlightenment with the insights of romanticism. For Freud tried to bridge the gap between the German romantics' profound preoccupation with the irrational, on the one hand, and the Western faith in liberty, equality, and fraternity, and in science as an instrument to their realization, on the other. But instead of recognizing in Freud a Good European and a great prose stylist who, like Nietzsche and Heine, wrote clearly, lucidly, and powerfully enough to be read outside of Germany, Jaspers completely overlooks Freud's radical individualism and—in 1931—links psychoanalysis with Marxism and racism as presenting "brutalizing demands" (p. 143).

Jaspers even denies outright that Freud is in any important sense carrying forward Nietzsche's work. In 1931, he writes, in the same popular volume on *Die Geistige Situation der Zeit:* "The self-reflection of the human being of integrity, which . . . had culminated in Kierkegaard and Nietzsche, has here degenerated into the uncovering of sexual desires and typical childhood experiences; it is the covering up of genuine, dangerous self-reflection by a mere rediscovery of already known types" (p. 139).

If this is a half-truth, the following claim seems almost entirely wrong: "Psychoanalysis, though this may not meet the eye, leads to the consequence of not thinking up, but of making one feel, the ideal that man return out of all schism and violence through which he might find the way to himself—return back to nature which no longer requires him to be human" (p. 139).

It is easy to counter such allegations with direct quotations from Freud—and it is relevant here to do so because Jaspers' position depends on attitudes that also mar his understanding of Nietzsche. Here, then, are three brief quotations from

Freud's *General Introduction to Psychoanalysis*, chapter 27:

> By raising the unconscious into consciousness, we overcome the repressions, abolish the conditions for symptom formation, and change the pathogenetic conflict into a normal conflict which must somehow find a resolution.

> Where there is no repression to be overcome, nor any analogous psychical process, there our therapeutics has no business.

> We hold that whoever has passed successfully through an education for truthfulness toward himself, will thereby be protected permanently against the danger of immorality, even if his standard of morality should somehow differ from social conventions.

Here Freud speaks as the heir of Nietzsche, and Jaspers' failure to see this is as revealing concerning his relation to Nietzsche as it is regarding his conception of Freud.

In 1950, Jaspers published a book on *Reason and Anti-Reason in Our Time* and, five years after Hitler's defeat, used Marxism and psychoanalysis as the two examples of anti-reason. The fact that most of his strictures against psychoanalysis are extremely well taken does not allay the apprehension that he shows a lack of historical perspective. Jaspers, of course, would not agree with the German reviewer who said of a collection of essays published in 1952 that they point to many wounds, but not to the main wound, the immoralization through psychoanalysis. Jaspers stays this side of the incredible. But he fails to recognize Freud's central intention: to help those who have lost their freedom to find it by teaching them to be honest with themselves, facing their problems instead of running away from them. Jaspers notes all the bad features that so often attend the formation of schools or sects but does not see how Freud has both given new meaning to the ancient conception of human equality, regardless of race, culture, or creed, and lent new impetus to the longing for a higher, but *attainable*, state of being.

It seems fair to add that, had Jaspers recognized Nietzsche's central intentions, he would have understood Freud's too. But following in the footsteps of Schlegel, Kierkegaard, and George and his Circle, Jaspers has romanticized Nietzsche: self-projection takes the place of understanding; basic purposes are disregarded; and positively stated conceptions are discounted as absurdities or as utterly empty, or again as "symbols" of which Jaspers says frankly: "Only via detours and with effort can one summon a significant content out of these symbols, by interpretation" (*Vernunft und Existenz*, pp. 15 f.). Thus Jaspers' critique of Nietzsche's conception of the overman, in *Nietzsche und das Christentum* (p. 54), presupposes the untenable interpretation of the George Circle, who had considered this ideal essentially *unattainable*, and completely overlooks the empirical, psychological content of the idea or its relation to "sublimation"—a key concept of Nietzsche's philosophy to which Jaspers, in his *Nietzsche*, devotes exactly half a page.

7

Summary of criticisms. My criticisms of Jaspers' interpretation of Nietzsche might be summarized as follows. First, Jaspers admittedly discounts Nietzsche's philosophy as opposed to his "philosophizing"; he refuses to take seriously overman and recurrence, will to power and sublimation, or any other definite concept.

Second, Jaspers fails, his intention notwithstanding, to introduce us to Nietzsche's philosophizing because he employs an untenable method. He makes no distinction, either in his references or in his evaluation, between Nietzsche's finished works and his fragments and notebook scribblings; and generally he makes no distinction between early or late passages either, but disregards the dates and thus necessarily also Nietzsche's intellectual development. He uses Nietzsche as a means to arouse us and to introduce us to *Jaspers'* philosophizing, not Nietzsche's. If we spread out Kant's writings, precritical, critical, and *Opus postumum,* we could also find one statement after another challenged by some statement elsewhere; and it would be little different with Plato. It may be a stimulating exercise, or even a deeply disturbing and shocking experience, to con-

sider contradictory statements, one after the other; it may, as
Jaspers says, make us aware of "authentic problems" and have
the power of "loosening" the mind; but all this should be
sharply distinguished from an introduction to Nietzsche's own
philosophizing. Jaspers' claim that concern with Nietzsche
"leads to no conclusion," but only arouses the reader, is clearly
a function of Jaspers' approach. If we studied Kant in this
manner, the result would be the same, except in so far as
Nietzsche's problems are of more obvious concern to laymen.

Third, Jaspers' frequent references to Nietzsche's "ambiguity" are misleading. He is taking up one of the central notions of Bertram's "Attempt at a Mythology," though he justly
repudiates this work. Nor does this seeming partial agreement
amount to any mutual corroboration. Jaspers uses the term
"ambiguity" in three different senses (cf. N., p. 373) of which
none corresponds entirely with the usual meaning of the word,
equivocality. Rather, "ambiguity" is one of Jaspers' favorite
words in his other works, too—even as it is a favorite with Sartre
and Simone de Beauvoir, whose book on *The Ethics of Ambiguity* is a good case in point. What is meant is the irreducibility of existence to any single system. To cite Jaspers' *Nietzsche* (p. 407): "Education by Nietzsche is as a *first training
in ambiguity*."

Fourth, Jaspers' interpretation of Nietzsche as "ambiguous"
does not only fail to do justice both to Nietzsche's philosophy
and to his philosophizing; it is also a chapter in a major historical tragedy. It contributed to the muting of a message that
was sorely needed. It helped to reduce to relative ineffective-
ness a philosophy that was unalterably opposed to the forces
that have determined recent German history.

Fifth, from a more strictly philosophic point of view, it is
regrettable that Jaspers dissolves all the more limited problems that Nietzsche posed and occasionally advanced toward
a solution. Nietzsche's philosophy of power, for example, is
certainly open to criticism, but can be made the point of departure for fruitful and precise philosophic reflection that may
lead to definite results. Jaspers' dictum, "But power is ambiguous" (*Nietzsche*, p. 267) is not incorrect but is admittedly
aimed to lead us away from precise conceptual thinking, in-

stead of making us think more rigorously than Nietzsche did.

All these criticisms are, in a way, condensed into a single sentence in Jaspers' essay "On My Philosophy": "Through my *Nietzsche* I wanted to introduce the reader into that loosening up of thought out of which *Existenzphilosophie* must spring" (*E.*, p. 157). Nietzsche is used to introduce us to Jaspers. It remains for us to consider Jaspers vis-à-vis Nietzsche.

8

Jaspers versus Nietzsche. First, there is the matter of style. Kant set a fateful and wholly unfortunate precedent when he departed from the lucidity of his magnificent essays to write his main works in a thoroughly graceless and often hopelessly obscure German. Fichte, obsessed with the desire to outdo Kant, naturally had to "better the instruction" in his *Wissenschaftslehre*, although he showed elsewhere how movingly he could write. Hegel, convinced that Fichte's pseudo-scientific rigor represented the only alternative to the romantics' raving lack of discipline, all but spoiled his grandiose *Phenomenology of the Spirit* by forcing it again and again into the spurious mold of "deduction." By then, a tradition had been created. Nietzsche, who loved to crack conventions, exploded this tradition, too, and showed that there is nothing about the German language that prevents it from being used brilliantly to illuminate the most obscure problems. In his *Zarathustra*, however, he went to the opposite extreme and created so dazzling a medium that it distracted from the ideas he sought to express. Elsewhere, too, his aphoristic style and often extreme emotional pitch introduce difficulties, but these are never in the tradition of sedate opaqueness established by Kant and frequently approximated by Jaspers. Almost every sentence in Nietzsche's works is crystal clear; his style is European. Jaspers, on the other hand, is often vague; and his sentences, frequently all but untranslatable. Here, too, he is closer to Kant than to Nietzsche.

Of course, comparing Jaspers' style with Nietzsche's is like juxtaposing contemporary painters with Van Gogh: one is reminded of Plato's saying, in the *Phaedrus* (245): "The sane man disappears and is nowhere when he enters into rivalry with the madman." Yet in philosophy much is to be said for sanity, and still more against madness. What makes an evaluation so difficult in this case is that what Nietzsche celebrated with such brilliant madness was precisely sanity—not the sobriety of the Philistine, but that of Socrates who could outdrink his companions at the symposium and yet go after his day's business. In Nietzsche's analyses the weaknesses of debauchery and abstinence alike stand revealed, while he points to the power of the passionate man who is the master of his passions. But his readers have been more struck with his own lack of control, his frantic gestures, and the pitch of his voice.

In Jaspers' work we find the opposite disharmony. Gravely, he describes the demonic type and, without raising his voice, speaks of those elected to live in this way. His style of reporting is often deceptively drab, even when he reports contradictions that to him indicate basic antinomies, the limits of reason, and the whirling rapids into which we are carried inevitably if we try to follow rational thought. And when he speaks of the realm beyond the rapids—the "Comprehensive" or "the space of possible existence which grows wider and brighter" —his style becomes not prophetic but involved and obscure.

Where Nietzsche, even under the spell of inspiration, denied himself the transport of the flight beyond reason, Jaspers, speaking more like a lecturer than a prophet, soars to God. He formulates his faith in brief assertions but tells us quietly that these are not to be accepted as a piece of knowledge, but as goals toward which we may direct ourselves. With seeming assurance, he speaks of ultimate mysteries or defines the significance of the great thinkers of the past in a single sentence each, but adds that his assertions are inadequate. Jaspers versus Nietzsche: didactic mysticism versus Dionysian enlightenment.

In his intense preoccupation with the individual and his *Existenz,* Jaspers is closer to Nietzsche than to Kant; yet it would be misleading to say that he follows Nietzsche. For Jaspers is more exclusively concerned with the individual and his state of being than European philosophy has ever been before; only a few thinkers who were religious writers first and

philosophers second—such as Augustine, Pascal, and Kierkegaard—approximate this exclusiveness. In Plato, on the other
hand, this preoccupation is accompanied by an equally intense interest in theoretical problems as such; this is also true
of Nietzsche. When Jaspers speaks of overcoming the whole
plane of philosophizing that characterizes Aristotle's work (cf.
section 3), he also dissociates himself, even if unknowingly,
from Plato, Kant, and Nietzsche, not to speak of most French,
British, and American philosophy.

Jaspers' concern with the limits set to us by "old age, sickness, and death" (*Einführung*, p. 21)—which reminds us of
the Buddha—and his repeated discussions of border situations
(*Grenzsituationen*), such as death, accident, guilt, and the un-
reliability of the world, are all closer to religion and literature
than to *most* Western philosophy, but they are certainly compatible with the dominant philosophic tradition and are characteristic precisely of some of the greatest minds. What separates Jaspers from such partly "existential" thinkers as Plato
and Spinoza, and also from Nietzsche, who still stands in this
tradition, is the exclusiveness of this concern and his resignation concerning precise conceptual thinking.

Such critical reflections, however, should be balanced by
an emphatic acknowledgment of Jaspers' strength. If he shares
some of Kant's shortcomings, he has also forwarded the best
elements in Kant's heritage. He has repeatedly spoken out for
the good elements in the Enlightenment—an unpopular cause
in Germany—and whenever he has expressly discussed it at
all, he has unequivocally denounced the recent German animus against scientific procedures and critical thinking. The
presence of elements in his own philosophy that seem to run
parallel with this animus cannot cancel such merits. And recently he has gone far beyond Nietzsche in also insisting on
the political and moral conditions under which alone free scientific inquiry can flourish. His consistent championship of humane attitudes and of respect for every human being as such,
certainly dwarfs many of the objections voiced above.

Then, Jaspers' *Nietzsche*, too, has made a contribution insufficiently suggested by the words of acknowledgment scattered through this essay. Reading it is a profound experience

that has the very effect at which the author aims: we find
every assumption we make dislodged; we are led to question
what seemed certain; we are constantly forced to think. Beyond that, the author's mastery of the relevant factual material—for example, that pertaining to Nietzsche's biography
—and his references to various sources of information make the
book most helpful for any student of Nietzsche. Finally, the
book brings to the reader's attention a wealth of enticing quotations from Nietzsche that do not fit previous interpretations
and attract to further study. Many of us are deeply indebted
to the book for this. Altogether I know of no other German
interpretation that is as well informed or suggestive.

Above all, Jaspers possesses an honesty of which Nietzsche,
for all his celebrations of intellectual integrity, would have been
quite incapable. Where Nietzsche resorted to the sarcastic hyperboles of *Ecce Homo*, Jaspers can judge himself with calm
and simple candor:

> In my last two years at school I stood alone. . . . That I
> behaved honestly but not heroically was the earliest shock.
> The consciousness of the limits of my self precluded the
> pride of defiant isolation. My character was penetrated by
> resignation which, in the form of knowledge of finitude and
> of the guilt of the free man, runs through my later phi-
> losophizing.
>
> At that time, my attitude was for the first time as it later
> remained peculiar to me, only partially justified by the lack
> of strength of my never healthy body. In the years of Na-
> tional Socialism, it remained the same. I have remained in-
> ternally free and did not yield to any pressure by commit-
> ting a bad act or saying a false word in public, but I did
> nothing in the fight against this crime. I omitted to do what
> my heart told me to do, while caution advised against it.
> In 1945, therefore, confronted with false tales on the radio
> and in the press which glorified my alleged deeds as ex-
> emplary, I had to publish a correction with the conclusion:
> I am no hero and do not want to be considered one.[4]

[4] "Mein Weg zur Philosophie" (1951), in *Rechenschaft und
Ausblick*, pp. 323 f.

9

Reply. These criticisms of Jaspers were originally written in 1952 for the Jaspers volume in the Library of Living Philosophers, which finally appeared in 1957. A brief explanation is required for repeating the same criticisms after Jaspers' "Reply to My Critics" at the end of that volume. For although most of section 1 is new and I have moved most footnotes into the text and made other minor changes, no criticism has been withdrawn.

The reason: While "communication" is one of Jaspers' key concepts, his incapacity for understanding other points of view has almost become legendary (cf. chapter 18 below). It is as if he copied single sentences on file cards and then composed his books and essays around these excerpts. A former student, still full of admiration, confirms that this is precisely what he does. In the process, the structure and meaning of the views he discusses occasionally escape him altogether.

His reply actually corroborates my criticisms. He insists on the wealth of his quotations from Nietzsche, as if I had not stressed this; but he does not discuss my attempt to show how, for example, he quite fails to grasp Nietzsche's image of Jesus. And the way he quotes and paraphrases me illustrates my charges. Where I say, "And some will suggest: everybody is entitled to his own Nietzsche," Jaspers quotes *me* as saying: "Everybody is entitled to his own Nietzsche." Using the same illicit method, he attributes to *me* the view that "I reject his Nietzsche, and he mine"; and then Jaspers scores the debater's point that, while I admit that I reject his Nietzsche, he, more generous, does not reject mine: "I appreciate the explanations of Kaufmann in his book on Nietzsche, which call special attention to aspects rarely noted (as, for example, the problem of sublimation)." As if I had shown no appreciation for anything at all in *his* book. From my remark—hardly controversial —that Kant's main works are written "in a thoroughly graceless and often hopelessly obscure German," he infers that I deny their greatness and significance. Then he proceeds to "say against Kaufmann" what I myself have said emphatically in my *Nietzsche,* in the first paragraph of chapter 2.

Jaspers' paragraph on Bertram ("I have read only through a few pages of Bertram's Nietzsche-book, because one recognizes immediately the type of spirit from which one gets no nourishment") and on the George Circle ("From my youth on I have kept clear of the George-circle") join no issue: I went out of my way to emphasize how uncongenial these men were to Jaspers.

Jaspers also makes a great deal of the "whirl" and says: "Of all this Kaufmann has noticed nothing." Surely, this only shows how hastily he read my essay. (See pp. 297, 301, 304, 306 above.)

He concludes his "reply" to me by saying that, according to my essay, Nietzsche and Freud "stood in the great world of the enlightenment, I not: I hope to be allowed to contradict this radically for my person." As I said expressly toward the end of my essay, Jaspers "has repeatedly spoken out for the good elements of the Enlightenment." But that should not blind us to what I went on to call "the presence of elements in his own philosophy" that are quite at odds with this tradition.

One final point: Jaspers supposes that his "thinking" is utterly "alien" to me. Without depreciating the differences, I probably go further than most philosophers in applauding Jaspers' central impulse: the opposition to finished philosophical edifices and the wish to communicate some sense for what in my *Critique of Religion and Philosophy* I called "the philosophic flight." Hence another Nietzsche scholar, with whom Jaspers would lump me as ignoring the "whirl" in order "to lift out of Nietzsche a supposedly essential positive element," would lump me with Jaspers.

What I find admirable in Nietzsche is precisely that he transcended the spurious alternative of scholasticism and romanticism. There is life and passion and development in his work, and his thought cannot be reduced, any more than Plato's, to a few doctrines that can be memorized; but for all that his concepts are not hollow symbols that do not matter, as if the "whirl" were everything.

This point transcends the interpretation of Nietzsche. We

need not choose between the dogmatism of those who believe that only a definitive doctrine can spell our salvation and the suspense of those who scorn all conclusions. Beyond the "shell," that Jaspers spurns and the "whirl" he seeks lies what makes life worth-while.

16

FREUD

Few writers have attained as much fame and influence in their lifetime as Freud, but relatively few people have any clear idea of the development of Freud's thought. Even psychiatrists often rely on secondary sources, and many of these are full of errors. It therefore seems useful to offer a brief sketch in which most of the major landmarks that are well known are indicated, so the reader can rapidly note their relation to each other. The inadequacy of Jaspers' portrait, discussed in the preceding chapter, should become apparent; also, and above all, Freud's significance for ethics.

That he loved Shakespeare and Goethe would not ensure him any attention here, but he is the heir of Goethe and Nietzsche in their opposition to resentment; and it is under his influence more than under theirs that education and penology have been *"delivered from revenge"* to some extent, to cite Nietzsche's phrase (see chapter 11). Freud's theories, as will be noted, are open to many objections; but in reading him we are reminded that greatness is possible in our time.

2

He was born in Freiberg (then Austria-Hungary, now Czechoslovakia) on May 6, 1856—the year Heinrich Heine died, and a year after Kierkegaard's death. Although he was only twelve years Nietzsche's junior, he published his first great book the year Nietzsche died, in 1900.

Being a Jew, he tells us, he learned early to discount the judgment of the compact majority. He studied medicine, took his M.D. in Vienna in 1881, specialized in brain anatomy, and in 1885 was made a lecturer for neuropathology. He studied hysteria with Charcot in Paris, and a little later came very close to establishing the use of cocaine as a local anesthetic. But he interrupted his work on this project to visit his fiancée, asking another man to continue where he had left off; and the other man procrastinated until the laurels went to a third party who had done similar work independently. Freud assures us that he never bore his fiancée any grudge on this account—an assurance that might not strike us as faintly comic, if Freud's later work had not changed our sensibility.

In 1886 he married after a long engagement. Then he studied hypnosis with Bernheim in Nancy and, back in Vienna, hysteria together with Breuer. Out of these studies he gradually developed his own theories, and in 1900 he published his first major work, which he continued to consider his greatest: *The Interpretation of Dreams*. Six hundred copies were printed, and it took eight years to sell them; but before his death the book went through eight painstakingly revised editions and was widely translated. More than any other single event, publication of this book marks the beginning of psychoanalysis, which Freud created and for which he coined the name. Nazi anti-Semites who belittled Freud's contribution sometimes claimed that Breuer was the real founder—not knowing that Breuer, too, was a Jew.

Before the First World War, Freud published several other fundamental works, including *The Psychopathology of Everyday Life*, his *Three Contributions to the Theory of Sex*, and *Totem and Tabu*. In 1911 and 1912 Alfred Adler and C. G. Jung seceded from Freud's school. During the war, Freud summed up his conclusions so far in a notable series of lectures, soon published and translated as *General Introduction to Psychoanalysis*—still by far the best introduction to the subject.

After the war Freud tried to systematize his theories, an attempt that led to some modifications and to the introduction of several new concepts, including the death impulse, the ego, the id, and the super-ego. These concepts represent afterthoughts; psychoanalysis does not stand or fall with them, and Freud's claim to fame might not have been greatly diminished had he stopped writing in 1920. Yet his attempt to systematize was by no means prompted by dogmatism: books like *Beyond the Pleasure Principle* and *The Ego and the Id* show a determination to examine the adequacy and sufficiency of the concepts previously employed and a willingness to effect even drastic revisions where necessary. Freud's lack of respect for those who broke with him was motivated by his conviction that their modifications of his theories were prompted less by evidence than by a false regard for public opinion and, in Jung's case, also by a penchant for the occult.

In his later works Freud applied his ideas to a critique of religion as a product of wishful thinking (*The Future of an Illusion*) and to general cultural criticism and philosophic anthropology (*Civilization and Its Discontents*). When the Nazis entered Vienna in 1938 he escaped to London, where he went on working until the last, in spite of cancer. During the last sixteen years of his life he was in almost constant pain and suffered thirty-three operations. He died on September 23, 1939, just after Hitler's conquest of Poland.

3

His relation to Nietzsche is of special interest. In his published works, Freud occasionally expressed his admiration for Nietzsche, "whose premonitions and insights often agree in the most amazing manner with the laborious results of psychoanalysis." But he seemed put off by Nietzsche's lack of humility and humanity. In his three-volume biography, Ernest Jones relates that some of Freud's remarks on Nietzsche still await publication and that Freud "several times said of Nietzsche that he had a more penetrating knowledge of himself than any other man who ever lived or was ever likely to live" (II, 344).

Jones also prints a letter in which Freud says of Nietzsche: "In my youth he signified a nobility which I could not attain. A friend of mine, Dr. Paneth, had got to know him in the Engadine [Jones adds in a footnote: "Probably in 1885"] and he used to write me a lot about him" (III, 460). Actually, Paneth met Nietzsche in Nizza, where he saw a great deal of him from December 26, 1883, until March 26, 1884, and the letters he wrote to his future wife during that time have been published in the Nietzsche biography written by the philosopher's sister. Presumably, what he wrote Freud was very similar.

In ' German, the passages on Nietzsche come to thirteen pages. A few quotations will show what impressed Freud.

There is not a trace of false pathos or the prophet's pose in him, as I had rather feared after his last work. Instead his manner is completely inoffensive and natural. . . . He told me, but without the least affectation or conceit, that he always felt himself to have a task and that now, as far as his eyes would permit it, he wanted to get out of himself and work up whatever might be in him.

He told me that through his physical pains he had got rid of his pessimism—from defiance, in order not to let himself by tyrannized by pain. . . .

There are many contradictions in Nietzsche, but he is a thoroughly honest human being. . . .

He is completely convinced of his mission and of his decisive importance. In this faith he is strong and superior to all misfortune, physical suffering, and poverty. Such a contempt for all external instruments of success, such freedom from all that smacks of cliques or advertising, is impressive.

There are human qualities that are far rarer than scientific discoveries. And anyone who looks at photographs of Freud's face, beginning with the dashing, handsome young man, and ending with the magnificent portraits of the old man—or who reads through Jones's biography—can hardly fail to see that Freud not only revolutionized man's thinking about man but that he also made of himself an abiding image of humanity.

4

Freud's stature as a human being is still insufficiently appreciated. All too often he is misrepresented as a stern and

humorless authoritarian, as a dogmatist who brooked no criticism, as a man quite lacking in humanity. It is the surpassing
merit of Jones's study of *The Life and Work of Sigmund Freud,*
and especially of the last volume (from which all of the quotations in this section have been taken), that, instead of piling
up worshipful epithets, it *shows* us Freud's courage and humor, his tenacity and tolerance, his attitudes toward his disciples and his own works, his response to suffering, fame, and
death. We are made to live through his troubled relationships
with Otto Rank and Sandor Ferenczi and savor greatness as
we read the detailed and wise letter to Ferenczi in which
Freud discusses his erstwhile disciple's deviations (pp. 163–
65). Frequently we are exasperated by the multifarious petty
problems, whether personal or financial, but we come to see
that the man's mettle has to be appreciated in this setting, and
the many straight quotations, mostly in the form of complete
letters but sometimes from conversations, leave no doubt that
few men were so memorable.

Soon after the first of his thirty-three facial operations for
cancer, one of his grandsons died, only four years old. "It was
the only occasion in his life when Freud was known to shed
tears . . . Heinerle had stood to him for all children and grand-
children. Since his death he had not been able to enjoy life;
he added: 'It is the secret of my indifference—people call it
courage—toward the danger to my own life'" (p. 92).

Freud did not only depreciate his own courage. He did not
consider himself a great man. "I am sure in a few decades my
name will be wiped away and our results will last" (p. 21).
"Fame," he said, "comes to us only after we are dead, and
frankly what comes afterwards does not concern me. I have
no aspirations to posthumous glory. My modesty is no virtue."
And when he was "asked whether it meant nothing to him
that his name should live, he replied: 'Nothing whatsoever,
even if it should live, which is by no means certain. . . . I
am far more interested in this blossom than in anything that
may happen to me after I am dead. . . . I am not a pessimist.
I permit no philosophic reflection to spoil my enjoyment of
the simple things of life'" (p. 126).

One might be tempted to call Freud a stoic. His many ref-

erences to "fate" and his fusion of resignation and courage
point in that direction. So does his refusal to submit in any
way to his almost intolerable suffering. He would not bow,
not even a little. "I prefer to think in torment than not to be
able to think clearly." Only during the last weeks "he consented
to take an occasional dose of aspirin, the only drug he accepted
before the very end" (p. 245).

This Roman stoicism which might bring to mind the early
Brutus or Mutius Scaevola is tempered by Freud's humor, his
humility, and his humanity. A single illustration may suffice.
He and his family had been bullied in a great many ways by
the Gestapo; but in order to receive his exit visa he had to
sign a statement that he had been treated "by the Gestapo
with all the respect and consideration due to my scientific reputation, that I could live and work in full freedom . . . that I
found full support from all concerned in this respect, and that
I have not the slightest reason for any complaint." Before sign-
ing, Freud asked whether he could add one sentence: "I can
heartily recommend the Gestapo to anyone" (p. 226).

To Freud himself, any attempt to classify him as a great
man without accepting his doctrines was almost incomprehensible—except possibly as a subtle form of resistance to psychoanalysis. To a writer who, in a book on great Jews, mentioned
Freud's name "together with the greatest names of our people
(which far transcends my ambition)" he wrote: "My impression is that if your objections to the conception of lapses are
justified, I have very little claim to be named beside Bergson
and Einstein among the intellectual sovereigns" (p. 450). And
on another occasion he said: "I ask nothing more from the
world than that it should leave me in peace and devote its
interest to psychoanalysis instead" (p. 179).

It is one of the great virtues of Jones's work that it makes
so abundantly clear how Freud's human greatness does not
stand or fall with the correctness of his theories. The nearest
parallel is surely Spinoza who is widely admired as one of the
noblest men of all time even by those who do not accept all of
his doctrines. Socrates furnishes another example. And though
Freud never saw himself in this perspective, he belongs with
these immortals.

His very refusal to admit that the development of an important scientific theory makes the author a great man is so rare that, paradoxically, it constitutes a sign of greatness. Lesser men make no distinction of this sort. Freud, like Einstein, did—not as a matter of theoretical insight but rather from instinctive modesty and from a deeply felt annoyance with "the hubbub on all sides of a popularity that" Freud, like Einstein, found "repellent" (p. 83).

If this image of Freud were right, he could not possibly have felt that his work was above all criticism, as so many of his critics have alleged he did. Those who have read Freud himself instead of secondary sources need no reassurance on this point: they know how he constantly revised his major work, *The Interpretation of Dreams,* and how full his later books are of admittedly tentative speculations. Still, it is noteworthy that Freud told a close friend that *The Future of an Illusion* "had very little value." And "to Ferenczi he was still more outspoken in his derogation of the book: 'Now it already seems to me childish; fundamentally I think otherwise; I regard it as weak analytically and inadequate as a self-confession'" (p. 138).

Freud was quite aware that the end of World War I marked a break in his work, and that his later speculations were not on a par with his pioneering studies. Far from being a despotic prophet, bent on excommunicating all who disagreed with him —Jones furnishes ample evidence, including letters, that ought to dispose of this myth—Freud was sharply critical of his own writings. An American admirer wrote in 1957: "His *Civilization and Its Discontents* at the zenith of his career (1930) is the most distinctive statement in the philosophy of existence and civilization which has been produced in the present century. By contrast to it . . . Comte and Spencer, Schopenhauer and Nietzsche . . . Dewey and Sartre . . . seem shades of yesteryear . . . Too few years are left in the present Century to exhaust the dimensions of his message . . ." And what might Freud have said to that? What did Freud in fact write Lou Andreas-Salomé (see chapter 12, section 1) about the very same book? "It strikes me, without doubt rightly so, as very superfluous in contradistinction from earlier works, in which there was always a creative impulse. But what else should I do? I can't spend the whole day in smoking and playing cards, I can no longer walk far, and the most of what there is to read does not interest me any more. So I wrote, and the time passed that way quite pleasantly" (p. 448).

One need not take this self-disparagement entirely at face value; one may detect some humor in it; one may seek the truth somewhere between these two extreme evaluations—and be grateful that Freud's is the modest one. Still, the author's criticism of his own book illuminates one of its stranger notions: that science, religion, and art are all palliatives that help us to endure an otherwise insufferable existence; that religion helps by way of self-deception, art by providing substitute gratifications, and science by being a diversion. This is not Freud at his best, and in an attempt to criticize these ideas one can actually cite some eloquent passages from Freud's earlier writings against them. (See section 97 of my *Critique*.)

Freud's last book, *Moses and Monotheism*, probably came as close as anything he ever wrote to being a bad book. Although it sustains excitement, the argument is extraordinarily flimsy—and it is a relief to learn from Jones that for a long time Freud himself thought of it as "an historical novel" (p. 193). Oddly, Jones rallies to a defense of the book and especially of its thesis that Moses was an Egyptian, although Jones has only scorn for Freud's hypothesis that Shakespeare's plays were written by the Earl of Oxford. On this point, Jones is far worse than Freud was: he cites as proofs the fantastic apologetics of Josephus and Eusebius, who lived more than thirteen centuries after the time of Moses; he enlists Max Weber as "the great Biblical scholar"; and he says that Ernst Sellin's claim that "he had found some evidence pointing to the murder of Moses . . . was immediately rejected by all Jewish scholars" (p. 373)—which is like saying that the theory about the Earl of Oxford was immediately rejected by all of the people of Stratford. As if Sellin's suggestion had been taken seriously by Gentile scholars!

On almost every aspect of Freud's life and work Jones is an expert, but not on Judaism. A remark he makes about Freud's father makes one wonder whether Jones knows that the Torah is the Hebrew term for the Five Books of Moses:

"Jacob Freud was, it is true, fond of reading the *Torah*, a book of Jewish philosophy rather than of religion; it was no doubt an indication of his interest in trying to unravel the knotty problems of life" (p. 350). And Jones thinks that the saying, "if a Jew says he enjoys fox hunting he is lying," illustrates the Jews' "ancestral traditions in feeling aloof from the animal world" (p. 306)—as if the point were not plainly that the Jew identifies himself with the hunted creature.

Such slips are rare in Jones's work on Freud and worth mentioning only because these three volumes will assuredly survive long after lesser works on Freud have been forgotten. Freud did not want anyone to write his biography: he thought biographies must necessarily be mendacious and hypocritical. When Jones undertook his task nevertheless, he was partly impelled by the luxuriant growth of untruths about Freud which called for a detailed, closely documented attempt to set the record straight. But he accomplished more than this: he set a new standard for biographers.

As we take leave of the man to think about his theories, let us turn to the high point of Jones's work, the Appendix that offers "Extracts from Correspondence," and quote Freud in a Shakespearean vein: "In the depths of my being I remain convinced that my dear fellow-creatures are—with individual exceptions—good for nothing [*Gesindel*]" (p. 449). This conviction did not prevent Freud from working for their benefit, trying to help them as best he could, without the least expectation of reward. The beginning of a letter to Schnitzler, the playwright, is no less Shakespearean: "Now you too have reached the age of sixty, while I, six years older, am approaching the end of life and may soon expect to see the close of the fifth act of this pretty incomprehensible and not always amusing comedy" (p. 443). He had nobility, he worked

> in a general honest thought
> And common good to all . . .
> His life was gentle; and the elements
> So mix'd in him that Nature might stand up
> And say to all the world, 'This was a man!'
>
> (*Julius Caesar*, last scene)

5

Psychoanalysis began as a therapeutic method when Freud abandoned hypnosis. Much has been made of his "determinism"; but the whole purpose of his therapy, if not of his life, was to restore their freedom to people who had become unable to do what they wanted to do, or to stop doing what they wanted to stop doing. Moreover, Freud abandoned hypnosis because it represents an encroachment on the patient's freedom and therefore does not lead to a permanent or complete cure: he did not want his patients to buy back their freedom at the price of permanent dependence on another human being. It is extremely doubtful whether Freud ever denied freedom in any sense in which it would be worth having.

The new method consisted first of all in question and answer, in the course of which Freud encountered frequent resistance and amnesia. The association of these two phenomena led to the conception of repression, which, as Freud himself pointed out, had been aphoristically anticipated by Nietzsche in section 68 of *Beyond Good and Evil*: " 'I have done that,' says my memory. 'I could not have done that,' says my pride and remains inexorable. Finally, my memory yields."

When he was able to overcome the patient's resistance and amnesia, Freud found that the repressed materials were very frequently concerned with sexual experiences of early childhood. Few of his contentions met with more initial opposition than the claim that young children are vitally interested in sexual functions, and few are such commonplaces today. Much more controversial is Freud's conception of the Oedipus complex, to which we shall return later.

To avoid prejudicing his results by leading questions, Freud came to replace the method of question and answer by recourse to free association and by the interpretation of dreams, which he called "the royal road to the unconscious." The central claim here is this: although internal physiological stimuli or external stimuli, like a noise, a smell, or a change of temperature, may trigger dreams, and although day residues turn up in dreams, every dream represents a wish fulfillment, al-

most always in disguised form. In the face of frequent mis-
representations, Freud insisted repeatedly that the wish need
not be sexual. He illustrated the *Interpretation of Dreams* with
Schwindt's "The Dream of the Prisoner," which shows grem-
lins sawing through the iron bars across the window and the
prisoner escaping; and Freud reports, for example, the dream
of a child who, after being denied a second helping of straw-
berries, dreamed of having it after all. Generally, however, the
overt dream must be distinguished from the latent content that
is disguised by an elaborate symbolism. Although some symbols are held to be almost invariable, a dream can be interpreted only with some knowledge of the dreamer's personal
background and associations. The symbolism as well as other
disfigurations of the latent content are charged to a "censor."

Even if one admits that the analysis of dreams, and of our
associations with various elements in a dream, is a royal road
to the unconscious, one may well question Freud's assumption
that the symbolism must always be explained in terms of self-
deception.

The central purpose of Freud's therapeutic interpretation of
dreams, however, and indeed of his entire treatment, should
not be overlooked. It is well stated in the twenty-seventh lecture of Freud's *General Introduction to Psychoanalysis:* "By
raising the unconscious into consciousness, we overcome the
repressions, abolish the conditions for symptom formation, and
change the pathogenetic conflict into a normal conflict which
must somehow find a resolution." "We hold that whoever has
successfully passed through an education for truthfulness toward himself, will thereby be protected permanently against
the danger of immorality, even if his standard of morality
should somehow differ from social conventions."

Although Freud says in the same context, "Where there is
no repression to be overcome, nor any analogous psychical
process, there our therapeutics has no business," he exerted
himself to show that repressions and analogous psychical processes were by no means confined to neurotics. Not only do
other men dream too, but there is what Freud called "the
psychopathology of everyday life." Here the key term is *Fehl-
leistung*, one of Freud's many felicitous coinages, inadequately

rendered as "error" or "slip." The coinage *mischievement* seems preferable. The theory here is that forgetting and slips in speaking, writing, or doing things, though triggered by tiredness or distraction, actually vent suppressed or repressed thoughts or wishes. A man who forgets his wedding, to give an extreme example, presumably does not wish to get married; and when Portia says to Bassanio, "One half of me is yours, the other half yours—Mine own, I would say," she shows that she has been thinking, though she did not mean to say it, that her whole heart belongs to Bassanio.

This last example is Freud's own and merely one instance among scores of illustrations from, or applications to, literature and art. Freud liked to show that what seemed fantastic to his contemporaries had long been known to Spinoza, Schopenhauer, and Nietzsche and utilized by Shakespeare, Goethe, Schiller, and Dostoevsky. He also tried to illuminate literary problems, as he did in his famous footnote on *Hamlet*, which was subsequently expanded into a book by Ernest Jones.

Most important, however, world literature furnishes powerful evidence against the common objection that the truth of Freud's theories is limited to the Vienna socialites around 1900 or, at best, to our own civilization. Sophocles' Jocasta soothes Oedipus, saying: "Many men have in their dreams had intercourse with their mothers." Plato says, at the beginning of the ninth book of the *Republic:*

> Of the unnecessary pleasures and desires some seem to me to be unlawful. They threaten to rise up in everybody; but suppressed by the laws and the better desires with the help of reason, they disappear completely in some people, or only a few weak ones remain, but in others they remain stronger and more numerous . . . those that awake in sleep when the other soul sleeps . . . but the bestial and wild part, overfull of food and drink, leaps up, shakes off sleep, and goes forth to satisfy its cravings. In such a state, as you know, he dares do anything, free of all shame and insight. He does not even think that he should shrink from intercourse with his mother. . . .

And Dostoevsky's Ivan Karamazov, whose brother has been

accused of murdering his father for the sake of a woman whom both father and son desired, shouts at the court: "Who doesn't desire his father's death?"

Such evidence, of course, does not establish the universality of these desires: only certain types in these civilizations, widely separated in space and time, might be troubled by such wishes; or such desires might be encountered only in some types of cultures, not in others. Freud argued powerfully, but not conclusively, that all men, regardless of race, color, or creed, are brothers under the skin. Those who disagree with him cannot rest satisfied with allegedly self-evident differences but must deal explicitly with the evidence adduced by Freud and others, notably including Otto Rank's *Das Inzest-Motiv in Dichtung und Sage.*

6

There remains Freud's later work in which the Oedipus complex becomes, if anything, more important. In his *New Introductory Lectures on Psychoanalysis* (chapter 5), he says of "the boy's Oedipus complex, in which he desires his mother, and wants to get rid of his father as a rival": "The threat of castration forces him to give up this attitude. Under the influence of the danger of losing his penis, he abandons his Oedipus complex; it is repressed and in the most normal cases entirely destroyed, while a severe super-ego is set up as its heir." The super-ego, which has been facetiously characterized as the part of the personality that is soluble in alcohol, is the psychoanalytic equivalent of the conscience. But the universality of the process here described, or even of the Oedipus complex, has never been established, nor have Freud's followers made systematic studies of orphans, semiorphans, children brought up by only one parent or neither parent, etc.

A theory suggested to Freud by Darwin, but long since abandoned by anthropologists, leads to Freud's least plausible thesis: "We cannot get away from the supposition that the guilt feeling of mankind is derived from the Oedipus complex and was acquired when the father was killed by the association of the brothers," he says in Section VII of *Civilization and*

its Discontents; and the notion of the murder of the primal
father by his sons plays an even more decisive role in Freud's
last book, *Moses and Monotheism.*

In the same section of *Civilization and its Discontents* Freud
suggests that besides the sex impulse there is another basic
urge, aggression. As the individual develops,

> aggression is introjected, made inwardly—really, sent back
> to where it came from, namely, turned against one's own
> ego. There it is taken over by a part of the ego which, as
> the superego, stands opposed to the rest of the ego; and in
> the form of "conscience" it now vents that same aggression
> against the ego which the ego would have liked to vent on
> other individuals. The tension between the severe superego
> and the ego subjected to it we call the consciousness of
> guilt; it finds expression in the need for punishment.

The wording depends on Freud's assumption that aggression
is, in its original form, directed against the self as a death
impulse.

Freud's theory of conscience is similar to Nietzsche's, which
is expounded in somewhat greater detail in the second essay
of the *Genealogy of Morals.* Freud himself says: "Nietzsche,
the other philosopher whose premonitions and insights often
agree in the most amazing manner with the laborious results
of psychoanalysis, I have long avoided for this very reason.
After all, I was less concerned about any priority than
about the preservation of my impartiality" (*Selbstdarstellung*).
Since his remarks about conscience do not represent "laborious
results" but bold speculations, it may have been unfortunate
that Freud did not give more careful attention to rival natural-
istic theories—and especially to Nietzsche's attempt to explain
in terms of a single basic drive the phenomena that led Freud
after World War I to modify his earlier psychological monism
by postulating a death impulse.

A few more quotations from the same section may round
out Freud's ideas about the genesis of conscience. "Evil is thus
originally that for which one is threatened with loss of love;
one must avoid it from fear of such loss." And a couple of
pages later: "Fate is considered as a substitute for the par-

ents; when one suffers misfortune this means that one is no
longer loved by this highest power; and threatened by this
loss of love, one submits again to the parent surrogate in the
super-ego which one was ready to neglect as long as everything went well." Even though it takes misfortune to make us
submit, Freud argues only a few pages later that, once the
super-ego is developed, the feeling of guilt becomes chronic:
"The denial of gratification does not help sufficiently, for the
wish remains and cannot be hidden from the super-ego. In
spite of the successful denial, therefore, a feeling of guilt will
develop. . . ." In the last chapter, finally, Freud says "that
the feeling of guilt . . . in its later phases is one and the same
thing as fear [*Angst*] of the superego."

Freud's later theories, here outlined, certainly give no adequate picture of his importance for ethics. At best they require
such sympathetic modification as, for example, David Riesman's suggestion in *The Lonely Crowd* that the super-ego account fits what Riesman calls the "inner-directed" person but
not the "tradition-directed" or "other-directed" type.

7

Freud's significance for ethics can perhaps be summed up
best in terms of a brief comparison first with Socrates and then
with Jesus. With Socrates he shares first of all the motto,
"Know thyself!" Freud lent substance to this demand when
he showed how ingeniously we deceive ourselves, hiding from
consciousness what pains us or does not meet with our
approval; and he suggested techniques for attaining self-
knowledge. Freud has often been censured for overemphasiz-
ing the dark side of man, a charge against which he defended
himself in the *General Introduction,* Chapter IX: "We dwell
on the evil side of man with greater emphasis only because
other men deny it, which makes man's psychic life not better
but incomprehensible." As a theory of human nature, psychoanalysis seems partial indeed: one might say that, unlike Kant,
Freud furnished a "critique of *un*-reason." To be sure, he did
not intend to deny man's reason: Robert Waelder recalls how
Freud said to him, "To me the moral has always seemed self-

evident"; and Theodor Reik recalls how Freud refused to accept Reik's pessimistic estimate of man's future. Even so, Freud's explicit comments on the aspirations of the artist, the seeker after truth, and the religious genius are simplistic, and his philosophical anthropology does not commend itself.[1] But it should not be forgotten that his reason for focusing attention on the irrational was that he had come to the conclusion that we must face and understand it before we could become autonomous. His approach was initially therapeutic and has pedagogical value, even though it does not yield a complete theory of human nature.

The second parallel with Socrates may be found in the belief of both men that virtue is knowledge—knowledge not of transcendent verities or of God but of ourselves. At this point Freud, like Socrates, is an optimist: the man who knows himself will not only cease to be neurotic but—and this passage was quoted above—he "will thereby be protected permanently against the danger of immorality, even if his standard of morality should somehow differ from social conventions."

The third and last parallel with Socrates concerns the maieutic method, the art of midwifery: Freud too seeks to give the needed knowledge, not by teaching, let alone preaching, but by way of eliciting memories. He tries to bring to light knowledge that is present in the subject but that cannot be "born" without help.

The parallels with Jesus can be stated summarily. There is first of all, to borrow a title from Stefan Zweig (the book contains a fine essay on Freud), "healing through the spirit." Freud's work is based on a radical antimaterialism that attacks physical symptoms via the psyche. Secondly, there is Freud's devotion to the despised and rejected, the outcasts of society. He had no liking for Jesus, Christianity, or the Jewish religion, and he argued that it was impossible to love one's neighbor as oneself, let alone one's enemies. Plainly, he valued honesty above both sentiments. But many Jews and Christians might well join in the wish that more men might love their neighbors in Freud's fashion!

[1]For a detailed critical discussion, see my *Critique*, §§42 and 96 f.

There remains yet the most important point of all. No man before Freud had given equal substance to one of the most striking sayings in the Gospels (found only in the fourth Gospel, and not even in the early manuscripts of that, but first related of a Stoic sage): "He that is without sin among you, let him first cast a stone." Nothing that Freud has done, and little that anyone else has done, is more relevant to ethics than is success in breaking down the wall between the normal and the abnormal, the respectable and the criminal, the good and the evil. Freud gave, as it were, a new answer to the Gospel query, "Who is my neighbor?" The mentally troubled, depressed, hysterical, and insane are not possessed by the devil but essentially "as thyself." Freud made men seek to understand and help where previous ages despised and condemned.

After Freud moral judgments become altogether questionable: they appear symptomatic rather than cognitive and tell us more about the judges than about those who are judged. In this respect Freud differs radically from Socrates and Jesus, and in many ways he is certainly closer to the Stoics and to Spinoza. The conception of moral judgments as symptoms can be found in Nietzsche: "Morality is . . . mere symptomatology" (*The Portable Nietzsche*, p. 501). But recent proponents of an emotivist theory of ethics probably owe more to Freud, and the French existentialists are equally indebted to both men.

Plato once defined justice as the health of the soul. Freud suggests that to have a healthy soul *is* to be ethical, the moral codes of mankind notwithstanding. Those who know themselves neither are wicked, according to Freud, nor call any man wicked: they are healthy and try to help the sick.

17

HEIDEGGER'S CASTLE

"Language is the house of Being," says Heidegger; but in truth his language is the house in which *he* hides, and his Gothic terminology is like a row of towers that frightens us away while it gives him a feeling of security. His philosophy is like a castle that, though certainly not beautiful, stands out from a generally dull landscape and catches the eye.

We should not dream of settling down beneath it to spend our lives, like Kafka's K., in futile efforts to penetrate the mysteries that, more often than not, are expressions of confusion rather than profundity. But we cannot get around the fact that his thought dominates philosophy, not only in Germany, but also in France and, to a lesser extent, in South America. Is it possible to unravel some of this mystery without giving one's life to it?

Since few of Heidegger's works have been translated, I shall quote him frequently. And since this chapter will be very critical, I shall in fairness quote relatively clear and suggestive passages. Those who are curious about obscure passages will have no trouble finding them in abundance in Heidegger's books.

2

Heidegger's books. Heidegger's main work, *Sein und Zeit: Erste Hälfte* (*Being and Time: First Half*)—the second half never appeared—was first published in Husserl's *Jahrbuch* in 1927 and was dedicated to him when it came out separately as a book. In two ways, however, it represented a marked departure from Husserl's phenomenology: Heidegger concentrated on describing various aspects of human existence, and he did this in order to achieve a better understanding of Being. The first of these points was widely noted and established his fame as one of the founders of existentialism: *Geworfenheit* (man's finding himself thrown into the world; cf. chapter 1, section 1, and chapter 5, section 1) and *Angst* (dread) became almost as popular as Freud's coinages, and Heidegger's discussion of care and conscience attracted wide attention, too. Yet it was by no means an afterthought when he insisted after World War II that he was no existentialist and that human existence had concerned him merely as the window through which man can peer into Being—though he did not use this image (cf. section 11 below).

In 1929 he published *Kant und das Problem der Metaphysik, Vom Wesen des Grundes,* and a seventeen-page lecture, *Was ist Metaphysik?* To this lecture he later added a nine-page postscript (1943) and then, in 1949, a remarkable fifteen-page introduction, which he considers an especially important self-interpretation. (This is available in English in my *Existentialism from Dostoevsky to Sartre.*)

After Hitler came to power in 1933, Heidegger accepted the *Rektorat* of the University of Freiburg. In his inaugural address, *Die Selbstbehauptung der deutschen Universität,* he welcomed the dawn of a new era and the abolition of academic freedom. He also dissociated himself completely from Husserl, who was a Jew.

His *Being and Time* had culminated in the challenge to face death with resolution. Resolution and courage never ceased to be central themes in his thought. In his inaugural address, analytic thinking is disparaged and spirit is defined as "primevally attuned, knowing resolution toward the essence of Being." And he continued to discuss courage in essays on Hölderlin's poetry (collected in one volume in 1944) and in a short essay *Vom Wesen der Wahrheit* (1943).

After the war, he published *Brief über den "Humanismus"* (1947) in which he repudiated Sartre and the label of existentialism, the previously mentioned self-interpretation, and *Holzwege* (1950), which comprises six essays, mostly exegetical. One deals with a passage in Hegel's *Phenomenology,* one with "Nietzsche's Word, 'God is Dead,'" one with a Rilke poem, one with Anaximander's sole surviving sentence. On the surface, he seemed to be concerned only with what others had said or not said and with what he himself had said or not said; but in Germany it became customary to speak of Heidegger's *Kehre,* his "turning," and to find a significant reversal in his postwar attempt to explore Being instead of continuing the analysis of man's existence begun in *Being and Time.*

Then, in 1953 and 1954, he suddenly published four new books. *Aus der Erfahrung des Denkens* (1954), a volume of twenty-odd pages, opens with a six-line poem and closes with an eight-line poem, two words per line. In between, every left page offers two or three lines, beginning "When," while every right page continues with four phrases that occurred to the author on the occasion named or that seem especially appropriate to him; e.g.,

When the evening light, falling somewhere into the
wood, gilds the tree trunks:

Singing and thinking are the trunks that are neighbors of
*   poetry.*
They grow out of Being and reach into its truth.
Their relation to each other makes us think what Hölderlin
*   sings of the trees of the wood:*
"And unknown to each other remain, as long as they stand,
*   the neighboring trunks."*

The three other books, like the other books Heidegger has published since, contain either essays and lectures—*Vorträge und Aufsätze* (1954)—or a course of lectures apiece, like *Was Heisst Denken?* (1954) and *Einführung in die Metaphysik* (1953). These books overlap very largely, and the author himself calls attention to this in the case of a lecture on Nietzsche in the first of these books, which is exceedingly similar to a section in the second. The many pieces on the pre-Socratics in the first collection overlap extensively not only the second volume but also the *Introduction to Metaphysics.*

There is no need to go on listing the occasional essays and

lectures that Heidegger has kept on publishing. Jaspers has given us two *Introductions:* first, his *Nietzsche,* which was subtitled "Introduction to an Understanding of his Philosophizing," and then his *Einführung in die Philosophie* (1950), of which the Yale University Press published an English translation under the title, *The Way to Wisdom.* These books hardly live up to their titles—not even the German titles—both are very definitely introductions to Jaspers' philosophizing. Heidegger's *Einführung in die Metaphysik* fits this pattern: it is an excellent introduction to Heidegger.

3

Heidegger and Nazism. When Heidegger's *Introduction* appeared in Germany in 1953, nothing excited more interest than the light it shed on his relation to the Nazis. The book consists of a series of lectures given at the University of Freiburg in 1935, and Heidegger assures the reader that nothing has been changed—except for minor stylistic revisions. What was written in 1935 but not said in the lectures is placed in parentheses, while material added during the following years has been placed in brackets—but there is very little of that.

The sentence that created a major newspaper controversy between *Allgemeine Zeitung,* Frankfurt, which found proof in it that Heidegger was still a Nazi, seeing that he had not changed this sentence, and *Die Zeit,* Hamburg, which came to his defense, reads:

> That, finally, which is offered today as the philosophy of National Socialism, but really does not have anything whatever to do with the inner truth and greatness of this movement (namely, with the encounter of technology on a worldwide scale on the one hand and modern man on the other) tries to catch its fish in these muddy waters of "values" and "totalities" [p. 152].

The Nazi party was often referred to as "the movement," and Heidegger does not claim that he spoke the words in the parentheses in 1935, only that they were written then—allowing possibly for minor stylistic revisions. Surely, it matters very little what precisely he wrote in 1935. What is obvious is that in 1933 he publicly embraced Nazism and that by 1935 he felt the need to dissociate himself from the "philosophy" of the party hacks. In the same vein, he said in connection with his own concern with Nietzsche:

> [His] philosophy is still immune against all the rude and crude obtrusiveness that characterizes the scribbling folk who are flocking around him today in ever increasing numbers. In fact, his work does not even seem to have weathered the worst abuses yet. When I speak of Nietzsche here, I do not want to have anything at all in common with all this [p. 27].

The Nazi Party Congress in Nürnberg that year, announced under the motto "The Triumph of the Will," also does not seem to have won his enthusiasm. On the contrary. He saw Europe "in the great pincers between Russia and America. From a metaphysical point of view, Russia and America represent the same thing: the same desperate race of unfettered technology and baseless organization of the man of normalcy." From a metaphysical point of view, the presence or absence of free speech does not matter any more than concentration camps, whether in Russia or in Germany. The *important* question is whether Germany, alone in an ocean of technology and normalcy, will face up to Being. In this context we find the scornful remark: "The numbers of millions participating in mass congresses are counted a triumph" (p. 28).

It seems clear that much of Nazism did not appeal to Heidegger. But there is absolutely nothing to suggest that the Nazis' systematic inhumanity or their contempt for all nobility, freedom, and honesty appalled him. Heidegger's disenchantment was not based on moral grounds: the triumphs were too shallow, the answers proffered too facile, and nobody seemed to care that the one event that truly mattered had not come to pass: the revelation of Being that would have permitted the completion of *Being and Time*.

Here is the final paragraph of the *Introduction to Metaphysics*:

Being able to ask a question means: being able to wait, even
one's whole life long. An age, however, which considers real
only what is fast and can be grasped with both hands believes that asking questions is "unrealistic" and does not pay.
But not numbers are essential but the right time, i.e. the
right moment and right endurance.

> "For the god
> who ponders, hates
> untimely growth." (Hölderlin)

In 1947, in his "Letter on 'Humanism,'" Heidegger insisted
—and there are several similar passages in his writings—"Until
today, thought, which in *Being and Time* attempted a few
steps, has not advanced at all beyond this treatise." Obviously,
this is not the fault of Heidegger, who at least advanced once
while nobody else in the world took any steps at all. That he
cannot complete his major work is the fault of our time (cf.
chapter 1 above).

Heidegger's initial attitude toward Hitler throws light on his
later thought. He once believed in a false messiah. Now he mis-
trusts all answers and celebrates the ability to wait as piety
itself. Not being able to wait is the sin against the spirit. The
second coming—rather the second half of *Being and Time*—
may seem overdue. But, though impious in other ways, most
English-speaking philosophers can wait.

In all his later writings, Heidegger insists on the importance
of questions and not on answers, on thinking rather than conclusions; but, unlike Jaspers, whom he resembles at this point,
he does not speak of "philosophizing" but of "being on the
way." He fills pages with scorn for the superficial answers
given by others but—again unlike Jaspers—argues that the impossibility of final answers is a feature of our age and keeps
alive the hope that, if we follow him—he does not say, into
the desert—some of us may yet enter the promised land.

In his little volume of "poetry" he says, "We come too late
for the gods and too early for Being" (p. 7), but in his lectures
he makes so much of the courage and tenacity of the attempt
to face Being that there is always some hope that, like Jacob,

after he had said "I will not let thee go, except thou bless me," he might prevail after all.

The fascination of his lectures and his books is due in no small measure to the way in which he manages to keep alive the hope that in just a few more pages, or surely before the course is over, we may see something that even now reduces any other enterprise to insignificance.

4

Introduction to Metaphysics. Let us follow Heidegger's quest all the way through his *Introduction* before considering his thought under systematic headings. The first of the four chapters of the book bears the title "The Basic Question of Metaphysics" and begins: "Why is there any being at all and not rather nothing?" Surely, Heidegger's inability to answer this question is not due to the age we live in but to certain peculiarities of the question. No previous age could have answered this question; and if a future generation should be able to answer it to its own satisfaction, it won't be because Being has revealed itself but because the intellectual conscience has gone to sleep.

One need not be a positivist to suggest that it is the philosopher's task to determine by an analysis of this question why it cannot be answered. Heidegger, however, proceeds as if Kant had never written his *Critique of Pure Reason* and as if the "why" of this question were unambiguous. The possibility that the question itself might be open to serious criticism is not even considered: the question is treated like an authoritative text—as a preacher might treat a verse from Scripture. It is expounded and extolled, circumscribed and circumvented, without ever being analyzed.

This question, which Heidegger calls the basic question (*Grundfrage*), is, he says, the first question "in rank." This can be shown in three ways: it has the widest scope, is the most profound and, finally, also the most original question. He takes up each claim in turn. To show, for example, that this is the most profound question, he says that the question asks about the ground (*Grund*) of what was Being. He speaks of *ergründen* (fathom) and *Gründung* (foundation) and distinguishes between *Ur-grund* (primal ground), *Ab-grund* (abyss), and *Un-grund* (bottomlessness?).

> This question with its Why does not move on one level or surface only but penetrates the underlying ["*zu-grunde*" *liegenden*] realms to their ultimate reaches, to the limits; it is opposed to all surfaces and all shallowness and strives for the depth; as the widest question it is also of all deep questions the deepest [pp. 2 f.].

This is rhapsody, not analysis; and the piling up of words with the same root—one of the most characteristic devices of Heidegger's style—induces a spurious sense of illumination, an unfounded conviction that something has been explained. When we become aware how many German words share the root syllable *Grund*, we feel that we now realize something we did not know before; we are apt to congratulate ourselves on seeing something and believe that the speaker is taking us on a voyage of discovery. But in fact nothing has been discovered except that several German words share the root syllable *Grund*. Heidegger's art is such that he maintains this sense of excitement throughout the book, and the suspense created by his initial paean on his question continues unabated for 157 pages.

On page 7, Heidegger admits: "Thus we really have not asked the question yet. We turned aside immediately into a consideration of the question. . . . With the considerations of this hour, therefore, we conclude our initial remarks." What was apparently the second lecture begins with a paean on philosophy that communicates an overwhelming sense of the importance of what he is doing. Some of the points Heidegger makes in this connection shall be considered later under appropriate topical headings. First, however, I want to try to reproduce the outline of the book.

The first chapter is full of fascinating observations: any number of them deserve careful reflection—but never receive it. They are like so many vistas that come into view as Heidegger sails, not toward an answer to his "basic question," but in the direction of a genuine asking of the question.

"Introduction to Metaphysics" means, as will be seen: leading into the asking of the basic question. But questions, and
especially basic questions, do not simply occur like stones
and water. Questions do not exist like shoes and clothes or
books. Questions are—and are only as they are really asked.
Leading into the asking of the basic question is therefore
not a walk toward something that lies or stands somewhere,
but the leading itself must awaken and create the asking.
Leading here means going ahead, asking, asking ahead. For
such leading there cannot be in the nature of the case any
following [*Gefolgschaft;* a dig at the Nazi conception of the
Führer with which the word *Gefolgschaft* was generally
associated. In his inaugural address Heidegger himself had
used the word constantly and with full approval.]. Where a
following appears and settles down in comfort—for example,
a philosophical school—asking questions is misunderstood
[p. 15].

The "existential pathos" of this appeal to the single human
being in his solitude is familiar from Nietzsche and Kierkegaard as well as Jaspers and Sartre. But Heidegger is by no
means content to get those who listen to him, or read him, to
ask a question genuinely. His concern is less with his audience,
less with the individual human being, than it is with Being.

The title "ontology" was coined only in the seventeenth
century. It designates the development of the traditional
doctrine of what has being into a discipline of philosophy
and a compartment of a philosophical system. . . . The
word "ontology," however, can also be taken "in the widest
sense and without agreement with contemporary ontological
tendencies" (cf. *Sein und Zeit,* 1927, 11). In that case "ontology" means the exertion to induce Being to speak . . .
[p. 31].

Nietzsche's Zarathustra said in the chapter "On the Afterworldly": "The belly of Being does not speak to humans at
all, except as a human. Verily, all being is hard to prove and
hard to induce to speak." Nietzsche suggests that the concern
with Being and metaphysics and the concern with God and

theology ("the afterworldly" is intended as a literal translation of "metaphysicians") are variations of a single attitude;
and we shall return to this theme later when comparing Heidegger's approach with that of theologians.

The second chapter is entitled "On the Grammar and Etymology of the Word 'be'" and deals separately first with the
grammar and then with the etymology. The first part (twelve
pages) does not appeal to ordinary language:

> That the development of occidental grammar originated in
> the Greeks' reflection on the *Greek* language—that gives this
> reflection unique significance. For the Greek language is (re-
> garding the possibilities of thinking) the most powerful and
> the most spiritual language besides German [p. 43].

The following discussion goes back to the origins of Greek reflection.

The three pages on "The Etymology of the Word 'be'" call
attention to the fact that "the vast multiplicity of different
forms of the verb 'be' is determined by three different roots."
There is *es* (cf. the Greek εἶναι, the Latin *esse*, the German
sein); there is *bheu* (cf. the Greek φύω, the Latin *fui*, the German *bin;* Heidegger does not mention the English *be*); and
finally *wes* (cf. the German *war, gewesen*, etc.). From these
three roots Heidegger derives three provisional meanings: live,
rise, abide (*leben, aufgehen, verweilen*).

Heidegger does not go beyond dabbling in etymology; and
an unkind critic could say that he is pulling all the stops, including etymology, always giving the impression that he
probes deeply when in fact he does not dig in anywhere. But
if we take this account as a programmatic suggestion, we must
concede that in one respect it is superior to a great deal of
contemporary analysis of English words: Heidegger calls attention to the important fact that a word may mark the confluence of several separate traditions. He does not emphasize
the moral: a word may be essentially ambiguous, and the ambiguity may be illuminated more decisively by a moment's
historical reflection than by pages and pages of examples from
ordinary language.

But Heidegger often substitutes etymologies for arguments

—and many of his etymologies are untenable; and many more, doubtful. Karl Löwith enumerates a few of the questionable ones in his little book, *Heidegger, Denker in dürftiger Zeit* (1953). The book marks his break with the master but bolsters the myth that Heidegger, for all his faults, is the one genuine "thinker in a paltry time."

The third chapter bears the title *Die Frage nach dem Wesen des Seins*, which might be translated: "The Question about the Essence of Being." But the German *nach*, which Heidegger employs instead of *über*, suggests something more like "The Quest for"; and *Wesen*, one of Heidegger's key terms, does not only mean "essence" but is also, as we have seen, one of the roots used in German in the conjugation of *sein* (to be). Moreover, *anwesend* means "present," and Heidegger likes to use *anwesen* and *wesen* as verbs to signify "being present."

The fourth and last chapter, "The Limitation of Being," takes up more than half of the book and is subdivided into four sections: *Sein und Werden* ("Being and Becoming"), *Sein und Schein* ("Being and Seeming," or "Appearance and Reality"), *Sein und Denken* ("Being and Thinking"), and *Sein und Sollen* ("Being and Ought," or "Is and Ought").

The first of these four sections (two pages) cites Parmenides, fragment 8, 1–6, first in Greek and then in Heidegger's German translation, and comments: "These few words stand there like Greek statues of the archaic period. What we still possess of the poem of Parmenides fits into a thin pamphlet which, however, refutes the claims of whole libraries of philosophic literature that they exist of necessity" (pp. 73 f.). Then Heidegger cites Heraclitus and asserts: "Heraclitus, who is supposed to be diametrically opposed to Parmenides insofar as the doctrine of Becoming is ascribed to him, really says the same thing Parmenides says" (p. 74). This will become clearer, we are told, in the following sections.

The section on "Being and Seeming" features a brief but suggestive discussion of Sophocles' *Oedipus Tyrannus*, admittedly derived from Karl Reinhardt's *Sophokles* (1933), and a long discussion of Parmenides, especially fragments 4, 6, and 1, verses 28–32.

The section on "Being and Thinking" (sixty-two pages) is the heart of the book. It raises the question, *Was heisst Denken?* (what is thinking?) on which Heidegger has published a separate series of lectures, and seeks to illuminate both Being and thought by a discussion of Heraclitus (pp. 96–104, *et passim*) and Parmenides' fragment 5, which seems to assert that thinking and Being are the same thing (pp. 104–11). Then Heidegger cites the second chorus (he calls it the first chorus) from Sophocles' *Antigone* (verses 332–75), in his own translation, to illuminate the nature of man (pp. 112–26); and then he brings together Sophocles, Parmenides, and Heraclitus. Plato signifies a "falling off [*'Abfall'*]." But "when we speak of a 'falling off' here we must insist that in spite of everything this falling off still remains at a height and does not sink down to what is low" (p. 141). In Plato, the earlier conception of truth (ἀλήθεια) as *Unverborgenheit* (unconcealedness, as Heidegger has long translated the Greek term) gives way to a conception of propositional truth, or, rather, correctness. Heidegger considers the role of Aristotle and Hegel in this development. From this later point of view, early Greek philosophy can no longer be understood.

The objection that the positions that Heidegger condemns are generally much clearer than what he admires would not surprise him: he is quite aware of the difficulty of saying, or of understanding today, what ought to be said. I shall quote one more passage from this section:

> We know from Heraclitus and Parmenides that the unconcealedness of what has being is not simply there. This unconcealedness occurs only as an accomplishment: the accomplishment of the word in poetry, the accomplishment of stone in a temple or statue, the accomplishment of the word in thought, and the accomplishment of the πόλις as the historic site which is the foundation and guardian of all this [p. 146].

One can share Heidegger's admiration for the Greeks and agree that a philosopher can learn far more from Sophocles, or for that matter Shakespeare, than from scores of professors (including Heidegger); and unquestionably the lone temple at

Segesta or an archaic torso of Apollo moves us more than volumes upon volumes of scholarly journals (or for that matter
Heidegger's prose). But why should the word "truth" be reserved for the peculiar excellence of works of art and denied
to propositions? After all, we have a large vocabulary to pay
tribute to works of art without calling them "true" (cf. my
Critique, §§22–25, and the discussion of "subjective truth" in
chapter 10 above). We can call them profound or exciting,
beautiful or sublime; we can say that they change our perception or sensibility and give us a deeper understanding of
things or of man's potentialities; and we can try to spell out in
detail what it is that works of art accomplish that propositions
cannot achieve. But to say simply that truth, which is really
unconcealedness, occurs in art, and that the conception of
propositional truth signifies a steep decline from the heights of
pre-Socratic Greece is making it rather easy for oneself. A philosopher should not be content with so little. Instead of extolling poetry and art and casting aspersions on science and
technology, he might illuminate the functions, the limitations,
and the dangers of each.

The final section on "Is and Ought" comprises only three
pages. Then another five pages wind up the book. The final
paragraph has already been quoted.

In the following pages I propose to offer some critical reflections under a number of topical headings. All the comments will be apropos of the *Introduction* but should throw
light on Heidegger's other work as well.

5

Repudiation of logic. Heidegger himself broadens his attack
on the conception of truth as propositional truth into an attack
on logic. He is aware of the criticisms that have been urged
against his discussion of "the nothing" in *Was ist Metaphysik*
and is apparently concerned with Carnap's critique in *Erkenntnis* (1929) in particular, although he does not mention it.
In defending the second part of his question ("Why is there
any being at all and not rather nothing?") Heidegger decides

that the laws of logic are at issue. This is how he sums up
the case of his critics:

> What is there to be asked about the nothing? Nothing is
> simply nothing. . . . Those who talk about the nothing do
> not know what they are doing. Those who speak of the noth-
> ing thereby turn it into a something. Speaking in this way
> they speak against what they themselves mean. They speak
> against, and contradict, themselves. . . . Such talk about
> the nothing is illogical. . . . Such talk about the nothing
> consists merely of meaningless sentences [p. 18].

But the "concern for the right regard for the basic laws of
thought" is based on a "misunderstanding," which in turn "is
rooted in a long prevalent failure to understand the question
about what has being. This lack of understanding, however,
springs from a more and more hardened *oblivion of Being*"
(p. 19).

The conception of the oblivion of Being (*Seinsvergessen-
heit*), which Heidegger italicizes, is deliberately ambiguous.
In his letter "On Humanism" Heidegger says:

> Thinking is *l'engagement par l'Être, pour l'Être,* I do not
> know whether it is possible in French to say both (*par* and
> *pour*) at once, like this: *penser, c'est l'engagement de
> l'Être.* The word for the genetive, *de l'—,* is here meant to
> express that the genetive is at once both *genetivus subjec-
> tivus* and *objectivus.* But "subject" and "object" are really
> unsuitable metaphysical terms which, by way of occidental
> "logic" and "grammar," have taken charge of the interpreta-
> tion of language at an early age. Today we are only begin-
> ning to apprehend what it is that is concealed in this process.
> The liberation of language from grammar, freeing it for a
> more original structure of essences [*in ein ursprünglicheres
> Wesensgefüge*] is reserved for thought and poetry [p. 54].

The oblivion of Being means not only that mankind has forgotten Being but also that Being has somehow withdrawn from
man; and the very distinction between our forgetting it and
its forgetting us is, according to Heidegger, a symptom of

man's fall from grace and a misrepresentation of an event that logical propositions are bound to falsify.

Heidegger himself follows up the sentence on the "oblivion of Being":

> It does not go without saying after all that logic and its basic rules can furnish our standards when we ask about what has being as such. It could be the other way around, and the whole of our familiar logic, which is usually treated like a gift from heaven, might be based on one very particular answer to the question about what has being. In that case any thinking that follows solely the laws of thought of our received logic would be quite unable from the outset even to understand the question about what has being, not to speak of really developing it and leading it toward an answer [p. 19].

Here more than anywhere else Heidegger's radicalism finds expression; here we gain the right perspective for understanding his determination to go to the roots—the roots of philosophy in the pre-Socratic age and the roots of words. He is looking for a pre-logical mode of thought. As it happens, this is not hard to discover, and there is an apt name for it: *associative thinking*. But Heidegger makes it seem very remote and profound (cf. pp. 91 f., 94, 144).

Heidegger happens to associate his protest against the adequacy of logically organized thought with his determination to talk about "the nothing."

> The nothing remains inaccessible on principle to any scientific approach. Whoever wants to speak in truth of the nothing, must necessarily become unscientific. But this remains a great misfortune only as long as one supposes that scientific thinking is the only really rigorous way of thinking, and that it alone can and must be made the standard of philosophic thinking too. But the opposite is the case. All scientific thinking is merely a derivative and eventually hardened form of philosophic thinking. Philosophy never originates out of, or through, science. Philosophy can never be made coordinate with the sciences. It belongs to a prior order, not

only "logically" or in a diagram of the system of the sciences.
Philosophy belongs to an altogether different realm and rank
of spiritual existence. Philosophy with its way of thinking
is in the same order only with poetry [p. 20].

To understand and evaluate Heidegger's repudiation of logic
we must consider the relation of philosophy and poetry.

6

Philosophy and poetry. The immediate context of Heidegger's contention that philosophy is more like poetry than like
science suggests that the nothing is not amenable to scientific
analysis; that it cannot even be discussed in logically ordered
discourse; and that only the poet and the philosopher can
speak of it in truth. "Genuine utterances about the nothing
must always remain unusual. It cannot be made common. It
dissolves when it is placed in the cheap acid of mere logical
acumen" (p. 20). As an example of a genuine utterance, Heidegger cites a passage from Hamsun:

Here he sits right between his ears and hears true emptiness.
Quite funny, a phantom. On the sea (formerly A. went to
sea a great deal) something (at any rate) would stir, and
there would be a sound, something audible, a choir of water. Here—nothing hits upon nothing and is not there, is not
even a hole. One can only shake one's head in resignation
[pp. 20 f.].

The experience of emptiness is one of the central themes of
Kafka, though Heidegger does not mention him. The *theological* interpretation of *The Trial* and *The Castle*, which claims,
following Max Brod, that these novels deal with K.'s relation
to the divine order, and Erich Heller's contention in *The Disinherited Mind* that it is not the divine order but the realm of
Satan both force Kafka's new wine into old skins. Kafka does
not suggest that his bureaucracies are subject to any over-all
purpose, whether benign or malicious. In fact, he exerts all
his very considerable power to suggest that they are not. And
the unforgettable atmosphere in these novels is due to the ab-

sence not only of a friendly power to which one might appeal but even of an opponent. To be accused of nothing; to be persecuted by nothing; to be pitted against nothing: that is the experience of K. Kafka communicates this experience splendidly; but this does not prove that only the poet can speak in truth of the nothing. What it does illustrate is, rather, that art is the language of the emotions: art is required to describe from the inside *any* emotional experience.

In Heidegger's declaration about "genuine utterances about the nothing" we can substitute any number of other words for "the nothing"; e.g., love, longing, contrition, despair—to wit: "Genuine utterances about love (or longing, contrition, despair) must always remain unusual. It cannot be made common. It dissolves when it is placed in the cheap acid of mere logical acumen." Heidegger's mistake is a very common mistake that has been made by many writers about mysticism. It is made by all those who consider the mystic experience uniquely ineffable (cf. my *Critique*, §§28 f. and 71 ff.).

Is it, however, the task of philosophy to communicate experiences? Most English-speaking philosophers would say: No. Yet some great philosophers have combined this function with the ability to analyze arguments and positions that are originally suggested by various experiences. The great philosopher is a poet too—but not only a poet.

Heidegger grants that "philosophy and poetry are not identical." But he claims that at their best both are marked by

an essential superiority of the spirit over all mere science. Out of this superiority the poet always speaks as if that which had being was expressed and addressed for the first time. In the poetry of the poet and the thinking of the thinker there is always enough world-space for everything— a tree, a mountain, a house, a birdcall—to lose altogether what might have seemed indifferent or common about it [p. 20].

This conception of the poet is, no doubt, strongly influenced by Rilke, and the last sentence echoes the ninth Duino Elegy:

> *Are we perhaps here just to say: house,*
> *bridge, well, gate, jug, fruit tree, window—*
> *at most: column, tower—but to say it, understand,*
> *oh, to say it as the things themselves never*
> *thought of existing intensely.*

Surely, these lines, influenced by the examples of Rodin and
Cézanne, and Heidegger's remarks on poetry, too, bring out
far better what poetry has in common with painting than what
it has in common with philosophy. Even if it were the poet's
function to communicate what is marvelous in a house or tree
—and this is certainly not entirely acceptable as it stands—this
is surely not the philosopher's task (cf. the final section of
chapter 13 above). And Heidegger never makes clear what
distinguishes philosophy from poetry.

A certain similarity between the artist and philosopher does
exist at this point; and it has been perfectly stated by Hegel
in the Preface to the *Phenomenology: Das Bekannte über-*
haupt ist darum, weil es bekannt ist, nicht erkannt (what is
known by acquaintance is not necessarily really known merely
because it is familiar). It is the philosopher's task, Hegel argues
both here and in the Preface to the *Philosophy of Right,* "to
comprehend what is." The philosopher, like the artist, shows
how little we know what we are most familiar with. This was
a point that Socrates drove home with inimitable sarcasm, and
it recurs, more or less prominently, throughout Western philosophy.

The great philosopher, like the great poet, has a vision. Philosophy is not all analysis and scrutiny and intellectual anatomy. Precisely the greatest philosophers have often sold carefulness short because it mattered less to them than did the
spirit's flight. They were concerned above all else with something they had seen, or were still seeing—something that
seemed to them to belong to a higher order than all mere
analysis. Analysis might come afterward, or might be used as
a steppingstone: it can never become a substitute for vision
any more than criticism can take the place of poetry. But Heidegger fails to see that his disparagement of logical scrutiny
and his scorn of "the cheap acid of mere logical acumen" open

the floodgates to fanaticism, superstition, and stupidity (cf. chapters 10 and 14 above and my *Critique*, §§14 and 24).

Heidegger points out, rightly, that the ability to learn is far rarer than the possession of information, and he says, in an epigram: "Knowledge means: *being able to learn*" (p. 17). Does Heidegger himself have this ability? Having found that resolution alone is not enough in the political realm, he has gone to the opposite extreme and claims that no answers at all can be given today, and that the contemporary philosopher can only ask questions and endure—and Heidegger takes no chances at this point and asks questions that rule out any answer, such as: what is thinking (by which, of course, he does not mean what Price or Piaget might mean)? or, who is Nietzsche's Zarathustra? or, why is there any being at all and not rather nothing? Heidegger sees that scrutiny is not enough, and goes to the opposite extreme, banishes logical discourse from philosophy, and breaks down all the dikes that we need to keep out madness and the many myths of the twentieth century.

Heidegger's insistence on the close relationship of philosophy and poetry culminates in the demand that we go back to the pre-Socratics.

In his posthumously published lectures on the pre-Platonic philosophers and in his fragment on "Philosophy in the Tragic Era of the Greeks," Nietzsche had suggested that a philosopher could learn a great deal from the pre-Socratics, including much that could not be learned from later philosophers. Jaspers took up this theme in his *Psychologie der Weltanschauungen* (1919), a book that Heidegger commended in *Sein und Zeit*. But Heidegger's attitude toward the pre-Socratics in his later works is not only different from Jaspers' and Nietzsche's, but quite unlike the attitude of any great philosopher toward his predecessors.

7

Invocation of the pre-Socratics. Why does Heidegger insist again and again that we must go back to the beginning of Western philosophy, to Anaximander, Heraclitus, and Par-

menides? When Paul had shaken off the yoke of the law he
soon saw himself confronted with immorality and strange doctrines and found that he could not do without some other
authority. In time, the Catholic Church supplied such authority in ample measure. Luther rebelled against it, only to find
himself face to face with all kinds of *Schwärmerei* in thought
and deed; and again a new authority was needed. Friedrich
Schlegel, like many another romantic, wound up his revolt
against the discipline of classicism by accepting Roman Catholicism. Heidegger, after his rejection of the authority of
logic, also needs an authority to rescue him from a tidal wave
of inane "intuitions"; and like many another romantic before
him he seeks refuge in archaism. We must go back to the beginnings.

This challenge heightens the excitement of his exposition.
The Greek words have changed their meanings in Latin translation: *natura* no longer retains the original meaning of the
Greek *physis;* and it was the Latin term that determined the
development of medieval philosophy. Our own words, "nature"
or *Natur,* obscure rather than reveal what we are seeking.
"We, however, shall leap over this entire process of deforma-
tion and decay and seek to reconquer the undestroyed power
of naming in the language and its words" (p. 11). Heidegger
invites comparison with an archeologist who promises to remove, first, the dust and dirt of recent years and, then, layer
after layer of previous ages until we finally recover some ancient glory of which we had previously had nothing but reflections in literature. But he never gets that far.

Suppose you lack Heidegger's admiration for the pre-
Socratics and see them more or less as John Burnet did:
"Then," says Heidegger,

> the beginning of Greek philosophy makes the impression
> which alone is, according to the everyday understanding,
> suitable for a beginning: it appears, to use another Latin
> root, primitive. In principle, the Greeks then become a kind
> of highgrade Hottentots, and compared to them modern sci-
> ence represents infinite progress. Quite apart from the par-
> ticular nonsense that is involved in this conception of the

beginning of Western philosophy as primitive, it must be
said: this interpretation forgets that the subject here is philosophy, something that belongs among the few great things
of man. Whatever is great, however, can only have had a
great beginning. Indeed, its beginning is always what is
greatest. Little is only the beginning of little things, and
their dubious greatness consists in belittling everything; little is the beginning of decay which can also become great
in the end, but only in the sense of the vastness of complete
destruction [p. 12].

Heidegger does not lack the characteristic romantic virtue of
feeling for the past. His interpretations of the pre-Socratics
are not reliable; but surely the pre-Socratics were neither
primitive scientists, as Burnet suggests, nor theologians, as
Werner Jaeger claims. They were men with insights for which
no vocabulary and no language was at hand; men who struggled with the language in an effort to say something that it
was not easy to say; men who frequently were not able to attain any final clarity and who left behind many puzzling and
perplexing statements that cannot be translated into basic English without gross falsification. Burnet does come close to turning them into a bunch of "highgrade Hottentots" who are not
very interesting. Heidegger, on the other hand, recaptures the
excitement of the first steps of Western philosophy, and his
translations, which are generally more obscure than the original fragments, avoid oversimplification and sustain the reader's
interest in the philosophers who are discussed. No one could
possibly say: so much for these men; I understand them and
see where they went wrong: now I am ready for something
else.

Heidegger is an excellent teacher in this respect: he does
not destroy an initial interest; he increases it. More precisely,
he awakens and maintains it. Anyone who reads the *Introduction* will understand why so many men who have studied with
him have kept for life a passion for philosophy, and why former pupils who are Marxists and Thomists agree that they
never had a more fascinating teacher.

Heidegger's attitude toward the pre-Socratics rules out any

facile escape from perplexity; and, as Plato remarked, and
Aristotle repeated, philosophy begins in perplexity. But,
where Plato and Aristotle considered perplexity a spur to seek
clarification, Heidegger scarcely deigns to distinguish between
perplexity and profundity. He is so contemptuous of the smug
Philistine who has never known perplexity that he encourages
a smugness in perplexity.

But the most serious fault of Heidegger's approach to the
pre-Socratics is that they become "authorities" for him. And in
philosophy there is no place for authorities. Indeed, Heidegger fails consistently to appreciate the greatest single contribution of the pre-Socratics: *they abandoned the exegetical mode
of thought that Heidegger revives.* Unlike most Indian thinkers,
they did not treat ancient writings as authorities.

8

Heidegger's authoritarianism. Although Heidegger suggests
at the end of the *Introduction* that he is condemned to endure in perplexity and that this is the human condition in our
time he really ends by "proving" this point with a quotation
from Hölderlin. It may be objected that the final quotation is
merely a pleasant stylistic device. But does Heidegger ever entertain the possibility that Hölderlin or Sophocles, Heraclitus or
Parmenides might be mistaken about anything? His attitude
toward these men is invariably one of humility before authority.

Any criticism of the pre-Socratics is out of the question. It
is assumed that they, living so near the beginning of Western
thought, knew what we do not know and would like to know.
When Heidegger explores the nature of man, he gives us a
translation of the wonderful second chorus from Sophocles'
Antigone and then interprets it. He proceeds exactly like a theologian who cites Scripture.

If Heidegger should say in his defense that he has chosen
texts that happen to contain the truth, texts in which the unconcealedness of Being is achieved, he would only set up his
own judgment as authoritative. It would be like saying that
his own claims happen to be true. You might cite another

chorus against the one selected by Heidegger, or pit Shakespeare against Sophocles.

Heidegger's admission that his interpretations are really not mere interpretations scarcely helps. "True interpretation must show what is not said in words but said nevertheless. At this point an interpretation must necessarily use force" (p. 124). This insistence on force (*Gewalt*), found in his book on Kant too, shows what would be obvious in any case: in the last analysis it is the interpreter who claims authority. Nothing else was to be expected once logic was rejected.

To be sure, Heidegger does not issue authoritative pronouncements that are meant to settle ancient issues. But he creates a sense of contentment and immeasurable superiority that might be expressed in some such words as these: we thank you, God, for making us like Sophocles and Heraclitus and not like other men. An authority is set up, and the follower is encouraged to consider himself superior because he accepts this authority. It is a matter of knowing the password and speaking the right language. Even if we sympathize with the lonely thinker who seeks comfort and courage and sustenance for his spirit in the early Greeks, there is little reason for feeling anything but alarm at his minions. Certainly Heidegger does not spread a critical spirit, or carefulness, or the virtues of the intellectual conscience.

9

Heidegger and theology. Heidegger spurns theology and exalts philosophy far above it, and yet his philosophy cannot be fully understood without reference to theology.

To ask the basic question, why there is any being at all and not rather nothing, is not a matter of repeating a few words: this is, according to Heidegger, the most original, the most primordial question (*die ursprünglichste Frage*), and to ask it genuinely we must leap (*springen*) out of the preceding security of our existence (p. 5). The Book of Genesis in the Bible does not answer the question at all and has no relation whatever to this question. "What is really asked in our question is for faith, a foolishness. Philosophy consists in this fool-

ishness. A 'Christian philosophy' is like wooden iron, a misunderstanding" (p. 6).

Heidegger does not explain why the assertion that God
created the world does not answer his question, but he is certainly right that it does not. To see this, we need only repeat
the question with a few additional words: Why is there any
being at all (including the divine being) and not rather nothing (not even God)? Heidegger suggests, more by innuendo
than by analysis, that philosophy is more radical and more
daring than theology, and that no other enterprise, except poetry, compares with philosophy.

As he talks about and around his original question without
ever coming close to answering it, he succeeds perfectly in
projecting his seriousness and his commitment to philosophy.

> It is entirely correct and quite in order: "one can't do any-
> thing with philosophy." What is wrong is merely the opin-
> ion that with these words the judgment on philosophy is
> complete. For there is still a little postscript in the form of a
> counter-question: whether, even if *we* can't do anything
> with it, philosophy might not in the end do something *to us*,
> provided we really engage in it [pp. 9 f.].

Heidegger says that philosophy "has no subject matter
whatever. It is an occurrence which must ever anew attain
Being (in the revealed openness that belongs to it)" (p. 65).
In the original, this sentence is as ambiguous as "the oblivion
of Being" (section 5 above). The sentence cannot only mean,
as my translation suggests, that philosophy is a reach for Being; it can also mean that it is an event that Being must effect
again and again. The distinction between the two interpretations is a function of grammar and logic and a symptom of
"the oblivion of Being."

> Being means appearing. That it appears is not, as it were,
> an afterthought, not something that sometimes happens to
> Being. Being occurs *as* appearing. With this the prevalent
> view of Greek philosophy collapses as an empty construc-
> tion: it is supposed that Greek philosophy was "realistic"
> and taught a doctrine of an objective Being in itself as op-
> posed to modern subjectivism; but this popular notion is

based on an utterly superficial interpretation. We must leave aside tags like "subjective" and "objective," "realistic" and "idealistic" [p. 77].

Many of Heidegger's statements about Being that are puzzling at first glance become clearer when we realize that Heidegger substitutes "Being" where theologians say "God." Here are a few more examples.

"Our questioning merely opens up the area," says Heidegger, in which Being can then break through (p. 23). Our task consists in making ourselves receptive for Being. "Is 'Being' a mere word and its significance a mere vapor, or is it the spiritual destiny of the Occident?" (p. 28). That "Being" is a mere word for us is "not as innocuous as the fact seems when we first state it"; it is due to the most sinister event: "that we have fallen out of that which this word designates and at present do not find our way back" (p. 30).

While theologians speak of our alienation from God, Heidegger suggests that our tragedy consists in the oblivion of Being. It is hard to give any precise meaning to this suggestion, and Heidegger does not exert himself in this direction; but even in the absence of any exact meaning, or perhaps owing to the absence of any exact meaning, his suggestion is evocative: it arouses associations with estrangement from God, without committing Heidegger to any particular belief.

Like Faulkner, Heidegger seems to feel that technology has estranged us, not only from poetry, but from the world itself. The two men share a rather murky, if generous, hatred of machines, science, and clarity; an anti-intellectualism that on occasion makes a virtue of reaction; a self-made theology that, however sincere, is a pretty muddy affair compared to the Book of Genesis. The lack of clarity and contempt for grammar that are functional and admirable in Faulkner's communication of unclear states of consciousness in his novels, but offensive in some of his pronouncements, border on obscurantism in Heidegger's philosophy of Being.

At the end of the *Introduction* Heidegger sums up what Being is as opposed to Becoming, Appearance, Thinking, and Ought: it is that which abides, that which is always the same,

that which is there, that which is extant. And Heidegger concludes his investigation by pointing out that all four of these
characterizations of Being "at bottom say the same: *constant
presence:* ὄν as οὐσία" (p. 154). It is interesting to note
that this may be the meaning of the Hebrew name of God,
which, according to Buber's interpretation of Exodus 3:14,
might be translated HE IS PRESENT (cf. my *Critique*, §89).
Heidegger's Being is, to use a Nietzschean phrase, the shadow
of God. Those who feel that they have known God himself,
either through a living religious tradition or through Scripture
or through personal experience, will hardly settle for his
shadow; and those who have not, will hardly understand Heidegger's attitude.

10

Heidegger and G. E. Moore. Heidegger's heavy dependence
on what others have said invites comparison with a statement
made by G. E. Moore in his "Autobiography" in the Library
of Living Philosophers:

> I do not think that the world or the sciences would ever
> have suggested to me any philosophic problems. What has
> suggested philosophical problems to me is things which
> other philosophers have said about the world or the sciences.

But Moore's concern has been to analyze and criticize such
statements, while Heidegger discusses passages that he reveres
—and reads his own views into them.

Heidegger's attitude toward his texts tends to be uncritical
while Moore's is hypercritical. Their attitude toward themselves differs in the same way: Moore has always been self-
critical to a fault, never afraid to say that he was mistaken or
even that he no longer knew what he could possibly have
meant when saying something; Heidegger, on the other hand,
never admits a mistake and never concedes that he does not
know what he meant, though his prose would invite such a
concession far more than Moore's (cf. chapter 2 of my
Critique).

Löwith, who knew Heidegger well in the period of *Being*

and Time, contends in his little book on Heidegger that Heidegger's later interpretations of his earlier work are quite at variance with what Heidegger himself meant in those days—and cites an extreme instance (pp. 39 f.). In his postscript to the fourth edition of *Was ist Metaphysik?* Heidegger said that Being continues "indeed" without all that has being, "but" that what has being never exists without Being. In the postscript to the fifth edition, six years later (1949), Heidegger says, without the least indication of this change, "that Being never exists without what has being" (p. 41).

Both positions look equally arbitrary, and one must ask what he could possibly have meant. Heidegger has once again substituted "Being" for "God" and transposed the old question whether God is immanent or transcendent. Is Being transcendent like the God of orthodox Christianity or—his later position —only immanent?

Heidegger's metaphysic of Being is a development of Christianity or, as some Catholic interpreters might say, a Christian heresy. His initial training, incidentally, was Catholic, and his first book was entitled *Kategorienlehre des Duns Scotus* (1916). It dealt with a work that, Heidegger assumed, was by Duns Scotus. As a matter of fact, it was not.

11

Heidegger's lack of vision. That Heidegger is, for all his faults, one of the most interesting philosophers of our time, there can be no doubt. What stands between him and greatness is neither the opaqueness of his style, of which it is easy to make fun, nor his temporary acceptance of Nazism, of which it is easy to make too much, but his lack of vision. After everything has been said, he really does not have very much to say.

From beginning to end, Heidegger's work is characterized by a fatal gap between promise and performance. He resembles the old Schelling of whom Kierkegaard records in his *Journals* that he began his lectures in Berlin by building up great expectations, which, as it soon appeared, he was unable to fulfill. Thirty years earlier, Friedrich Schlegel had acquired a reputation for the same fault, and Hegel had divined in the Preface to his *Phenomenology* that this is one of the characteristics of romantic philosophy. Impatience with careful analysis and a contempt for intellectual scrutiny will always appeal to a large audience, but praise of profundity is no substitute for detailed achievement. In Hegel's words: "But even as there is an empty breadth, there is also an empty depth, . . . an intensity void of content."

This criticism may not seem to apply to *Being and Time*, which features a wealth of detail and almost scholastic exactitude. But here, too, the excitement is generated and maintained by unfulfilled promises and by the insistence that what is being done is infinitely more profound than meets the eye or is, in fact, the case. Heidegger's analysis of everyday existence, of chatter and curiosity, care and anxiety, is introduced —to give a single example—by a reiteration of one of the leitmotifs of the book:

> With reference to these phenomena, the remark may not be superfluous that this interpretation has a purely ontological intent and is far removed from any moralizing critique of everyday existence and from all the aspirations of "cultural philosophy" [p. 167].

It is this central theme of the book that probably accounts for the fact that it has remained a fragment that Heidegger cannot complete. For 438 pages Heidegger built on the expectation that he would unravel Being and accomplish what Western ontology since Aristotle had been unable to do. Whether his psychological analyses were tenable did not matter as long as he insisted that they were *not* psychological at all. But, having given his account of human existence, Heidegger had, as a matter of fact, *not* unraveled Being. Hence the need for the "Second Half" of *Being and Time*—which has never appeared.

In his *Introduction* Heidegger would still like to unravel Being, and is still unable to do it. This is certainly not due to the age we live in. Heidegger finds no answers to his questions because he does not ask answerable questions. The questions he poses are questions in the same sense in which we speak

of a "Jewish question" or "the question of homosexuality."
They are exciting but utterly vague—not really questions at
all in the ordinary sense, but labels for vast complexes of problems that must be distinguished before any answers can be
attempted. Heidegger does not even offer penetrating insights
apropos of his questions.

It is Heidegger's lack of vision that condemns him to turn
to texts and write more and more about what others have
written: Hölderlin and Rilke, Anaximander, Heraclitus, and
Parmenides, Hegel and Nietzsche. This is the nemesis of romanticism. After rebelling against the rules of classicism and
endorsing profundity, the early German romantics, too, had
little to offer that was profound—and hence became translators,
historians, and interpreters, if they did not have the good fortune of being poets or composers.

Even Heidegger's interpretations lack substance. Perhaps
Sophocles' second chorus in the *Antigone* can tell us more
about human nature than the adage that man is a rational
animal, which, as Heidegger points out, is really a very inadequate translation of Aristotle's suggestion that man is ζῷον
λόγον ἔχον. But Heidegger's fourteen pages on Sophocles'
chorus do not add to our understanding of human nature. A
reading of the *Antigone* or of *Lear* does, but Heidegger does
not. He reminds us that man is not altogether rational but
uncanny; but when his lectures were delivered in 1935, and
when they were published in 1953, few of us were unaware
of this.

To ask a question that is neither trivial nor unanswerable
may be a mark of genius. Heidegger boasts of not being banal,
but he seeks security from triviality in a lack of precision.
When we ask in the end what has really been said, we come
up either with nothing or with trivialities.

12

The Castle. Heidegger's pronouncements are generally perplexing but then again encouraging; they are not always consistent, but haunt the mind. Why should we assume, like
Kafka's K., that there is any surpassing wisdom behind this

apparent confusion? Like Kafka's officials, Heidegger commutes between the outer chambers of the castle and the village in which he is respected as coming from "up there"; but he has lost all contact with the Count.

One should recall the name of Kafka's Count, mentioned only once, on the second page of *The Castle:* Westwest—exactly the characterization Heidegger gives of Being when he says, *es west.* Franz Overbeck commented on Harnack's *Wesen des Christentums:* it is only since Christianity is dead that people make so much of its *Wesen.* The word generally means essence (Harnack's meaning); the verb once meant being present (Heidegger's meaning); but this is archaic and one's initial association is with *verwesen,* which means decomposing (Overbeck's meaning). Kafka's Count was surely dead; and Kafka probably meant that—in Nietzsche's words—God was dead; that the world was abandoned to confusion and absurdity without any governing purpose (cf. my *Existentialism,* p. 122, for further evidence).

Heidegger is "on the way," as he himself would put it, but he looks for a chimera, "Being"—the shadow of God. He thinks that if only he could really get in touch with the pre-Socratics Being would become clear to him; and he seeks contact with the pre-Socratics through Rilke and Hölderlin. But in fact the pre-Socratics themselves did not have any saving knowledge: though men of genius, they were human beings like ourselves, with some insights we lack, perhaps, but without other insights that we owe to their successors.

If there is one thing above all that we have learned since their time—and especially in our time—it is this: although reason has its limitations, those who would abandon it on that account might as well pluck out their eyes because they are not able to see *everything,* or perhaps do not see things as they "really" are. They are like men protected from the ocean by a dike who tear it down because it does not reach the heavens.

It did not take Heidegger to discover that reason cannot build a metaphysical Tower of Babel; but it did take Heidegger to infer that poetry, or some sort of intuitive, associative, but hardly really poetic, thinking should replace rational dis-

course and become immune against critical reason. There are
many men at all times who are willing to be done with reason,
and especially with critical reason. There will always be a
ready audience for all who denounce it as essentially a para-
site. In truth, the critical function of reason is our best safeguard against fanaticism, inhumanity, and terror.

Knowing that the greatest poets have not been romantic enemies of reason, Hegel quoted Goethe's Mephistopheles when
he wished to make this point:

> *Have but contempt for reason and for science,*
> *Although they truly are man's best reliance,*
> *And let the Prince of Lies confound confusion*
> *By luring you toward magic and illusion—*
> *And you are on the road to hell.*

18

GERMAN THOUGHT AFTER
WORLD WAR II

A decade after World War II, the situation in Germany is almost the exact reverse from what it was after World War I. Then she was economically prostrate and unable to achieve political stability, but few countries could equal her vitality in music, painting, poetry, and architecture, or theology, the novel, and philosophy. Now it is the economic and political recovery of West Germany that nobody would have considered possible when the war ended; but there are no cultural achievements of comparable significance.

Even those Germans who are concerned about the current bleakness in the arts and *Geisteswissenschaften* generally share in the popular repression of any memory of the Hitler years. One simply does not mention the loss through emigration of Freud and Mann and Zweig; Buber, Barth, and Tillich; Hindemith and Schoenberg; Carnap and Cassirer; the Bauhaus architects, and countless others. People far prefer to blame the heavy losses of *potential* geniuses during the war. This dodge, of course, fails to explain why Germany is holding her own in the natural sciences. The striking fact that the sciences and the theaters flourish in East Germany, too, reminds us that both can survive totalitarian regimes; but the humanities cannot: they are all but dead in East Germany, and in West Germany they have not recovered from the blow that Hitler dealt them. West Germany is doing a brisk business on all fronts, but culturally she is living on her capital.

This thesis might be illustrated in a great many ways. The challenge represented by the dozens of bombed cities has generally been met economically, but not artistically. The thriving stores and hotels that flourish in the ruins of yesterday around the great cathedrals are, at best, not too offensive; but they certainly do not merit a second look. One is stunned by the amount of rubble that has been cleared away, by the evidence of prosperity, and by the lack of all creative imagination.

There are scores of repertoire theaters, but they rely largely on classics, and the few living authors are generally French or American. Bert Brecht, who returned to East Berlin from California, was the outstanding exception: since his death, nobody in Germany would claim that there is another German dramatist of equal stature—one to compare with Sartre or with Anouilh, with Miller or with Williams. Nor is there a German poet to rank with Benn, who died in 1956, not to speak of Rilke or George, who published some of their best verse after World War I.

It would be tedious to survey field upon field. Instead, let us look a little more closely at philosophy. This is by no means unfair, for the picture in philosophy compares favorably with that in most other areas. Where else can the Germans still boast of two such names as Heidegger and Jaspers?

Outsiders are apt to think that Jaspers and Heidegger belong to the same school of thought—namely, existentialism— and that they are presumably equally influential. Both assumptions are quite wrong. Existentialism is a label that both men repudiate. Moreover, each of them repudiates the other. For several years now, both of them have published book upon book—Heidegger usually slim essays of well under a hundred pages, Jaspers bulky tomes that range from three hundred pages to more than one thousand. Jaspers no longer reads Heidegger's publications, and Heidegger reciprocates. Even so, both find their readers—but by no means the same readers. At the German universities, for example, you will find scarcely a course that deals with Jaspers, even briefly, but a great many that deal with Heidegger at length.

Not since the death of Hegel has a German philosopher during his own life wielded an influence comparable to Heidegger's. This is partly due to the fact that so many chairs of philosophy are occupied by his old students, while not one such chair is held by one of Jaspers' or of Nicolai Hartmann's or Cassirer's students. To understand this situation, one must keep in mind the methods followed at the German universities.

The forte of the German professor and student of the *Geisteswissenschaften* is, in one word, *referieren*—reporting, summarizing, outlining. Those addicted to this method generally read a manuscript: the German *Vorlesung* (lecture) is, much more often than not, quite literally a *Vorlesung*—a reading out loud. And the students try to copy into their notebooks as much as possible of what the professor reads out of his. Of necessity, he reads either what he has already published, or what he is about to publish, or what he himself does not consider good enough to publish. Today it is the last technique that is by far the most popular. It should be added that most professors do not repeat their lectures, and that practically none offer the same courses year after year as is so often done at American universities. As a result, most German professors are busy during the term writing their lectures for the week and have no time to talk with students. Indeed, at most of the best universities the students have exceedingly little contact with their professors.

The classes are generally large, and the professors have a direct financial interest in attracting a great many students since the students still pay *Hörgelder*. There is, moreover, a close relationship between the size of a man's classes and his prestige. Given a widespread interest in Heidegger, it is therefore tempting for philosophy professors to announce a course of lectures featuring Heidegger's name in the title. A course on more prosaic subjects is likely to attract few students.

By far the most philosophy courses are historical, and there are hardly any courses at all on such subjects as ethics, theory of knowledge, logic, or philosophy of science. Told that Americans have such courses, a German professor replied that these subjects were dated by Heidegger; and a German student, who was working on his doctoral dissertation with a professor who had spent the war years teaching philosophy in the United States, exclaimed, "Apparently, you are still in the eighteenth century!"

The few courses that have systematic rather than historical titles usually turn out to be historical surveys. And almost in-

variably the Herr Professor *referiert*. Needless to say, his summaries and paraphrases are by no means always unexception-
able.

But the students are not likely to notice this, as there are
no reading assignments or discussion groups.

In place of the latter, the professor usually offers a seminar
in connection with his course of lectures, and some of the more
advanced or specialized students come to that, too. Often,
these seminars are much too large for any discussion. In a theology seminar one may encounter as many as two hundred
students, though that is too many even for the professor. He
admits only one-third of these as active members, has them sit
in the front rows, and then asks them specific questions about
the text at hand, while the rest listen reverently from the back
rows.

In the seminars a text is read: sometimes a whole book,
sometimes a few pages. The professor offers his interpretation
and assigns topics for reports, which are read by the students
and criticized by him. If the text is French, Latin, or Greek,
a good deal of time may be spent on the mechanics of translation; and in any case the discussion is almost invariably about
points of interpretation. Sometimes one overhears students
wondering whether the professor's reading of a certain sentence
is really tenable—but only in conversation with each other after
the seminar is over.

To be suitable for a seminar, a text must, of course, be difficult—a condition met admirably by the works of Heidegger.
In this respect, Jaspers is unquestionably inferior to him. Moreover, Jaspers' books are full of reports of what other people
have said, according to Jaspers; and these summaries, while
often very questionable, are usually clear. Small indeed is the
temptation for the German teacher of philosophy to summarize
Jaspers' summaries. What matters most to Jaspers, to be sure,
is the appeal to the reader to change his life, but this hortatory
element of all his writings lends itself still less to classroom
presentation.

Heidegger deals no less often with what others have said,
but never to summarize or paraphrase it, let alone to make it
clear. What Heidegger holds up to scorn is precisely the super-

ficiality of all the clear interpretations of the past, and his own
exegesis is invariably much darker than the text from which
he took off. He himself says that he sets out on the way toward that point from which the right questions may some day
be asked, and what seems obscurantism to those who do not
like him seems exciting and profound to many a German student and professor.

Close criticism of a text is practically unknown. The task is
to understand it. Before you could possibly criticize Heidegger
or Hegel, Kierkegaard or Kant, Pascal or Plato, Nietzsche,
Aristotle, or Augustine—to name the approved philosophers
who are studied widely—you would have to read all their writings in the original to begin with. For you must understand
before you can presume to criticize. Asked whether he agrees
with Kant, or even whether he considers a particular argument sound, the student who has studied Kant for one or two
semesters is most likely to repudiate this question as ridiculous,
naive, and utterly subphilosophic. If you tried to press the
point by presenting the student with some contradiction between two of his approved authorities to show him that he
cannot agree with both Kant and Leibniz on some point, he
would, no doubt, dodge into history. He would explain that
Kant did not really criticize Leibniz but only the school philosophy of his own time, or he might enter into an exegesis of
the two apparently conflicting texts: in either case he would
end up by pointing to the need for further study of the historical background. The result is almost certain to be incon-
clusive: what will be established is the need for more historical
research.

There are two acceptable attitudes toward the great philosophers: either uncritical empathy or wholesale rejection in
the name of history. In the latter case, the key word is *überholt*,
dated. Kant is dated by idealism, idealism is dated by existentialism, and the big question is whether Heidegger is possibly
already *überholt*. Detailed criticism of an argument is almost
unknown among German philosophers today.

The professors themselves are authorities and firmly convinced for the most part that their students are in no position
to discuss with them, let alone to criticize them; and in phi-

losophy at least there is a strong tendency to exclude rival points of view. Professor X's mission is to turn out *X-Schüler,* and his success and prestige is measured in large part by the number of people, and especially *Privatdozenten,* who will say for the rest of their lives—much as an American might say, "I went to Harvard"—*Ich bin X-Schüler,* I am a student of X. As long as X was Kant or Hegel, or even Husserl or, for that matter, Heidegger, this may have made some sense. Today, however, it often sounds ridiculous.

If these attitudes produced a wealth of sound and interesting historical studies, the situation would be very different from the way it is in fact. The Hegelian tradition that established Germany's supremacy in the historiography of philosophy is decidedly a matter of the past. Not only are there no heirs today to Zeller, Erdmann, and Windelband, with their great scope, but the profoundly uncritical climate of thought favors unsound studies.

The very alternative of empathy and criticism is unsound. If we really wish to understand a text, we cannot dispense with criticism: we must find out with what problem the author tried to deal, and this leads to the question of how successfully he dealt with it. That, however, is decidedly not the approach cultivated at the German universities today, and this is due above all to the precedents set by Heidegger and Jaspers.

2

Heidegger has done more than any other man to establish the philosopher's immunity from criticism and the standards of mere correctness or accuracy. What he is after is truth—not correctness—and truth was to the Greeks *aletheia,* which, he says, means unconcealedness or openness. It is, no doubt, ironical that a philosopher who speaks so much of unconcealedness and openness should be so lacking in openness—not only openness to criticism and to other ideas but also candor; for example, about his intellectual debts and his political past. He has consistently resisted all suggestions from his friends and former students that he should make some frank statement about his behavior during the Hitler years and his notorious lecture on *Die Selbstbehauptung der deutschen Universität*. You might as well expect the Delphic oracle to criticize itself.

Heidegger thrives on the fascination of ambiguity, he loves mystery, and he never tires of insisting that he is misunderstood. He claims that his interpreters, including his old friends and students, have quite failed to get the point of *Being and Time*, the early work on which his reputation largely rests. If he were right, could we help concluding that he is a virtuoso of concealment?

In conversation he will suggest that the best of Nietzsche is to be found in incompletely published notes that are now inaccessible in East Germany. Heidegger has photostats of this material, hidden in a safe place: there can be no thought of publication now. Why? Because nobody knows Nietzsche's handwriting well enough. Actually, the top expert on Nietzsche manuscripts is a professor of philosophy at Darmstadt, in Western Germany: Karl Schlechta.

Heidegger's penchant for the obscure is evident in his historical studies, which form the bulk of his work since *Being and Time*. There can be no doubt at all about his preference for pliant notes and fragments. On the sole surviving sentence of Anaximander he has written a famous essay of forty-eight pages, and in his widely discussed exegesis of "Nietzsche's Word 'God is Dead'" he systematically ignores the over-all development of Nietzsche's thought as well as the context of the many notes he cites to prove that Nietzsche was the last great metaphysician of the West. Rilke scholars are impressed by the great erudition of these efforts; Nietzsche experts find his Rilke exegesis most suggestive; and the classical philologists reserve their admiration for his modern studies. In this respect there is a certain parallel to Toynbee.

Unfortunately, in Heidegger's case, too, the abysmal unsoundness of his method is rarely noted. What meets the eye is that his interpretations are vastly more interesting than the often pointless summaries and paraphrases of his colleagues. That his exegeses are untenable seems to matter less than that they are exciting. But it is hardly difficult to be exciting and even original if one spurns mere correctness.

Heidegger hopes to crown his life's work with a major book

on the pre-Socratics. Substantial samples of this effort have by now been published in various collections, notably in *Holzwege* (1950), *Einführung in die Metaphysik* (1953), and *Vorträge und Aufsätze* (1954). Devoted former students who are now full professors and still yield to none in admiration for the early *Being and Time* confess, though for the most part only privately over a glass of wine, that they are appalled by these interpretations; and those who pride themselves on being classical philologists as well as philosophers insist that his readings are based on outright mistakes. When such mistakes are pointed out to him in manuscript, he is said to respond gruffly, "So it is all wrong"—and then the text appears in print without the least alteration.

Heidegger claims that philosophy is much more closely related to poetry than to science, but his prose fares no better if we judge it as poetry. His realm is the realm of magic.

During the winter semester 1955/56, he offered a course of lectures for the third time since the war and the first time in three years. He spoke for forty-five minutes every Friday afternoon on *Der Satz vom Grund,* which might seem to mean "the principle of (sufficient) reason." *Satz,* however, can not only mean sentence or principle, but also, if rarely, jump or leap, though *Sprung* is a more common word for that. Before long Heidegger announced: *"Der Sprung ist der Satz aus dem Grundsatz vom Grund in das Sagen des Seins."* Surely, this is closer to *Finnegans Wake* than to the *Critique of Pure Reason;* but is it poetry? Would it not be far more accurate to say that Heidegger refuses systematically to distinguish between mnemonic devices and arguments?

From the beginning of the semester until the end, Heidegger filled not only the aula of the University of Freiburg but also two other large auditoria to which his lectures were carried over a public address system. He did not play up to the crowd but read his manuscript slowly and clearly without any gestures. The atmosphere in the aula was electric when he entered, though many people slept during the lectures. In the two other auditoria, on the other hand, there were some students who were able to transfer into their notes his Greek quotations. The course of lectures has been published since.

The size and persistence of the audience gives some indication of the prestige of philosophy in Germany, which is comparable to the prestige of democracy in the United States. The Germans tend to think of philosophy as something peculiarly their own. Indeed, as they see it, there are only two kinds of philosophy: Greek and German. Medieval philosophy and French philosophy are more or less marginal phenomena, while English-speaking philosophy is all but a contradiction in terms. As for Hume, we all know that he aroused Kant.

3

Jaspers' lack of influence among German philosophers is almost total. Ten years after the war, there were among German university teachers of philosophy one Jaspers-Schüler and one Hartmann-Schüler, and both were unable to obtain a chair, though there were vacancies. In courses, Jaspers was ignored entirely, but in conversation his steady stream of books insured him some attention. The professionals, however, were ill-disposed toward his recent publications.

When he published a full-length study of *Schelling* in 1955, nothing excited more interest than the question whether it was an oblique polemic against Heidegger. Those close to Jaspers vouched that it was not. But the fact remains that the central portion of the book deals with Schelling's question, why there is any being at all and not rather nothing—a question widely associated with Heidegger, who has devoted two books to it without ever mentioning Schelling in this connection. It is also striking that Jaspers comments at length on Schelling's interest in politics, by way of criticizing him, and most people had not even been aware that Schelling had had any such interests, while Heidegger's relation to the Nazis was common knowledge.

What puts off the German philosophers more than anything else is Jaspers' insistence on criticizing the men with whom he deals; but his criticism does not take the form of any detailed analysis of arguments. Schelling, for example, is condemned for his attempt to offer spurious knowledge—a point that Jaspers has made elsewhere against Heidegger. Schelling's entire philosophic enterprise is rejected.

Jaspers' frequent insistence on "communication" invites comparison with Heidegger's talk of "unconcealedness": what Jaspers so beautifully calls "a loving struggle" is almost nowhere in evidence in his own work. He never appears as a combatant who exposes his own views to the point of view which he attacks. He writes as a judge and passes sentence from an unquestioned base of unique moral integrity that he is quite unwilling to concede his victim. Nothing shocked the German philosophers more than his proclamation at the one hundredth anniversary of Schelling's death: "He lacked a noble soul"—unless it was his critique in his book of Schelling's first marriage.

Much more serious, though not widely noted, is the basic unsoundness of Jaspers' whole approach. He completely disregards Schelling's intellectual development—a failing that this book shares with his two earlier books on Nietzsche. This is fatal in the case of two men who in their late works reached positions so different from their early works that they felt called upon to criticize their early books. Another, smaller point deserves notice only because no critic seems to have taken exception to it, and some young German scholars have begun to follow Jaspers' precedent. Although he acknowledges the expert and reliable help of a Privatdozent who assists him with technical details, Jaspers says on the last page: "My Schelling quotations are not philologically exact. Omissions are throughout not indicated by any dots. Words have been transposed wherever the context of my presentation made this convenient."

Jaspers' failure to do justice to points of view different from his own and his lack of any talent for communication are most glaringly in evidence in his book on *Reason and Anti-Reason in Our Time,* where Marx and Freud are pictured—to a German audience in 1950—as *the* two representatives of anti-reason in our time. His professional colleagues, however, were much more embarrassed by Jaspers' polemic against Bultmann, published in a little book on *Die Frage der Entmythologisierung* (1954. Published in English as *Myth and Christian-*

ity, 1958). Here he deals with a contemporary with whom it is relatively easy to communicate: Bultmann readily understands objections and is willing to discuss them with the utmost fairness. In the book, however, no communication is established.

Bultmann's program of demythologization, which has stirred up German Protestant theology, was first presented in a short essay in 1941 (for a critical discussion, see my *Critique,* §§54 ff.). Since then, no German theologian has had any other idea that has attracted a comparable amount of interest. Bultmann's idea is that Christianity represents a call to make a decision. To present this call, theologians and preachers must demythologize the challenge, stripping away the myths, which are merely the language of the age in which Jesus and the early Christians lived.

Among these myths Bultmann mentions the "three-storey view of the world" with a heaven above us and a hell beneath. A bishop in Norway was almost deposed over the question of demythologizing hell, and this problem was discussed at the German universities, too. The discussion was centered in the interpretation of specific passages in Scripture; for example, whether the fire in Luke 16 means real fire. The compatibility of some form or other of eternal agony and punishment with Christian love and God's love was not even mentioned, nor was Bultmann's declaration—probably in conversation only— that he should not care to go to heaven if he believed that even a single soul was suffering eternal punishment. What interests people is exegesis; and demythologizing, no less than Heidegger's essays on Hölderlin and the pre-Socratics, fits in with this preoccupation.

That Jaspers' polemics are above comparison with the often minute squabbles that have filled many an issue of the German journals scarcely needs emphasis. What is distressing is that he should give most of his time and energy to historical and critical studies without ever producing either a definitive critique or an exemplary historical study. One feels, however unjustly, that one has the right to expect more from him, and then is disappointed. His colleagues, however, have long ceased being disappointed. They take his preoccupation with history as a sign that he has nothing more to say.

4

There are, of course, a great many philosophers not mentioned here, and many are solid and careful. But not one rivals the impact of a Jaspers, Heidegger, or Bultmann on postwar German thought. Not one is widely discussed either by the public or by his professional colleagues.

On the editorial front the situation is different. Good critical editions that are certain to replace their predecessors keep appearing and—to stick to men considered in the present book—the new editions of Hegel, Nietzsche, and Rilke include some hitherto unpublished items.

In the case of Karl Schlechta's three-volume edition of Nietzsche's works the novelty was actually vastly overestimated in the press—first in Germany and then in the United States, too. The editor worked in the Nietzsche archives in Weimar before World War II. The first two volumes contain all the works that Nietzsche himself finished, printed on thin paper. In a very few places, the texts of the *Antichrist* and the *Dionysos Dithyramben* have been corrected from the manuscripts, in line with previously published information. It is the last volume that constitutes Schlechta's signal contribution to Nietzsche scholarship; but since it contains only a small selection from the voluminous essays, notes, fragments, and letters published in previous editions it cannot supplant them, at least for scholarly purposes.

The three features of the third volume that nevertheless make it important are, first of all, that the selection of 278 Nietzsche letters includes over a dozen not previously published, though these are not of special interest. Secondly, the editor has completely rearranged those of Nietzsche's notes that the philosopher's sister published in her own arrangement as *The Will to Power*. He says expressly that "*The Will to Power* contains nothing new—nothing that could surprise those who know everything that Nietzsche published or prepared for publication" (p. 1403). This is actually an exaggeration, but Schlechta is concerned to do away with the last pretense that it consists in anything more than "Notes of the Eighties" —the title under which he prints these notes in the random order in which they were found in Nietzsche's notebooks. Nietzsche used his notebooks chaotically, and the entries do not reflect the order of composition. Indeed, the two best previous editions gave the approximate date of every note in an appendix, which Schlechta fails to do. Nor are the numbers that each note had in *The Will to Power* given. In this new edition one can no longer check quickly what Nietzsche had to say about morality, Christianity, or theory of knowledge. If, as a result, most readers should instead turn to the finished works, Schlechta would, no doubt, be satisfied.

The third interesting feature of Schlechta's edition is his detailed account, in his "Philological Postscript," of the forgeries that Nietzsche's sister perpetrated. He lists thirty-two "letters to mother and sister" of which there were no originals in the archives "but only copies in the sister's hand," or edited by her, and usually drafts in Nietzsche's hand. He relates how he discovered erasures in the addresses and signatures of these drafts and then found that "Dear Mother" had often been changed to "Dear Sister."

Both the nature of *The Will to Power* and the sister's role were clear before this and described and documented fully in my *Nietzsche* (1950). In the Viking *Portable Nietzsche* (1954), moreover, notes that the sister printed in *The Will to Power* are integrated in the chronological sequence and headed, for example, "Note (1884)," with a footnote reference, furnishing the number which the note bears in *The Will to Power*. But Schlechta's detailed demonstration of the sister's outright forgeries is new and was received in Germany as a sensation. In sum, his edition does not change the Nietzsche picture available before, nor does Schlechta claim that it does. But he has driven the last set of nails into the coffin of the Nietzsche legend woven by Elisabeth Förster-Nietzsche.[1]

[1] A forgery that has been justly ignored in Germany is still catalogued as Nietzsche's work in many American libraries: *My Sister and I* (1951), published by Samuel Roth, who achieved fame in 1927 when Bridges, Croce, Einstein, Eliot, Gide, Hamsun, Heming-

Schlechta's subsequent little collection of a few miscellaneous essays, *Der Fall Nietzsche* (1958), does not add much.
Schlechta shows little feeling for Nietzsche. He is no great
historian or interpreter, but a scrupulous editor.

5

Could it be that the Germans, once the people of *Dichter
und Denker*, composers and historians, have become a people
of editors and businessmen? Or are there perhaps new talents,
and possibly even men of genius, who have not attracted notice yet?

Some people feel that the situation is much the same
throughout the West. In the United States, too, the age of
James and Santayana, Dewey and Whitehead has passed. The
age of the giants is gone, and the age of the pygmies is at
hand. But any such conclusion is unwarranted.

In the United States, there is a vitality in philosophical discussion, and enthusiasm coupled with critical power, which,
quite apart from occasional constructive efforts, represents an
altogether different atmosphere. In literature, too, there are
not only a couple of Nobel Prize winners but also a great
many young writers who, no less than our young philosophers,
are enthusiastic critics. In Germany, the critical spirit atro-
phied during the Hitler years; and as long as any recollection
of the recent past is repressed, the climate of thought will
scarcely change. One should not look at the great names only
but listen hard whether the "untimely" voice of criticism and
of truly new creation is not to be heard somewhere. What
is needed is not magic but honesty, the courage of self-
knowledge, and the criticism of illusions.

" 'I have done that,' says my memory. 'I could not have
done that,' says my pride and remains inexorable. Finally, my

way, and 160 other famous men of letters signed a protest against
him. After my detailed exposé of the forgery in *Partisan Review*,
May–June, 1952, some glaring anachronisms were deleted, with the
space left blank, in the next printing. For a few brief comments on
that, see *The Philosophical Review*, Jan., 1955.

memory yields." Thus wrote Nietzsche in *Beyond Good and Evil;* and the trouble is that it is not only the memory that yields. The whole fiber does. The economic recovery is deceptive. Culturally, Germany is living on her capital.

19

TOYNBEE AND SUPER-HISTORY

The existentialist historian. Since we left Shakespeare, we have concentrated on the European continent and considered Goethe and Hegel, Kierkegaard and Nietzsche, Rilke and Freud, Jaspers and Heidegger. Our two major themes in moving from Shakespeare to existentialism were, first, the relationships between religion and poetry and philosophy, and, secondly, the falsification of history. But while it seemed feasible to concentrate on the Continent in connection with the first theme, Toynbee has a right to be considered in any extended discussion of the falsification of history. For in his work the falsification of history is no longer incidental to the writing of philosophy or poetry or criticism: his whole reputation rests on it.

Toynbee's work also exemplifies our other theme. Here we find a vast literary effort that falls between religion and poetry—as between two chairs. The dissatisfaction with any one genre and the attempt to fuse two or more is common to Kierkegaard, Nietzsche, and Plato. As we have seen, it is enormously dangerous, and most attempts fail wretchedly. In conclusion, one such failure should be considered in detail.

It may seem that at this point we leave behind existentialism. But Toynbee furnishes a classical example of the kind of thinking that the later Heidegger demands in place of logical and scientific thinking: *andenkendes Denken,* a thinking that recalls the past, relying heavily on intuition, an associative thinking that is closer to *Dichtung*—to fiction if not to poetry—than it is to science. Of course, Toynbee is in no sense a follower of Heidegger, and neither has the least admiration for the other. Indeed, Toynbee seems to see himself as something of a social scientist—at least in A *Study of History*—and we shall have to consider this claim. But the dangers that await those who are lured by Kierkegaard's and Heidegger's disparagement of critical thinking could hardly be illustrated better than by an examination of Toynbee.

One could do worse—and soon I shall—than to call Toynbee an existentialist historian. He offers us Kierkegaard's curious blend of epical digressions with religious urgency; he entertains us with no end of stories, but would have us know that our salvation is at stake. And because salvation is at stake, objective truth is considered pedestrian and not ultimately important. Unashamed subjectivity emerges. History is rewritten in accordance with the writer's homiletic needs, and his personal circumstances and the trivia of his life obtrude at every turn.

For all that, Toynbee is no Kierkegaard. What is lacking is the humor of the Dane and, though this sounds paradoxical, the full measure of his seriousness, too. Kierkegaard's laughter is as ultimately serious as Toynbee's grave seriousness is often laughable—or would be if it were not for his vast prestige and influence. To cite Luke 6:26, almost "all men speak well of" Toynbee, while Kierkegaard, unlike Toynbee—and unlike Heidegger and Jaspers—sought martyrdom. When a powerful newspaper, which he despised, spoke well of him, Kierkegaard asked it to pillory him, which it did. And instead of stressing his agreement with the religion of his fathers, he wore himself out writing and peddling the pamphlets that were later collected in *Attack on Christendom;* and, taken to a hospital, he refused the ministrations of his church. If such seriousness, such "engagement," such a fusion of life and thought, is part of the meaning of "existentialism," then, of course, Toynbee is no existentialist—any more than Heidegger or Jaspers.

Indeed, Toynbee is hard to classify. Before venturing a positive suggestion in the next chapter, let us first find out what he is not.

2

The lion and the centipede. Judged by low standards, *A Study of History* is an impressive and often interesting work. Judged by the standards that color Toynbee's judgment and have molded his performance, it is supercolossal: a cast of thousands, ranging from churches and civilizations to the author and his family; ten volumes compared to Spengler's two; and forty-eight pages of "Contents," no more analytic than the text but mystifying and titillating. He offers us an enormous screen and entertainment coupled with religious significance, all based on lots of research. This research, to be sure, does not preclude amazing oversights and errors, but the author is not writing for the historians, who have by now roundly condemned his work.

For whom does he write? He writes for posterity, for generations centuries hence who will read him after all the other writers of our time have been forgotten. Again and again he takes posterity into his confidence with words like these: "As for the writer's use of the traditional language, . . . he might say, for his readers' information, that his regular and deliberate practice was to continue to employ traditional language unless and until he could find new words that seemed to him to express his meaning more clearly and more exactly. In the writer's day the resources of language were still utterly inadequate" (VII, 421). But can the inadequacies of Toynbee's style really be blamed on "the writer's day"?

Sir Ernest Barker judges that Toynbee "writes English almost as if it were a foreign language, in long periodic sentences, with one relative clause piled on, or dovetailed into, another"; and he adds: "The reviewer found himself tempted, again and again, to break up and re-write the long rolling cryptic sentences: in particular he found himself anxious to banish . . . the 'ornate alias,' and to substitute, for instance, the words 'St. Paul' for 'the Tarsian Jewish apostle of Christianity *in partibus infidelium.'*" And A. J. P. Taylor, the Oxford historian, remarks that "adjectives are piled on with all the ruthlessness which the Egyptians used when building the pyramids."

If we considered Toynbee as in the main a poet, such criticisms of his style would certainly be pertinent; but is he not really a historian? The enormous difficulty of doing justice to Toynbee is due to his determination to mix genres. If you find fault with him as a historian you are likely to be told that he is really a social scientist who is a pioneer in a new field and out to discover hitherto unknown laws; and it is only when his method has been shown to be a travesty of science that apologists are apt to say he is a poet.

Today there is a wide demand for the integration of knowledge, for "a whole view," for the supradepartmental course; but surely there is no special virtue whatever in a fusion of poor history with unsound science and wretched poetry, even if it is spiced with ever so frequent references to God. The fallacy here is exactly the same one that leads some people to suppose that five invalid proofs of God's existence are better than one valid proof. Or would you rather be a centipede than a man? The answer to this infatuation with quantity has been given long ago in one of Aesop's fables: when a vixen boasted of the size of her litter and asked the lioness about the size of hers, the lioness replied: *hen alla leonta*—one, but a lion.

3

The historian—and the Renaissance. Let us consider Toynbee first as a historian. Two examples, which could be multiplied at random, may illustrate his procedure. Both are selected to obviate the objection that I am merely pitting my view against his or dealing with abstruse and remote incidents about which it is easy to make some small mistake. In both cases the author is dealing with material that is well known to millions of his contemporaries and shows that he utterly lacks the conscience of the sound historian.

Example I: Part X deals with "Contacts between Civilizations in Time" and is subtitled "Renaissances." On the first five pages we are told, with a wealth of metaphor, analogy, and simple repetition, that:

In using the word *renaissance* as a proper name, we have
been allowing ourselves to fall into the error of seeing a
unique occurrence in an event which in reality was no more
than one particular instance of a recurrent historical phenomenon. The evocation of a dead culture by the living
representatives of a civilization that is still a going concern
proves to be a species of historical event for which the
proper label is, not "the Renaissance," but "renaissances."

There follows "A Survey of Renaissances" in which these turn
out to be a particularly repulsive form of necromancy—a word
that is used over and over, together with the metaphors that
it invites. After Toynbee's indictment has taken up "Renaissances of Political Ideas, Ideals, and Institutions"; "Renaissances of Systems of Law"; "Renaissances of Philosophies"
(five and a half pages on China and two and a half on Aristotle); and "Renaissances of Languages and Literature" (seven
subheadings), we finally do get to "Renaissances of Visual
Arts" and *our* Renaissance. At this point one wonders how
Toynbee will make good his indictment. It is always interesting to find an intelligent person with a fresh perspective, and
you want to see what Toynbee will have to say about Leonardo, Michelangelo, Titian, and a dozen others. But he can't
quite spare five pages for "Renaissances of Visual Arts"; and
though he indicts the Italian Renaissance, he simply does not
mention Leonardo, Michelangelo, Titian, or the other great
painters and sculptors of the period.

Toynbee, of course, has every right to dislike these artists,
and an intelligent critique is bound to be more fruitful than a
conventional appreciation. As it happens, Toynbee is not at all
interested in them, and in his whole ten volumes he has absolutely nothing to say about any of them. This, too, is his
privilege, though it certainly diminishes his competence as a
student of Western civilization and raises severe doubts about
his critique of renaissances—especially "of visual arts." But
what is irresponsible and unjustifiable is that he should support his indictment of the Italian Renaissance by passing over
in silence what does not readily fit his case.

4

The historian—and the Jews. The second example of Toynbee's lack of the historical conscience may be found in his discussion of "Contacts between Civilizations in Space (Encounters between Contemporaries)," which constitutes Part IX
of his work. I shall confine myself to section 5: "The Modern
West and the Jews."

He begins not with the modern West but with antiquity and
after that spends some time on the Jews in Spain under the
Visigoths and later under Muslim rule. This discussion should
be most interesting, seeing that Toynbee had committed himself to all sorts of implausible theses in his earlier volumes:
we must make civilizations the unit of study, he had said, because unlike nations they can be studied in isolation from each
other; Western civilization and Islam are two civilizations
that are autonomous in this sense, and the Jews are a fossil
(the word is his) of a third, so-called Syriac, civilization.
What, then, will Toynbee make of the apparent fusion of these
three civilizations? What will he say about Judah ben Halevy,
Gabirol, and Maimonides' relation to scholasticism? Alas, he
does not as much as mention any of them. He might of course
plead that he is mainly concerned with "The Modern West
and the Jews," though in view of his implausible theses he
ought to say something about events that seem to refute them
so clearly. What, then, does he have to say about Spinoza?
Again, not a single reference in 334 pages of indices. Perhaps
Spinoza is not modern enough. What happens when we come
to the nineteenth and twentieth centuries? What will Toynbee
say about the remarkable behavior of this fossil after the
emancipation, about the scores of Jewish scientists and thinkers, about the way in which the Jews suddenly entered into
Western civilization and made major contributions? Nothing,
absolutely nothing. If medieval Spain does not fit his scheme,
he ignores it; and if the Jews are a living refutation of his
theories, attack is the best defense.

Toynbee tries to establish the word "Judaical," mainly by
using it in this fashion, as a synonym of "fanatical" (by way

of contrast with "the gentle and unaggressive ethos of Christianity"), as when he speaks, for example, of "a series of anti-Jewish enactments of a Judaically fanatical ferocity"—enacted by Christians, of course. Toynbee likes to use the epithet "Judaical" for elements of Christianity of which he does not approve. If this prejudice, however unworthy of a historian among all people, is at least common, Toynbee also suggests again and again that "Jew" and "businessman"—not to use a less polite term—are synonymous. This, coupled with his failure to mention in this context a single Jewish scholar, scientist, poet, philosopher, or artist, amounts to a grotesque falsification of history and a complete perversion of the relations between "The Modern West and the Jews."

When he finally comes to "The Fate of the European Jews and the Palestinian Arabs, A.D. 1933–48" and his thesis that "On the Day of Judgement the gravest crime standing to the German National Socialists' account might be, not that they had exterminated the majority of the Western Jews, but that they had caused the surviving remnant of Jewry to stumble," he shows as much contempt for history as any Hollywood director ever did. It is not the merits of Zionism that are at issue here. An intelligent and honest indictment always deserves a hearing, though what one has the right to expect from a historian is first of all an honest account of what happened. Such an account should make us understand what previously we did not understand; it should enlarge our horizon and affect our prejudices and valuations.

Does Toynbee explain the origin of Zionism with which he deals at great length? Decidedly not. But it is one of the great oddities of his work that he prints, in footnotes and appendices, critical comments by scholars who have read parts of his manuscript—and again and again these comments invalidate the text but are left standing without any reply by the author. In the present instance, James Parkes, a Gentile student of anti-Semitism, throws more light on the origin of Zionism in three lines on page 294, not to speak of his two-page "Annex," than does Toynbee in his daydreams and sermons in the text. Similarly, to give just one other example, Parkes points out in another note, two pages later, that Toynbee is mistaken about a date in the text; but Toynbee continues for pages and pages to use this date just the same.

I am not advocating a pedestrian lack of imagination. A historian should put himself into the place of the men whose decisions he discusses and ask himself what went on in their minds—but naturally after having first used all the available data as the necessary context and clues. Toynbee, however, ignores the most relevant data; and for the sake of his system or sermon he spurns them even after Parkes has called attention to a few of them.

There is no reason why Toynbee should know a great deal about Zionism or Judaism; but as long as he does not, why does he insist on writing about both at such great length? The indices of Volumes VI and X (which take care, between them, of all but the first three volumes) contain over four columns of references to the Jews, and a column apiece about "Judaism" —but not a single reference to Hillel or Akiba, not to speak of lesser men or such contemporary representatives as, for example, Buber.

Actually, the name of Hillel is mentioned once in Toynbee's indictment of Zionism: "The image and superscription of this new human coinage was not Hillel's but Caesar's." But a few sentences later, on the same page (311), he pontificates:

> This mystical feeling for an historical Eretz Israel, which inspired the Zionist pioneers with the spiritual power to move mountains, was entirely derived from a diasporan orthodox theology that convicted the Zionists of an importunity which verged upon impiety in their attempt to take out of God's hands the fulfilment of God's promise to restore Israel to Palestine on God's own initiative.

Clearly, Toynbee does not know one of Hillel's most celebrated dicta: "If I am not for myself, who will be? And if I am for myself only, what am I? And if not now, when?" Nor does Toynbee see the weakness of his own conception of religion, which would indeed turn it into a mere opiate by so unhesitatingly divorcing God's initiative from man's.

What is most unjustifiable is surely Toynbee's report to posterity about what happened in Palestine after the British left.

In the text he gives the impression that the Jews did to the
Arabs precisely what the Nazis had done to the Jews. In a
footnote he belatedly admits that "the cold-blooded systematic
'genocide' of several million human beings . . . had no parallel
at all in the Jews' ill-treatment of the Palestinian Arabs." But
they deprived of "their homes and property" and reduced to
the status of "displaced persons" some 684,000 Arabs. In a note
this figure is qualified and the Jews are blamed for only 284,-
000; but these "expulsions," we are told, "were on the heads
of all Israel." Did they occur during a war or in the midst
of peace? Toynbee does not say, but throughout he gives the
consistent, if fantastic, impression that the Jews attacked inno-
cent Arabs to vent the aggressive feelings accumulated during
their own persecution by the Nazis. That any Arab had ever
fired a shot on a Jew in Palestine before 1948, or that the
Arab states had declared war on Israel the moment the British
had left their former mandate, and that the Jews were fighting a war in self-defense against armies pledged to extermi-
nate them to the last man, woman, and child—all that is not
only not mentioned but brazenly denied by implication.

So is the fact that the Arab leaders repeatedly called upon
the Arabs in Israel to leave Israel—both to paralyze the new
state by their exodus and to facilitate a wholesale slaughter
of the Israelis—and promised them the whole land within a
few weeks.

Judged by high standards, some of the things the Israelis
did certainly deserve censure, as does our systematic bombing
of civilians toward the end of World War II, not to speak of
Hiroshima or, worse, Nagasaki. But those who are fighting for
their life and liberty can at least plead extenuating circumstances. What can the historian plead who willfully falsifies the
history of events with which no man required him to deal?

5

The scientific approach. So much for the historian. Surely,
A. J. P. Taylor is too kind when he says: "Professor Toynbee's
method is not that of scholarship, but of the lucky dip, with
emphasis on the luck." But in a recent note on "What I am

Trying to Do," in the same issue of *International Affairs* in which Sir Ernest Barker offers his strictures, Toynbee tells us: "One of my aims in *A Study of History* has been to try out the scientific approach to human affairs and to test how far it will carry us."

What he proposes to show, as is well known by now, is that some twenty-odd civilizations exemplify certain patterns in their development. Taylor has suggested that Toynbee's scheme was, in fact, a generalization from classical antiquity: "If other civilizations failed to fit into this pattern, they were dismissed as abortive, ossified, or achieving a wrong-headed *tour de force*." This criticism is valid as far as it goes, but it does not bring out the full enormity of Toynbee's method.

In the first place, Toynbee's anthropomorphic conception of civilizations is superstitious: the question how many civilizations there are is like asking how many sciences there are, and the question when a particular civilization originated is on a level with the query when art began. Worse still, the conceit that civilizations are not only individual entities but the only units that can be studied historically one at a time, without referring beyond them, is the height of naïveté. Only a few completely isolated societies can be studied thoroughly without reference to other societies; but any unit whatever, whether a civilization, a nation, a city, a university, or a railroad can be made the object of a historical study in which outside entities are introduced as sparingly as possible. Specifically, no "Syriac Civilization," for example, ever existed, though it may possibly be convenient in some contexts to lump together the many kingdoms that existed between ancient Egypt and Mesopotamia and to give them some such name as this; but this fictitious civilization could hardly be studied very fully without reference to its two mighty neighbors. It should be added that the untenable thesis that civilizations are the only self-contained "intelligible fields of historical study," which Toynbee had argued with much rhetoric and little logic on the first fifty pages of Volume I, is quickly, though not pointedly, abandoned at the beginning of Volume VII.

Secondly, if you want to verify the presence of a certain pattern in the geneses, growths, breakdowns, and disintegra-

tions of twenty-odd civilizations, the scientific approach would
seem obvious. You have to consider your twenty-odd items in
turn, admitting frankly where we either lack sufficient evidence or find what does not fit our pattern. But Toynbee
spurns this pedestrian approach. He finds his illustrations in
nations and individuals, in Goethe's *Faust* and the New Testament; and he is not beyond illustrating the genesis or growth
of a civilization from the fate of a nation, or even a small part
of a nation, such as New England, during a period when the
civilization to which it belonged was, according to Toynbee,
breaking down and incapable of any further growth in any of
its parts. His procedure, in short, is unsystematic and inconsistent in the extreme. In this manner no historical laws could
possibly be established, even if there were any.

Toynbee's delight at finding several examples of this sort
that fit, or seem to him to fit, into his scheme is generally increased by their waywardness. Thus he shows for some seventy
pages how civilizations grow, by finding examples of "with-
drawal and return" in the lives of Philopoemen, Leo Syrus,
Ollivier, Clarendon, Ibn Khaldūn, Kant, and Hamlet, among
many others. This sort of thing pleases him so much that he
forgets altogether that, to take a single example, Kant, who
perhaps lived a withdrawn life, never returned. That students
went to Königsberg, which he had never left, is hardly a return; but if it were, what would this prove about the pattern
of the growth of civilizations?

That illustrations of this kind could be adduced at random
for any theory or pattern whatsoever, Toynbee does not realize
any more than that a truly scientific approach would require
him to go out of his way to deal specifically (1) with evidence
which on the face of it appears to contradict his theories, and
(2) with rival constructions of that evidence which, as *he* construes it, does fit.

Consider Part VI, on "Universal States," with which the last
four-volume batch begins. It contains a lot of miscellaneous
data, but no survey at all of Toynbee's twenty-odd civilizations. Instead of taking them up one by one, Toynbee offers
such chapter headings as "The Doom of Tithonus" and "The
Price of Euthanasia."

To be sure, in this case he also offers a "Table" of "Universal States," reprinted without change from Volume VI. Now, this table had been criticized some years ago by Pieter Geyl in a brilliant essay on the fatal flaws of "Toynbee's System of Civilizations"—an essay that was reprinted in a book, *The Pattern of the Past*, together with the text of a debate between Toynbee and Geyl. Geyl is passed over in silence in the last four volumes. The only major critic with whom Toynbee deals at length, in a very amusing "Annex" that, however, shows no understanding at all of his critic's position, is R. G. Collingwood. But to return to the fatal table: Geyl had called attention not only to the triteness and vagueness of Toynbee's so-called laws but also to the startling fact that, according to this table, there was universal peace in Western Europe from "A.D. 1797–1814," and in the area of "The Danubian Hapsburg Monarchy A.D. 1526–1918." Yet Toynbee did not see fit to revise these claims; his system takes precedence.

6

The poet. Confronted with this sort of thing, it has become customary to say that Toynbee is really a poet. But is not that rather like saying that Senator McCarthy was a poet? The splashy fifty-page claim that is, much later, abandoned quickly in a few sentences, points in the same direction. So does the method he follows, as we have seen, in some of his indictments.

Let us be friendlier: is not calling Toynbee a poet rather like saying that Cecil B. De Mille is a poet? The Napoleonic wars don't fit, so Toynbee rewrites history. And how much De Mille there is in such a sentence as this:

In the field of encounters in the Time-dimension an Antaean rebound that wins from Necromancy an anticipatory communion with the Future has its antithesis in an Atlantean stance in which a Necromancer who has yielded to the legendary Epimethean impulse of Lot's wife is petrified by the hypnotic stare of a resuscitated corpse's Medusan countenance into the rigidity of a pillar of salt pinned down by the incubus of the Past [IX, 363].

What a cast!
Is Toynbee really a poet? Toynbee himself says:

As a consequence of his fifteenth-century Italian education, the writer's spiritual home was, not a post-Christian Western World, but a pre-Christian Hellas; and, whenever he was moved to put his deeper and more intimate feelings into words, they found expression in Greek or Latin verse, and not in the English vernacular that happened to be his mother tongue [IX, 411].

Indeed, Volumes I and VII begin with two long poems written, respectively, in Greek and Latin; but "intimate feelings" are also expressed frequently in the vernacular of the text in which the author feels less at home. But is it poetry when the author informs us, after giving a reference in a footnote: "My aunt Gertrude's copy, with my name written in it in her handwriting, dated 'September 1906,' is here on my desk in May 1951"? And there are a great many similar passages.

Surely, people begin to think of Toynbee as a poet only where he has raised other expectations and then failed to fulfill them. At the end of Part XI, for example, after well over two hundred pages about "Law and Freedom in History," one expects some resolution of the conflict between those who affirm and those who deny the presence of laws in history. But Toynbee concludes:

Since the God who is Love is also Omnipotence, a soul that loves is liberated by the maker and master of all laws from a bondage to laws of the Subconscious Psyche which Babylonian souls used to project on to inexorable stars in their courses and which Hellenic souls used to personify as malignant *kêres* and daimones; and a liberating truth which had once proved potent to set free [John VIII. 32] fast-fettered Hellenes and Babylonians might once again be taken to heart by the children of a post-Christian World which had been vainly seeking to ban those dread psychic principalities and powers [Rom. VIII. 38; Eph. III. 10 and VI. 12] in the name of a Science that was as impotent to exorcize them as any pre-Christian magic.

I have put the footnotes into brackets and might add that probably more than half of Toynbee's footnotes are of this nature. But is this poetry or merely murky?

7

The theologian. It might be suggested that Toynbee is really a theologian. In this capacity, however, he ranks with the friends of Job. To vindicate the justice of God, he regularly infers, as they did, that misfortune is a proof of a prior moral transgression; and evidence to the contrary does not deter him. Thus he speaks, for example, of churches that "committed spiritual suicide by going into politics" and forfeited the chance of "playing a church's authentic role"; and he continues: "Cases in point were the syncretistic Egyptiac Church . . . Zoroastrianism, Judaism, Nestorianism, and Monophysitism, which had allowed themselves to be used by a submerged Syriac Civilization as weapons in its warfare against a dominant Hellenism." Elsewhere, too, Toynbee sharply condemns the Jewish uprising of 135 A.D. But did not Islam and Christianity go into politics and wage wars—and not merely to defend a threatened way of life, but aggressive wars? No, says Toynbee in the very same passage from which I have just quoted: "Islam alone had partially succeeded in retrieving a false step into which it had been led in its infancy by its Founder" (VII, 532). Islam has flourished; so Toynbee infers, after the manner of Job's friends, it must have been virtuous. And when our gentle scholar comes to the Crusades, only thirty-five pages after his indictment of the Zionists, he develops all the enthusiasm of a Sunday-morning quarterback as he pictures the victories that might have been, if only the Crusaders had followed his strategy.

In his footnotes Toynbee carries on a prolonged theological discussion with one Martin Wight, a Christian, who eventually draws from our author an admission that he is no longer a Christian. Toynbee's position is developed in an "Annex" on "Higher Religions and Psychological Types." The types are those of Jung (Freud is not listed in any of the indices), and the "higher" religions are the four with the largest following.

Toynbee's religious outlook also finds expression at the end of Part XIII (the last part of his work) when, after piling up quotations in different languages for several pages, he concludes with a long prayer of his own that alternates between Latin and English. I quote two of its twenty stanzas:

Sancta Dei Genetrix, intercede pro nobis.
Mother Mary, Mother Isis, Mother Cybele, Mother Ishtar,
Mother Kwanyin, have compassion on us, by whatsoever name
we bless thee for bringing Our Savior into the World.

It would be hard to guess whom this will offend more: Catholics or Protestants? But if syncretism hitherto usually meant an attempt to offend no religion, consider Toynbee's bow to Islam:

Sancte Petre, intercede pro nobis.
Tender-hearted Muhammad, who are also one of the weaker
vessels of God's grace, pray that His grace may inspire
us. . . .

For any who might wish to commemorate the event, Toynbee finished this prayer in "London, 1951, June 15, 6.25 P.M., after looking once more, this afternoon, at Fra Angelico's picture of the Beatific Vision." (Throughout his work, Toynbee frequently informs us of the exact date when, for example, a footnote was written. Fra Angelico, of course, is not mentioned in the discussion of "Renaissances.")

To find inspiration in many religions is one thing; to find godlike a deity with whom so many must intercede is another and brings to mind Toynbee's favorite book: "But thou, when thou prayest, enter into thy closet, and when thou hast shut thy door, pray to thy Father which is in secret. . . . But when ye pray, use not vain repetitions, as the heathen do: for they think that they shall be heard for their much speaking."

Toynbee's religiousness, like the rest of his work, is spectacular, has a huge cast, and is, for all its ostentatious humility, charged with self-importance. And his conceit is essentially different from the self-stylization of Socrates in his Apology or of Nietzsche or Shaw: there is neither sarcasm in it nor any discrimination between what is representative and what is

trivial. In the first two indices, little space was given to the
author, and hardly more to God. In the new index both have
attained to two whole columns, and many items under "Toynbee, Arnold Joseph" are on the level of "Kensington Gardens,
visits to" (4 references) and "curiosity of" (2 references).

8

Our new illiteracy. There are many good things in these
volumes, including not only some of the contributions of Toynbee's critics, which he had the good grace to print, but also
occasional thought-provoking judgments, many fascinating
quotations and observations, and several good anecdotes.
More's the pity that it all does not add up to a great work
but only to a huge smorgasbord in which many of the dishes
are poisoned. Far from being more scientific than Spengler,
whom he calls a "pontifical-minded man of genius," Toynbee
is more pontifical, less original, and endowed with an essentially eclectic and digressive mind. What suggests the possibility of greatness in Toynbee's case is mainly the lavish expendi-
ture and sheer size of his undertaking. Beyond that, the
fashionable taste for a mixture of almost any kind of religion
with erudition has helped to make Toynbee one of the idols
of our new illiteracy.

This illiteracy does not know the distinction between erudition and scholarship, between irresponsibility and poetry, between assurance and evidence. One reads Toynbee's indictments and is impressed by the wealth of footnotes, and one
does not notice that they sometimes refer to nothing but other
passages in which the same unfounded claims are made, supported by similar cross-references—or that a spectacular figure
is cut down to less than half its size in a note; or that a splashy
fifty-page claim is unostentatiously dropped in a few sentences,
much later. In an age in which similar techniques beset us so
sorely, the scholar bears a greater responsibility than ever.
Toynbee advocates admirable virtues. "The voice is the voice
of Jacob, but the hands are the hands of Esau."

20

TOYNBEE AND RELIGION

A failure of conscience. On the heels of Toynbee's ten-volume work, *A Study of History*, two books of criticism appeared as well as a new book by Toynbee himself: *An Historian's Approach to Religion.* The two critical books differ decisively from the many studies that are now devoted to poets, philosophers, and theologians: they represent crushing exposés of Toynbee and question not only his methods but even his honesty.

In the first of these books, *Toynbee and History: Critical Essays and Reviews,* edited by Ashley Montagu, we find the staid London *Times Literary Supplement* arguing that Toynbee "frequently" relies on "radical distortion of the facts," and that his central thesis is downright absurd and "reinforced by a vast hodge-podge of subsidiary theories, arguments and explanations which are by no means always mutually compatible." In the same volume, Geoffrey Barraclough, who has since succeeded to Toynbee's chair of international history at Chatham House, London, also attacks Toynbee's "inconsistency and his arbitrary use of historical evidence," and explicitly agrees with other scholars that Toynbee's vaunted empirical method is "mere make belief." Barraclough also ridicules Toynbee's "hotch-potch of the platitudes of current social and political analysis, combined with wishful thinking and dubious speculations." And Hugh Trevor-Roper, the Oxford historian, concludes: "Helping out his conjuring tricks with imperfect light, distracting noises and a certain amount of intellectual hanky-panky, he pretends that he has proved what he has merely stated. This seems to me, in so learned a man, a terrible per-

version of history." While some of the Americans represented
in the book take a kindlier view, and most of them hedge their
strictures with tributes to Toynbee's erudition, none of them
have answered these crucial charges.

Toynbee's fantastic treatment of the Jews is the subject of
the second book, Maurice Samuel's *The Professor and the Fossil*.
Before one reads it, one wonders whether there is much
point in a single author's devoting a whole book to Toynbee's
books, and at that a book that deals mainly with a single
theme. But once you start reading Samuel, there is no stopping:
compellingly written, this book, with its rich humanity,
is no mere critique but a positive contribution to the understanding
of Judaism and the Jews from biblical times to our
own. What is criticized, moreover, is so monstrous that it is
good to have such an able exposure to set the record straight.

Toynbee's failure is in part a failure of conscience. There
are many who quite fail to see this and object that some selection
is imperative, that some mistakes are unavoidable, and
that scope, originality, and human interest are ample compensations
for such common failings. This is one of those half-
truths with which the road to hell is paved. It is the conscience
alone that raises sweep and novelty above mere fantasy and
daydreams. Popularity with a vast audience in the face of opposition
from the scholars is no proof of truthfulness. Goebbels'
well-known dictum that big lies are more readily believed
than little ones reminds us of the dangers of unscrupulous
originality and scope.

Samuel shows how Toynbee based his notoriously untruthful
version of the Israeli war of independence on "the account
prepared by Mr. George Kirk for the *Survey of International
Affairs*" of which Toynbee himself was the editor from 1920
until 1946, but that Toynbee used only what, taken out of
context, seemed to give some substance to his certainly very
original theses, while he left out all the crucial points that gave
the lie to his account. Any talk of Toynbee's erudition is irrelevant
at this point. Nobody questions that. What he lacks is the
scholar's conscience.

2

Prophet or symptom. Sharp polemics are not popular in the
United States today: witness the difference between Toynbee's
critics in America and England. In the United States, mere
corrections of errors are usually shrugged off as unimportant,
and questions of method are considered academic. While an
avowal of agnosticism would ruin a politician's career, glaring
misstatements of fact, false promises, and mendacious accusations are expected and excused. Clearly, truthfulness is considered much less important in America today than theism, success, and some semblance of charity. Toynbee has these three
essential virtues of the politician, and like politicians is forgiven
for his lack of truthfulness.

Like Heidegger, Toynbee is opposed to positivism to the
point where he no longer cares about correctness. A striking
illustration has been cited in the last chapter: in the sixth volume of his *Study,* first published in 1939, he printed a Table
of Universal States on which he maintained that Western civilization had two branches, and that the western part had experienced universal peace, or as he prefers to say, *"Pax
Oecumenica* A.D. 1797–1814"—when, as Toynbee surely knows,
there was scarcely a single year of peace. The eastern branch,
the area of "the Danubian Hapsburg Monarchy" had its *"Pax
Oecumenica* A.D. 1526–1918." There is a certain boldness in
the figure 1918. A more timid man might have said 1914,
hoping that the reader would forget the Thirty Years' War
and the Seven Years' War and Napoleon's wars and others,
more or less remote. Pieter Geyl called Toynbee's attention
to these striking errors—and a host of others—but the table is
reprinted without change in 1954 in Volume VII.

By some strange logic, there are many people who suppose
that a man who is so wrong about the past is more likely than
others to be right about the future. On the jacket of Toynbee's
new book an American historian is quoted as saying what we
have been told again and again: "He is more than a historian:
he is a great deal of a prophet." In his articles no less than his
books Toynbee himself has cultivated the impression that he

can foretell the future, but he usually avoids all interesting and tangible predictions—his chapter on "The Religious Outlook in a Twentieth Century World" is a case in point—and in the early volumes of his big work we do not only fail to find forecasts fulfilled meantime, but we find that Toynbee was much less perceptive than a great many contemporaries. After a long interview with Hitler, for example, Toynbee declared in 1936 that he was "convinced of his sincerity in desiring peace in Europe."

Now, it might be suggested that Toynbee harks back to the Hebrew prophets, who were less concerned with forecasting the future than they were with the morals of their people. Their prophecies were, most characteristically, conditional. They said: change your ways; your present course will lead to such and such results. And the one prophet who failed to understand this crucial point was instructed about it by God: Jonah. To be sure, Toynbee is a moralist of sorts, but he could hardly be more remote from the distinctive ethos of the prophets, who were more self-effacing than any men of comparable stature in all history. They disappeared completely in their message and sacrificed their lives to it. No historian, on the other hand, has ever made a greater show of his learning than Toynbee, or attached one-tenth as much importance to the small minutiae of his life.

You need only examine the Index of his Volume X with its two columns of amazing references to Toynbee, Arnold Joseph: ". . . critical faculty, awakening of" down to "walking, liking for." There is no need to labor this point, seeing that Toynbee himself clearly does not find the pre-Exilic prophets congenial: not one of the indices to his ten-volume *Study* lists a single reference to even one of them—which, of course, does not keep Toynbee from posing as a top authority on Judaism or from giving the appearance that he is thoroughly at home in the Bible from which the same passages are quoted again and again and again.

Surely, Toynbee is not more than a historian. Toynbee is less than a historian; he is a symptom: a symptom of the worship of size; a symptom of the eclipse of scruple; a symptom of the widespread hunger for vast spectacles, for men of learning who come out for any version of religion whatsoever, and above all for assurance that history has a meaning. Sparked by the futility of so much human suffering, by a deep ambivalence over the mechanization of modern life, and by profound confusion in the face of more and more specialized experts, there is a desperate demand for a royal road to meaning. And, while the men of impeccable methods generally avoid questions of meaning, vast masses of people who will not be put off turn to commentators, columnists, and editorials; and to popular accounts by men who have consulted experts; and to Toynbee. As long as there is even some small promise of significance, people willingly put up with vagueness, inconsistencies, and errors.

If a single factor accounts more than any other for Toynbee's popularity in the United States, it is surely his concern with religion—not simply the fact of his concern but above all the nature of his concern. In an age in which books become bestsellers because they seem to prove scientifically that the Bible is right, Toynbee could hardly fail to be a popular success. His frequent references to God and Christ and his thousands of footnote references to the New Testament, which record his every use of a biblical turn of speech, assure the Christian reader that the Bible is proved right, while his growing hope for a vast syncretism pleases those who feel that the one thing needful is a meeting of East and West. Toynbee makes a great show of religion, which the Hebrew prophets did not, but he presses no unequivocal or incisive demands, which the prophets did. Unlike the religion of most, if not all, of mankind's great religious figures, Toynbee's religion is ingratiating—like that of the politicians and our most successful magazines. He offers us history, social science, anecdotes, schemes, entertainment—all this and heaven, too.

An Historian's Approach to Religion is thus no mere appendage to his major work. Here we have Toynbee's considered reflections on one of his central interests. In less than three hundred pages he sums up what is scattered over ten volumes of twice that length each in his previous work. Constant references to those sections of the ten volumes in which "the subject of this chapter has been dealt with in greater detail" make it quite clear that these Gifford Lectures on religion, which he delivered at the University of Edinburgh in 1952 and 1953, represent the ultimate conclusions to which his vast *Study* has led him.

3

One-upmanship. The first conclusion that emerges from a reading of this new book is how little Toynbee has to say: much less than any number of previous Gifford Lecturers. Both of the critical books on Toynbee are far more instructive and exciting. Eight times the course of lectures is interrupted by an "Annexe" (*sic*), and there are pages upon pages of un-interrupted quotations, especially from Pierre Bayle, but also from John Locke and Thomas Sprat. What these long quota-tions prove, or what theses they might be required to support, remains unclear. Stripped of these quotations and of Toynbee's inveterate repetitions, little remains, except space he might have used to state his theses clearly and to adduce some evidence.

Toynbee's interest is confined to six religions, of which he says at the outset:

> In the world of A.D. 1956 the greatest cultural gulf was not the rift between Judaic Western Liberalism and a Judaic Western Communism; it was the chasm between the whole Judaic group of ideologies and religions—Communism, Lib-eralism, Christianity, Islam, and their parent Judaism itself —on the one hand and the Buddhaic group of philosophies and religions—post-Buddhaic Hinduism, the Mahayana, and the Hinayana—on the other hand.

There is nothing in the book to persuade the reader who is not content to accept this verdict without argument. If anyone should wonder about the "cultural gulf" between the Western world and the Arab world, or the colored peoples of Africa, or the Chinese, he will find that Toynbee has nothing to say about all that. He is interested in Judaism, Christianity, and Islam, and in Hinduism and Hinayana and Mahayana Buddhism; and he finds it convenient to lump these together in two groups of three each.

Now one might expect some concentrated treatment of the six religions that do interest him. One might suppose that he will consider them either one by one or at least three by three. And one might hope that he will increase our understanding of these six religions. All three of these hopes are disappointed. It is of the very essence of Toynbee's method, or rather his lack of method, that he does not take up in turn his six religions —or the twenty-odd civilizations in his *Study*—and that he does *not* base his generalizations on inductions. His whole style of thinking is inseparable from his habit of moving freely and allusively among his six religions, substituting words like "proved" and "must" and "therefore" for the least attempt at serious demonstration. Many of his statements are not only metaphorical but qualified beyond the point of still retaining a clear meaning, and a great deal of what he says is contradicted elsewhere, exemplifying what Maurice Samuel has politely called "the blurring effect." Elusive as the Delphic oracle itself, Toynbee concludes the book without either adding to our knowledge of his six religions or substantiating some illuminating generalization.

Part One, which takes up the first half of the book, is entitled "The Dawn of the Higher Religions." Toynbee manages to discuss this dawn without a single mention of Moses, the Upanishads, or the Bhagavad-Gita. Needless to say, he throws little light on the dawn of Judaism or Hinduism, either pre- or post-Buddhaic, or for that matter the dawn of any other religion, high or low. Toynbee informs posterity, evidently just in case his book alone should survive from our time: "What Man's original religion may have been is a question that was still under debate in A.D. 1956." The third sentence after this begins: "It is, indeed, conceivable that Man did not begin to worship Nature until he had begun to be able to manipulate her." And the following sentence reads in full: "The worship of Nature will have had its *floruit* in the long age during which Man felt himself to be neither wholly impotent in the face of Nature (so that it was now no longer quite useless for him to try to influence her) nor wholly master of her (so that to try to influence her was still worth his while)." Surely, this is not only "conceivable" but a truism, and we may note that the long age described by Toynbee has not ended yet, nor ever will as long as men survive. But a very large part of the book is filled with inferences of this sort which are made to sound bold by some such phrase as, "It is, indeed, conceivable," which at the same time serves to qualify what Toynbee says in such a way that, pressed, one simply could not say what Toynbee tries to tell us.

In any case the first five chapters antedate the "dawn" and it may be unfair to expect clarity and light. From "The Worship of Nature" we progress to three kinds of "Man-worship": "The Idolization of Parochial Communities," "The Idolization of an Oecumenical Community," and "The Idolization of a Self-sufficient Philosopher." Then the darkness lifts for "The Epiphany of the Higher Religions." Evidently Toynbee thinks, and would have us believe, that this was the historical sequence of events; but to enable us to judge if this is so or not, he should, albeit briefly, demonstrate how each of his six religions was preceded by these four benighted stages. Far from doing anything remotely like this, Toynbee does not even date the dawn of each approximately; and according to the seventh volume of his *Study*, Judaism is not at all a higher religion, and Buddhism is *one* religion, not two.

"The epiphany of the higher religions" is deduced, not demonstrated; and the deduction is characteristically unconvincing. "Human power, in all its forms, is limited and, in the last resort, illusory." If you fail to see the last point, Toynbee says absolutely nothing to persuade you. "The idolatrous worship of an oecumenical state leads to a policy of keeping Suffering within bounds by force, and so to the paradox of inflicting Suffering for the sake of limiting it." What "oecumenical state" has ever shown any profound concern to limit suffering? Did the Roman Empire? It is not considered. Nor does Toynbee show what is paradoxical about, say, inoculating people to limit suffering. This alleged paradox, however, is crucial for Toynbee's argument, which proceeds:

Since an oecumenical state is the most estimable kind of

state that Man has succeeded in creating so far [I for one should rather live in any number of "parochial" states than in the "oecumenical" Roman Empire], the moral paradox inherent in an oecumenical state is a verdict on states of all kinds: in its worse and its better varieties alike, the state is the nemesis of Original Sin.

Is it? And what does this mean? Has it been established by argument? Or is all this suggestive double talk?

Original Sin, which is in fashion once again today, is mentioned frequently throughout the book; but only toward the end, on page 267, are we told that it is merely "another name for self-centredness." While this peculiar definition might persuade us that the author is an authority on this evil (in view, for example, of his two columns of stunning references to his name in Volume X), it makes nonsense of the sentence that refers to the state's attempt to limit suffering.

Toynbee's main point is that "the failure of both the idolization of the self-sufficient philosopher and the idolization of the oecumenical community to meet the challenge presented by the failure of parochial-community-worship opens the way for a rejection of the worship of human power in all forms." But instead of briefly surveying the actual origins of the higher religions, Toynbee drowns us in a flood of capitals and rhetoric, concluding:

The infliction of such extreme suffering on the grand scale is a self-indictment of the society in which these atrocities are committed, and in the Westernizing World of the twentieth century of the Christian Era [his system of capitalization is baffling] there was a subconscious self-defensive conspiracy to minimize the painfulness of deracination by the euphemism of calling the sufferers "displaced persons." [Toynbee himself likes to call the Jews "fossils"—to underscore the painfulness of being uprooted?] In the Hellenic World of the fifth century B.C., Herodotus did not flinch from calling them *déracinés* outright. [Good old unflinching Herodotus with his flair for showing off his French!] This has been the human seed from which the higher religions have sprung.

To be sure, the Buddha does not seem to fit this picture; but he left his father's palace and became "a voluntary *déraciné.*"

What exactly is Toynbee trying to say? Less than a page before, he has claimed that the great philosophers were "born into the middle, or even the upper, class of Society" while, "by contrast, the founders of the higher religions have mostly arisen in the ranks of the vast majority of the" *déracinés.* Now, there are, according to Toynbee, only four, or five, or six higher religions: Confucius is enlisted as a philosopher, Lao-tzu is read out of history, and the rank of Judaism is left unclear, while Hinayana and Mahayana Buddhism are sometimes counted as one religion and sometimes as two. Naturally, one wonders whether it is true that the founders of these four, or five, or six higher religions "have mostly arisen" among the uprooted. One or two were founded by the Buddha who "was the son of a parochial prince," and post-Buddhaic Hinduism (a very doubtful conception in any case) did not have any founder. That leaves at most three out of six, and perhaps only two out of five, and Toynbee does not say which of these qualify for his word "mostly." Was Jesus *déraciné?*

If Toynbee stooped to list "the founders" before he generalized about them, he would save space and ensure precision, but, alas, destroy his thesis. He excels even professional politicians in the gentle art of saying nothing, with a flow of rhetoric, and stating patent falsehoods without being readily found out.

Is there really any difference along the lines suggested by Toynbee between the great philosophers and the founders of the great religions? Or is the difference rather in their following? When Toynbee says (p. 139), "Of all the philosophies thrown up by all the civilizations up to date, only two—Confucianism and the Hinayanian school of Buddhism—are still in the field today," he implies, quite unreasonably, that even a philosophy is "in the field" and deserves consideration only when it has gained the allegiance of vast masses of people. It should be noted that not even Thomism qualifies. But what makes little sense in the case of philosophies is not altogether unreasonable in the case of religions. Without in the least accepting Toynbee's occasional implication that the "higher" re-

ligions are, of course, the four with the most members (see his
Volume VII), one may concede that in common speech the
word "religion," unlike the word "philosophy," is usually reserved for mass movements. Indeed, when a philosophy becomes a mass movement, as Toynbee's own examples indicate,
we often refer to it as a religion. And a mass movement,
whether religious or not, depends on the adherence of the
masses, notably including the lower classes. Now one may go
on to ask what predisposes the masses for a mass movement,
and it may well be the case that "displaced persons" are especially receptive. Toynbee does not furnish much evidence one
way or the other, but Eric Hoffer, in *The True Believer:
Thoughts on the Nature of Mass Movements,* has listed a great
many similar factors to which this might well be added,
though hardly as either a necessary or a sufficient condition.
It might also be argued, and was in fact argued at length by
Nietzsche, that there are two kinds of morality and religion:
the kind that develops among the lower classes and the kind
that originates in the ruling class, like Hinduism and Buddhism.

Toynbee's famed erudition manifests itself not in a disciplined awareness of important treatments of his subject matter, let alone rival hypotheses or facts that do not seem to fit
his own account, but in a flair for quaint allusions. His method
is what Stephen Potter calls "one-upmanship." Where a red
herring might be recognized and challenged, the queer fish
that Toynbee introduces with an air of mildly bored authority
silence all opposition—unless you either happen to know about
them or have the patience to find out.

In the chapter on "The Epiphany of the Higher Religions"
we soon encounter two examples. In fact, the reader who does
not know Toynbee might well suppose that the following sentence comes from Stephen Potter: "This alloy of Archaism in
Futurism partly accounts for the failures of Aristonicus in a
Roman Asia and of his contemporaries, the insurgent Syrian
slave-kings Eunus, Cleon, and Athenio in a Roman Sicily."
Another similar attempt is made a little later on the same page:
"In Jewish history the classic gentle archaist is Rabbi Johanan
ben Zakkai." Then we are treated to a story about Rabbi

Johanan. The reader is likely to conclude that Toynbee, even
if he does not quote the pre-Exilic prophets, is at home in
Talmud and Rabbinic literature. But in fact this seems to be
the only rabbi known to Toynbee. He never once refers to
Hillel's teachings or Akiba's, for example; and all he knows of
Rabbi Johanan is this one story that he quotes from Burkitt's
book, *Jewish and Christian Apocalypses* (1914). As Maurice
Samuel shows, Toynbee's interpretation of this story is untenable; but Samuel charitably fails to mention that Toynbee uses
this one story no less than nineteen times.

It is quite unclear what the rabbi has to do with the "epiphany" of his religion, which presumably occurred more than a
thousand years before his time. It is clear, however, that Toynbee believes that "Johanan ben Zakkai's inspiration has enabled
Judaism to survive in diasporà." This last word, "diasporà"
(dispersion), shows that the "subconscious self-defensive conspiracy" is not confined to "the twentieth century of the Christian Era" but goes back to the Greeks, the unflinching Herodotus notwithstanding. It also shows that Toynbee does not mind
joining this conspiracy, at least against "fossils."

Toynbee believes that "The survival of the Zoroastrian and
Jewish diasporàs" proves "the effectiveness of Archaism as a
social cement when it is compounded with the spirit of gen-
tleness." Nevertheless, Toynbee strongly disapproves of "the
meticulous observance of an archaic ritual law" and calls this
"a form of Man-worship that has been found to be a bad
religion by the general experience of Mankind; and . . . spirit-
ually sterilizing."

Are we supposed to be quite staggered by the closeness of
the parallel between the Jews and Parsees—so staggered that
we fail to notice that his reference to "Man-worship" is a
gratuitous, unfounded, and base insult? Does he expect us to
shed tears over the spiritual sterility of the Jews when we
compare it to the spiritual fertility of other peoples? Is this
really "An Historian's Approach to Religion"?

4

Self-centeredness. Toynbee finds self-centeredness the greatest vice of man, calls it our Original Sin, and believes that the
historian can help others become less self-centered. With this
last point I could not agree more. Surely, a study of history
may shatter our parochial prejudices by acquainting us with
people and ideas quite remote from our own environment. We
need not accept completely the modest, but faintly ironic, alternative that the great nineteenth-century historian, Ranke,
posed in the Preface to his first great work: "To history has
been assigned the office of judging the past, of instructing the
present for the benefit of future ages. To such high offices
this work does not aspire: It wants only to show how things
actually happened." By doing just that, no more, the historian
can perform a crucial moral function and quite change our
valuations.

Toynbee's work, on the other hand, is marred from beginning to end by his singular inability to transcend his idiosyncrasies. The one idea that, as he sees it, he shares with the
Eastern ("non-Judaic") religions is their tolerance and openness to syncretism; but this eclectic orientation he himself acquired elsewhere. And his tediously repetitive praise of Mahayana altruism, too, is an instance of his willingness to praise
in other religions only what he himself has believed all along.

Toynbee's tolerance consists in sometimes giving credit to
others where they happen to agree with him. Of any serious
effort to do justice to other views one finds no trace. Although
he writes as if he had accomplished some sort of Copernican
revolution by discovering that world history does not revolve
around the nation in which the historian happens to be born,
he is in fact much more parochial than was Ranke when he
wrote that "every epoch is immediate to God." And if, as
Ranke said, "the true historian . . . must feel a participation
and pleasure in the particular for itself . . . [and] a real affection for this human race in all its manifold variety" while keep-

ing clear of "preconceived ideas,"[1] then Toynbee is a poor historian indeed.

It may seem unfair to judge Toynbee by Ranke's standards, but this is an internal critique of Toynbee that does not depend on standards he himself rejects. Speaking of the chasm that allegedly divides the Judaic and the non-Judaic religions and ideologies, Toynbee says expressly at the outset of his book:

> In the bridging of this chasm the contemporary historian has a part to play which is as difficult as it is important. The self-correction through self-transcendence, which is the essence of his profession, no doubt always falls short of its objective; yet, even so, it is something to the good; for to some extent it does succeed in . . . widening the mental horizon of an innately self-centered living creature.

And a great many more words to the same effect.

By the end of that same first chapter, we find Toynbee stubbornly resisting "self-correction through self-transcendence" when he attacks the critics of his own attempt to find historical laws as men who have given "a superficial answer," and he offers arguments against the "historians of this antinomian Late Modern Western school" that are not only preposterous but evidence an utter failure to understand, let alone do justice to, the people he attacks. It is this early failure rather than the fine statement of principle that sets the tone for the rest of his book.

Surely, Toynbee would have advanced the cause of tolerance and self-transcendence ever so much more if he had followed Ranke's humble example and told "how it actually happened" by way of making his vast audience understand the ethos of the Hinayana and the Hindus, of the Diaspora and of Zionism, of the early Christians and Islam, of the neo-orthodox and of Liberal Protestantism. Instead of doing all, or some small part, of this, he sits in judgment without ever questioning his standards. He cannot refrain from airing once again his

[1] Cf. the Ranke chapter in *The Varieties of History*, edited by Fritz Stern, pp. 54 ff., and my own *Nietzsche*, p. 395.

well-known humbug on the Jews; he puts the Buddha in his
place by finding him "illogical" and "inconsistent" over and
over and over again (would that Toynbee himself were half
as logical, consistent, and compassionate as the Buddha! and
that he really substantiated his charge just once instead of
bolstering conviction by sheer repetition!); he charges Hinayana Buddhism with superficiality; he informs us that Mo-
hammed fell into a fatal error; and he would persuade us by
his tireless reiteration that the Mahayana and Christianity are
superior to the other high religions, not to speak of low ones.
This is surely a strange triumph over his innate self-centeredness!

5

Some very widespread prejudices. Without agreeing that
self-centeredness in the bad sense is as universal as Toynbee
insists, one may concede that many of his prejudices are widespread, and there may be some point in calling particular attention to a few of these. It is my very point that many readers
will agree with Toynbee, and there is no chance here of re-
futing all these prejudices. I merely want to advance the cause
of "self-transcendence through self-correction" by pointing out
that these assumptions should be questioned.

Speaking of the higher religions generally, Toynbee declares
ex cathedra that "a church's mission is to preach the gospel to
every creature" (p. 109); and later he tells us, still in *An
Historian's Approach to Religion:* "The true purpose of a
higher religion is to radiate the spiritual counsels and truths
that are its essence into as many souls as it can reach, in order
that each of these souls may be enabled thereby to fulfil the
true end of Man. Man's true end is to glorify God and to
enjoy Him for ever" (p. 269). By these standards, among
others, Toynbee passes judgment. This, of course, is a partisan
approach which from the outset is not open to what other
religions might consider their purpose or the best aim of human life. It is not a historian's approach but a theologian's.
But to qualify as good theology, Toynbee's opinions would
require some rational explication as well as some reasons. And

the historian, even if reluctant to go into the history of his own standards, should bring to life the ethos of nonmissionary religions like early Hinduism and early Judaism. By doing that, he would perform a major service to theologians, philosophers, and mankind at large.

Toynbee maintains a naïve, popular, pragmatic view and insists on a "practical test. 'By their fruits ye shall know them.'" He quite fails to see that the next question, even if we go along, is bound to be: And by what standards shall we judge the fruits? In unhesitatingly applying his own standards, he is guilty of the very parochialism that he has gone forth to slay.

Sometimes Toynbee considers success an indication of superior value. Nothing could be more popular today, but few things could be more unforgivable in a historian, and an avowedly religious historian at that. It is surely one of the major functions of a historian to expose the frequently unedifying causes of success with neither fear nor favor. Toynbee, on the contrary, sides with Job's friends, inferring prior virtue from success, and guilt from suffering.

His partisanship for Christianity also leads him frequently to falsify the facts. Here is a pretty stark example: "the Christians were the only people in the Roman Empire, except the professional soldiers, who were prepared to lay down their lives for the sake of an ideal" (p. 101). Rather more subtle, and still more popular, are the distortions in Toynbee's account of the development of Christianity out of Judaism. Here he compounds widely accepted errors with fantastic innuendo.

> This Christian vision of God is a heritage from Israel. . . . Before Yahweh became the parochial god of a community of Nomads . . . he would appear to have been a god embodying one of the forces of Nature. Perhaps he was a volcano or perhaps the weather, to judge by the traditional account, in the Pentateuch. . . . A god who had . . . led his "Chosen People" in an aggressive war of expropriation and extermination against the inhabitants of a country that had been neither Israel's to take nor Yahweh's to give, might not seem to have been a promising medium for an approach to Reality. Yet the sufferings inflicted on Israel and Judah

by Assyrian and Babylonian hands during a time of troubles
that dragged on from the eighth into the sixth century B.C.,
inspired the Prophets to see, through the wraith of Yahweh
the parochial war-god, another Yahweh who had more in
common with the god in the Sun who was worshipped by
Ikhnaton, Aristonicus, and Aurelian.

This Atonian Yahweh was Justice and Mercy as well as Power,
and his Power and Justice were . . . omnipotent, ubiquitous,
impartial. . . . But the vision had still to be clarified by the
further insight that the God Almighty who was Justice and
Mercy was also Pity and Love; and though the greatest of the
Prophets beheld Pity and Love incarnate in a Suffering Serv-
ant, it was a stumbling-block to the Jews when Christianity
identified this human figure with the sublime God who had
made His epiphany through Yahweh's forbidding lineaments
[pp. 88 f.].

Again, is this a historian's approach? Has any other historian of any repute claimed that Yahweh "was a volcano or
perhaps the weather"? Does Toynbee's interpretation of the
Pentateuch inspire confidence in his interpretation of other,
less widely known, documents? Have the five Books of Moses
no moral significance whatsoever? Was Moses himself, who is
altogether ignored here, nothing but "the leader of the Exodus"
(as the Index to Volume X identifies him)? And does not the
last sentence of Toynbee's first paragraph give the strange impression that between the eighth and the sixth century B.C.
the Jews at last came close to catching up with the superior
wisdom of such men as Aristonicus and Aurelian who, as a
matter of fact, lived many centuries later and distinguished
themselves as leaders in aggressive wars? And what sense does
it make to say that the prophets stressed justice and mercy
but not pity and love? Is there some sharp distinction between
mercy and pity? And is Toynbee seriously suggesting that the
prophets failed to speak of love, again and again and again?
If anything can equal this succession of distortions, it is the
final sentence that somehow gives the impression that the Jews
could not accept the attribution of pity and love to "the sublime God." After all, what they balked at was the identification

of a "human figure," whatever his qualities might be, with God. Nor do the Gospels picture Jesus as "Pity and Love incarnate." Indeed, the Jesus of the Gospels is not half so compassionate as Hillel or the Buddha. And is the God of hell and judgment, the God of Jesus and Augustine, of Dante and Calvin, less "forbidding" than the God of Jonah?

Even when it is freed from all insinuations, Toynbee's central thesis here is highly questionable. In a footnote in his big *Study* (V, 119), it is stated, unadorned: "Christianity stands, not side by side with Judaism, but on its shoulders, while they both tower above the primitive religion of Israel. . . . Before and below the Prophets, the Biblical tradition presents us with a Moses. . . ." The great popularity of this idea does not make it sound. Here are but a few reasons for rejecting it.

First, Toynbee accepts uncritically one of the pseudo-Darwinistic dogmas of the nineteenth century when he assumes without argument that religion is like science, and unlike art, in exemplifying progress. If Judaism is at all like other religions, there is not only no overwhelming presumption that Moses must surely have been far inferior to the prophets, but, on the contrary, the analogy with other religions makes it probable that a towering figure, perhaps never equaled since came at the outset. Moreover, the prophets themselves testify consistently that the morality that they proclaim is not original with them. They all say more or less what Micah says: "You have been told, O man, what is good and what the Lord requires of you."

Secondly, Toynbee's notion that one religion stands on the shoulders of another and represents, as Toynbee says occasionally, the culmination of its predecessor, is profoundly questionable in principle, quite apart from the case at hand. Even in the nineteenth century when this idea gained wide popularity, the greatest historian and the greatest Christian thinker both repudiated it. Kierkegaard insisted that the superiority of Christianity cannot be demonstrated in this manner and that Christianity represents an alternative among others, necessitating a decision. And Ranke wrote: "Every epoch is immediate to God."

Thirdly, Toynbee is compelled to distort facts to create even a presumption in his favor. In addition to his overt distortions in the long passage cited, he never faces up to the radical discontinuity between the prophets and Jesus. The prophets were not concerned with individual salvation, they did not assume a life after death, let alone eternal damnation, and they did not address themselves to the question, "How can I enter the kingdom of heaven?" Their central theme was the will of God and social love and justice. They stressed the rights of the widow and the orphan and the stranger, and denounced injustice at the international level, too: "They shall beat their swords into plowshares. . . . Nation shall not lift up sword against nation, neither shall they learn war any more." Toynbee gives us no inkling of all this, or of the vast differences between the prophets and Aurelian, Aristonicus, and Ikhnaton, and he ignores Jesus' decisive break with this prophetic heritage. Surely, there is a very important sense in which Jesus' Gospel is self-centered, while the message of the prophets was not. (The problems raised here are discussed more fully, without reference to Toynbee, in my *Critique of Religion and Philosophy*.)

In *An Historian's Approach to Religion*, these matters might well deserve discussion. And if anyone should plead a lack of space, let him reflect on Toynbee's annexes, quotations, and redundancies, and his lengthy report on how a "hope kindled into a flame in the writer's heart on the 13th October 1953, when, on the eve of a Round Table Conference . . . he was . . . [in] Sacro Speco . . . and . . . he prayed . . ." (pp. 154 ff.). On the basis of Toynbee's books we might be able to fill a calendar with dates like these,[2] but we could not construct anything remotely resembling a history of the higher religions.

The next distortion, again not confined to Toynbee, is also connected with the rise of Christianity. He argues, chiefly in

[2] This paragraph, like a few others, had to be omitted at the last minute for reasons of space when this essay first appeared in *Commentary* in April, 1957. Since then Trevor-Roper has made the most of this point in a brilliant satirical essay on "Arnold Toynbee's Millennium" in *Encounter*. His essay is reprinted in his *Men and Events* (1957).

chapter 9 of his new book and in Volume VII of his *Study*
(pp. 465 ff.), that "the translation of the gospels of Christianity and Islam into terms of Hellenic metaphysics has had awk-
ward consequences because it ignored the distinction between
two facets of Truth which cannot be focussed into unity by
. . . the Human Mind." These two facets are poetic truth
and scientific truth. What Toynbee proposes invites comparison with Rudolf Bultmann's "demythologizing," but Toynbee's
erudition, with its flair for esoteric tidbits, stops short, as usual,
before the most relevant discussions of his subject matter.
What he recommends is this: "Strip the Christian and Islamic
gospels of their incongruous and outworn Greek scientific
dress; resist the temptation to put them into an alternative
scientific dress of a Western cut which will also be incongruous
and ephemeral; and take the truth that they express in the
non-scientific poetical sense that is the natural sense in this
context." This may be appealing, but Toynbee's way of putting
the issue depends on his misrepresentation of the facts. He
asks: "In what sense did Christians, in those very early days
before the statement of Christian beliefs began to be Hellenized, mean that Jesus was the Son of God, that He rose from
the dead, that He ascended into Heaven?" Is it impertinent to
ask a historian to what time he is referring?

Scholars agree that Greek ways of thinking affected some
of the last books of the Old Testament and, even more, the
Judaism of Jesus' time. The demonstration of the close affinities
of original Christianity with Judaism does not prove that it
was pre-Hellenistic. Moreover, Toynbee himself has shown in
over 150 pages, in an "Annex" to Volume VI—which is much
more interesting than his new book but which has been generally ignored—that the story of Jesus is inseparable from Hellenistic folklore and beliefs: detail after detail in this story
and in some of the most poignant sayings, too, is shown to be
a commonplace in Hellenistic literature before the time of
Jesus. Reviewers have remarked on Toynbee's development
from the religion of his fathers in the first six volumes to the
syncretism of the last four, but without calling attention to
this Annex (in those days he still spelled it without the final
"e"), which seems to account for the change.

Toynbee lost the faith of his fathers and the belief in the uniqueness of Christ when he discovered that Christianity itself was syncretistic. If Christianity was the result of syncretism, how could it now shut itself off against a further, worldwide syncretism? This suggestion, of course, does not preclude the possibility that Toynbee's divorce in 1946 may have contributed to his conviction that Catholicism is too exclusive.

Toynbee fails to grasp two crucial consequences that, on his own showing, he cannot escape. He cannot cling to the popular idea that the Hellenic dress and everything that appears theological were added to Christianity at a late date. This is a prejudice of many Protestants who recall that Luther had no patience with Aquinas and with Aristotle and tried to go back to original Christianity. But Luther's original Christianity was profoundly Hellenic, as is evidenced, briefly, by his repeated estimate that "the evangelist John is a master above all the other evangelists" and "that he alone might well deserve to be called an evangelist." Toynbee ought to face the question whether it was not "Hellenized" Christian beliefs rather than any higher morality that led to the break with Judaism: for according to the Book of Acts in the New Testament it was the Christians who broke with Judaism, long after the crucifixion. He rejects and ridicules theology, but he should ask whether the crucial beliefs that distinguished the Christians in those days, and ever since, or at least until about one hundred years ago, were untheological.

Toynbee's attempt to demythologize, moreover, assumes without argument that these beliefs—of which he himself has shown that many are encountered widely in pre-Christian literature in connection with many different pagan heroes—have a hard core. "In trying to correct the mistranslations of the essence of religion into the transitory vernacular languages of a succession of past times and places," Toynbee warns, one is yet doomed "to make a mistranslation of his own"; for we, too, are the children of our age. He assumes, without argument as usual, that there is some univocal core, not only of Christianity but of religion in general, which can be variously translated. This assumption is utterly gratuitous.

Even if Micah's famous words, "only to do justice and to

love mercy, and to walk humbly with your God," were the
essence of Judaism and all the rest were a mere mistranslation
of this essence, this is certainly not the essence of Christianity:
else, as Paul told the Galatians, "Christ has died in vain." Paul's
theology is not a misguided attempt to translate the prophets'
concern with social justice into his vernacular. And the attempt
to fight social injustice is not only not a part of Buddhism—
Hinayana, Mahayana, or Zen—but is incompatible with the
ethos of Buddhism.

Toynbee's attempt to disengage "the Essence from the Nonessentials in Mankind's Religious Heritage" is another instance
of his taking up a popular idea without in the least illuminating
it. He glosses over the differences between the world's religions
and gives the impression that these differences are merely
quantitative and permit us to arrange the great religions on a
scale, with the Mahayana and Christianity at the top. The
price they have to pay for this singular honor, however, is
that they cease to be themselves: indeed, Toynbee flays them
alive, as Rabbi Akiba was flayed by the Romans (although
we have seen that, according to Toynbee, the Christians had
a monopoly in the Roman Empire on dying "for the sake of
an ideal"). Toynbee would skin the great religions as one peels
an onion (his own metaphor). Only that one notion in each
that meets with Toynbee's favor may remain. The rest is mistranslation.

The "Christian-Mahayanian vision" has, Toynbee thinks,
"brought to light something else in God's nature and action
which, in the vision of the other three religions [I am not sure
which three qualify for second honors at this point], is perhaps
latent but is not explicit. Both Christianity and the Mahayana
hold that a superhuman being [no capitals] has demonstrated
His love for human beings in action, and this at the cost of
the suffering that is inseparable from being a self." Surely,
these are strange grounds for according highest honors. The
candidates who receive only a B from Professor Toynbee
might well argue that Christianity and the Mahayana are here
guilty of a mistranslation and express a worthwhile point in
faulty language, inasmuch as they take poetry for history. Actually, there is a huge difference in this respect between Chris-

tianity and Buddhism, which Toynbee glosses over because
it does not fit. But is Toynbee justified in rebuking the Jews
again and again for rejecting the teachings of the early Christians, who, if he is right, were guilty of mistaking poetry for
fact? Why does he find such harsh words for the Jews
throughout their history, while he is so lenient with the Crusades and the Inquisition and the Christian emphasis on
dogma, faith, and sacraments? Why, in his redundant homilies
about suffering, is he so unwilling to show some compassion
for the religion whose members have suffered by far the most
for their religion? He often seems to belong with those who
deny charity only to those who need it, show it only where it
will attract attention, and above all like to *talk* of it.

6

Conclusion. It would, of course, be utter folly to claim that
there is nothing good in Toynbee's work or in his latest book.
R. H. S. Crossman said in a review in *The New Statesman,*
evidently not entirely aware of the full implications of his
judgment: "Far the most valuable part of this book is the
series of lengthy Annexes," with their copious quotations from
John Locke and Thomas Sprat. Bayle might be added to the
list. It may be, as Crossman seems to think, that by bringing
such passages to the attention of his wide audience Toynbee
has struck a blow for tolerance, enlightenment, and—against
traditional Christianity. Similarly, his repeated references to
Mahayana Buddhism, though not at all enlightening to the
scholar—on the contrary—may make a large public aware of a
religion whose very name they had not heard before. Toynbee's discussion of essentials and nonessentials, although un-
helpful for philosophers and theologians and for almost anyone
who has reflected on the subject, may make a few thousand
people conscious of a problem. And so forth.

It would be easy to add further points of the same kind, but
this is faint praise indeed. We should not hesitate to say as
much for our most successful magazines. Indeed, that is what
people say who would defend the comic-book editions of the
classics: having read *Hamlet* in this fashion, many who would

not have dreamed of reading it in the original will probably go on to read it. Will they? And will Toynbee's readers go on to think seriously about his problems and eventually forget his errors? Surely, the converse is much more likely.

If these comparisons should seem invidious, the reader should reflect if Toynbee's work is not insidious. It is entertaining and seems instructive, but really is not instructive because it is utterly unreliable. It is ingratiating and seems religious, but genuine religion is never ingratiating. It is moralistic and preaches tolerance and ridicules parochialism, but it is full of parochial prejudices, deeply intolerant, and based on a staggering lack of scruple.

Many people suspect all critiques of Toynbees. Why? First, because some feel, as Toynbee does, that success is a proof of virtue. They overlook that Toynbee's huge success is confined to the United States where public opinion is heavily influenced by magazines with staff-written reviews and huge pictorial displays. In England the situation is very different. Second, Toynbee seems to be religious without being a fanatic, and there is a widespread feeling that this makes a man immune to all criticism. Third, and most important, there are few who have read his major work. Those who have read only the one-volume abridgment, which established his success in the United States, assume that everything is proved in the ten volumes. Many critics who have checked some sections only in the large work and found Toynbee open to a host of criticisms think the other parts are surely better and wind up their criticisms with a tribute to his scope and erudition, which confirms the Toynbee legend. In his new book, Toynbee constantly gives the impression that his theses have been proved in his big *Study*. Those equipped to criticize his history think that in view of his success he must be a superior theologian or a prophet.

As a theologian and historian, as a scientist and poet, Toynbee fails. But if anyone thinks seriously that Toynbee is a prophet, let him ponder whether Toynbee is not one of the false prophets of whom there is never any dearth. He offers us more than we have any right to ask and yet demands nothing from us and, alas, too little from himself. It is unlikely that many agnostics, Jews, Muslims, or Buddhists will accept him. And Christian readers would do well to think about these words of Jesus: "Beware of false prophets which come to you in sheep's clothing."

Bibliography

A

Preliminary versions of many chapters have appeared in various books and journals. I am grateful to the publishers for permission to present them now in revised form and am also happy to have this opportunity to thank all those whose comments encouraged and helped me. In the following list, one asterisk indicates that one or more sections have been added to the version previously published, while two asterisks signify particularly extensive revision. *All* chapters have undergone *some* revision. But some of the "new" material is old and was omitted at the time of periodical publication for reasons of space.

In the following list, the first number denotes the chapter.

1 & 2: Not previously published in any form.
*3: *Partisan Review*, Nov.–Dec., 1952, and *The New Partisan Reader 1945–1953*, Harcourt, Brace & Co., 1953.
**4: Based on articles in *Journal of the History of Ideas*, Oct., 1949, and *Encyclopedia of Morals* (ed. V. Ferm), Philosophical Library, 1956.
**5: Based on an essay in *Monatshefte* (University of Wisconsin), Nov., 1949.
6: Not previously published in any form.
**7, **8: *The Philosophical Review*, Oct., 1951, and Jan., 1954.
9: New; but I have made use of some material I published in German in *Zeitschrift für Philosophische Forschung*, 1956.
*10: *The Kenyon Review*, Spring, 1956.
11: *Encyclopedia of Morals* (cf. 4 above).
12: *The Kenyon Review*, Winter, 1955.
13: *Partisan Review*, Winter, 1955.
**14: A draft appeared in German in *Offener Horizont: Festschrift für Karl Jaspers*, Piper, Munich, 1953.
*15: *The Philosophy of Karl Jaspers* (ed. P. Schilpp), Library of

Living Philosophers, Tudor Publishing Co., 1957; German
ed., Kohlhammer, Stuttgart, 1957.

*16: *Encyclopedia of Morals* (cf. 4 above) and B.22 below.

**17: A draft appeared in Hebrew in *Iyyun* (Israel), Jan., 1958,
and also in a book, *Divrey Iyyun*, dedicated to Martin Buber
on the occasion of his eightieth birthday, The Magnes Press
of the Hebrew University, Jerusalem, 1958.

*18: *The Kenyon Review*, Winter, 1957; *The Philosophical Review*, Apr., 1958; *Texte und Zeichen* 16, 1957.

*19: *Partisan Review*, Fall, 1955, and *Toynbee and History* (ed.
Ashley Montagu), Porter Sargent, 1956.

20: *Commentary*, Apr., 1957.

B

Books cited in the present volume are listed here. English translations
of German titles are listed for the convenience of students, but the translations in the text are my own.

Barker, Sir Ernest; "Dr. Toynbee's *Study of History*," review in *International Affairs*, vol. 31 (1955), pp. 5-16; reprinted in *Toynbee and
History*. See Montagu.

Barnes, Hazel; *The Literature of Possibility: A Study in Humanistic Existentialism*; University of Nebraska Press, 1959. (A detailed study of
the literary works of Sartre, Camus, and de Beauvoir that stresses
the relation of these works to their respective philosophies. I have
reviewed this book in *The American Scholar*, Summer 1960, and, at
greater length, in *Ethics*, July 1960.)

Barraclough, Geoffrey. See Montagu.

de Beauvoir, Simone; *The Ethics of Ambiguity*; transl. Bernard
Frechtman; Philosophical Library, N.Y., 1948.

Bertram, Ernst; *Von der Freiheit des Wortes*; Insel, Leipzig, n.d.

——; *Nietzsche: Versuch einer Mythologie*; Bondi, Berlin, 1918.

Bornkamm, Guenther; *Der Lohngedanke im Neuen Testament*;
Heliand-Verlag, Lüneburg, 1947.

Bultmann, Rudolf. See under Jaspers below.

Bradley, A. C.; *Shakespearean Tragedy: Lectures on Hamlet, Othello,
King Lear, Macbeth*; Macmillan, N.Y., 1949 (1st ed., 1904);
paperback ed., Meridian Books, N.Y., 1955.

*   *   *

Bradley, F. H.; *Appearance and Reality*; Sonnenschein, London, 1893; and rev. ed., with an appendix, 1897.

Bretall, Robert (ed.); *A Kierkegaard Anthology*; Princeton University Press, 1946; reprinted Modern Library, N.Y., 1959.

Brod, Max; *Heidentum, Christentum, Judentum*; Kurt Wolff, Munich, 1922.

Carnap, Rudolf; "Überwindung der Metaphysik durch logische Analyse der Sprache," in *Erkenntnis*, vol. II.4, pp. 219-41. (Includes a critique of Heidegger's *Was ist Metaphysik?*—and ends with a handsome compliment to Nietzsche.)

Carrit, E. F.; "Discussion, Hegel and Prussianism," in *Philosophy*, April, 1940, pp. 190-97; July, 1940, pp. 313-17. Included in Kaufmann, *Hegel's Political Philosophy*.

Cassirer, Ernst; *The Myth of the State*; Yale University Press, 1946; paperback ed., Anchor Books, N.Y., 1955.

Collins, James; *The Mind of Kierkegaard*; Regnery, Chicago, 1953. See also my review in *The Kenyon Review*, Summer 1954.

Croce, Benedetto; *What is Living and What is Dead of the Philosophy of Hegel*; transl. Douglas Ainslie, from the 3rd Italian edition, 1912; Macmillan, London, 1915.

Cross, F. L. (ed.); *Oxford Dictionary of the Christian Church*; Oxford University Press, 1957.

Crossman, R. H. S.; "Prodigal's Return," review of Toynbee's *An Historian's Approach to Religion*, in *New Statesman and Nation*, Sept. 22, 1956.

Diels, Hermann; *Die Fragmente der Vorsokratiker*; 2 vols. in 3; 2nd ed.; Weidmannsche Buchhandlung, Berlin, 1906-1910; greatly improved 6th ed., ed. Walther Kranz; 3 vols; *ibid.*, 1951-1952.

Dilthey, Wilhelm; *Die Jugendgeschichte Hegels*; Teubner, Leipzig and Berlin, 1921.

Dowden, Edward (ed.); *The Sonnets of William Shakespere*; K. Paul, Trench, Trübner, London, 1881.

Eliot, Thomas Stearns; *After Strange Gods; A Primer of Modern Heresy*; Harcourt, Brace, N.Y., 1934.

——; *Idea of a Christian Society*; Harcourt, Brace, N.Y., 1940.

——; *On Poetry and Poets*; Farrar, Straus and Cudahy, N.Y., 1957.

——; *Shakespeare and the Stoicism of Seneca*; Oxford University Press, 1927; reprinted in *Selected Essays 1917-1932*; Harcourt, Brace, N.Y., 1932.

——. *See also* Knight.

Fergusson, Francis; *The Idea of a Theater*; Princeton University Press, 1949; paperback ed., Anchor Books, N.Y., 1953.

Fischer, Kuno; *Hegels Leben, Werke und Lehre*; 2 vols.; Winter, Heidelberg, 1901.

Förster-Nietzsche, Elisabeth; *Das Leben.Friedrich Nietzsches*; 2 vols. in 3; Naumann, Leipzig, 1895-1904.

Fox, Marvin; "Kierkegaard and Rabbinic Judaism," in *Judaism*, April, 1953.

Freud, Sigmund. 1856-1939. There are two German collected editions:

———; *Gesammelte Schriften*; 12 vols.; Internationaler Psychoanalytischer Verlag, Leipzig, Wien, Zürich, 1924-34.

———; *Gesammelte Werke*; 18 vols.; Imago Publishing Co., London, 1940-52.

———; *The Standard Edition of the Complete Psychological Works*; ed. James Strachey and others; 24 vols. Hogarth Press and Institute of Psychoanalysis, London, 1953ff.

———. *See also* Jones.

Fries, Jakob Friedrich; *Über die Gefährdung des Wohlstandes und Charakters der Deutschen durch die Juden*; published simultaneously as a pamphlet and in *Heidelbergische Jahrbücher der Litteratur*, 1816, pp. 241-64, where it is printed as a review of a book by Friedrich Rühs and does not have the above title.

Fromm, Erich; *Psychoanalysis and Religion*; Yale University Press, 1950.

Geyl, Pieter; "Toynbee's System of Civilizations," in *Journal of the History of Ideas*, January, 1948, pp. 93-124; reprinted in *The Pattern of the Past: Can We Determine It?* by Pieter Geyl, Arnold J. Toynbee and Pitirim A. Sorokin; Beacon Press, Boston, 1949; also in *Toynbee and History. See* Montagu.

Gilson, Etienne; *The Unity of Philosophical Experience*; Scribner's, N.Y., 1937.

Glockner, Herman; *Hegel*; 2 vols.; Frommanns, Stuttgart, 1929-1940.

Goethe, Johann Wolfgang von. 1749-1832. There is a vast number of German editions of the works, of which three are listed here, followed by the most inclusive edition of Goethe's conversations. The Conversations with Eckermann are also available singly in a variety of editions. There are too many translations, mostly inadequate, to list here.

———; *Werke: Vollständige Ausgabe letzter Hand*; Cotta, Stuttgart & Tübingen; 40 vols., ed. under Goethe's supervision, 1827-31, plus 15 vols. of *Nachgelassene Werke*, 1833-34, and 5 more vols., 1842; Index vol. for vols. 1-55; ed. C. T. Musculus; 1835.

———; *Werke: herausgegeben im Auftrage der Grossherzogin Sophie von Sachsen* (so-called *Sophienausgabe*); 143 vols.; Böhlau, Weimar, 1887-1919. (Includes diaries, 15 vols., and letters, 50 vols.)

———; *Gedenkausgabe der Werke, Briefe und Gespräche*; ed. Ernst Beutler; 24 vols., thin paper; Artemis, Zürich, 1949. (Includes 4 volumes of letters and 3 vols. of conversations, those with Eckermann comprising vol. 24. An excellent edition.)

——; *Gespräche*; ed. Woldemar Freiherr von Biedermann; 10 vols. in 5; F. W. von Biedermann, Leipzig, 1889-91; rev. ed., with many additions; 5 vols.; ed. Flodoard Freiherr von Biedermann and others; *ibid.*, 1909-11.

——. See also Gräf, Pniower.

Gräf, Hans Gerhard; *Goethe über seine Dichtungen: Versuch einer Sammlung aller Äusserungen des Dichters über seine poetischen Werke*; 9 vols.; Literarische Anstalt, Frankfurt a. M., 1901-1914.

Gundolf, Ernst; *Nietzsche als Richter unserer Zeit*; Hirt, Breslau, 1923.

Günther, Hans F. K.; *Platon als Hüter des Lebens: Platons Zucht und Erziehungsgedanken und deren Bedeutung für die Gegenwart*; J. F. Lehmann, Munich, 1928.

Haering, Theodor; *Hegel, Sein Wollen und Sein Werk; eine chronologische Entwicklungsgeschichte der Gedanken und der Sprache Hegels*; 2 vols.; Teubner, Leipzig and Berlin, 1929-1938.

Harnack, Adolf; *Das Wesen des Christentums*; Hinrichs, Leipzig, 1908; Engl. transl. T. B. Saunders; *What is Christianity?*; Harper Torchbooks, N.Y., 1957.

Hartman, R. S. *See* under Hegel.

Hegel, Georg Wilhelm Friedrich. 1770-1831. Published only four books, as follows:

——; *Die Phänomenologie des Geistes*; published originally as *System der Wissenschaft: Erster Theil, die P. d. G.*; Bamberg und Würzburg, 1807; Engl. transl. J. B. Baillie; *The Phenomenology of Mind*; 2 vols., 1910; 2nd rev. ed., in one vol., Allen & Unwin, London, and Macmillan, N.Y., 1931.

——; *Wissenschaft der Logik*; 3 parts; Nürnberg, 1812-16; Engl. transl. W. H. Johnston and L. G. Struthers; *Science of Logic*; 2 vols.; Allen & Unwin, London, 1929. The third part was translated earlier by Henry S. Macran as *Hegel's Doctrine of Formal Logic, being a translation of the first section of the Subjective Logic*; Clarendon Press, Oxford, 1912; and *Hegel's Logic of World and Idea, being a translation of the second and third parts of the Subjective Logic*; Clarendon Press, Oxford, 1929.

——; *Encyklopädie der philosophischen Wissenschaften im Grundrisse*; Heidelberg, 1817; 2nd, completely rev. ed., Heidelberg, 1827; 3rd rev. ed., Heidelberg, 1830. The book has three parts, of which William Wallace translated the first as *The Logic of Hegel*; 2nd rev. ed., Clarendon Press, Oxford, 1892; and the last as *Hegel's Philosophy of Mind*, Clarendon Press, Oxford, 1894.

——; *Grundlinien der Philosophie des Rechts*; Berlin, 1821. Translations, entitled *Philosophy of Right*, by S. W. Dyde; George Bell & Sons, London, 1896 and by T. M. Knox; Clarendon Press, Oxford, 1942.

In German there are three major collected editions of Hegel's works, of which the second agrees largely with the first, while the third is a critical edition and, on the whole, a triumph of modern scholarship.

——; *Werke: Vollständige Ausgabe durch einen Verein von Freunden des Verewigten;* 18 vols.; Duncker und Humblot, Berlin, 1832-45. Several vols. appeared in rev. 2nd eds., 1840-47. In the *Encyklopädie* and *Philosophie des Rechts*, Hegel's text was supplemented, section by section, with "additions" based on his students' lecture notes. Hegel's lectures on the philosophy of history, on aesthetics (vol. 10, actually comprising 3 vols.), on the philosophy of religion (vols. 11 and 12), and on the history of philosophy (vols. 13-15) were included in this edition, on the basis of his students' notes. Vol. 9, *Vorlesungen über die Philosophie der Geschichte* was edited by Eduard Gans in the 1st ed., 1837; by Karl Hegel in the 2nd and 3rd eds., 1840 and 1843. In 1887, a 19th vol. was added: *Briefe von und an Hegel*, ed. Karl Hegel.

——; *Sämtliche Werke: Jubiläumsausgabe in 20 Bänden;* ed. Hermann Glockner; Frommann, Stuttgart, 1927-30. This edition was supplemented by a very useful 4-vol. *Hegel-Lexikon*, 1935-39; 2nd rev. ed. in 2 vols., thin paper, 1957; also by a volume, *Dokumente zu Hegels Entwicklung*, ed. Johannes Hoffmeister; 1936; but Hegel's correspondence was omitted.

——; *Sämtliche Werke: Kritische Ausgabe;* begun by Georg Lasson, continued by Johannes Hoffmeister who re-edited some of Lasson's volumes; Felix Meiner, Hamburg. This edition, nowhere near completion in 1959, developed out of Lasson's fine critical editions of single works, among which his early edition (1907) of *Die Phänomenologie des Geistes*, with a superb introduction, deserves special praise. Lasson's introductions are among the best things written on Hegel in any language. His edition of the lectures on the philosophy of history is notable for its incorporation of Hegel's own, newly discovered MS material in the long introductory portion, published in a slim volume as *Die Vernunft in der Geschichte*, 1917; 2nd rev. ed. (1920); R. S. Hartman's translation; *Reason in History*; The Liberal Arts Press, N.Y., 1953, is *not* a translation of this volume but a translation of Karl Hegel's edition into which excerpts from Lasson's edition have been fitted in places which Professor Hartman considered suitable.

——; *Briefe von und an Hegel*; ed. Johannes Hoffmeister; 4 vols.; Felix Meiner, Hamburg, 1952, 1953, 1954; index volume to 1960. These volumes form part of the preceding edition and contain ample notes which constitute a major contribution to our knowledge of the whole period from 1785 to 1831.

——; *Hegels theologische Jugendschriften*; ed. Herman Nohl; J. C. B. Mohr, Tübingen, 1907. A new edition is to form part of the critical edition of the works. Partial translation, entitled *Early Theological Writings*, transl. T. M. Knox; long introd. and trans. of some fragments by Richard Kroner; The University of Chicago Press, 1948.

——. *See also* Carrit, Croce, Dilthey, Fischer, Glockner, Haering, Heidegger, Knox, Kroner, Löwith, Lukács, Marcuse, Mueller, Mure, Rosenzweig, Royce. The Hegel items under Kaufmann contain more biographical information.

Heidegger, Martin. 1889-1976. Only the books cited in the present vol are listed.

——; *Aus der Erfahrung des Denkens*; Neske Pfullingen, 1954 (written 1947).

——; *Einführung in die Metaphysik*; Niemeyer, Tübingen, 1953.

——; *Introduction to Metaphysics*; transl. Ralph Manheim; Yale University Press, 1959. (Instead of rendering *Sein* as "Being" and *Seiendes* as "beings," as I did in *Existentialism from Dostoevsky to Sartre* with Heidegger's enthusiastic approval, Manheim renders the former as "being" and the latter occasionally as "what is" but generally as "essents.")

——; *Erläuterungen zu Hölderlins Dichtung*; Klostermann, Frankfurt a. M., 1944; 2nd ed., with additional chapter, *ibid.*, 1951.

——; *Holzwege*; Klostermann, Frankfurt a. M., 1952. (Contains: *Der Ursprung des Kunstwerkes; Die Zeit des Weltbildes; Hegels Begriff der Erfahrung; Nietzsches Wort "Gott ist tot"; Wozu Dichter; Der Spruch des Anaximander.*)

——; *Kant und das Problem der Metaphysik*; Schulte, Frankfurt a. M., 1934.

——; *Die Kategorien-und Bedeutungslehre des Duns Scotus*; Mohr, Tübingen, 1916.

——; *Platons Lehre von der Wahrheit: mit einem Brief über den "Humanismus"*; Francke, Bern, Switzerland, 1947, 1954; Original ed., of the Plato essay, 1942.

——; *Der Satz vom Grund*; Neske Pfullingen, 1958.

——; *Sein und Zeit: Erste Hälfte*; Niemeyer, Halle, 1927.

——; *Die Selbstbehauptung der deutschen Universität: Rede gehalten bei der feierlichen Übernahme des Rektorats der Universität Freiburg i. Br. am 27.5.1933*; Wilh. Gottl. Korn, Breslau, n.d. (1933).

———; *Vorträge und Aufsätze*; Neske Pfullingen, 1954.

———; *Was Heisst Denken?*; Niemeyer, Tübingen, 1954.

———; *Was ist Metaphysik?*; Friedrich Cohen, Bonn, 1929; 5th ed., with added Introduction and Postscript; Klostermann, Frankfurt a. M., 1949; transl. of the introductory essay by Walter Kaufmann in *Existentialism from Dostoevsky to Sartre*; transl. of the lecture by R. F. C. Hull and A. Crick; "What is Metaphysics?," in *Existence and Being*; intr. Werner Brock; Regnery, Chicago, 1949.

———; *Vom Wesen der Wahrheit*; Klostermann, Frankfurt a. M., 1949.

———; *Vom Wesen des Grundes*; Klostermann, Frankfurt a. M., 1955.

———. *See also* Carnap, Löwith.

Heller, Erich; *The Disinherited Mind*; Dufour & Saifer, Philadelphia, 1952; 2nd ed., Farrar, Straus and Cudahy, N.Y., 1957.

Hesse, Hermann; *Gesammelte Schriften*; 7 vols. Suhrkamp, Frankfurt a. M., 1957; *Der Steppenwolf*; Fischer, Berlin, 1927; Engl. transl. Basil Greighton; *Steppenwolf*; Holt, N.Y., 1947; reprinted, Ungar, N.Y. Engl. transl. of two of his other novels are available in paperback eds.; *Siddharta* (New Directions) and *Journey to the East* (Noonday). It is to be hoped that *Steppenwolf, Demian, Death and the Lover (Narziss und Goldmund)*, and the Nobel-Prize-winning *Magister Ludi (Das Glaperlenspiel)* will follow soon. They are among the great European novels. [Since this was written in 1958, Hesse's other novels have been translated.]

Hoffer, Erich; *The True Believer: Thoughts on the Nature of Mass Movements*; Harpers, N.Y., 1851; paperback ed., Mentor Books, N.Y., 1958.

Hofstadter, Richard; *The American Political Tradition and the Men Who Made It*; Knopf, N.Y., 1948; paperback ed., Vintage Books, N.Y., 1954.

Holtorf, H.; *Platon: Auslese und Bildung der Führer und Wehrmänner: Eine Auswahl aus dem "Staat"*; 2nd ed., Teubner, Leipzig and Berlin, 1936.

Hubler, Edward; *The Sense of Shakespeare's Sonnets*; Princeton University Press, 1952.

Hulme, T. E.; *Speculations: Essays on Humanism and the Philosophy of Art*; ed. Herbert Read; Routledge, London, 1924, 1936, 1949.

Jaspers, Karl. 1883-1969. Comprehensive bibliographies of his voluminous writings may be found in the vols. cited in A.14 and A.15. Below only the books cited in the present volume are listed.

———; *Allgemeine Psychopathologie*; Springer, Berlin, 1913; 2nd rev. ed., 1920; 3rd rev. ed., 1922; 4th entirely rev. ed., 1946.

———; *Einführung in die Philosophie*: Artemis, Zürich, 1949; Engl.

transl. R. Manheim; *The Way to Wisdom*; Yale University Press, 1951.

——; and Bultmann, R.; *Die Frage der Entmythologisierung*; Piper, Munich, 1954; Engl. transl. *Myth and Christianity*; Noonday Press, N.Y., 1958.

——; *Die Geistige Situation der Zeit*; Walter de Gruyter, Berlin and Leipzig, 1931; 5th rev. ed., 1933; Engl. transl. E. and C. Paul; *Man in the Modern Age*; Routledge, London, 1933.

——; "Zu Nietzsche's Bedeutung in der Geschichte der Philosophie," in *Die Neue Rundschau*, 1950. 3; Engl. transl. Stanley Godman; "The Importance of Nietzsche, Marx and Kierkegaard in the History of Philosophy," in *The Hibbert Journal*, April, 1951; Engl. transl. Ralph Manheim; "Nietzsche and the Present," in *The Partisan Review*, January-February, 1952.

——; *Nietzsche: Einführung in das Verständnis seines Philosophierens*; Walter de Gruyter, Berlin and Leipzig, 1936; 2nd ed., 1947, "unchanged," but with a new preface.

——; *Nietzsche und das Christentum*; Seifert, Hameln, n.d.

——; *Philosophie; 3 vols.*; I. *Philosophische Weltorientierung*, II. *Existenzerhellung*, III. *Metaphysik*; Springer, Berlin, 1932; 2nd ed., in one vol., 1948; 3rd ed., in 3 vols., with new Postscript, 1956.

——; *Der Philosophische Glaube*; Piper, Munich, 1948; Engl. transl. Ralph Manheim; *The Perennial Scope of Philosophy*; Routledge; London, 1950.

——; *Psychologie der Weltanschauungen*; Springer, Berlin, 1919.

——; *Rechenschaft und Ausblick: Reden und Aufsätze*; Piper, Munich, 1951.

——; *Schelling*; Piper, Munich, 1955.

——; *Strindberg und Van Gogh: Versuch einer pathographischen Analyse unter vergleichender Heranzielung von Swedenborg und Hölderlin*; J. Storm, Bremen, 1949.

——; *Von Ursprung und Ziel der Geschichte*; Artemis, Zürich, 1949; Engl. transl. M. Bullock; *The Origin and Goal of History*; Yale University Press, 1953.

——; *Vernunft und Existenz*; J. B. Wolters, Groningen, Batavia, 1935; Engl. transl. William Earle; *Reason and Existenz*; Noonday Press, N.Y., 1955. Two chapters are reprinted in my *Existentialism from Dostoevsky to Sartre*.

——; *Vernunft und Widervernunft in unserer Zeit*; Piper, Munich, 1950; Engl. transl. S. Godman; *Reason and Anti-reason in Our Times*; Yale University Press, 1952.

Jones, Ernest; *The Life and Work of Sigmund Freud*; 3 vols.; Basic

Books, N.Y., 1953ff. *See also* my review of vol. III in *Judaism*, winter 1958.

Kaufmann, Walter; *Cain and Other Poems*; Doubleday, Garden City, N.Y., 1962; Enlarged Edition, New American Library, N.Y., 1975.

———; *Critique of Religion and Philosophy*; Harper, N.Y., 1958; Double-day Anchor Books, Garden City, N.Y., 1961; Princeton University Press, 1978, with a new preface.

———; *Discovering the Mind*; vol. I: *Goethe, Kant, and Hegel*; vol. II: *Nietzsche, Heidegger, and Buber*; vol. III: *Freud versus Adler and Jung*; McGraw-Hill, N.Y., 1980, 1980, 1981.

———; *Existentialism from Dostoevsky to Sartre*; Meridian Books, N.Y., 1956; revised and expanded, New American Library, N.Y. 1975. (Writings, some translated into English for the first time, by Dosto-evsky, Kierkegaard, Nietzsche, Rilke, Kafka, Jaspers, Heidegger, Sartre, and Camus, with brief prefaces and a 41-page introduction.)

———; *Existentialism, Religion, and Death*; New American Library, N.Y., 1976.

———; *The Faith of a Heretic*; Doubleday, Garden City, N.Y., 1961; New American Library, N.Y., 1978, with a new preface.

———; *The Future of the Humanities*; Reader's Digest Press, N.Y., 1977.

———; *Goethe's Faust: A New Translation*; Doubleday, Garden City, N.Y., 1961. With a long introduction and the original text on facing pages.

———; *Hegel: Reinterpretation, Texts, and Commentary*; Doubleday, Garden City, N.Y., 1965. In 2 vols., *Hegel: A Reinterpretation* and *Hegel: Texts and Commentary*, Doubleday Anchor Books, Garden City, N.Y., 1966, and University of Notre Dame Press, Notre Dame, Indiana, 1977, 1978.

———; *Hegel's Political Philosophy*; Atherton Press, N.Y., 1970. Ten es-says by S. Avineri, E. F. Carritt, S. Hook, W. Kaufmann, T. M. Knox, and Z. A. Pelczynski, with introduction and notes.

———; *Man's Lot: A Trilogy*. Photographs and Text. Reader's Digest Press, distributed by McGraw-Hill, N.Y., 1978. The three parts were also published simultaneously in 3 paperback vols.: *Life at the Limits, Time is an Artist*, and *What is Man?*

———; *Nietzsche: Philosopher, Psychologist, Antichrist*; Princeton Uni-versity Press, 1950; fourth edition, again extensively revised, 1974.

———; *Religion from Tolstoy to Camus*; Harper, N.Y., 1961; englarged softcover edition, 1964.

———; *Religions in Four Dimensions: Existential and Aesthetic, Historical and Comparative*. Text and Photographs. Reader's Digest Press, distributed by McGraw Hill, N.Y., 1976.

———; *Tragedy and Philosophy*; Doubleday, Garden City, N.Y., 1968; Princeton University Press, 1979, with a new preface.

———; *Twenty-five German Poets: A Bilingual Collection*, edited, translated, and introduced; W. W. Norton, N.Y., 1975. The original poems and my translations appear on facing pages, Goethe on pp. 18-59, Nietzsche on 144-75, Rilke on 200-51.

———; *Without Guilt and Justice: From Decidophobia to Autonomy*; Peter H. Wyden, N.Y., 1973; Dell paperback, N.Y., 1975.

———; see also the translations listed under Nietzsche.

Keynes, John Maynard; *Essays and Sketches in Biography*; Meridian Books, N.Y., 1956.

Kierkegaard, Søren. 1813-55. I list the Danish collected editions, the German collected editions, and, there being no English collected edition, the English works actually cited in the present volume. A list of all works available in English may be found in the Modern Library edition of Bretall (see above).

———; *Samlede Vaerker*; 15 vols.; Gyldendal, Copenhagen, 1920-36. (Vol. 15 contains a comprehensive Index.)

———; *Papirer*; ed. P. A. Heiberg and V. Kuhr; 9 vols.; Gyldendal, Copenhagen, 1909-20.

———; *Gesammelte Werke*; transl. Emanuel Hirsch (with prefaces and helpful notes); Diederichs, Düsseldorf, 1950 ff. At least 16 vols. had appeared by 1958. The total number of vols. contemplated is not easy to infer, as "7., 8., und 9. Abteilung," for example, appear in a single vol. of 219 pp., while "1. Abteilung," for example, constitutes a single vol. of 510 pp. *Die Schriften über sich selbst* (1951) comprises "Section" 33; and "Section" 35 contains *Briefe* (1955).

———; *Die Tagebücher: 1834-1855*; selected and transl. Theodor Haecker; Hegner-Bücherei, Kösel-Verlag, Munich, 1949.

———; *Attack upon Christendom*; transl. Walter Lowrie; Princeton University Press, 1944.

———; *On Authority and Revelation: The Book on Adler*; transl. Walter Lowrie; Princeton University Press, 1955.

———; *The Concept of Dread*; transl. Walter Lowrie; Princeton University Press, 1946.

———; *Concluding Unscientific Postscript*; transl. David F. Swenson and Walter Lowrie; Princeton University Press, 1944.

———; *Either/Or: A Fragment of Life*; 2 vols.; vol. I transl. D. F. and L. M. Swenson; vol. II transl. Walter Lowrie; Princeton University Press, 1944.

———; *Fear and Trembling*; transl. Walter Lowrie; Princeton University

Press, 1941, 1954; page references in the text refer to paperback
ed., Anchor Books, N.Y., 1954.

——; *The Journals*; ed. and transl. Alexander Dru; Oxford University
Press, 1938.

——; *Philosophical Fragments*; transl. David F. Swenson; Princeton
University Press, 1946.

——; *The Point of View for My Work as an Author*; transl. Walter Lowrie; Oxford University Press, 1950.

——; *Sickness unto Death*; transl. Walter Lowrie; Princeton University
Press, 1941, 1954; page references in the text refer to paperback
ed., Anchor Books, N.Y., 1954.

——; *Stages on Life's Way*; transl. Walter Lowrie; Princeton University
Press, 1945.

——. *See also* Bretall, Collins, Fox, Jaspers, Lowrie, Thomte.

Knight, G. Wilson; *The Wheel of Fire: Essays in Interpretation of
Shakespeare's Sombre Tragedies*; Oxford University Press, 1930;
4th rev. ed., Methuen, 1949; 5th rev. ed., paperback, Meridian
Books, N.Y., 1957. Introd. by T. S. Eliot, 1930.

Knox, T. M.; "Hegel and Prussianism," in *Philosophy*; January, 1940,
pp. 51-64; July, 1940, pp. 313-17. Included in Kaufmann, *Hegel's
Political Philosophy*.

Kohn, Hans; *The Idea of Nationalism*; Macmillan, N.Y., 1944.

——; *The Twentieth Century*; Macmillan, N.Y., 1949.

Kolnai, Aurel; *The War Against the West*; Viking Press, N.Y., 1938.

Kroner, Richard; *Von Kant bis Hegel*; 2 vols.; Mohr, Tübingen, 1921-
1924.

Levinson, R. B.; *In Defense of Plato*; Harvard University Press, 1953.
See also my review in *The Journal of Politics*, February 1955.

Löwith, Karl; *Von Hegel zu Nietzsche*; Europa, Zürich and N.Y., 1941.

——; *Heidegger, Denker in dürftiger Zeit*; Fischer, Frankfurt a. M.,
1953.

Lowrie, Walter; *A Short Life of Kierkegaard*; Princeton University
Press, 1942; paperback ed., *ibid.*, 1958. *See also* under Kierkegaard.

Lukács, Georg; *Der junge Hegel, und die Probleme der kapitalistischen
Gesellschaft*; Europa, Zürich, 1948; with different pagination,
Aufbau-Verlag, Berlin, 1954.

——; *Die Zerstörung der Vernunft: Der Weg des Irrationalismus von
Schelling zu Hitler*; Aufbau-Verlag, Berlin, 1953; with some corrections, *ibid.*, 1955.

——. *See also* Watnick.

Marcuse, Herbert; *Reason and Revolution: Hegel and the Rise of Social*

Theory; Oxford University Press, 1941; 2nd ed., Humanities Press, N.Y., 1954.

Maritain, Jacques; *Scholasticism and Politics*; translation ed. by Mortimer J. Adler; Centenary Press, London, 1940, 1945.

Marx, Karl, and Engels, Friedrich; *Die Deutsche Ideologie: Kritik der Neuesten Deutschen Philosophie in ihren Repräsentanten, Feuerbach, B. Bauer und Stirner*; Verlag für Literatur und Politik, Wien and Berlin, 1932.

Montagu, Ashley (ed.); *Toynbee and History: Critical Essays and Reviews*; Porter Sargent, Boston, 1956.

Moore, G. E.; "Autobiography," in *The Philosophy of G. E. Moore*; ed. Paul Schilpp; The Library of Living Philosophers, N.Y., 1942; 2nd. ed., Tudor, N.Y., 1952.

Mueller, Gustav E.; "The Hegel Legend of 'Thesis-Antithesis-Synthesis,' " in *Journal of the History of Ideas*, June, 1958 (vol. XIX.3).

Mure, G. R. C.; *An Introduction to Hegel*; Clarendon Press, Oxford, 1940.

——; *A Study of Hegel's Logic*; Clarendon Press, Oxford, 1950.

Niebuhr, Reinhold; *An Interpretation of Christian Ethics*; Harpers, N.Y., 1935; paperback ed., with a new preface; Meridian Books, N.Y., 1956.

Nietzsche, Friedrich. 1844-1900. A bibliography is included in my *Nietzsche* (Princeton University Press, 1974, pp. 483-510).

——; *Gesammelte Werke*; 23 vols.; Musarion Verlag, Munich, 1920-29.

——; *Werke in drei Bänden*; ed. Karl Schlechta; 3 vols., thin paper; Carl Hanser, Munich, 1954-56.

——; *The Complete Works of Friedrich Nietzsche*; ed. Oscar Levy; 18 vols. incl. Index vol.; Macmillan, N.Y.

——; *The Portable Nietzsche*. Selected and translated, with an introduction, prefaces, and notes; The Viking Press, N.Y., 1954; paperback ed., with new postscript, 1958. (Includes complete new translations of *Thus Spoke Zarathustra, Twilight of the Idols, The Antichrist*, and *Nietzsche contra Wagner*, and selections from 12 other books and from Nietzsche's notes and letters.)

——; *Beyond Good and Evil; The Birth of Tragedy and The Case of Wagner; On The Genealogy of Morals and Ecce Homo*; all translated with commentary by Walter Kaufmann; Vintage Books, Random House, N.Y., 1966, 1967, 1967. Also together in one volume, *Basic Writings of Nietzsche*, Modern Library Giant, Random House, N.Y., 1968.

——; *The Will to Power*, a new translation, edited with commentary by Walter Kaufmann; Random House, N.Y. 1967.

——; *The Gay Science*, With a Prelude in Rhymes and an Appendix of Songs, translated with commentary by Walter Kaufmann; Random House, N.Y., 1974.

——; *My Sister and I*; allegedly translated and introduced by Oscar Levy; Board's Head Books, N.Y., 1951; rev. ed. 1953. A forgery. See p. 383 above and Kaufmann's Nietzsche (1974), p. 502 and the footnote on 503.

——. *See also* Bertram, Carnap, Förster-Nietzsche, Gundolf, Heidegger, Jaspers, Löwith.

Otto, Rudolf; *Das Heilige*; Klotz, Gotha, 1917, 1926; Engl. transl. J. W. Harvey; *The Idea of the Holy*; Oxford University Press, 1923, 1946, 1950; paperback ed., Galaxy books, N.Y., 1958.

Plato. *See* Günther, Heidegger, Holtorf, Levinson, Wild, B.1, B.20, and B.21.

Pniower, Otto; *Goethes Faust: Zeugnisse und Excurse zu seiner Entstehungsgeschichte*; Weidman, Berlin, 1899.

Popper, Karl R.; *Die Logik der Forschung: Zur Erkenntnistheorie der modernen Naturwissenschaft*; Springer, Wien, 1935.

——; *The Open Society and Its Enemies*; 2 vols.; Routledge, London, 1945; rev. ed.; 1 vol.; Princeton University Press, 1950. All references in the present vol. are to the rev. ed.

Rank, Otto; *Das Inzest-Motiv in Dichtung und Sage: Grundzüge einer Psychologie des dichterischen Schaffens*; Deuticke, Leipzig, 1912.

Reinhardt, Karl; *Sophokles*, Klostermann, Frankfurt a. M., 1933.

Riesman, David; with Nathan Glazer and Reuel Denney; *The Lonely Crowd: a Study of the Changing American Character*; Yale University Press, 1950; paperback ed., abridged by the authors, Anchor Books, N.Y., 1955.

Rilke, Rainer Maria. 1875-1926. After the completion of an early 6-vol. ed. of *Gesammelte Werke*, a lot of new material was made available—a few items at a time—which was often integrated into collections of previously published material. In 1955, finally, a superb new edition of *Sämtliche Werke* in 6 vols., thin paper, was begun by Insel-Verlag, Leipzig. Vol. 1 (1955) contains all the books of poetry which Rilke himself published, superbly indexed, with the dates of composition furnished for every poem. Vol. 2 (1956) offers the poems not published by Rilke in book form. Vol. 3 (1959) contains poetic juvenilia; 4-6, Rilke's prose. There are many volumes of English translations. Their adequacy varies from poem to poem. There is no collected English edition.

Robinson, Edwin Arlington; *The Town Down the River*; Scribner's, N.Y., 1910.

Rosenberg, Alfred; *Der Mythus des Zwanzigsten Jahrhunderts*; Hoheneichen, Munich, 1930; total ed., by 1940: 878,000 copies.

Rosenzweig, Franz; *Hegel und der Staat*; 2 vols.; Oldenbourg, Munich and Berlin, 1920.

Royce, Josiah; "Hegel's Terminology," in *Baldwin's Dictionary of Philosophy and Psychology*; Macmillan, N.Y. and London, 1901.

Samuel, Maurice; *The Professor and the Fossil: Some Observations on Arnold J. Toynbee's A Study of History*; Knopf, N.Y., 1956.

Sartre, Jean-Paul; "The Childhood of a Leader," in *The Wall and Other Stories*; transl. Lloyd Alexander; New Directions, N.Y., 1948; paperback ed.; *Intimacy*; Avon, N.Y., n.d.; Berkeley, N.Y., 1956.

Shakespeare, William. *See* Bradley, A. C., Dowden, Eliot, Fergusson, Hubler, Knight.

Stallman, Robert W.; *Critiques and Essays in Criticism*; Ronald Press, N.Y., 1949.

Stern, Fritz (ed.); *The Varieties of History, from Voltaire to the Present*; Meridian Books, N.Y., 1956.

Taylor, A. J. P. *See* Montagu.

Thomte, Reidar; *Kierkegaard's Philosophy of Religion*; Princeton University Press, 1948.

Times Literary Supplement. *See* Montagu.

Toynbee, Arnold Joseph; *An Historian's Approach to Religion*; Oxford University Press, 1956.

——; *A Study of History*; 10 vols.; under auspices of Royal Institute of International Affairs; Oxford University Press, London, N.Y., Toronto; vols. 1-3, 1934; vols. 4-6, 1939; vols. 7-10, 1954.

——; "What I am Trying to Do," in *International Affairs*, vol. 31 (1955), pp. 1-4; reprinted in *Toynbee and History*. *See* Montagu.

——. *See also* Barker, Crossman, Geyl, Montagu, Samuel, Trevor-Roper, and my article on Toynbee in *Collier's Encyclopedia*, 1959.

Trevor-Roper, Hugh R.; *Men and Events: Historical Essays*; Harpers, N.Y., 1957. *See also* Montagu.

Vuillemin, J.; "Nietzsche Aujord'hui," in *Les Temps Modernes: Revue Mensuelle*, ed. Jean-Paul Sartre, May, 1951, pp. 1921-1954.

Watnick, Morris; "Georg Lukacs," in *Soviet Survey*; No. 23 (January-March, 1958), pp. 60-66; No. 24 (April-June, 1958), pp. 51-57; No. 25 (July-September, 1958), pp. 61-68. To be continued.

Wild, John; *Plato's Modern Enemies and the Theory of Natural Law*; University of Chicago Press, 1953.

Zweig, Stefan; *Die Heilung durch den Geist: Mesmer, Mary Baker-Eddy, Freud*; Inselverlag, Leipzig. 1931.

Index

Index